We wish to pay tribute to the fine coaches who have contributed chapters to this book and to the coaches and administrators who have made comments and suggestions concerning its contents and writing. In addition, we appreciate the many comments from coaches and players who recognized the need for a book on baseball strategy and urged that such a book be written.

Bob Bennett
Jack Stallings

Contents

Preface vi

Setting the Stage for Strategic Baseball ix
Andy Baylock

PART I Offense 1

1 Determining the Lineup and Batting Order 3
Richard "Itch" Jones

2 Scouting and Studying the Opposition 15
Chuck Hartman

3 Using Signals for Hitting and Base Running 25
Mike Gillespie

4 Hitting Strategy 31
Mark Johnson

5 Base-Running Strategy 53
Danny Hall

6 Decision-Making in Specific Offensive Situations 67
Jack Stallings

PART II Pitching 93

7 Shutting Down Hitters 95
Keith Madison

8 Stopping Base Runners 115
Bob Bennett

9 Fielding the Position 139
Geoff Zahn

10 Working a Game 155
John Winkin

11 Handling Pitchers 179
Steve Hertz

PART III Defense 201

12 Setting the Lineup: Positions 2 Through 9 203
Jim Morris

13 Defensive Positioning 219
George Horton

14 Defensive Tactics 243
Bob Morgan

PART IV Fine-Tuning Your Strategic Approach 277

15 Adjusting for Different Levels of Competition 279
John Herbold

16 Adapting the Game Plan for Different Situations 297
Dick Birmingham

17 Playing the Game the Right Way 317
Bobo Brayton

Index 333

About the ABCA 339

About the Editors 341

About the Contributors 343

Preface

What? Another book on baseball? And a book on baseball strategy! Why? Because many baseball people who have been involved in the game for a long time say that strategy is the most misunderstood aspect of the game. Books, videotapes, magazine and newspaper articles, and clinic presentations usually focus on the skills and fundamentals of the game. Certainly those aspects of the game are much needed in our efforts to improve the coaching and playing of the game. In recent years, more emphasis has been placed on the psychology of coaching. Many coaches now understand better how to motivate players and develop their mental skills.

But anyone who has seen a coach bring his infield in with a runner on third and a four-run lead in the ninth inning will immediately conclude that a book on baseball strategy is badly needed! This book focuses on the various aspects of baseball strategy and what goes into the thoughts of a coach or player as he makes a strategic decision during a game. Most baseball books are about *doing*—throwing or hitting the curveball, turning the double play, or throwing to the cutoff man. This book is about *thinking;* if you think first, you will know the correct thing to do.

This book is unique in that it addresses every aspect of baseball strategy under one cover. It is written for coaches, players, and fans of baseball, by some of the best coaches in the sport. They share the expertise they have acquired over years of successfully competing and coaching at the highest levels. The writers make up a veritable *Who's Who* in the baseball-coaching world. Their experience and skills in coaching baseball make each uniquely qualified to contribute to this book.

This book is for the ballplayer or coach who is interested in reaching his full potential, and that means sharpening physical and mental skills and developing a good understanding of baseball strategy. This book is written for coaches *and* players because players must understand proper strategy if they are to play the game aggressively and make those split-second decisions needed during a game. Players enhance their instincts and reactions to game situations when they understand the strategy needed at a particular time in the game. Because players know ahead of time what to do, they can act quickly, correctly, and confidently. Some would say they act instinctively, but they really act not on instinct, but through knowledge and understanding of strategy.

What percentage of the time does the average coach spend teaching strategy? What portion of his time does a player devote to thinking about strategy? Is it 10 percent? Is it 5 percent or 3 percent? Whatever the total, it usually isn't much, so players must either guess what to do (and often guess wrong) or rely on signals and instructions from the coach, a process that is slow and at times confusing. All coaches teach players *what* to do, many also teach them *how* to do it, but the best coaches also teach them *why* they do it, and that means teaching proper strategy.

Baseball Strategies is a book you can read once and then turn back to repeatedly. Read a section or chapter that interests you and come back to it again in a few days or weeks. When something comes up in a game that was confusing and led to some indecision, turn to the appropriate chapter to find out what one of the authors has to say about that particular situation.

The book is divided into four parts. Part I deals with offensive strategy and includes advice on setting the lineup and batting order, scouting the opposition, establishing an effective signaling system, and executing sound hitting and base-running strategies. You will also learn what factors to consider when planning a strategic move and which strategies are most successful in specific offensive situations.

Part II deals with the strategy of pitching and includes shutting down hitters, stopping base runners, the pitcher's role in fielding, working a game, and the all-important handling of pitchers.

Coaching a pitching staff is challenging work. How many pitches should be thrown in practice and in games? How can each pitcher get enough work to be and stay effective? Along with dealing with the pitching staff, the coach has the even greater challenge of managing the game. Ideas and examples that have stood the test of time are carefully brought to light.

The third part deals with baseball defense and includes setting the lineup of the defensive players, positioning defensive players, and defensive tactics. Some coaches and players seem to have a knack for knowing how to play each hitter. Some are uncanny at compiling and putting to use pages of statistics and other details to help defend against their opponents. Some of the greatest defensive minds in college baseball offer their methods and systems of defensive tactics. They will show us regular and special defenses and help us devise our own methods and systems.

The fourth part has to do with fine-tuning your strategy by adjusting it for different levels of competition, adapting the game plan for different situations, and playing the game the right way. The same strategy may not work for all situations. Adjustments may be necessary. Part IV is one of the most valuable parts of the book. Learning how to adapt to different situations is one of the true lessons in life. Baseball is no exception. The authors of these chapters will tell wonderful stories about their experiences. Each of us can gain insight into how this game should be played. We can also gain much from the words concerning how to fine-tune strategy.

Coaches must understand the percentages of baseball; we all know that nothing will be successful all the time, but we want to understand what will be successful *most* of the time in a particular situation. A coach may occasionally make a snap decision that really doesn't make any sense and have success, but it doesn't happen often. Coaches should make strategy decisions by considering the *percentages,* based on the situation and abilities of the players involved, both their players and their opponent's players. Walter Rabb, the veteran coach at the University of North Carolina, used to say, "You will do OK if you just remember that you don't coach baseball, you coach *baseball players!"* Perhaps the most common mistake coaches make in reaching strategic decisions is failing to think about the most important thing—the abilities of the players involved.

Strategy can be as simple as a basic move in a game of checkers or as involved as the most difficult move in a chess match. Strategy is constant. It is everywhere and in every inning. It involves decision making. Some decisions are easy to make, whereas others are difficult. Decisions made from a background of knowledge produce the best results. When both the coach and the players have knowledge and understanding of the strategy, teamwork blossoms and the likelihood of a successful outcome improves. Pete Beiden, the late Hall of Fame coach from Fresno State, used a simple offensive signal system to teach his players about strategy. His signals were either "Yes" or "No." When he flashed a "Yes" signal, he expected the batter or runner to execute the proper play for that particular situation.

There is more than one way to approach any situation in the game. This book is filled with examples of how coaches may approach a problem in different ways, but they all use sound thinking, based on percentages, to solve the problem. One coach will make no move, while another coach may make several moves in the same set of circumstances. Either may be right or wrong. The important issue is the thought process that went into making the decision. If the strategy used was based on sound fundamental principles and was developed based on percentages that applied to that situation, chances are that a good decision was made.

Setting the Stage for Strategic Baseball

Andy Baylock

"JOE SMITH GOES 4-4 TO LEAD HUSKIES IN ROMP"

"LUIS TORRES HURLS GEM 3-HITTER IN WIN"

"JASON LINDSTROM'S 9TH-INNING HOMER IS THE DIFFERENCE AS HUSKIES WIN"

These three headlines are troublesome to coaches. The lead-ins all focus on one player's performance as the reason for victory rather than the play of the entire team. Like any good headline, however, they introduce an article describing what occurred in a baseball game. That article will have all the particulars of journalism, including the who, what, where, when, and why. But the most important aspect of the outcome of the game, the how, will most likely be forgotten. The how might not matter in the newspaper articles, but it is critical to success in both coaching and playing. The how is strategy, which often goes unnoticed by the casual observer or the newspaper reporter, but without it a coach or player cannot realize his full potential.

A strategy is a vision for success, a plan of attack, a road to your goals. A good coach never loses sight of his vision for success. Whether it be moving the runners over with nobody out, recruiting the left-handed pitcher who could make the difference, or reaching the fund-raising goal, the coach is the point man for what former President George Bush called "the vision thing." And although coaches may choose a certain strategy, achieving success with it requires that players understand it and implement it.

Offensive strategies enhance a team's ability to have batters become base runners and to have base runners advance or be advanced by subsequent batters. Defensive strategies enable a team to stop the advancement of runners. Keep the double play in order; never let second base go uncovered; work fast, throw strikes, change speeds—these dictums are all parts of strategies that coaches apply at all levels of competition.

Keys to Success in Implementation

You can apply strategies that stop your opponent from interfering with what you are going to do by first establishing a sound base of discipline (communication) and respect. The "eternal triangle" (figure I.1) illustrates the qualities you need before you can successfully implement different strategies. You need an acceptable level of talent, concentration, and commitment before you will be capable of making things happen—forcing the action and not just waiting for it to happen. In most situations the difference between teams is not significant. Little mistakes determine wins and losses.

Talent involves the ability to run, throw, field, hit, and hit with power. Concentration is the ability to block out all internal and external distractions while executing a skill, and commitment is a promise to do all in one's power to get the job done. Providing all ingredients are of the highest caliber, your team will be successful. A shortcoming in one or more areas, however, decreases the probability for consistent success.

The key to success in the implementation of strategies is to select your offensive and defensive plan (your vision), live it, adjust and amend it, and have patience with it, because it won't always work to perfection. Understand percentages and trust your system, evaluate your offensive and defensive tendencies, and then install your system.

At the same time, you need to ask the following questions:

- Is your talent capable of executing the tactics and techniques essential to the success of the system?
- Do you have the time, staff, facility, and environment to develop it in practice?

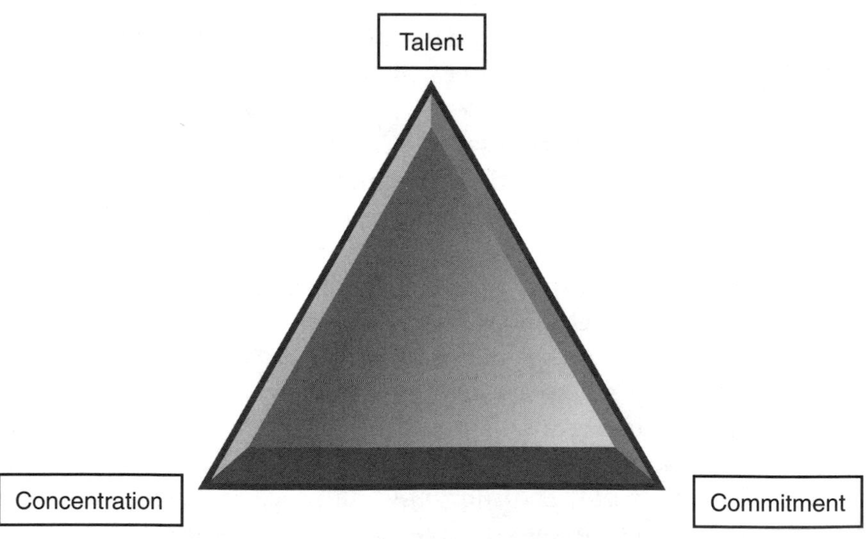

FIGURE I.1 Three qualities essential to the success of a strategy.

- Do your players and staff respect the game by always hustling?
- Do they truly believe that "it ain't over til it's over?"
- Do you have positive leadership by upperclassmen that can show the way in dealing with adversity?

If a team has good communication and respect among coaches and players, you are ready to put in as much strategy as possible and review it whenever you have time and opportunity. You should practice the plan in pressure situations so that on game day everything is second nature.

Fine-Tuning Your Approach

Coaches should consider several important questions when fine-tuning their strategic approach:

- What are the NCAA, NAIA, or high school regulations regarding how much prep time you are allowed (hours per week, number of weeks, and so on)?
- Do you have a veteran team?
- Do you have a committed team?
- Are your players coachable?
- Do you have team cohesion? Do players accept and understand their roles as defined by the coaches?
- Do your players demonstrate poise? How do they react when something bad happens?
- Can they handle failure and make adjustments?
- Do you have commitment and trust from players and staff, and not just when it's convenient?

A coach should believe in and be committed to specific strategies, but must be open to adjustments to those strategies when confronted with variables that could alter the master plan (e.g., not playing for the big three-run home run inning when incapable of producing such).

Effective Practice Methods

Your staff should think through methods for preparing strategies during practice sessions. You must determine the critical position or critical phase of the skill (hit, throw, field) or play (bunt defense, first-and-third defense, and so on). Teach all movements to that point and then let the player finish it off. A coach who is proficient in teaching the mechanics of the swing, making the pitch, fielding the ground ball, etc., will show players the most efficient ways to get to the point of contact, point of release, ball into glove, etc. At that point, the player is responsible for executing the skill consistently.

Slow down the game so that each pitch is a separate contest. Repeat, reinforce, refine. Build confidence by constantly drilling in gamelike competitive situations. That way, when players face the same situation in competition, they can say, "We've been here, we've practiced it." Don't be afraid to make adjustments against the toughest competition. Baseball is a game of many failures. To enjoy the game and be successful, you must adjust. Therefore, conduct pressure practices. Anyone can play; not all can win. Diligence and faith in your system will earn you "Nice plays" rather than "Nice tries." Your system becomes amendable, leading to consistency and constancy.

Some of the finest baseball coaches to have coached and taught the amateur game have written this text about baseball strategy. Their intent is to stimulate you to apply various strategies to make something happen rather than simply waiting for something to happen.

PART I

OFFENSE

Determining the Lineup and Batting Order

Richard "Itch" Jones with Eric Snider

Each year when the University of Illinois baseball players report to the clubhouse for the first day of fall baseball practice, we as a coaching staff watch each player walk through the door. As they pass by, questions fly through our minds. Have our returning players improved from last year? Will our incoming freshmen be able to make the adjustment from the high school game to Division I college baseball? What will be the ideal lineup for the team this year? Will we have team speed? Will we have power? How will we handle the bat? What type of offensive response will our team have?

From that point on, the coaching staff will endlessly debate the lineup for the new season. Our evaluation of fall practice, winter workouts, and the early nonconference schedule is crucial. That assessment will help us weigh the pros and cons of our players' individual abilities and define what our athletes can and cannot do. Once we establish the potential of our players as individuals we can decide on a lineup. Ideally, that lineup will reflect a basic philosophy that we follow as a coaching staff—that a successful offense consists of four qualities:

1. Speed
2. Power

3. Bat control
4. Offensive response

The better teams in baseball have lineups that feature a combination of athletes with those four qualities. Therefore, the first step in establishing the ideal lineup for any season is to determine if the team has one, two, three, or all four of the qualities and to combine the team's strengths from there.

Evaluating Players' Strengths and Weaknesses

To discover how many of these qualities a team possesses each year, the coaching staff must evaluate each athlete's individual abilities. At Illinois this evaluation begins during fall practice and continues until the beginning of the Big Ten season at the end of March. Establishing an offensive strategy is critical during this time. Therefore, in practice during this stretch we do drills during intrasquad games so that they are gamelike in nature. We do this because we want our athletes to feel the so-called pressure during practice. We believe that if they become accustomed to feeling game pressure day in and day out, they will have the ability to respond immediately and correctly when we put them in any situation during a game. At Illinois we have found that daily gamelike practice settings that cover base running, base stealing, hitting the ball in positive-count situations, bat control, situational hitting, and offensive response end up emphasizing our players' strengths while helping to identify their weaknesses. By identifying these strengths and weaknesses in practice, we as a coaching staff are better able to develop our team's offensive strategy, enhance the offensive success of our program, and establish our lineup before the heart of the season begins. This approach affords the team its best opportunity to reach its goals because less guesswork is required during the conference season.

Speed

We define a speed player as an athlete who will not consistently drive the ball deep into the outfield but who, when he does reach base, is a constant threat to steal. The old saying "Speed never slumps" illustrates why this quality is essential to offensive success. We teach base running to each of our players, and each becomes fundamentally sound in his running techniques. After evaluating our team in the speed area, we identify the players who possess good speed. We then take this group and work with them on their base-stealing techniques:

- Stealing second and third
- Reading pitchers and catchers in steal attempts
- Reading pitchouts
- Deciding when to run and when not to run

During our intrasquad games all players work on their base-running techniques in reaction to our hitters, and our base stealers also work on their base-stealing techniques in reaction to our pitchers and catchers. We never neglect the players who lack speed when it comes to base-running drills. Each player works on getting out of the batter's box, running as hard as he can, and cutting each base as efficiently and precisely as possible. The ability to advance a base on a bobbled ball or an overthrow of a cutoff man can make the difference in a close game.

Power

We define a power hitter as a player who makes hard contact and regularly hits doubles, home runs, or deep fly balls but often lacks speed. As a staff we know power when we see it, as do all baseball coaches, and when we have a player who has the ability to hit the ball out of the ballpark, we encourage him to make hard contact. The all-or-nothing approach is not acceptable in the offense we employ. At Illinois we feel that power hitters will accumulate more walks than strikeouts. These players are normally good fastball hitters, and we have them work diligently in getting themselves into a positive hitter's count (3-1, 2-0, and 1-0). During our intrasquad practices we constantly remind our players to get good pitches to hit. We want them to learn to hit the fastball, lay off the change-up, and hammer the breaking ball that starts directly at them waist high or higher.

Bat Control

We define a contact hitter as a player who often puts the ball in play, doesn't strike out much, handles the bat, is a good base runner, and hits for a high average. The ability to bunt for hits, sacrifice, squeeze, slash, hit-and-run, and hit behind runners are some of the key elements in this player's game. Typically, a hitter is either a power hitter or a bat-control hitter, and we evaluate each of our players to determine which type he fits. Those we identify as being strong in bat control work on executing their game during our intrasquad practices. We emphasize to this group that they have one opportunity to perform these bat-control skills and that they must deliver. We even ask our power hitters to perform bat-control skills because we will call on them to do so over the course of a normal game and season. Having both bat control and power is essential to the offensive success of any team and for those players who wish to move on to the next level.

Offensive Response

We define offensive response as the ability of individual players or the team to respond immediately and correctly in every game situation. As a staff we feel that combining team speed, power, and bat-control skills in our daily practices will develop offensive response. Because we incorporate all of our drills into our live intrasquad games, we do offensive-response drills on a daily basis with the hope that they will become second nature to our players. A few of the drills that we incorporate into our intrasquad games follow. These drills develop the four qualities essential to a successful offense and help us determine our ideal lineup. The possible situations are endless.

Base-Running Drill

To develop base-running skills during a live intrasquad game, we have one or two players at each base working on leads, reads, and reacting to live hitters and live defense. These players are not live during the game. The base runners react to the live hitter, as does the defense. To improve our base-running techniques, each player works at each base daily and throughout the entire intrasquad game. If the batter gets a base hit, he becomes live to the defensive team. If he is a base-stealing threat, we tell him that we are down a run and that he must steal second or third to put himself into scoring position. All of our base stealers have the green light, permission to steal on their own. Our base stealers also know that they are responsible for working on stealing second and third throughout the intrasquad game, whether they are live or not. During these intrasquad games we have no base coaches or umpires, and the players must know what inning we are in, what the score is, and the number of outs. They must react and make their own decisions, forcing them to improve their ability to read various game situations.

Power Drill

To develop power, we put our hitters into positive-count situations. We start each inning with the bases loaded and one out with an 0-0, 2-0, or 3-1 count. The hitter's sole goal in this situation is to drive the ball into the outfield, resulting in a run scored while avoiding a rally-killing double-play ground ball.

Bat-Control Drill

To develop bat control, we often use the same situations that we do for power. We start the inning with the bases loaded and one out. The hitter's sole goal in this situation is to squeeze, bunt, or hit to the right side, scoring the run while avoiding the double play. Another situation is to start each inning with a runner on second and no one out. We ask the batter to hit behind the runner to move him over. If the batter is successful in moving the runner, he comes back to home plate immediately and gets another live at-bat with a runner on third base. The batter will then have the opportunity to react to whether the infield is in or back. If the infield is in, we want a fly ball. If the infield is back, we look for a ground ball hit toward short or second, reinforcing to our team that positive outs score runs. If the hitter fails to move the runner on second, we have a situation with a runner on second and one out. The goal for the next hitter becomes getting a hit that scores the game-winning run from second.

Again, we cover all of the aspects of a potent offense (team speed, power, bat control, and offensive response) during these intrasquad games. In doing so we have the opportunity to evaluate our players' strengths and weaknesses every day at practice.

Setting the Lineup

After we have incorporated our offensive strategy and evaluated our team's progress during our fall intrasquad games, winter workouts, and preseason games, we as a staff are ready to put together our ideal lineup for the ballclub. The approach is simple. We put our best hitters at the top of the order, ensuring that these players will get the extra at-bats at the end of the game. With the game on the line, we want our strongest hitters at the plate to give our team the best chance to win.

The following sections describe the specific things we look for when developing an offensive lineup. The batting order would ideally consist of the following traits in each spot of the order.

Leadoff

Over the course of a game and season the leadoff hitter will bat the most. The player in the leadoff slot needs to create havoc and put pressure on the defense and the pitcher, starting with the first pitch of the game. The ideal leadoff batter hits right-handed and left-handed pitching equally well. We look for someone who can consistently make hard contact (power) that produces extra-base hits. The leadoff hitter in our lineup has strong knowledge of the strike zone and will have the highest on-base percentage on the team. Assuming he makes consistent, hard contact, he will have a low strikeout percentage. The leadoff hitter needs to be patient at the plate and aggressive enough to lay down bunts or produce hits and RBIs. The leadoff hitter should be the best base runner in the lineup with instincts that tell him when to run and when not to run. His aggressiveness allows him to go from first to third on virtually any ball hit into the outfield, and his ability to read pitchers and steal a base when called upon is crucial. Our leadoff hitter is unselfish and willing to take a walk or get on base in any way possible while also being a good RBI guy with two outs. Overall, the leadoff hitter in any lineup needs to have the ability to beat a team with his power, bat control, base running, speed, and knowledge of the game.

Two Hole

Ideally, we look for a left-handed batter in the second spot for two reasons. First, chances are that he will be able to pull the ball through the right side when the first baseman is holding the runner on. Second, a left-handed hitter to some extent blocks the catcher's vision with a runner on first base, giving us a better chance to steal a base. As a rule our left-handed hitter in the two hole is on the plate and has the ability to pull the ball to the right side. He also needs to have the ability to hit the ball through the left side either to beat out a hit with his speed or to execute the hit-and-run. The ability to hit the ball to either side of the infield is crucial. If the hitter is right-handed, we want the batter off the plate, making it easier for him to go the other way. A right-handed batter in the two hole should also have the ability to pull the ball.

Whether the two-hole batter is right-handed or left-handed, he must be patient and selective so that our leadoff hitter can steal bases. Ideally, the number two hitter also hits both right- and left-handed pitching equally well. Outstanding bat control comes into play because this hitter has to move runners over. Good foot speed is important so that he can stay out of the double play. The power we expect out of the two hole is doubles. This hitter will most likely see fastballs because of the base-running skills and speed of the leadoff batter. To have a successful offense, the two-hole hitter must have the ability to handle the fastball, be a good hitter with two strikes, be a good RBI guy with two outs, and be able to get a bunt down consistently. Like the leadoff batter, this hitter will have good base-running skills and the ability to steal a base when the situation dictates.

Three Hole

Our best overall hitter will bat third. The three-hole hitter has power, the lowest strikeout percentage on the team, and hits both right- and left-handed pitching. His combination of power and bat control over the course of a season will dictate the success of a team. He is the best contact hitter in the lineup, is patient and selective at the plate, and always takes good swings. The three-hole hitter has good knowledge of the strike zone and the ability to hit the fastball, off-speed pitches, and breaking balls to all fields. Because he is the best contact hitter on the team, he hits for a high average. The three-hole hitter will have good base-running skills, and with the heart of the order coming up behind him, he should have enough speed to stay out of an inning-ending double play.

This hitter is aggressive, likes pressure, and wants to drive in runners, especially with two outs. He wants to be at the plate in the toughest situations, and he makes the pitcher come to him. He seldom hits pitcher's pitches.

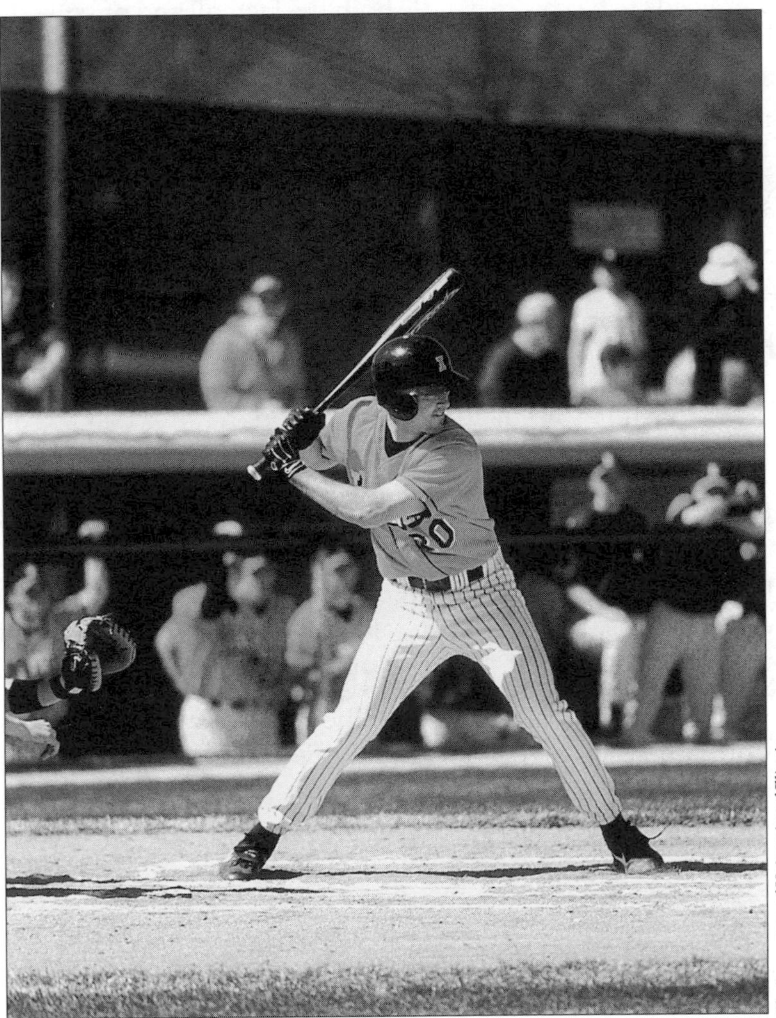

Photo courtesy of University of Illinois

The ideal three-hole hitter has both power and bat control and thrives under pressure.

Instead, this hitter seems to get his pitch more often than the rest of the lineup does, and he usually produces when he gets it. The ideal three-hole hitter seldom chases bad pitches because he can recognize pitches and deliveries. His patience and discipline at the plate make him the toughest out in our lineup. Overall, the three-hole hitter in any lineup needs to have the ability to beat a team with his power, bat control, base running, and knowledge of the game.

Four Hole

The four-hole hitter needs to be a good enough hitter to protect the batter ahead of him. This hitter has power, and he's a good, hard contact hitter. This batter needs to be able to handle both the fastball and off-speed pitches. He has good knowledge of the strike zone, enabling him to collect more walks than strikeouts. We want this hitter to have good base-running skills and enough speed to stay out of the double play. He is an RBI hitter with the ability to drive in runners from second base. The cleanup batter will usually come up with a runner or runners on base, so he must have the knack of either driving in those runners with a single or hitting the ball out of the park.

Five Hole

The number five hitter needs to be a good enough hitter that the opposing team cannot pitch around the cleanup hitter to get to him. The five-hole hitter will have extra-base power, but he is more of a free swinger and more aggressive than the hitters in front of him. The five-hole hitter should be the second- or third-leading RBI guy on the team. He needs to have the ability to handle both the breaking ball and off-speed pitches. The five-hole hitter will have decent base-running skills, along with the mental discipline to hit a fly ball or even strike out rather than hit into an inning-ending double play. Like the two hitters in front of him, the five-hole hitter wants RBIs, and when he makes contact he usually produces runs.

Six Hole

The ideal six-hole hitter has some power and hits for a high average. Because he is hitting behind the team's best hitters, he will have excellent bat-control skills that allow him to hit behind runners. He will handle the fastball and has the ability to hit to all fields. Hitting behind the top offensive threats on the team, the six-hole hitter needs to move a runner or produce a run when he makes contact.

Seven, Eight, and Nine Holes

The bottom part of the batting order can make or break the lineup. If the bottom part of the order can make the pitcher work, put pressure on the defense, get on base by any means possible, move runners, and set the table for the top of the order, a team will always have a chance to win games. On the other hand, if the bottom three hitters are so-called dead outs, the chances of winning are slim. For example, if these hitters are dead outs and each bats three times in a nine-inning game, we will virtually be playing a six-inning, 18-out game against an opponent who is playing a nine-inning, 27-out game. In this scenario our opponent will get 27 chances to score runs compared with our 18 chances to score. The odds of our scoring more runs than our opponent are solidly against us.

Ideally, we want the seven-, eight-, and nine-hole hitters to have the same skills as our top two hitters. Although they will probably lack power and the ability to make consistent, hard contact, these three hitters need to have decent speed and good bat control. Their goals are to get on base in any way possible, make the pitcher work, score runs, move runners, and set the table for the hitters at the top of the order. If a pitcher's pitch count increases appreciably during these players' at-bats, the top of the order has a better chance to do some real damage. The seven-, eight-, and nine-hole hitters need to be able to bunt, hit to the opposite field, and execute the hit-and-run correctly. They are fundamentally sound base runners who have the ability to steal bases when needed. These hitters will consistently move runners or get themselves into scoring position. If these three are able to do their job, the top of the order will have a chance to do theirs, which is to produce runs.

Pinch Hitting

Pinch hitting is one of the most difficult jobs in baseball and it takes a special kind of player to be accomplished at this skill. A good pinch hitter is a player who is mentally prepared to enter the game at any time. He must also have confidence in himself and his ability because he will get only one at-bat, and that one at-bat generally comes at an important time and situation in the game.

There are three categories of pinch hitters that are used in three different types of situations. The first category is the hitter that has a good eye at the plate, makes contact, and has the ability to reach base a good percentage of time. It is essential that this pinch hitter have a high on-base percentage. This hitter needs to be willing to battle the pitcher, making him go deep into the count, in order to increase his chances of getting on base. He can do this because he should also be a good two-strike hitter. He must be able to put the pressure on the pitcher to throw strikes, but still be able to make contact if the pitcher is finding the strike zone. This person knows his role is to get on base so that the top of the order will have an opportunity to knock him in.

The second category of pinch hitters is an athlete that makes regular contact and has a history of success hitting with runners on base, advancing runners, and collecting RBIs. Usually a line-drive hitter, this player has gap power and hits well under pressure.

The third category is a hitter that has home-run power but has a tendency to strike out more than the contact hitter discussed above. This player is usually called upon in situations where his long ball can tie the score or put his team ahead. He will normally enter the game from the seventh inning through the end of the game. This person is usually a good fastball hitter, as he will be called upon frequently to hit against the opponent's closer. In professional baseball, if a choice had to be made, a right-handed hitter might be preferable in this situation over a left-handed hitter because, as a rule, right-handed hitters hit right-handed pitching better than left-handed hitters hit left-handed pitching.

Right- and left-handed batters are another important consideration to take into account when inserting pinch hitters. As a manager, you would like to have the option of left-handed and right-handed hitters coming off the bench. At the high school and college levels, however, this is often difficult. Normally you will have your best hitters already in the lineup. It is not uncommon to see trades in professional baseball being made that ensure a team's bench has hitters that swing both from the left and right sides of the plate.

Another consideration to take into account when setting a lineup and thinking of possible pinch hitting situations is whether there is a player on the team that hits a certain pitcher consistently. Some managers, when they have such a hitter, will keep that player on the bench until the team gets runners in scoring position. At that point, the manager may insert this person as a pinch hitter for a weak hitter, hoping that he will produce a hit and drive in a few runs to keep a big inning alive.

The point of substituting a pinch hitter into a game is to put him into an important situation where he can make a difference in a ballgame. He is entering the game because he has a better chance of getting on base and driving in runs than the person he is replacing. Pinch hitters are most likely to be used in one of the following scenarios.

The first pinch hitter, the one that makes consistent contact, has good knowledge of the strike zone and is not afraid to take the pitcher deep into the count. By doing this he gives the pitcher a chance to do his work for him, which is reaching base any way he can, if the pitcher cannot throw a strike. He is likely to be used early in the game or when his team needs the tying or winning run on base. As stated in the description of this first category, this pinch hitter is used in an attempt to start a rally.

Pinch hitter number two is the good contact hitter with gap power who hits well under pressure. This player's value is most evident when hitting with runners on base. He has the ability to hit and advance runners, as well as a high percentage of driving runners home. This pinch hitter, often used in game-winning situations, is called upon to keep a rally alive. Although he can and does drive in runs, he makes contact often enough that he won't often strike out. Even if his contact doesn't drive in a run or result in a hit and thus him reaching base, odds are good that his contact will be enough to move a runner over, giving the next hitter in the lineup another chance to drive home an important run.

The third pinch hitter, the one with home-run power who frequently strikes out, usually enters the game late with the score tied or one run behind. His role is to try and get a pitch that he can drive out of the ballpark to tie the score or give his team the lead. This is the hitter who is called on when his one at-bat is the one that can and will shift the momentum of the game to one side or another.

In most close games pinch hitters are needed and will be used. A team that has a few good hitters coming off the bench will see their presence leading to additional wins over the course of a long season. As a coach or manager, when you are selecting your team, consider the last person or two that you keep. Think about whether one of the athletes you are choosing between fits into one of the pinch hitting categories described above. If one does, it may be in your interests to find him a spot on your team.

To create a lineup that gives a program its best chance of being successful, a coaching staff needs to be able to identify the players who are able to produce when called upon. By incorporating the four offensive qualities of an ideal lineup—speed, power, bat control, and offensive response—into everyday practice sessions, we are able to identify each of our players' strengths and weaknesses. We can thus name our top hitters, whom we put at the top of the lineup so that they get the extra at-bats in the later innings, when we hope we will be in a position to win the game. Building a lineup around these four qualities will help develop a team's offensive strategy, enhance the success of a program, and establish a consistent lineup.

Scouting and Studying the Opposition

Chuck Hartman

Having information on your opponent may give your team a better chance of winning a game. Information should be based on previous games, scouting reports, and observations you make both before and during the game.

If you have played your opponent in the last couple of years, information from the charts or the computer can be helpful. Look for pitching patterns or tendencies on certain counts. When pitching patterns are unambiguous, you can use the information as an offensive focus for your team. Tendencies that occur most often come on 0-0, 1-0, 2-0, 3-1, and 3-2 counts. You must analyze these counts with bases empty and with men in scoring position. In preparing the charts, use a regular pencil with no one on base and a colored pen or pencil with men on base.

Figure 2.1 shows that no definite tendency occurs on the first pitch (0-0). Every hitter except English and Bauder received a different pitch during the second time at bat. A couple of tendencies do occur. Nine out of 12 pitches with an 0-1 count were off-speed, seven out of eight 0-2 pitches were fastballs, and all 2-0, 3-1, and 3-2 pitches were fastballs. All 2-2 pitches were breaking balls. The hitter should be aware that against this club (or this pitcher), off-speed pitches are likely on 0-1 and 2-2 counts. Your hitters should be sitting on fastballs on the 2-0, 3-1, and 3-2 pitches.

Figure 2.2 shows that the pitcher's best pitch is obviously the fastball because he threw the fastball 81 times out of the 118 pitches. In addition, he started 21 of the 30 hitters with fastballs. The real tendency in this chart is that the 1-0 pitch was a fastball to 28 of the 30 hitters. With men on base, this pitcher stayed with his best pitch, which was obviously his fastball.

Hitter's Tendency Chart

Hitter	0-0	1-0	0-1	0-2	2-0	1-1	1-2	2-2	2-1	3-1	3-2
Stanton	1,2,2,1,1	1,1	3			1			1		
Tugwell	2,1,1,1	2,2	3		1	4			1		
West	1,2,1,3	1				4	3		1,1		
Toregas	2,1,4,1		4	1		3	1,3	3			
Bauder	2,4,3,1		1	1,1		4			1		
English	1,1,1,3	2,4	2,3	1		2,1,3	1	2	4		
Hutchison	1,4,1,1	1,3,1	1	1	1,1	4	4	3	4		1,1
Harris	2,1,1,1	2,1	4,3			1,1	1,3		1	1	1
Winterfeldt	1,2,1,1		1,3,3	4,1,1				3	1		

FIGURE 2.1 Use the charts to help identify pitching patterns and tendencies on certain counts.

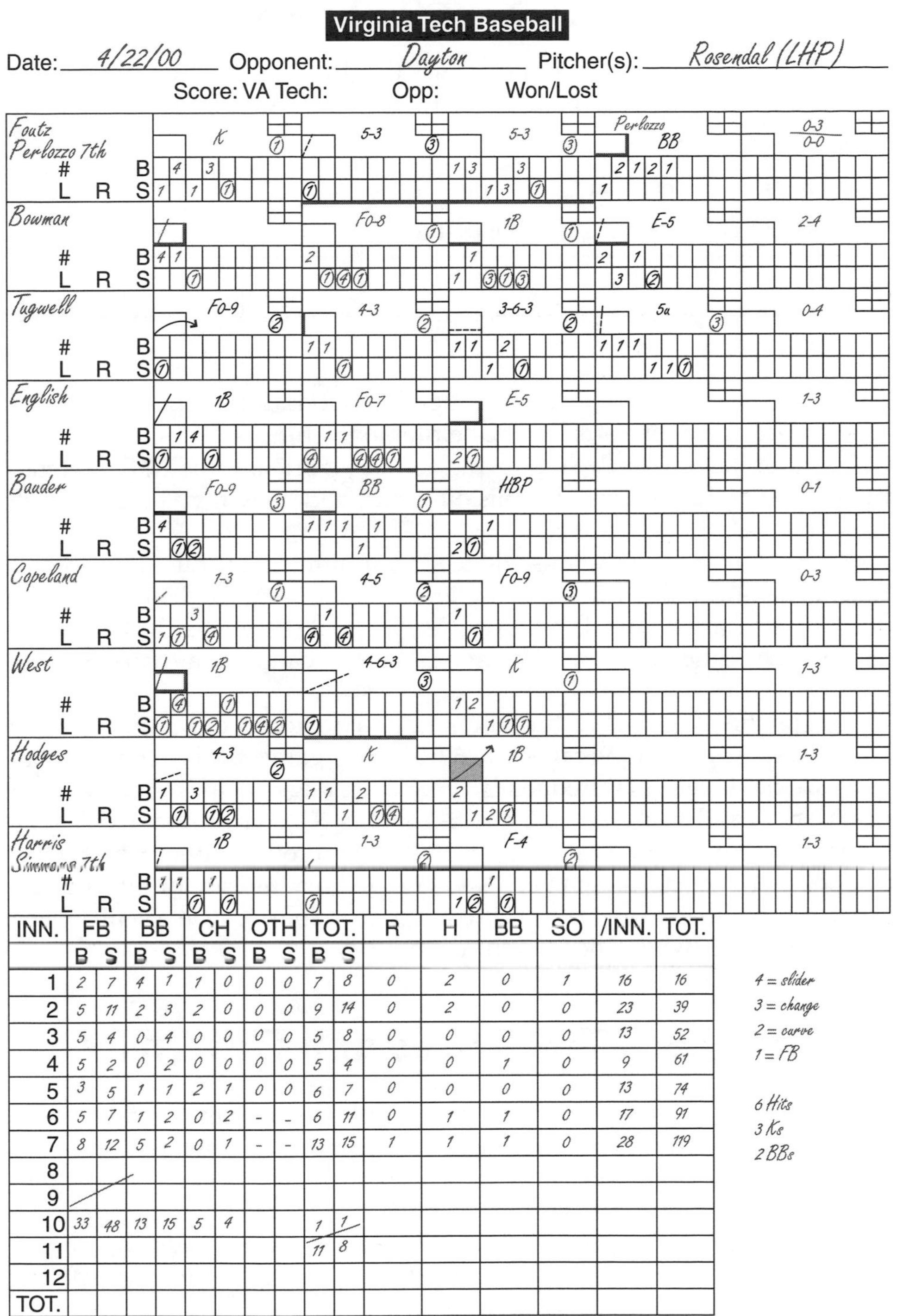

Virginia Tech Baseball

Date: 4/22/00 Opponent: Dayton Pitcher(s): Rosendal (LHP)

Score: VA Tech: Opp: Won/Lost

Foutz / Perlozzo 7th	K	5-3	5-3	Perlozzo BB	0-3 / 0-0
Bowman		F0-8	1B	E-5	2-4
Tugwell	F0-9	4-3	3-6-3	5u	0-4
English	1B	F0-7	E-5		1-3
Bauder	F0-9	BB	HBP		0-1
Copeland	1-3	4-5	F0-9		0-3
West	1B	4-6-3	K		1-3
Hodges	4-3	K	1B		1-3
Harris / Simmons 7th	1B	1-3	F-4		1-3

INN.	FB B	FB S	BB B	BB S	CH B	CH S	OTH B	OTH S	TOT. B	TOT. S	R	H	BB	SO	/INN.	TOT.
1	2	7	4	1	1	0	0	0	7	8	0	2	0	1	16	16
2	5	11	2	3	2	0	0	0	9	14	0	2	0	0	23	39
3	5	4	0	4	0	0	0	0	5	8	0	0	0	0	13	52
4	5	2	0	2	0	0	0	0	5	4	0	0	1	0	9	61
5	3	5	1	1	2	1	0	0	6	7	0	0	0	0	13	74
6	5	7	1	2	0	2	-	-	6	11	0	1	1	0	17	91
7	8	12	5	2	0	1	-	-	13	15	1	1	1	0	28	119
8																
9																
10	33	48	13	15	5	4			1	1						
11									11	8						
12																
TOT.																

4 = slider
3 = change
2 = curve
1 = FB

6 Hits
3 Ks
2 BBs

FIGURE 2.2 This chart shows the pitcher's tendency to use the fastball.

Pitcher's Stuff and Control

One thing to remember about pitchers is that they are creatures of habit. A couple of important factors are his stuff and his control. Questions to be answered here are these:

- What is his best pitch?
- What is his approximate velocity?
- Does his ball move?
- Does he have good off-speed pitches? If so, what type of spin do these off-speed pitches have?

Coaches and players should discuss these questions during the game. Good communication in this area can be helpful to the hitters.

Another key is identifying the pitcher's best pitch. Usually, the pitcher has one pitch that he considers his out pitch, and he will go to it in clutch situations.

Answers to these questions will feed your hitters lots of useful information. If the pitcher is throwing 90 miles per hour or more, the hitters must get the bats started quickly. On the other hand, if the pitcher has good off-speed pitches, the hitters must be able to stay back and hit the ball deeper in the strike zone.

The pitcher's control factor will have a tremendous effect on offensive strategy. If the pitcher averages 4 to 6 walks per game, the coach will probably use the take signal frequently. The coach might want to take a lot of first pitches and pitches on 2-0 and 3-1 counts. This approach enables the team to put runners on base and run up the pitch count. Either result could be enough to win a close game. Sometimes the pitcher cannot throw a certain pitch or pitches for strikes. Hitters can then look for a particular pitch to hit, especially when ahead in the count.

Pitcher's Tendencies and Patterns

Catchers, and even the coaches who call pitches, sometimes have tendencies. The previously discussed charts showed some of the tendencies and patterns. These patterns can be helpful to the coach in developing his offensive strategy. For example, if the first pitch is a strike and the tendency is then to go with an off-speed pitch, breaking ball, or splitter, this becomes a good pitch to start a runner. If the 0-2 pitch tendency is a curve or splitter, this is also a great time to start a runner.

Pitchers often go to their best pitch with runners in scoring position. The first pitch thrown to a hitter with runners in scoring position is often the pitch that the pitcher will use to try to get that hitter out. If the first pitch is a ball (1-0), many pitchers will not throw off-speed pitches for fear of getting further behind. Of course, if he is an off-speed pitcher, this pattern will be different. Teams can find out early by observing their charts to see if the pitcher will go off-speed on 2-0 or 3-1 counts.

Control of the Running Game

In determining how the pitcher controls the running game, don't forget that he is a creature of habit. One of the first things that all coaches do is determine the pitcher's time in delivering the ball to the plate. If the ball reaches the catcher more than 1.3 seconds after the pitcher first commits to the plate, you can steal bases. You must know your runners. An excellent coaching device is to time your runners from their leads to second base or third base. If the pitcher's release time plus the catcher's time to second base is higher than or equal to your runner's time, you can usually steal the base. For example, if your runner's time is 3.3 seconds to second base, the pitcher's time is 1.4 seconds, and the catcher's time is 2.0, your runner can steal the base.

You must observe the pitcher's moves to first base. How quick is it? Does he move to first while going into the stretch? Does he hold the ball for a time and then go to first? If a pitcher doesn't throw over much, he usually doesn't have a good move. Pitchers with good moves throw to first base often.

The timing or looks of a pitcher often fall into a pattern. He may look only once or twice at a runner. When your first runner gets on base, your players should focus on the pitcher, looking for a pattern, the timing, and the move to first. If one of these players then becomes a base runner, he has a picture of what to look for. He shouldn't have to ask his coach.

Defensive Strengths and Liabilities

One of the more important aspects of the defense is the catcher's throwing ability. His accuracy and arm strength can dictate your offensive strategy. If he throws well, then you should use the bunt, hit-and-run, or run-and-hit strategies. If he throws poorly, the better base runners should be able to steal. You should not have to use the sacrifice bunt against a weak-throwing catcher.

Players and coaches should observe outfield arm strength during pregame. Their strength or weakness can be the determining factor in whether you can take the extra base or not. Players and coaches, through their pregame observations, can make good decisions on running to the next base.

Likewise, players and coaches should watch the third baseman in the pregame and note his agility, arm strength, and ability to make the play on a slow roller. During the game, they should find answers to several questions about the third baseman's play:

- How does he play the hitters?
- Does he play deep, medium, or short?
- Does he move back after a strike on the hitter?

Your good drag bunters should observe all these factors to help determine when to use that part of the offensive game.

During the game, observation of the defensive alignment can be helpful to the offensive players. The alignment can be one of the best indicators of how the opponent is going to pitch to a hitter. If the opponent is playing the hitter to be late, they are probably going to try to pitch away. Of course, if the opponent is playing the hitter to pull, they may be trying to keep the ball inside.

The play of the middle infielders can offer opportunities to the offense. If neither of the middle infielders moves toward second base after a pitch with a man on first base, the opponent is susceptible to the delayed steal. On the steal or hit-and-run play, do both infielders move before the pitch reaches the plate? If they do, you should try hit-and-run plays because the vacated spots left by the middle infielders are where most ground balls are hit. On the hit-and-run play, does the infielder covering the base leave early? Does he leave before the pitch gets to the plate? If he does, then the vacated space may indicate that the opponent is susceptible to the hit-and-run. The fake steal is a good way to check this out.

Another observation you should make is how well they turn the double play. If they are good, coaching strategy might involve a sacrifice bunt or hit-and-run to avoid being taken out of the inning by the ground ball. On the other hand, if they are not very good and you have a decent runner at the plate, you may want to swing away.

Observations During the Game

Most of the scouting reports and previously discussed items must be observed. How is the pitcher's control? What kind of zone does the umpire have? Is the zone large or small? These three questions must be answered to determine game strategy.

If the umpire has a small zone, the hitter can be patient in waiting for his pitch. On the other hand, if the zone is large, the hitter must open up his strike zone, particularly with two strikes. The type of zone can also dictate coaching strategy. A small zone might suggest using the take signal, and a large zone might call for the hit sign.

As previously discussed, hitters must know the pitcher's tendencies and patterns. Each hitter in the lineup should understand from the scouting report and his game observations how the opposing team is attempting to get him out. Hitters should observe the 0-2 counts closely because many teams will use the same strategy on every 0-2 count. The hitter should develop a focus for this situation.

How is the opposing pitcher controlling the running game? What are his habits that your team should know? The team and coaches should be observing the types of moves the pitcher uses. Does the right-handed pitcher move early, or does he hold the ball? His move should be timed. Any move over 1.0 seconds indicates to the runner that he can extend the lead. In dealing with left-handed pitchers, several anatomical factors should be considered:

- Position of head when throwing home or throwing to first base. The left-handed pitcher will often look at first base and throw home or look at home and throw to first. Sometimes, the left-hander will tilt his head back when throwing to first base.
- Knee of the front leg. The left-hander will open up his front knee when throwing to first. When throwing home, the knee is straight up and approximately in line with the rear leg.
- Trunk position. Sometimes left-handers will tilt back when throwing to first base. They do this to clear their hips.

Of course, players and coaches must all note the pitcher's time to the plate and the catcher's time throwing to second base.

Hitter's Adjustments

Hitters must be observant and talk to other hitters during the game. They should discuss whether the fastball has movement. If so, what kind of movement? They should talk about the off-speed pitches. What kind of action does the ball have? Is the spin 12 to 6? Can the hitter see the spin on the curveball or slider?

The pitcher on the opposing team will usually have an out pitch. Hitters must understand what this pitch is. They should be observing game charts to see if pitching patterns are developing during the game. Hitters should be aware of the pitches used during various counts, particularly 0-2, 2-0, 3-1, and 3-2. They must develop a two-strike approach against the opposing pitcher.

Most important, the hitter has to understand how the pitcher is attempting to get *him* out. If the pitcher is pitching away with all his pitches, the hitter may have to move closer to the plate or try to hit to the opposite field. If the pitcher is giving him a steady diet of curveballs or off-speed pitches, the hitter might move up in the box and try to hit the ball deeper in the

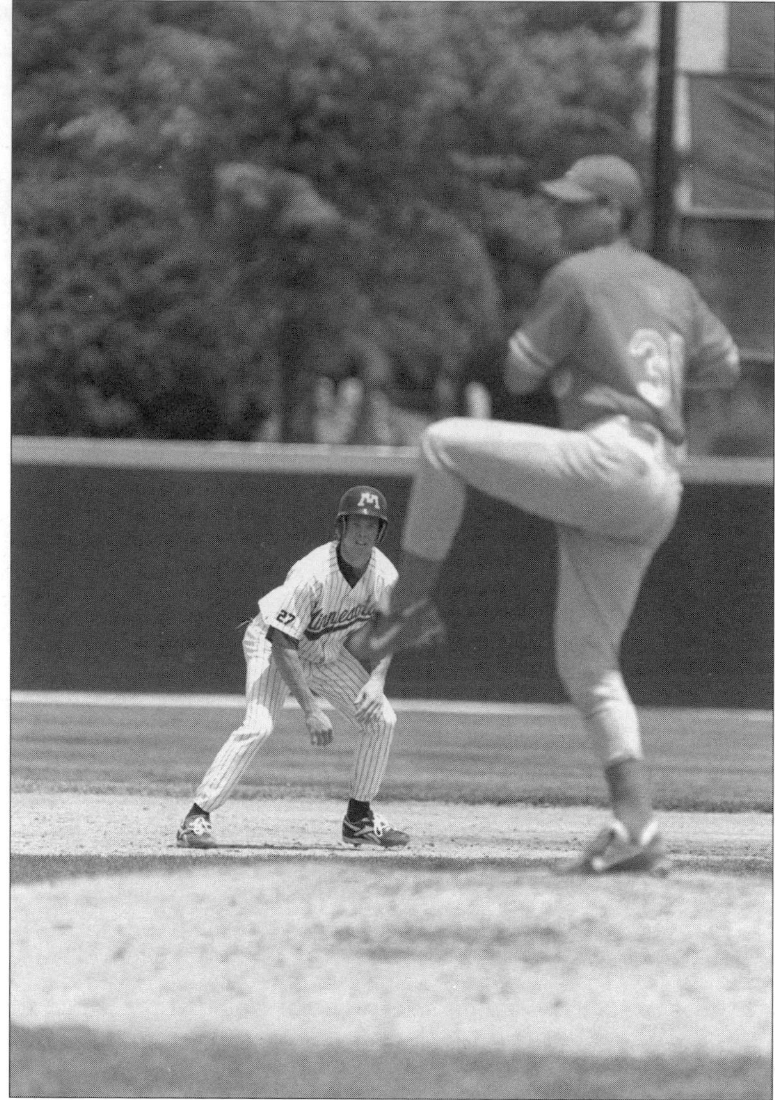

Before attempting a steal, it's important to know the pitcher's time to the plate plus the catcher's time to second. If it's higher than or equal to the runner's time, you can usually steal the base.

zone. The hitter should realize that the first pitch thrown to him with men in scoring position is most likely the pitch that the opposition feels they can use to get him out.

Finally, the hitter must analyze the game situation. For example, with a runner on second base with no outs, the opposing pitcher will try to prevent the hitter from hitting to the right side of the diamond. The pitcher will throw off-speed pitches or pitch inside to right-handed batters. He will pitch the left-handed hitters away with fastballs or backdoor sliders.

When the double play is in order, the pitcher will attempt to get a ground ball, usually with pitches down in the zone. If the hitter is a pull hitter, the pitcher will probably try to keep the ball away in hopes of having the hitter roll over and hit a ground ball to the second baseman or shortstop, depending on whether he is right-handed or left-handed. The preceding would also apply with a runner on third base and less than two outs. If the pitcher gets two strikes on the hitter, he may go for the strikeout. With a runner on third base the hitter should not forget which is the pitcher's best pitch.

Players who understand how pitchers are trying to get them out, know all the information available on the opposing pitcher, and understand the dictates of the game situation will be better offensive players. Of course, better offensive players create a better offensive team. Base runners must know the arm strength of the outfielders and the catcher. The complete offensive player knows that the pitcher is a creature of habit. If players and coaches observe the abilities and tendencies of the opposition and use the information intelligently, their team will have a competitive edge. Using these focus points during the game should make them a much better offensive team.

Using Signals for Hitting and Base Running

Mike Gillespie

Because we ask our players to do so much offensively, we have many signs and must constantly review them with the team. We have found in college baseball that our opponents are tireless in their efforts to pick our signs. So although we want to keep our system simple, we must be deceptive enough to ensure that someone outside our group cannot determine the meaning of our signs. Consequently, we find it helpful to have alternate systems or at least to change indicators game to game or inning to inning. One option is to have different signs for different players. Coaches must continually review their signs with the team and regularly alternate systems if they expect their players to know the systems and execute with confident aggressiveness whatever it is they are being asked to do.

Establishing a Functional System

Our communication of a sign may be as simple as talking to the hitter or possibly the on-deck hitter before he leaves the dugout. For example, we may tell the hitter that if he gets on, we will steal or hit-and-run on the first pitch so he should ignore what might be a dummy sign. Some teams use the on-deck hitter or hitter in the hole to communicate to the hitter information gleaned from the catcher, that he's setting up in or away, for example.

We ask that the on-deck hitter look for a sign before he leaves the on-deck circle. Once he becomes the hitter we want him to drop one foot out of the box to look for a sign after every pitch or pickoff attempt. Before he gets back in the box, he should allow the runner to take his lead. We demand that the batter do this quickly, and we attempt to give signs promptly to avoid slowing the tempo of the game unnecessarily. Some teams ask that the hitter and base runners acknowledge signs to ensure that no one has missed a sign.

When "situational hitting" is called for, such as when we have a man at second with none out or a man at third with less than two outs and one or more infielders back, we communicate to the hitter that we expect him to "play the game" by selecting a pitch that he can hit to the right side, up the middle on the ground, or other appropriate tactic. We likewise specifically convey to the runner at third what he is to do on a ground ball. Of course, we as coaches must be mindful of a player's capabilities before we ask him to execute a specific skill.

We expect a base runner to look for a sign immediately upon reaching a base, after every pickoff attempt, or after any foul ball, and he must anticipate a verbal sign from the base coach. The runner should be mindful that the hitter is waiting to get into the box until the runner takes his lead. Once he has his lead, the runner must be reading the catcher's signs and the pitcher's grips. The runner's system of relaying signs might be a movement of either hand or foot, or a turn or tilt of the head. The runner will first communicate that he has picked a catcher's signs or a pitcher's grips by calling out a phrase or using some hand sign. We will then alert the hitter.

Deciding Who Calls Pitches

In college baseball it is not uncommon for either the head coach or the pitching coach to call the pitches, rather than having the catcher call the game. Those who go by this philosophy believe the coaching staff has a greater knowledge of the scouting report than does the catcher and is better suited to match a pitcher's strengths with a hitter's weaknesses. The coaches may also have experience with a particular opponent that tells them when a team likes to hit-and-run, squeeze, or attempt a certain first-and-third play, and they call pitches accordingly.

Those who prefer that the catcher call pitches believe the catcher has a better feel for how the pitcher is throwing and has a better perspective of any adjustment a hitter is making. These same coaches feel that traditionally the catcher runs the game much like the quarterback in football. Has anyone noticed that the quarterback virtually never calls the game anymore? Nor does the middle linebacker call the defense, or the point guard determine the offense or defense in basketball.

The suggestion that players offensively decide whether or not to hit-and-run, squeeze, or double steal would be met with much skepticism, to put it mildly. Why is pitch calling different? I have also noticed that if the team loses, it is the coach, not the catcher, who gets fired.

Sign, Sign, Everywhere a Sign

Our system of sign giving to call pitches to the hitter has been limited only by our imagination. We make liberal use of verbal signals, typically using a phrase that is common baseball terminology— "line drive," "base hit," "good hitter," and "come on now," to name a few. Sometimes we use a dummy phrase, meaning nothing.

Our offensive touch system makes use of an indicator. The hot sign may be two signs after the indicator, and we may use a double indicator and require that we lock in the sign with some specific touch at the end of the sequence. A wipe-off may start the sequence over, and there will always be one or more "nothing's on" signs. The player should have a sign to ask for a repeat of the coach's sign. We use an "ignore it" sign, which means "ignore the sign I'm about to give," and we also use a "thinking about it" sign to tell our player that we are considering a certain play within the next couple of pitches. We make particular use of this sign when we are considering a squeeze, steal of home, or first-and-third play.

Another method of sign giving we like is using a separate set of signs between the head coach and the first-base coach, who employs his own verbal signs to the runner for a steal or delayed steal. This is simply another way of protecting against the possibility that our opponent will pick our signs.

Picking Opponents' Signals

Like so many teams, we are seeking to pick the signs and pitches of our opponent, and we must constantly be on the alert for the other team's attempts to pick us. We listen for a word, phrase, whistle, or other form of communication, and we try to locate the source from which it is coming. Commonly it is someone in the dugout, a base runner, a base coach, or a player in the bullpen, but we've encountered teams that put someone behind the outfield fence or in the stands behind the catcher. Some opponents even have someone studying TV monitors in the dugout or clubhouse. We also scout ourselves: Can we pick our own coach, pitcher, or catcher? Does our pattern of sign giving or some telltale body language give us away? We must remember that by videotaping games on television, our opponents have the opportunity to study our signs, so we must prepare accordingly.

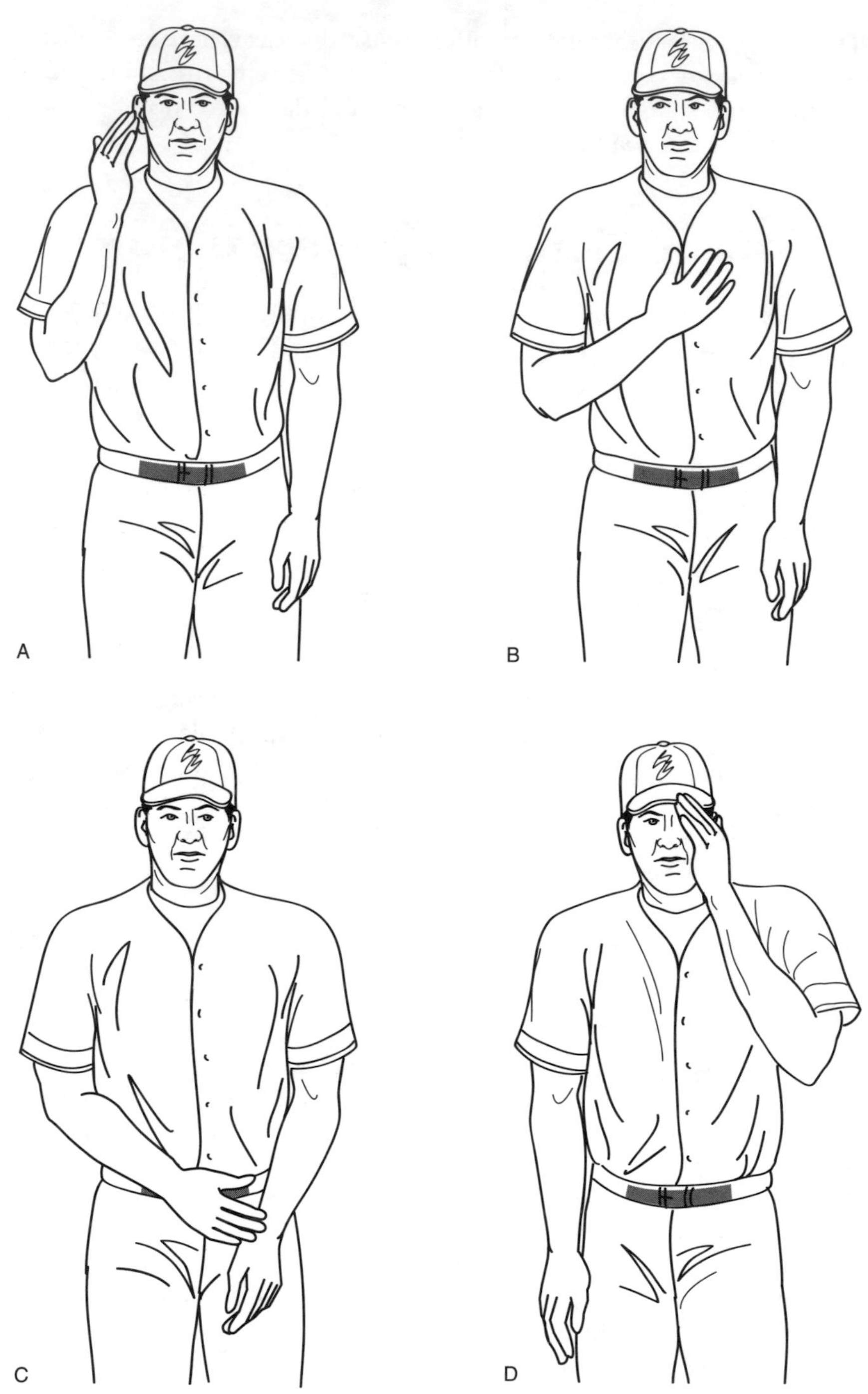

A sample set of signs: The indicator is the right hand touching the left wrist, and the steal sign is the left hand swiping the bill of the hat on the next touch. To complete the set, the coach must wipe his chest in a downward motion with either hand on the last touch. So, *(a)* the coach touches his ear, *(b)* wipes his hand across the chest, then *(c)* touches his left wrist with

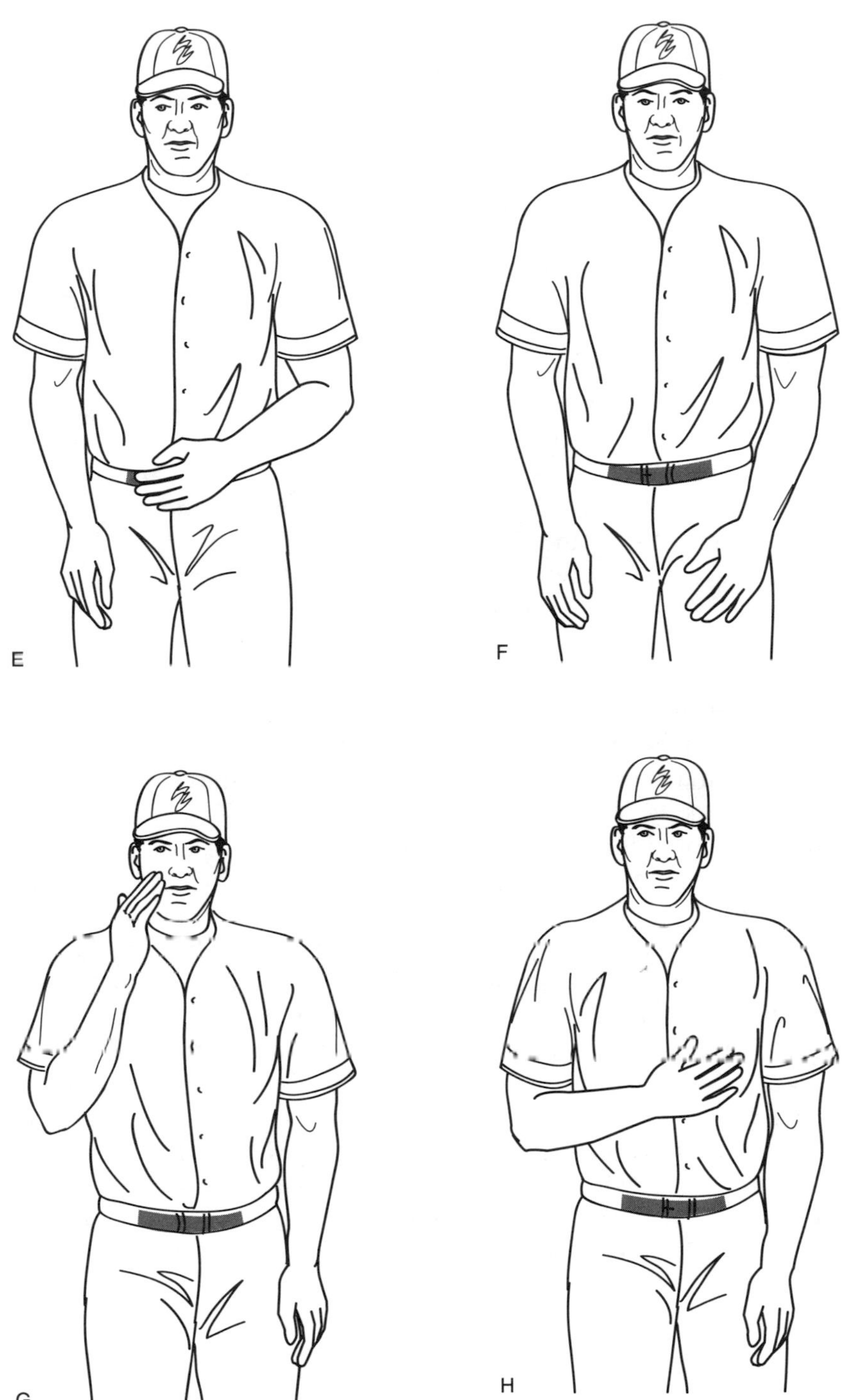

his right hand (indicator). This is immediately followed with *(d)* a swipe of the bill of the hat by the left hand (steal), *(e)* a touch to the belt, *(f)* a wipe down the leg, *(g)* a touch of the face, then *(h)* a wipe down the chest to "lock-in" the sign and complete the set.

When trying to steal our opponents' signs or a pitcher's pitches, we have had our greatest success when we have coaches or players on our team committed to the task of searching for some pattern or telltale movement. This obviously requires patience and sticking to it.

We typically chart the touches utilized by the coach in an attempt to associate a certain touch or sequence of touches with a particular play. Certain signs such as the "take" or "swing-away" are often very simple with no attempt at camouflage or deception, and some coaches get careless about how they use their indicator; careful charting may reveal these parts of a sign system.

We have found that an effective method of decoding a catcher's system is for a runner to return to the dugout and report the sign and pitch sequence to our "007," our code breaker. For example, the runner may report that the catcher flashed 4-1-2-3-2 and the pitch was a slider, and then flashed 1-2-4-1-3 and the pitch was a change. "007" records it and may determine that the first sign after a 2 indicates the pitch. Complex systems may require many runners to report to the code breaker what they observed.

We expect everyone on the team to be involved in picking pitches. The most common give-aways are a pitcher's show of different grips or hand movements, subtle changes in his motion, finger movement of the glove-hand forefinger that is outside the glove, and even facial expressions and flexed forearm muscles. Catchers may have their fingers exposed to base coaches, they may move to a target early, or they may hold the glove a certain way on certain pitches.

Sometimes infielders are moving or talking, and on rare occasions an outfielder's movement can betray what the pitch is. When the pitches are called from the dugout, we assign a group of at least three players the task of trying to break the system. Through a process of charting the coach's touches or actions, we occasionally are able to determine what's coming. We find that picking pitches is often simple and that determination and tenacity make the difference in whether we are successful in this area.

We've also found it effective to make dummy calls, that is, to make calls as though we have pitches when in fact we don't. A pitcher may become distracted, lose focus or concentration, and make a mistake that results in a hit.

We have observed that teams who are complete in their preparation are ready to exploit any opportunity to get an out on defense or enhance their offense. Having hitters know what's coming is just one area that might be a difference maker.

Signs are the vehicle by which communication is accomplished in baseball. Games might be won or lost for no reason other than a sign that is successfully delivered or missed completely. The challenge is to be simple in the design of a sign system, yet complex enough to keep opponents from being able to decipher the system.

4

Hitting Strategy

Mark Johnson

A baseball fan may go to the ballpark, watch a game, enjoy it, and go home completely unaware that he missed the game! Of course, the fan saw the obvious aspects of the game, but he may have missed the inner part, the game within the game—the emotions, the matchups, the strategies of the game on and after every pitch. The outcome of the game involves much more than running, throwing, fielding, and hitting. It's not that simple. The beauty of baseball is often found in the interplay of emotions, matchups, and strategies that unfold with each passing moment.

Why would a team bunt in the second inning of a scoreless game with a man on first, no outs, and the five-hole hitter at the plate? Why would a team play the infield in during the second inning of a scoreless game with runners at second and third and the three-hole hitter at the plate? Most managers will not play their entire hand early in a game, but they do lay down some cards that others can see. The preceding hypothetical situations could provide clues about how the manager feels about both teams' pitchers, offenses, bullpens, and defenses. Remembering a manager's early decisions may be useful as the game progresses because they can provide valuable insight into a team's strategy.

Baseball fans are said to second-guess more than the fans of any other sport. Many fans have played the game in one form or another—at a picnic, in the backyard, or in some type of organized league. Many see it as a rather simple game of pitch, hit, run, catch, and throw. Baseball also has the enduring quality of time between pitches. The game is *made* for second guessing. Its structure gives people a second chance to make a decision after they have seen the results of the first decision. And unlike many other sports, baseball often offers only two choices. If the first choice failed, a second-guessing fan could end up a genius—and many fans do! And why not?

Second-guessing is one of the great pleasures in going to the ballgame, and yes, it brings a fan closer to the game within the game.

Guidelines for Effective Hitting Strategy

A rock-solid rulebook on hitting strategies does not exist. Too many variables change from pitch to pitch. Each player has different talents and abilities. Few can execute all the skills needed to set the rule. Some can execute the hit-and-run, some can bunt, some are difficult to strike out, some can hit behind the runner, some can hit for power, and some can hit for a high percentage. But few can do it all! Some hitters match up better with certain pitchers. Also, players tend to hit better at some times than they do at others. Players are influenced by the moments they have just passed through. Some players, if they have just come through a negative experience, will respond with more determination, whereas others will break down and call it a bad day.

Conversely, hitting strategy may have absolutely nothing to do with the hitter. A strategy may be designed simply to test a weakness of the opponent. Variables will always be present, and, of course, they are what make the game entertaining and intriguing. Most people who have been around the game a long time can attest to witnessing some successes with a strategy that broke the rulebook. They've seen the first-and-third, two-out suicide squeeze with the third baseman playing even up with the bag. They've seen an unsuccessful steal attempt with two outs and a nine-hole hitter batting .125 at the plate. They've seen a successful first-and-third double steal with no outs and a speedy three-hole hitter at the plate. At this point we should simply note that a good manager will play percentage baseball until the variables change his thoughts.

We should also realize that a good manager and a good hitter have more information to assist their decision making than anyone else does, including fans, parents, and, yes, baseball men. The manager and hitter are aware of variables that no one else knows about. They may not bunt in a bunting situation simply because the hitter is a poor bunter or because the next hitter does not match up well with the pitcher. Or a manager may bunt with a man on second and no outs simply because the hitter cannot hit the ball to the right side.

Despite the many variables that affect hitting strategy, the manager or coach should know some simple general rules. These are guidelines to consider when developing a strategic plan, and they can be adjusted to fit each unique situation.

- *Consider the skill level of the players.* Strategies vary greatly with the level of play. In the lower level of skill development (preadolescents and adolescents), games are usually lost more than they are won. In other words, teams usually beat themselves with poor defensive plays, lots of bases on balls, poor base running, and so on. Teams that end up in the win column usually put the ball in play and force defensive mistakes with bunts, steals, and hit-and-run plays. At this level, the more ground balls that are hit, the better the chances for victory. Make the defense play.

As the skill level rises to a good high school level or certainly to the college level, defensive skills are much better. The double play becomes an inning-ending feature, catchers hold down the running game, pitchers have better moves to first base on pickoff attempts and a quicker delivery to home plate, and the first-and-third double steal doesn't work as well. Simply put, the defense will not offer as many opportunities or outs as it does at the younger level of play. A coach or manager must pick spots for strategic hitting more wisely.

At the professional level, of course, the defense seldom gives an opponent more than three outs. The skill level is so good that rarely do you see an attempted first-and-third double steal. The players control more of the game because of their skill level. Gambles do not often pan out at this level. Opponents will not lose the game; they will force a team to win the game. More often than not, a manager's role is concerned with matchups.

Therefore, good hitting strategy for one level may be poor strategy for another. Pay attention to the skill level of the players as you plan strategies.

- *Don't overstrategize.* Young coaches, in particular, tend to do too much maneuvering and do not allow the players to control the outcome of the game. They neutralize their team's talent by dominating the games with bunts, hit-and-run plays, and so forth. The talent of the players wins or loses most games, not the strategies of the coach or manager! Once the game starts, coaches and managers increase their chances for victory by letting their players play rather than forcing the action with a lot of strategic moves.

- *Set the right tempo.* Managers sometimes use hitting strategies simply to set the tempo for the team, to let players see the manager's aggressiveness and belief in the players. Some strategies are set not necessarily to win the game at that moment but to establish the mind-set of the players, their roles, and their responsibilities. A manager may allow a hitter to hit on a 3-0 count. This tactic sends a message not only to that hitter but also to the entire team. This approach goes against percentage baseball, but it may pay dividends in the mind-set of the players. In like manner, a manager may hit-and-run in the first inning to set the tempo.

- *Play for the big inning early and be more aggressive.* Many games are won in one big inning. In the early innings of the game, managers should play for that big inning. Sacrificing outs to move runners rarely produces big innings. With no outs early in a normal game, unless an excellent bunter or hit-and-run player is at the plate or an excellent base stealer is at first, play the game out and let the hitter hit.
- *The more outs there are, the more a team should gamble.* If you have three outs to work with and a man on first, play it out for a big inning. As the number of outs increases, the team must do something that is against percentage baseball. Hit-and-run plays and steals should occur more after one out. If the team is well behind midway or late in the game, however, gambles are not recommended.
- *The latter part of a game belongs more to the manager.* Managers pay closer attention to matchups that might require pinch hitters, pinch runners, or better bunters. Most managers will give up some defensive skills to produce a key run late in the game. Remember, in baseball you cannot hold the ball or run out the clock. The pitcher must throw to the hitter. If you are at the key spot, substitute offense for defense and then hope the ball doesn't find your offensive move when that player takes the field!
- *Play the short game early when facing a dominating pitcher.* Use the bunt, try the hit-and-run, and move runners.
- *When behind late in the game without the tying run at the plate, play straight-up baseball.* Of course, the objective in hitting strategy in baseball is always to get ahead or stay even with your opponent as the game materializes. That way, all hitting strategies are alive and well. When behind late in a game and with the tying run not at the plate, most teams must play the game straight up because they cannot afford to give up outs to advance runners. A team is at the mercy of lower percentage baseball; that is, they must rely on extra-base hits, bases on balls, and multiple hits in an inning. They may even have to change their hitting strategy in counts by taking a called first strike in the latter part of a game.
- *Avoid falling into patterns.* Although most managers and coaches have philosophical beliefs and tendencies in hitting strategies, they should avoid falling into a pattern. An aggressive bunt defense can improve percentages to get a lead runner out if the defensive team can anticipate that a bunt is going to be attempted. A pitchout on a hit-and-run can ruin an inning if the defensive team calculates correctly. In like manner, the defense can switch the middle infielders if the offensive team always tries the hit-and-run in certain situations. Managers would be wise not to fall into patterns.

Role of Hitters in the Lineup

Itchy Jones, the Hall of Fame coach from the University of Illinois, has done a tremendous job of identifying how to determine lineups in chapter 1. Unfortunately, once the game starts, roles change because the lineup is usually different every inning.

Should the mind-set be different for the hitter depending on where and when he bats in the current inning? Yes, it should. We have often heard that every at-bat is different—different pitcher, different circumstances in the game, different counts, different situations facing the hitter. The role of the hitter in an inning changes because of his place in the lineup. As we discuss this, realize that a team does not want to weaken the talent the hitter brings to the plate by asking him simply to fill a role, but a team must establish a collective mind-set so that everyone understands the requirements of the various roles.

The ultimate leadoff hitter in an inning is one who will force the pitcher to throw strikes and, in most cases, force the pitcher to throw five or six pitches in the at-bat. This hitter can take a strike and not panic. He knows he can put the ball in play. He will often take a strike on a 2-0 or 3-1 count unless it is his pitch, in his zone. In some cases he will take it anyway.

Unfortunately, the leadoff hitter in your batting order sometimes leads off only in the first inning. Within a span of five or six games, everyone in your batting order will probably lead off some innings. The surest way to get on first base is by way of a base on balls. The chance that a team will score increases dramatically when the leadoff hitter reaches first base. For that reason coaches always say to the pitcher, "Get the leadoff man out, and your inning is halfway over!" The leadoff man must force the pitcher to throw strikes, and if the pitcher gets behind in the count, he must be willing to take a strike.

The hitter who comes to the plate with no one on base and two outs faces a different situation. On the 0-0, 2-0, or 3-1 count, he is looking to drive the ball with the idea of getting into scoring position. He knows that although a base on balls is good, it will still take a couple more hits to score him.

The leadoff hitter must realize that he can make a huge contribution to his team's chances of having a big inning by getting on base. Taking the 3-1 strike is frustrating to an "individual" hitter, but not to a situational hitter. He realizes that the pitcher has missed on three of his last four pitches. The percentages say he will not now throw two strikes in a row.

If the leadoff hitter gets on, the key player in that inning will always be the next hitter. To keep the inning alive, the objective of the second hitter is to move the base runner into scoring position and, if possible, get on base as well. If he makes an out but moves the runner, the at-bat is still solid. Hitting the ball to the right side will increase the chances of moving the runner because the hole there is larger with the first baseman holding the runner and because the throw to second from a right-handed first baseman or second baseman is a lower percentage throw than the throw from the shortstop or third baseman, who are on the left side of the infield. That said, it is not wise, particularly early in a game, to take hitting strengths away from the hitter. At most levels of play the hitter should hit with his strengths and not give himself up to hit to the right side. If the runner is critically important, the manager can ask the hitter to execute a sacrifice bunt.

Obviously, the role that the three-hole hitter plays in the inning depends on the situation. If the runner remains at first with one out, a hit-and-run may be his objective that inning. If the runner has advanced to scoring position, the hitter's objective is to drive in the run. If the three-hole hitter comes up with no one on and two outs, he looks for pitches to drive, and he aggressively but intelligently gambles on turning a single into a double.

Plan Before Going to the Plate

Year in and year out, a larger percentage of games will be won by the team with the highest on-base average rather than the team with the highest slugging percentage. Many studies have been conducted concerning productivity of ground balls, fly balls, and line drives. Studies at the NCAA Division I level conclude the following:

- For every 10 ground balls hit, 3 will fall in for a base hit, and the on-base average is 42 percent.
- For every 10 line drives hit, 8 will fall in for a base hit, and the on-base average will be 84 percent.
- For every 10 fly balls hit (including all home runs), 2 will fall in for a base hit, and the on-base average will be 29 percent.

Keep in mind that these statistics apply to top amateur baseball players who are skilled defensively and play on surfaces that are usually better than those of other amateur fields. One could certainly argue that the batting averages and on-base averages would increase with less skilled defenses or with poorly manicured fields. And although either condition would mean more base hits on fly balls, the increase for ground balls and line drives would be even greater. It is simply easier to catch a fly ball than it is to catch a ground ball, throw it accurately to a base, and have it be caught. In like manner, line drives are harder to catch than fly balls; fly balls can be run down more easily than line drives.

If you are playing any level of amateur baseball and believe that on-base average wins more games, then line drives and ground balls are the route to take.

As a reference point to ensure understanding, hitters should normally

- hit the inside pitch to the pull side (figure 4.1a),
- hit the outside pitch to the opposite side (figure 4.1b), and
- hit the pitch down the middle to the middle of the field (figure 4.1c).

This set of guidelines is an absolute in hitting. Successful hitters rarely deviate from this absolute, although there are exceptions for exceptional hitters.

Unless a hitter is in a guess count (3-1, 2-0), his initial thought is to work from a plan that the next pitch will be in the middle of the plate and high in

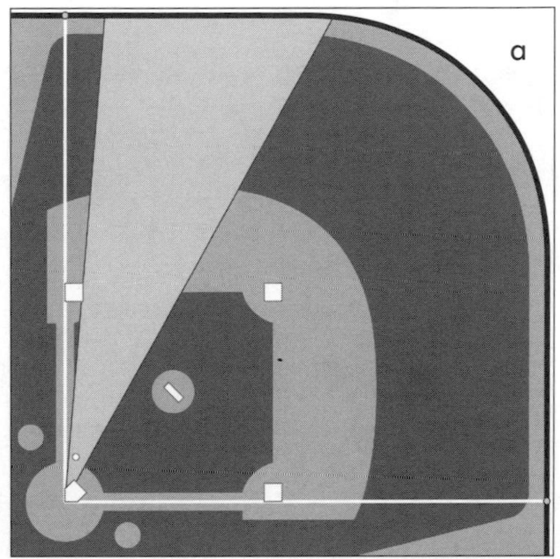

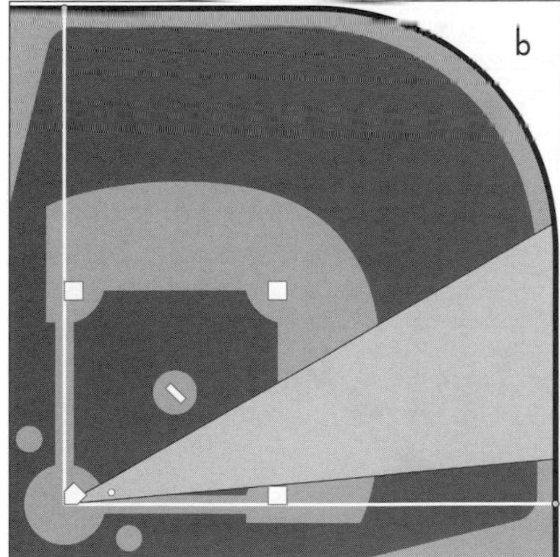

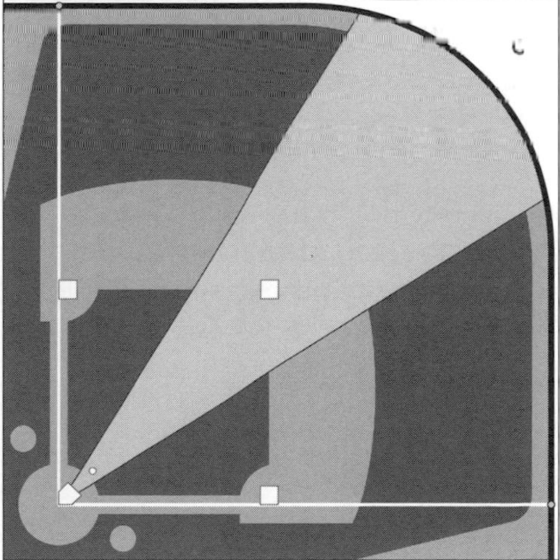

FIGURE 4.1 Hitters should normally *(a)* hit the inside pitch to pull side, *(b)* hit the outside pitch to the opposite side, and *(c)* hit the pitch down the middle to the middle of the field (right-handed hitter).

the strike zone. His mental plan will be to hit a line drive up the middle. Although plans do not always work out, the hitter should note that with this plan he can more easily make adjustments as the pitch is thrown. If we say that the middle of the plate is 10 inches wide, then we must adjust to around 3 1/2 inches for the outer half and 3 1/2 inches for the inner half of the plate (see figure 4.2). In reality, most hitters, either consciously or unconsciously, work from the premise that the pitch will be more toward the inside. Obviously, in this case greater adjustments to the outside pitch in the strike zone become necessary and are often unsuccessful. In like manner, a hitter will have fewer pop-ups or foul balls if he starts with the expectation that a ball will be pitched up in the zone. Adjusting the swing down is much easier than adjusting the swing up, and the results are normally more productive.

Successful hitting requires aggressiveness. The pitcher starts the action; he throws the first blow. The hitter must be prepared to respond aggressively. Aggressiveness will overcome many flaws in a swing.

The hitter has only a little time to make the decision to swing the bat. He should plan on swinging! Aggressive, good hitters have already made half of that decision. Rather than making two decisions, either to swing or not to swing, the aggressive hitter will make only one decision—not to swing. He is already planning to swing.

Good hitters will primarily use the middle of the field. That is, the balls they hit will travel between the shortstop and second baseman or to the power alleys in the outfield. Although there are exceptions, you will find that high-average hitters do not consistently pull or push. Pitchers have a much easier time beating the pull hitter or push hitter. The tough hitters are those who consistently use the middle of the field.

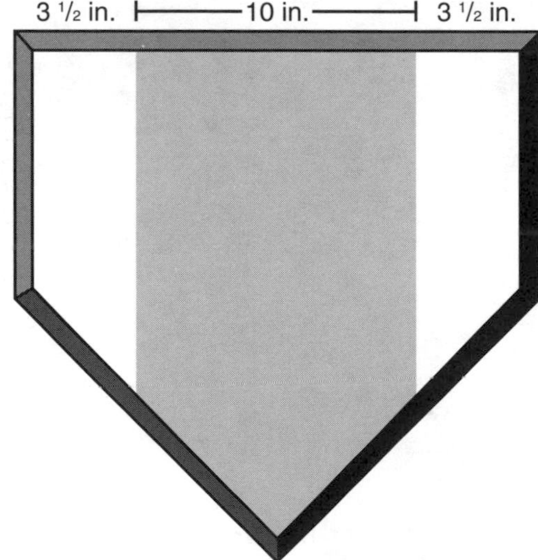

FIGURE 4.2 In a 0-0 count, look for a pitch in this zone and adjust off this location.

Few hitters, even good hitters, can control both sides of the plate. It is simply too wide an area. Thus hitters must make a choice. Most will pick the inside area to just past the midway point of the plate. Unless the hitter is exceptional, choosing the inside part of the plate is a poor approach. If we chart and study pitchers, particularly in amateur baseball, we will notice that over 70 percent of the pitches in the strike zone are from just inside the midway point of the plate to the outside corner (see figure 4.3). Many more outs are made on the outside half of the plate. When learning to control the width of the plate, a wise choice is to choose the area that includes a little inside the midway point of the plate toward the outside corner.

Note also that when a hitter is trying to increase the area of the plate that he can control, he should work from the area he *can* control toward the more poorly controlled area. If he can control the outside half of the plate and wants to enlarge his skill at controlling more of the plate, he should not go to the inside corner. He should work on increasing his control from the middle of the plate slightly toward the inner half (see figure 4.4). The good hitter will tell you that RBI hits are usually hit to the middle of the field or opposite side because most pitchers, with a runner in scoring position, will work the outer half of the plate with fastballs, curveballs, or sliders. For the pitcher, that's where the outs are. Obviously, we are talking percentage baseball here, but this trend has been around since the game began.

As long as we are discussing percentage baseball, we must also point out that with few exceptions, the fastball is an easier pitch to hit than the breaking pitch. The hitter should make an effort to hit a fastball. Ralph Garr, a former major-league hitter who has held some Atlanta Braves' offensive records, once made a statement that relates to this premise concerning the fastball. "The best way to hit the curveball is not to miss the fastball!" He

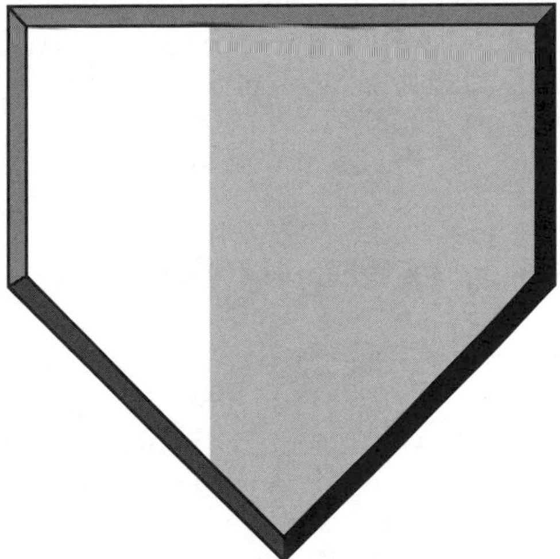

FIGURE 4.3 Seventy percent of strikes are in this zone (right-handed hitter).

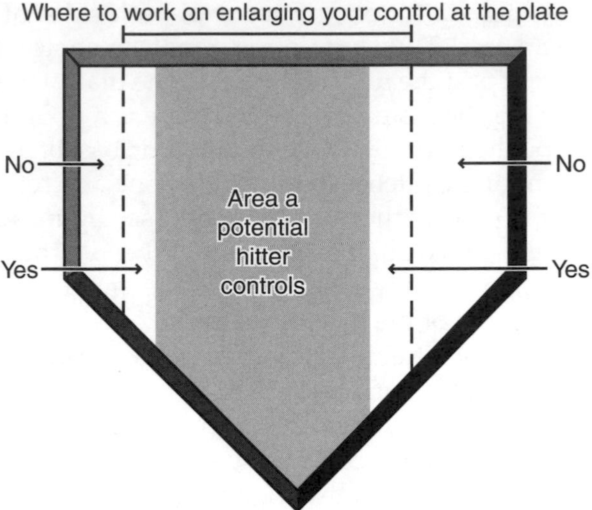

FIGURE 4.4 When a hitter is trying to increase the area of the plate that he can control, he should work from the area he *can* control toward the more poorly controlled area.

made every effort to hit the fastball because he knew he could hit it better than he could the curveball. Early in the count, it is wise to give away both corners of the plate (two to three inches on both sides) and look for a fastball to hit to the middle of the field. Many good hitters make a living doing just that. The hitter can't win every at-bat, but he can put the percentages in his favor.

We've discussed a lot of the thinking that goes on as a player walks from the on-deck circle to the batter's box. Having a plan and visualizing it is critical. But once the pitcher releases the ball, the hitter has no time to think and hit. The hitter must be relaxed and focused enough to let his reflexes take over in the mental picture that he has established. Thinking and having a high-percentage plan is critical, and it must be rehearsed in mental pictures. The hitter must visualize his plan, his swing, and where the ball will go. If he wants success, he must first visualize it.

How to Work the Count

Simply put, the hitter must make the pitcher throw strikes. A base on balls has a 100 percent on-base average! The batter should not help the pitcher by swinging at balls out of the strike zone. The success ratio for a hitter over a full season is often in direct correlation with the count when he hits the ball. This is proven every year as researchers, coaches, and players survey results in relationship to the count. When the hitter is behind in the count (1-2, 0-2), the batting average will normally be 150 to 200 points lower than when the hitter is ahead in the count (3-1, 2-0). The critical counts, the 0-0 and 1-1 counts, swing the success-failure rate at a greater range than any other count. In short, swinging at balls out of the strike zone can greatly increase the success ratio for the pitcher.

A hitter may face 12 counts on each at-bat. Some counts increase the hitter's chances, some favor the pitcher, and others are neutral. Table 4.1 presents the three categories of counts. Obviously, the object is to stay out of the pitcher's counts. How does the hitter do that? He knows the strike zone and does not swing at balls that are not strikes. In addition, he stays off solid pitcher's pitches when in hitter's counts.

Working the count correlates heavily with the confidence of the hitter. Good hitters can still hit when behind in the count, although they know that the percentages are not quite as good. Remember, some at-bats belong totally to the pitcher. If he has good stuff and controls the corners of the plate, he will win. Fortunately for the hitter, most pitchers will make mistakes. The hitter must be ready.

Ways to Advance Runners: Situational Hitting

Few observers doubt that the emphasis placed on situational hitting has diminished over the past 15 or 20 years. With the advent of the higher powered aluminum bat, the designated hitter (DH), and high salary premiums placed on home runs, RBIs, and slugging percentage, the element of the game involving situational hitting has become somewhat lost at most levels of play. For the baseball purist, situational hitting is one of the beauties of the game. That facet of baseball is still there, however, and careful observation will reveal that most championship teams use this important area of the game. Anyone can win blowout ballgames, but the championship teams are crowned because they win a larger percentage of the close games. In many cases they win because they execute situational hitting. Teams that

TABLE 4.1 Twelve Counts a Hitter May Encounter

HITTER'S COUNTS	PITCHER'S COUNTS	EVEN COUNTS
1-0	0-1	0-0
2-0	0-2	1-1
2-1	1-2	
3-0	2-2	
3-1		
3-2		

advance to the playoffs do so because they have good pitchers who can beat good hitters. If the hitters have the ability to execute situational hitting, they can still win!

Situational hitting simply means that hitters hit to the situation presented on that particular at-bat. With no one on base and no outs, the at-bat is different from the same situation with two outs. With a man on second base and no outs, the at-bat is different from the same situation with one out. In most cases situational hitting does not require as much talent as pure hitting does. Consequently, players can learn situational hitting and use it with some success against dominating pitchers.

Situational hitting brings these other important advantages to the team:

- Less skilled offensive players can contribute to the team's offensive success.
- The player who gives his at-bat to the team concept through situational hitting is identified as a team player.
- Teams that work on situational hitting in practice will learn how to control the bat and the strike zone at a faster rate than those who do not work on this area of hitting.

Baseball includes many distinct situational hitting areas. The following are some of the major situations that the manager or coaches can emphasize to the team.

Bunting and Fake Bunting

The sacrifice bunt, drag bunt, fake bunt slash, fake bunt slash hit-and-run, safety squeeze, and suicide squeeze are all forms of situational hitting because they move base runners.

The sacrifice bunt is the purest way to advance runners. Normally, it also has the highest probability of producing an out on the batter-runner. The drag bunt is a little more risky, but if done well it will increase the chance that the batter-runner, as well as the base runner, will be safe. The fake bunt slash, like the drag bunt, throws in an element of surprise and can catch the defense out of position. This play is not as high a percentage play as the sacrifice bunt, but it can lead to a big inning. The fake bunt slash hit-and-run, which adds a steal attempt by the base runner and a required swing, is even more risky, but it too can lead to a big inning. Use these strategies with no outs and, with the hit-and-run, use a 0-0, 1-0, 1-1, or 2-1 count because the pitcher is more likely to be throwing a strike.

The safety squeeze is executed with a runner on third. The hitter executes this bunt in much the same way he does the sacrifice bunt although he puts more emphasis on bunting away from the pitcher and perhaps more firmly, particularly if the corners (first baseman and third baseman) are play-

Photo courtesy of Texas A&M Sports Information

The drag bunt can be a good way to advance runners and, when done well, will increase the chance of the batter being safe as well.

ing back. The suicide squeeze is an all-or-none play in which the runner on third commits to home plate before the batter bunts the ball. Obviously, the suicide bunt is much more risky, and a manager must pick a count when he can expect a decent pitch to bunt. Normally, both of these bunts are done with one out. (The best times to bunt and hit-and-run are covered in more detail later in this chapter.)

Man on Second in a Nonforce Situation, No Outs

The two main situational hitting areas are at-bats that occur with a runner at second and no outs and with a runner on third and less than two outs.

With a man on second, no one on first, and no outs, the hitter must step up for the team. His at-bat must move the runner to third or possibly score him. The objective is to hit behind the runner. One school of thought says that the hitter must hit all balls to the right side. Another, and perhaps better, approach is to try to hit the ball to the right of where the runner on second leads off. This larger target gives the hitter a better chance to control a wider area of the strike zone with authority and perhaps drive the runner in for a score. One drawback of hitting to that area is that the ball hit back to the pitcher will not move the runner. The base runner's rule is always to advance to third on a ball hit at him or behind him, except if the ball is hit to the pitcher. Take your chances on the latter school of thought. You'll not only move more runners but also drive in more runs.

In this situation the right-handed hitter must lay off the strike thrown on the inner third of the plate early in the count. He should look for a pitch

Photo courtesy of Texas A&M Sports Information

The left-handed hitter hits the inside pitch to pull side to advance the runner on second base in a non-force situation with no outs.

thrown on the outer two-thirds of the plate. The hitter must be sure to keep his power base (keep his weight within both feet) and let the ball get a little deeper (closer to the plate as opposed to out in front of the plate). He wants to be sure to lead with the knob of the bat so that that he stays on the inside of the ball. The hitter should not completely give away his at-bat. He must be aggressive and drive the pitch. Obviously, the surest way to get the runner to third is by sacrifice bunting, but particularly early in a game, the team should go for more than one run. The hitter must just remember to stay off the inside pitch that requires him to pull the ball.

A left-handed hitter should stay off the pitch in the outer third of the plate early in the count. He is looking for a pitch that he can drive to the middle or right side of the field. He has it easier than the right-handed hitter does.

Teams should work on this area of situational hitting. With less than two outs there are many more ways to score from third than from second.

Man on Third, Less Than Two Outs

This circumstance requires a different kind of at-bat. Remember that RBIs are always better than hits! Get the runner in for the score.

Let's look at the infielders. Are they back, halfway, or in? Regardless of where they are playing, the hitter's point of emphasis should be to stay above the ball in the approach and not overswing. What he must avoid is popping up or striking out.

With the infield back a simple ground ball will almost always score the runner unless it goes back to the pitcher. Many coaches emphasize hitting to the middle of the field because the shortstop and second baseman are too far away from the plate to throw out a runner trying to score, whereas a ground ball hit hard to the corner infielders may get the runner thrown out at the plate trying to score. Although this concern is legitimate, an emphasis on hitting up the middle may be too restrictive for some hitters. Emphasizing line drives or ground balls with good bat control is a good rule. More experienced hitters sometimes like to drive the ball in the air for at least a sacrifice fly or even more. This approach may produce too many pop-ups or short fly balls, so unless the hitter is highly skilled, I do not recommend it.

With the infield playing in or halfway, the hitter should approach the situation the same way. The probability of driving a ball through the infield increases when the infielders play closer to the plate. For that reason, coaches don't like to play in. They don't want to help the opposition create big innings.

This situation does not require a great offensive player. The hitter should stay on top of the ball, control his swing, and put the ball in play. He should stay out of the strikeout count by hitting early in the count and not being as selective on thrown strikes. A hint for the hitter is that every coach becomes annoyed when a hitter takes a called third strike in this situation. The batter must give in and put the ball in play! The chances for good things to happen are great, even on poorly hit balls.

Hit-and-Run

A well-executed hit-and-run is another play that the baseball purist rates highly. The offense uses the hit-and-run in two situations. The traditional one is with a man on first or men on first and third. The other hit-and-run situation is with men on first and second.

Man on First or Men on First and Third

To execute the hit-and-run, signal the man on first to attempt to steal second. Either the second baseman or shortstop will break to the bag to receive the throw from the catcher. The hitter swings and tries to hit the ball to the unoccupied area, either second or shortstop. Normally, the second baseman will cover second with a right-handed hitter, and the shortstop will cover second with a left-handed hitter. For our purposes, we will assume this to be the case.

The hitter has a clearly defined situational hitting objective. He must address three areas:

1. He should swing at the pitch unless it is in the dirt or so far out of range that he cannot make any contact. In both of these situations, the pitches will be so poorly thrown that the catcher will be unlikely to catch the ball cleanly and throw the runner out. The hitter must remember to swing at the pitch. Even if he misses the ball, the catcher will have a somewhat tougher time throwing the runner out at second.
2. The hitter should hit the ball on the ground. If he cannot hit the pitch to the proper area of the infield, he should at least hit it on the ground. The runner will make it to second and will be in scoring position. A fly ball can create double plays and in most cases will result in an out without advancing the runner to scoring position.
3. He should hit the ball to the designated area. Besides swinging at the ball and hitting it on the ground, he must hit to the unoccupied area of the infield.

To execute the hit-and-run properly, the hitter must not overswing. The priority must be a solid, controlled swing. His power base (keeping his weight within both feet) must remain solidly intact. He must make an extra effort to stay on top of the ball. This requires approaching the ball with the barrel above the hands and the hands higher than the front elbow. He leads the swing with the knob of the bat toward the ball and allows the ball to get depth (closer to the plate). He must attempt to stay inside the ball on the swing. The idea is to hit the top half and slightly inside the ball. The hitter must stay back and avoid overswinging.

Men on First and Second

Essentially the same execution is desired in this situation although hitting the ground ball to a particular area of the infield receives less emphasis. Remember that the third baseman will now be moving to cover third and another hole is available. The hitter should put the ball on the ground.

When to Bunt, Fake Bunt, and Hit-and-Run

This section covers the best times to put different hitting strategies into action, including the bunt, fake bunt slash, fake bunt slash hit-and-run, hit-and-run, safety squeeze, and suicide squeeze. When contemplating these six strategies, remember that variables weigh in heavily. What is right for one team or one level of play may not be right for another team or a different level of play. We cannot escape this dilemma by saying, "All things being equal, this is the strategy," because all things are never equal; there are simply too many variables. With that stipulation, we will address the various strategies in general terms.

Sacrifice Bunt

Very simply, the manager or coach should sacrifice bunt when he deems the run important to the outcome of the game. If a manager is willing to give up an out and in most cases an inning for the run, it must be important. Variables? If the defense can't handle the bunt, bunt more. If you have an ace on the mound who has a chance to hold the opposition's runs to a minimum, bunt early and often. If the opponents have an ace on the mound, bunt more because your team is less likely to produce multiple hits in an inning. Normally, you should play for the big inning in the early part of the game and use your short game in the latter part of the game. If you have a ball club that hits poorly, bunt more. Have your weaker hitters bunt more than your good hitters. Try to bunt when you have good hitters coming up next in the lineup. Normally, sacrifice bunt only with no outs. With the DH in the lineup, you should not have any dead-out hitters. When behind by two or more runs late in the game, the sacrifice bunt is not a good strategy. The list can go on almost forever. Remember, the general rule is to bunt when one run is important to the outcome of the game.

With men on first and second, a team should elect to bunt only when none are out. In this case the manager normally regards the man on first to

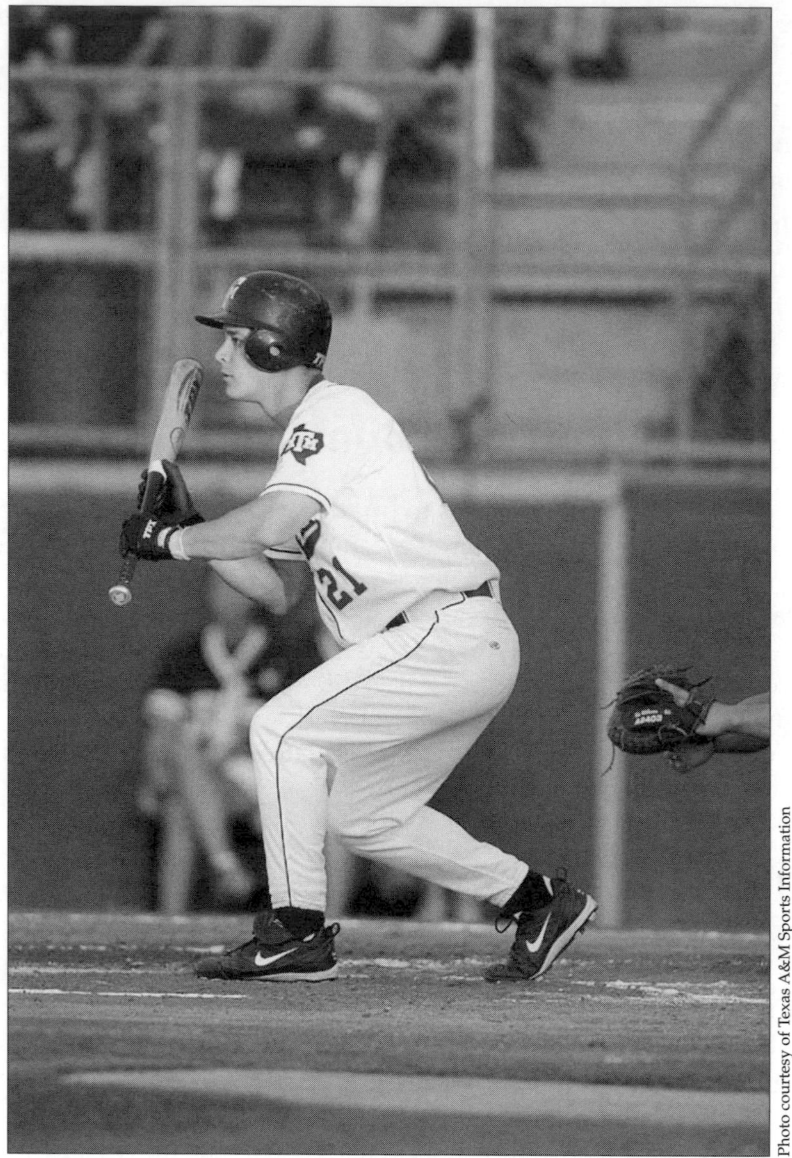

Photo courtesy of Texas A&M Sports Information

Sacrifice bunt when it is deemed that the run is important to the outcome of the game.

be a critical run. This strategy will usually keep the offensive team from hitting into the double play and allow the team two outs to drive in the two runs as opposed to three outs to drive in one or possibly two runs. This strategy is usually employed with a weaker hitter at the plate and better hitters coming up next. The batter normally executes the sacrifice bunt on 0-0, 0-1, 1-0, or 1-1 counts. Some coaches let their good hitters swing away until they get a strike.

Fake Bunt Slash

The hitter executes the fake bunt slash by showing a bunting stance to the defense in the hope that they will charge the corners of the infield and perhaps even that the second baseman will start toward first to cover that bag. The hitter then draws back to his hitting stance and proceeds to hit if it is a strike. Obviously, this strategy works best in what the defense perceives to be a bunting situation. The manager will usually use this strategy rather than the sacrifice bunt when he feels that the run is not as critical to the outcome of the game. He may also use it if he feels the defense is playing aggressively for a sacrifice bunt. Remember, a general rule is not to allow the defense to take the sacrifice bunt away from you when you consider the run critical. This play is less likely to move the runner than the sacrifice bunt; however, if it does work, you've moved the runner and increased your chances that the batter-runner will be safe at first. This play can be used earlier in a game than the sacrifice bunt, when the idea of playing for the big inning is still intact. This play, like the sacrifice, should be used with no outs and on 0-0, 1-0, 0-1, or 1-1 counts. This play can discourage the opposition from employing an aggressive bunt defense.

Fake Bunt Slash Hit-and-Run

This strategy follows the same philosophy as the fake bunt slash with the additional feature that the runner will attempt to advance to second base as the pitcher throws to home plate. The hitter must attempt to hit this pitch, preferably on the ground. The gamble, of course, is that he must get a decent ball to hit and not swing and miss. This play can present havoc to a defense if they bite on the fake bunt and the shortstop breaks to cover second on the apparent steal attempt. The play leaves many potential holes in the infield and normally takes away the inning-ending double play. This play can also be used with men on first and second and no outs. Most managers prefer not to use this play with a left-handed hitter with men on first and second because the catcher's throw to third is easier if the hitter misses the ball. Use this play when the count is 0-0, 1-0, 1-1, 2-1.

Hit-and-Run

As with all hitting strategies, the ability of the hitter to execute the relevant skill is a critical variable. This play can be incorporated with no outs or one out. If the batter hits the ball on the ground, the play has an excellent chance of advancing the base runners. Although the hitter is not sacrificing an out to move runners as he does when bunting, the play often results in the hitter making an out, so it is not a wise play with two outs. The manager normally calls this play with one out. The hit-and-run is executed with the runners attempting a steal and the hitter hitting a ground ball to the vacated area, normally to the side opposite his hitting side. That is, a right-handed hitter normally hits to the second-base area because the second baseman normally covers second on steal attempts when a right-handed hitter is batting. The batter must swing on the pitch if it is catchable by the catcher. He must try to hit the ball on the ground to the vacated spot. If the batter executes the play properly, runners should end up on first and third. Most managers prefer to hit-and-run with right-handed batters because the base runner has a better chance to reach third on balls hit to the right fielder than he would with a left-handed batter hitting balls to left field. In the second situation, the left fielder would have an easier play at third. The hit-and-run is an excellent way to avoid double plays. Most managers will hit-and-run when they feel that the pitcher will throw a strike. Consequently, the strategy works best on 0-0, 1-0, 1-1, and 2-1 counts. The 2-0 count favors the hitter so much that many managers will simply let the hitter hit away. Obviously, the 0-1, 0-2, or 1-2 counts are not good gambles.

The situation with runners on first and third with less than two outs is also a good time to hit-and-run because the play provides a great chance to stay out of the inning-ending double play as well as score a run from third. This play is executed the same way as the play with a man on first except that the runner at third reacts to the hit ball.

Some managers also like to hit-and-run with runners on first and second with a right-handed hitter at the plate. The gamble increases with a left-handed hitter because a swing and miss usually presents an easy throw from the catcher to third. The play does create early movement of coverage on the steal attempts, which opens more areas of the infield. The hitter should simply try to hit the ball on the ground in this play.

Safety Squeeze

The hitter executes the safety squeeze by bunting in a direction away from the pitcher. The runner on third commits to advance to home when he reads that the ball is down and not toward the pitcher. The hitter does not bunt if he does not get a good pitch. This play is normally called with one out, less than two strikes, and the infield, particularly the corner infielders, not playing the in positions. The offense can execute the play with the pitcher in the stretch or windup position.

The offense can also execute the safety squeeze with men on first and third and one out. This play reduces the possibility of an inning-ending double play, scores a run, and moves the runner on first into scoring position. One of the drawbacks is that the runner at third has difficulty getting a good jump on mediocre bunts. The runner has an easy read if the ball is bunted close to the foul lines, but he can run into an out at home plate if the bunted ball rolls toward, but not directly at, the pitcher, and he gets a bad read or poor jump on the bunted ball. The play also has the potential of placing the hitter in a pitcher's count if he fouls off the first attempt. Many hitters will elect to bunt on any pitch because they are afraid they will lose the element of surprise. This is usually a poor decision. The safety squeeze is normally used to increase a small lead. The runner at third may represent the key run, but most managers will use the suicide bunt in that case. This play is used early in the count with less than two strikes.

Suicide Squeeze

The hitter executes the suicide squeeze by bunting at the pitched ball regardless of where it is. The runner at third base will take a walking lead and break for home plate after the pitcher's arm starts back. This manager uses this play with one out. It works best if the pitcher is working from the windup position and the corner infielders are playing behind the base paths between their respective bases and second base. This all-or-none play is used when the run is deemed critical to the outcome of the game. The offense must disguise the play well. An early show of the play by the batter or runner can result in a pitchout. This play works best with a right-handed hitter because early detection of the play with a resulting pitchout is made away from the runner attempting to score. Obviously, the perfect scenario for the squeeze does not always exist. The infield can be in, and the pitcher can be working from the stretch. Although those conditions reduce the margin for error, the play can still work if the execution is good. The squeeze can also be run in a first-and-third situation. Even if the bunt fails, it prevents the double play and advances the runner to scoring position. The play is normally run on 0-0, 1-0, 1-1, and 2-1 counts.

How do we score runs without the help of our opponents? In answering that question, our minds immediately travel to a picture of a hitter in the batter's box hitting a frozen rope. In many cases that scenario is the answer to the question, but if we agree with the familiar phrase that "good pitching will beat good hitting," we must realize that the offensive side of baseball must encompass more than just hitting a baseball. Teams that do not have a high team batting average can still score runs and win championships! They are usually highly skilled at executing a hitting plan, can work the count, and can advance runners through situational hitting and proper hitting strategy. Let the game within the game begin!

5

Base-Running Strategy

Danny Hall

Base-running strategies must be formulated before the game starts. As a coach I want to make sure that I watch the infield and outfield to see how all the position players throw. I watch the outfielders to judge their arm strength, their accuracy, and how quickly they get rid of the ball. An outfielder may have a strong arm, but if he takes all day to throw the ball we will run on him. I also pay close attention to all the infielders, especially the catcher. If the middle infielders do not throw well we know we can run on them on relays and possibly double steals. If the first baseman does not throw well we might employ a double-steal play and run on his arm. I also want to get a release time on the catcher and judge his throwing accuracy. These judgments and observations help me formulate a base-running strategy for the game.

Home to First

The key to getting a good jump out of the batter's box is taking a good fundamental swing and staying on balance. Once the batter hits the ball he should step with his back foot toward first base. If the ball is a ground ball in the infield, the hitter should only glance at the ball on his third stride out of the box. After this initial look he focuses on the front of the base and tries to step with either foot on the front of the base while leaning with the upper body, much like a sprinter breaking the tape at the finish line. If the hitter looks at the batted ball while in the box, spends too much time looking at the ball while running down the line, or steps on the backside of the base, his running time will be slower.

After the hitter crosses first base he should break down and look over his right shoulder in case of an errant throw to first base. Doing this will make it easier to advance to second on an error. The farther the hitter runs toward the outfield after crossing the base, the less likely it is that he will be able to advance on an error.

On a line-drive base hit or a fly ball to outfield, the hitter will immediately start to round the base as he leaves the box. His path will look like a semicircle (see figure 5.1). If the hitter hits a ground ball that goes through the infield, he will do a question mark turn at first (see figure 5.2). As he approaches first, he steps on the inside corner of the base and tries to be in a straight line toward second. He should always think that he is going to second unless the outfielder stops him by catching the ball or making a good relay throw. If the outfielder makes a good throw the batter-runner stops and returns to first while keeping his eye on where the ball is. The good base runner always knows where the ball is.

As a rule the turnaround rest will be short if the ball is in right field and longer as the ball moves from center to left field. If the outfielder catches the fly ball, I ask our runners to sprint three more steps after the catch. This

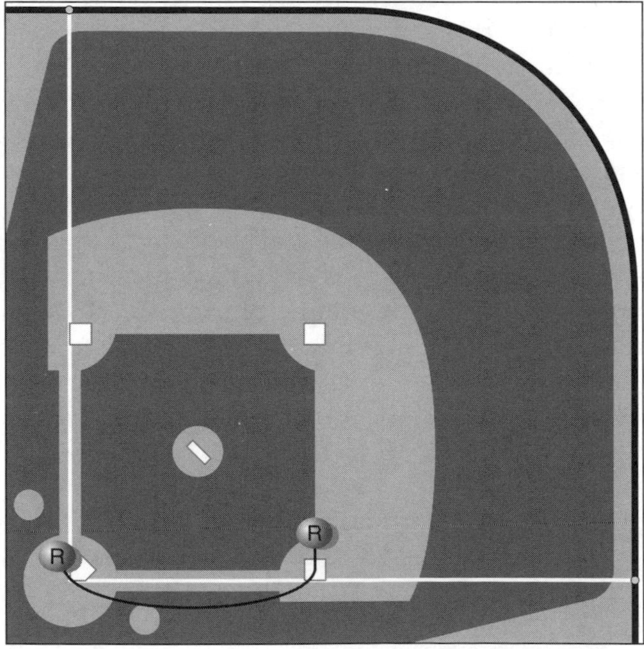

FIGURE 5.1 On a line-drive base hit or a fly ball to outfield, the hitter will start to round the base immediately out of the batter's box. His path looks like a semicircle.

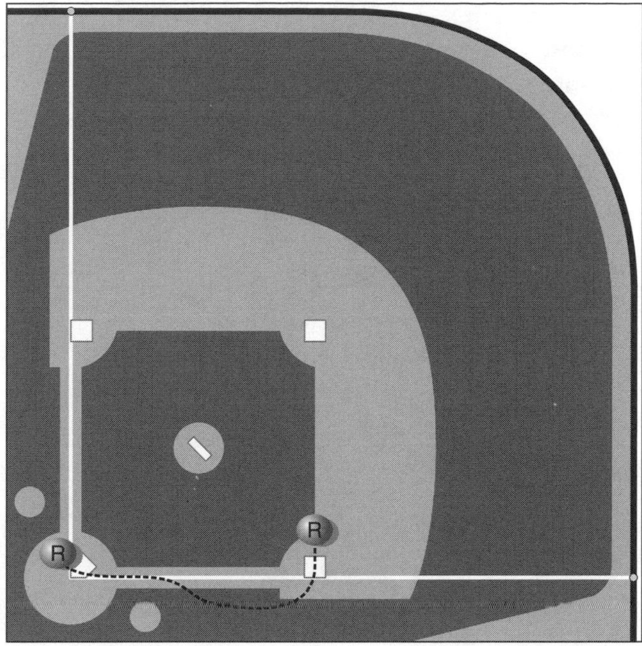

FIGURE 5.2 On a ground ball that goes through the infield, the hitter will do a question mark turn at first. He starts to first, then rounds the base.

practice prevents the runner from slowing down in anticipation of the catch. We call it the three-step rule, and I know we advance some extra bases because of it after dropped or missed fly balls.

Base Runners' Responsibilities and Keys

I ask our players to look to the third base coach immediately after reaching a base. I like to get the sign to them early so that they can concentrate on their keys for steals. Giving the sign promptly also allows the hitter a chance to see it and then concentrate on executing at the plate. The coaches will remind them of the number of outs and tell them to see the line drive through the infield before breaking for the next base. This simple reminder helps the runner focus.

First to Third

One of the best and most exciting plays in baseball is the runner going from first to third on a base hit. This is an important play with no outs or one out because if the runner gets to third, he can score without benefit of a base hit. The decision to go or not to go is up to the base runner unless the ball has been hit behind him down the right-field line. In that case the runner must look at the third-base coach for the sign to advance or stop at second. In all other cases the runner can see the ball and the outfielders to determine his chances of getting to third. Runners should remember several general rules:

- If the outfielder fields the base hit while moving toward third, the runner may not be able to advance.
- If the outfielder fields the ball moving away from third base, the runner can advance.
- The depth of the outfielder and quality of his arm are always determining factors.
- The runner must never make the first or third out of an inning at third base.

Leadoffs

When leading off first base the base runner takes his lead when the pitcher contacts the rubber with his pivot foot. The runner walks off the base with his left foot first and then his right foot as the pitcher looks to the catcher for the sign. He increases his lead by reaching with his right foot toward second while keeping his weight on his left foot. He replaces his right foot with his left until he has a lead that feels safe and comfortable. Ideally, he would have a 12- to 15-foot lead. By measuring his lead as described earlier, the base runner knows exactly how far he is from the base. He never takes his eye off the pitcher and never crosses his feet. His ability to read the move of the pitcher and return to first base dictates the size of his lead.

Primary Lead

The primary lead is the lead that the runner uses to get off the base. He uses caution so that he doesn't get picked off while taking his lead. He always keeps his eyes on the pitcher and measures his lead with his feet so that he knows exactly how far he is from the base. Several factors dictate how far off the base he gets:

- The size of his primary lead is dictated first and foremost by his agility and reaction time. The good base runner who is quick and can react can take a bigger lead than the guy who is slow to react.
- The pitcher's move also dictates the size of his lead. If the pitcher has a quick move to first, he takes a shorter lead. If the pitcher has a slow move to first, his lead is larger.

- If he can react and dive back to the base, he can take a 12- to 15-foot lead. If he has to come back to the base standing up, he must take a shorter lead.

If he returns to first standing up, he should return with his right foot on the inside corner of the base. This technique makes it difficult for the first baseman to retrieve the errant pickoff attempt that is into the field of play. If he dives back to first, he should take a step back to first with his left foot, cross over with his right, and dive for the back corner of the base. The runner should turn his head to the outfield side and look for the errant pickoff attempt.

Secondary Lead

The base runner takes his secondary lead as the pitcher is making the pitch. The runner executes the secondary lead by shuffling his feet to gain ground

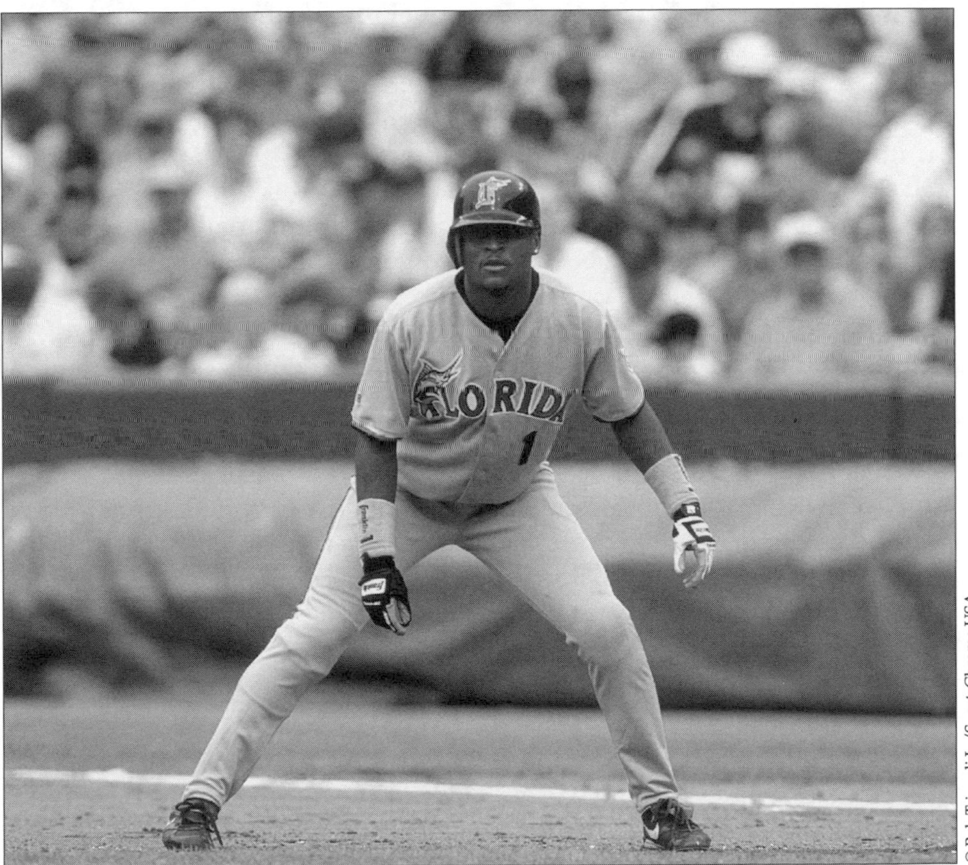

When leading off, runners should keep their eyes on the pitcher at all times and know the exact distance they are from the base.

toward the next base. He keeps his hips square to home plate and shuffles until the hitter makes contact or the catcher catches the ball. The runner must not stop until the catcher secures the ball. If he observes the catcher dropping to his knees, he keeps shuffling with the idea that he may advance on the ball in the dirt. As a general rule, we want our good base runners breaking for second base on all balls that the catcher attempts to block by going to his knees. It is difficult for the catcher to block and recover the ball in time to throw to second to get the runner out.

Secondary lead: Return to first. As the base runner shuffles on his secondary lead and reads a take by the hitter, he stops and returns to first immediately. He must keep his eyes on the catcher at all times. If there is a pickoff attempt, the first-base coach will alert the runner that the first baseman is coming to the base. The good base runner knows where the ball is at all times.

Secondary lead: Advance to second. As the base runner shuffles on his secondary lead and reads ground-ball contact, he immediately advances to second base by crossing over his right foot. If the ground ball is caught by an infielder, the base runner tries to beat the throw to second. If the ground ball goes through the infield, the base runner rounds the base and advances to third (figure 5.3) or stays at second base.

Secondary lead: Line drive. The general rule of thumb is that the base runner will freeze on all line drives. We tell them to see the line drive through the infield before advancing to second. If they follow this simple rule, they will avoid getting doubled off of first base.

Secondary lead: Fly ball. If the base runner reads a fly ball to the outfield, he advances toward second base with caution. If the ball is in right field, he cannot advance too far off of first. The more the ball is into center and left field, the closer the runner advances toward second. If the ball is caught, he returns to first quickly but must make sure to keep his eyes on the ball while returning. By keeping his eyes on the ball, the runner can advance to second on an errant throw by the outfielders. If the fly ball takes the outfielder away from the infield and away from first base, the base runner advances with caution to second base and possibly beyond second if it is a deep fly ball to left center or left field. We tell the runner to keep advancing as long as the outfielder has his back to the infield. Remember that if the base runner advances beyond second, he must retouch the base before returning to first on a caught fly ball. By advancing to second or beyond, the runner increases his chances of scoring on the fly ball that gets over the outfielder's head.

One way lead. This lead is used to bait the pitcher into throwing over to first base. The base runner takes a larger lead to entice the pitcher into throwing over. As soon as the pitcher makes a move, the base runner breaks back toward first base. The idea is to see the pitcher's move to first base.

Lead at second: Advancing to third. The runner at second will receive help from the base coaches with his lead at second. He should always keep his

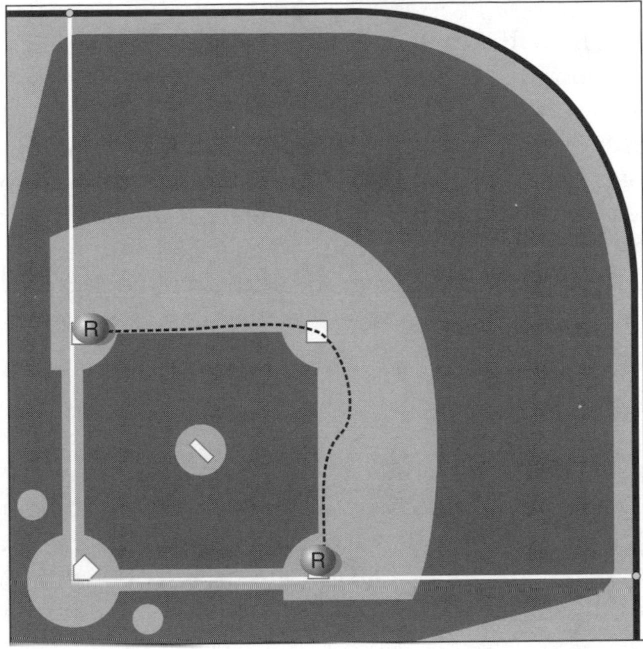

FIGURE 5.3 The runner rounds the base with a question mark turn when heading to third.

eyes on the pitcher and listen for instructions from the coaches on increasing or decreasing his lead. Keep increasing until the coach yells "hold" or "caution." If the coach reads a pickoff attempt, he will yell "back." The secondary lead at second is exactly like the secondary at first base. The runner shuffles until the ball is either caught or hit. If the hitter takes, he should stop his shuffle and return to second immediately. If the ball is in the dirt, he must read the catcher's block and only advance if he is sure he will be safe. He is already in scoring position at second; therefore he needs to use good judgment when advancing on a ball in the dirt.

Secondary lead at second: Groundball reads. The runner advances to third from second on all ground balls to the right side of the pitcher's mound. On ground balls that are hit directly toward the pitcher, the runner advances to third only after seeing the ball get past the pitcher. On a ground ball that gets past the pitcher on the third-base side of the mound, the runner advances to third if the ground ball is behind him. If the ground ball is to the left side of the infield, the runner must see the ball through the infield into the outfield before advancing to third. The runner may advance to third on a slow-hit ground ball to the third baseman. This is an exception to seeing the ball through the infield. The runner may also advance to third on backhand plays by the third baseman or shortstop when they must make a long throw across the field.

Advancing to third on fly balls. The base runner will always be trying to get to third on a fly ball if there are no outs. Our rule is to always tag up on a fly ball to the outfield with no outs. If the runner can advance to third on the catch, he can score easily from third with one out. He advances to third on fly balls using the keys discussed later in "Tag-Ups." If there is one out, he usually assumes a position off the base that allows him to advance to third or home if the ball is not caught by the outfielder. If the ball is caught, he is still in scoring position at second and should only tag and advance if he can stand up at third base. Remember, do not make the first or third out in an inning at third base.

Lead at Second

With less than two outs the runner at second will lead straight off the base. A good rule is to take a 15-foot lead or whatever the middle infielder will allow. The runner keeps his eyes on the pitcher and lets the coaches watch the middle infielder. The runner steals third on the pitcher and, to a certain degree, the middle infielder. To key off the pitcher he looks for the following:

- The pitcher who is 1.5 seconds or greater to the plate. Left-handed pitchers are normally slower to the plate.
- The pitcher who looks once to second and then pitches or the pitcher who does the same thing each time before pitching.
- If the middle infielders are not holding the runner, the runner can get a big lead, which means that we can even steal on the pitcher who is quick to the plate.

With two outs the runner takes a two-out lead. He takes his normal lead and then backs up two or three steps toward the outfield. This positioning allows for a sharper turn at third base and allows the runner to stay in the base line from third to home.

Lead at Third

The lead at third, like the lead at first, should be 12 to 15 feet. The runner must be aware of the possible pick at third by the pitcher or catcher. If the third baseman is close to the base, then the runner knows that chances are good for a pickoff attempt. If he is behind the bag by more than four steps, the runner can take a bigger lead and a bigger secondary lead. The secondary lead at third is a walking lead; the base runner tries to have his body facing the hitter and his right foot down as the ball arrives in the hitting area. If the runner has been instructed to go on the ground ball, a good walking lead will allow him to get a great jump to the plate.

When a runner gets to third, his number one objective is to score. The coach must remind him of the number of outs. The coach also reminds him to see all line drives through the infield before advancing to home. The coach also reminds him to tag up on all fly balls to the outfield. The only fly ball that the runner will not tag up on is the shallow fly ball or pop-up in between an outfielder and infielder. In this case, the runner will probably go halfway toward home or as far as he can get off of third and still return safely if the ball is caught. The coach will also tell the runner when to advance to home on ground balls. This scenario is often dictated by the number of outs, score of the game, inning in the game, and position of the infielders. Examples include:

- *Runner at third, no outs, infield back.* The runner advances to home on all ground balls that he sees. On the ground ball toward the pitcher, he must see the ball past the pitcher.
- *Runner at third, no outs, infield in.* The runner stays because there are no outs. He must see this ground ball through the infield.
- *Runner at third, no outs, corner infielders are playing in.* The runner advances on all ground balls hit to shortstop and second base, but must hold on ground balls to the third baseman or first baseman. Remember to see the ground ball past the pitcher.
- *Runners at first and third, no outs.* The runner advances to home on all ground balls to avoid the double play being turned. If a play is made on the runner at home, he should try to get in a rundown and allow the other runners enough time to get into scoring position at second and third.
- *Runner at third, one out, infield in.* The coach must decide whether he can risk the chance of the runner being thrown out at home. If he tells him to go on ground-ball contact, then he probably doesn't have a good feeling about the next hitter scoring the runner with two outs.

Reading the Pitcher

Pitchers are creatures of habit. One of the important things to observe early in a game is what the pitcher does in the stretch.

- *What is his time to home plate?* We calculate this by starting the stopwatch when the pitcher picks up his lead foot and stopping the watch when the catcher catches the ball. A time of 1.3 seconds or less means that the pitcher is quick to the plate. A time of 1.4 is average, and 1.5 seconds or more is slow. Knowing this time helps us determine who can steal and who can't.

- *Does he use a slide step?* The slide step is a quick step to the plate by the pitcher, in contrast to a normal lift of the knee and then a step to the plate. Our rule is that we never steal on a slide step, even after we have given the steal sign.
- *Does he throw over to first?* If so, are his feet quick or slow? Does he throw over coming up with his hands? Going down with his hands? From the set position? After setting, does he hold and throw over? Does he have a step-off move? Does he routinely hold the ball in the set position for the same length of time before he delivers to the plate; that is, does he use the one-thousand-one, one-thousand-two pitch?
- *Left-handers are different altogether; is his kick to the plate the same as his kick to first?* Usually the kicks are different. Does he look in the same spot when throwing to home and to first? Does he look to first and throw home? Look to home and throw to first? Does he have a step-off move? Does he break the plane of the rubber when he is going home?

The runner must observe and calculate all these factors before taking a lead. To get back to first standing up, the base runner crosses over with his right foot, steps with his left, and then steps on the inside corner of the base with his right foot. This technique forces the first baseman to go around him to catch an errant throw. If the runner dives back, he crosses over with his right foot and dives for the base. The key on the dive is to stay low to the ground.

Steals

This section describes different strategies for stealing bases, including the straight steal, the delayed steal, letting a runner steal on his own, and stealing home.

- *Straight steal.* The straight steal occurs when the coach gives the steal sign because he feels that the base runner has an excellent chance of being safe. The coach may have observed a slow release by the pitcher or catcher, or he may feel that an off-speed pitch is coming. Ideally, the coach should know the speed and running time of the base runner from first to second.

For example, pitcher's release (1.5) + catcher's release (2.2) = 3.7 seconds.

Base runner with 12-foot lead and slide at second = 3.4 seconds. *Go!*

- *Steal on your own.* In this steal the coach gives the smart base runner a sign. The thought is to let the runner determine when he can get a good jump on the pitcher. The runner should have observed all the factors described in this chapter and get the feel or rhythm to steal the base. Our percentages of being successful are much better using this steal and trusting the runner.

- *Delayed steal.* This steal takes advantage of the lazy catcher and inattentive middle infielders who put their heads down after the catcher catches the pitch. The runner at first does not break immediately on the pitch. Instead, he delays to decoy the catcher and middle infielders. The technique is shuffle, shuffle, and break for second. The base runner goes from primary lead to secondary lead and then breaks for second. The delayed steal offers a great element of surprise for the runner who is not fast or not expected to steal.
- *Stealing home.* The steal of home is one of the most exciting plays in baseball. The runner steals on the pitcher who fails to look at him while winding up to deliver the pitch. The runner must get a big lead, but he must be careful not to tip the pitcher or third baseman that he is stealing. One way to do this is to bluff a steal of home before the steal itself. The hitter is instructed to swing at the pitch late to

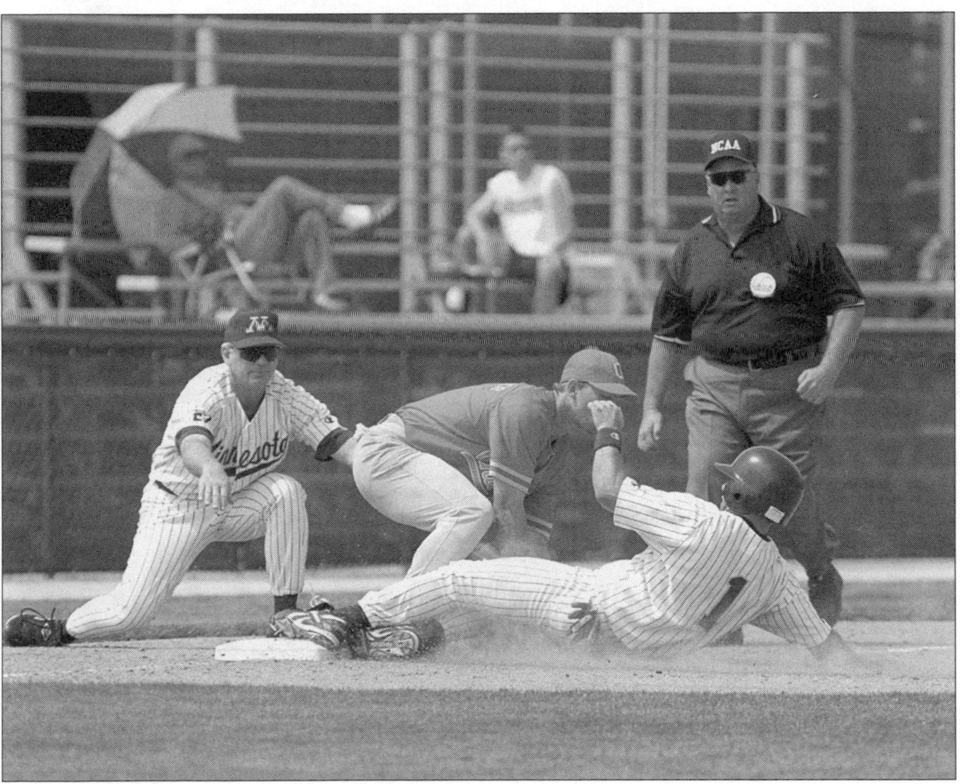

The percentages of being successful are much better using the "steal on your own" signal and trusting the runner.

keep the catcher from catching the ball out in front of home plate. If we know that we may attempt to steal home, I have found it advantageous to inform the home-plate umpire that we may attempt it. This way he is on his toes and expecting it rather than being caught off guard.

Tag-Ups

The base runner uses a tag-up when the batter hits the ball in the air and the runner feels that he can advance to the next base. The runner can advance to the next base once the ball contacts the fielder's glove. The runner should watch the play himself and keep one foot on the bag until contact occurs between the ball and glove. I prefer that the runner determine when to leave the bag rather than not watching the ball and listening to the coach. The runner should tag at first base when he feels that a deep fly ball is going to stay in the park and be caught. With no other runners on base he might be able to advance to second if the outfielder does not throw well or is not anticipating an advance by the runner. If the runner at first has any doubts that the ball will be caught, he should not tag up. Instead, he should go as far toward second base as he can without risking being doubled off first base.

The tag-up at second base is more complicated. The number of outs is a key factor in whether to tag or not. With no outs the goal is to get to third base with one out. Therefore, the runner is more likely to tag up and try to advance on the catch. Key factors on whether the runner can advance are the following:

- Depth of the fly ball.
- Strength of the outfielder's arm.
- The runner's speed.
- The positioning of the outfielder. Is he moving toward third base or away from the base? A general rule is that if he is moving away from third, the runner can advance on a medium-depth fly ball, and if he is moving toward third, the runner cannot advance.

The runner on second should be aware of two other possibilities. If the outfielder is running hard away from the base, the runner may assume a position off the base that allows him to score if the ball goes over the outfielder's head and to tag up and advance to third should the outfielder catch the ball. Should the runner determine that a deep fly ball is going to be caught and he knows that he can advance to third easily, he should be aware that he might be able to score from second base. Key factors here are a weak outfield arm or poor relay throw.

Special Plays

The following list describes the most successful strategies for common special plays.

- *Rundowns.* The key to staying in a rundown and ultimately getting safely to a base is the ability to run with the eyes on the guy with the ball. The idea is for the runner to change direction quickly once he reads the release of the ball by the fielders. With some luck he can force the fielder into a mistake and get to a base safely. If the runner gets picked off first and breaks back for second, he tries to line up the infielder at second and hopes that the first baseman makes a wild throw or hits him in the back. He shouldn't give up until the play is over.
- *Ball four, runner at second, wild pitch.* Sometimes the runner on second can score an easy run on a pitch that gets by the catcher on ball four. The hitter sprints for first and continues to second, hoping that the catcher tries to make a long throw from the backstop to second. If the base runner at second hustles to third and reads the throw from the backstop all the way to second, he should score easily.
- *Squeeze play.* On a safety squeeze the base runner at third will read the bunt by the hitter before advancing. Any bunt that doesn't go right at the pitcher should allow the base runner to score. On a bunt directly to the pitcher, the base runner will hold. On a suicide squeeze the runner at third will break for home plate when the pitcher's lead knee commits to the plate. We count on the hitter to bunt the ball on the ground.

  The double squeeze occurs with runners at second and third and one out. Both base runners break on the pitch as they would in a suicide squeeze. We instruct the hitter to bunt the ball down the third-base line. With a good bunt and a good runner at second, both runners may score on this play.
- *Extended lead, first and third, versus left-handed pitcher.* The base runner at first takes one more step on his lead, trying to draw a pickoff move from the lefty. The runner at third will extend his lead and break for home as soon as the lefty picks up his foot to move toward first. The runner at first will jab back to the base for one step in hopes that the first baseman will delay throwing home. A good time to use this play is when the lefty pitcher has a big kick to the plate or when the first baseman has a weak arm.
- *Extended lead versus right-handed pitcher.* The base runner at first takes one more step on his primary lead than normal in an effort to draw a pickoff throw from the pitcher. When the pitcher throws to first, the

runner sprints toward second base, hoping to draw a throw from the first baseman all the way into second. The base runner at third will get a good secondary lead on the pickoff throw to first and break for home as soon as he reads the release of the baseball by the first baseman. A good runner at third will almost surely score if the first baseman throws the ball all the way to second.

Hit-and-Run Play

The key thing for the base runner on the hit-and-run is to remember that we are betting on the hitter to do his job of making contact. The runner is not trying to steal the base; therefore, he should never get picked off. I suggest that the runner take a half-step shorter lead to give the impression that he is not going anywhere. After reading the pitcher's delivery to the plate, the runner should break for second base using a good crossover step. On the third step the runner should glance at the hitter to see if he has made contact and, if he has, to try to follow the ball. The runner should keep running unless the hitter pops the ball up or hits it in the air to the outfield. If the runner loses the sight of the ball he should look to the third-base coach for help.

A good base-running team can win a lot of games that they otherwise might have lost. The ability of a team or a player to steal a base puts a lot of pressure on the defense. It also means that you don't have to give up an out by bunting or executing a hit-and-run to get that player into scoring position. By saving outs, you give yourself more scoring opportunities. The team that knows when to advance to the next base on fly balls, ground balls, and base hits also creates more scoring opportunities. Use base running as a weapon.

6

Decision-Making in Specific Offensive Situations

Jack Stallings

Strategy decisions, in any sport, need to be based on good fundamental principles and on percentages that will give the team and its players the best chance of success. A coach may have a gut feeling about what might work in a certain situation, and sometimes (by heeding that gut feeling) he may make an impulsive strategic decision that seems to be contrary to all common sense or strategy percentages, yet it works that time! But to be consistently successful over a long period, a coach needs to make decisions that are most likely to be successful given the abilities of the players of both teams, all the factors of the situation, and the percentages of baseball.

Coaches must also understand that when they make a strategy decision, it is a good or bad decision at the time it is made based on the players' abilities, the situation, and the percentages, not on whether the play was successful or unsuccessful! Coaches make decisions based on all the factors available to them, and then the players have to execute the play called by the coach. How the players perform their skills on a particular play has nothing to do with the wisdom of the coach's decision. The coach must make his decision before he knows how the players will perform (known as first guessing), but the fans, parents, and media have the luxury of waiting until a play is over and then determining if the decision was a good or bad one (known as second guessing). Fans, parents, and the media are therefore *never* wrong on a strategy decision!

Assessing Players' Abilities

In making offensive strategy decisions, coaches must understand that they are not coaching baseball but are really coaching baseball *players*, so strategy decisions revolve around who is doing something more than what is being done. Understanding the situation of a game is obviously important in making strategy decisions, but knowing the abilities of the players involved is even more important. A coach must know as much as possible about the abilities of his players, as well as the abilities of the players on the other team.

Your Players

Baseball strategy will be more consistent when it is based on the abilities of your team's players rather than on the abilities of the players of the opposing team. A coach will be much more familiar with the abilities of his players and he can control pretty well what they do or try to do, but he can't control the players on the other team at all.

A coach should carefully and constantly study the strengths and weaknesses of each of his players, especially in practice, because if a player is not capable of executing a skill well in practice most of the time, he is not going to be able to execute that same skill well in games, at least not often. The old explanation, "Coach, I know I didn't make that play very well in practice today, but in a game I'll turn it up a notch and show you I can get it done," usually doesn't work. A player who uses that approach is making an excuse for the failure to work hard in practice and prepare properly to play the game well. Nobody sprinkles magic dust over the baseball field when they play the "Star-Spangled Banner" so that ordinary players become great performers. As an old minor-league manager used to say, "You can't push a button and turn a practice donkey into a Kentucky Derby thoroughbred."

Many coaches are naturally optimistic about their players. Because they work with the kids every day, they often overestimate their skills, especially if the players are nice guys. Coaches must be realistic in evaluating the members of their team so that they have an accurate idea of what each player can do.

A baseball cliche that probably goes way back to Wee Willie Keeler and Tinker-to-Evers-to-Chance is "Know the strengths of your players and take advantage of them." A team will win many more games by having Babe Ruth or Mark McGwire swing away in a tight ballgame rather than having him sacrifice bunt. A coach certainly wants to be aware of the strengths of each of his players and try to put those players in positions where they can do their thing and take advantage of their strongest and best skills in various situations in the game. A coach should know their limitations as well and avoid asking players to do something that he knows they cannot do well a good percentage of the time. As the old New York Yankees and New York Mets manager Casey Stengle said in his peculiar way of using the English language, "Why ask a player to execute if he can't execute?" Earl Weaver, the great manager of the Baltimore Orioles, said it another way: "Remember a player's capabilities and incapabilities and never ask a player to do something that is beyond him." Failure to evaluate the weaknesses of his players is a common and often serious problem of many baseball coaches.

For a coach to know the abilities of his players well, he must teach them the skills they will be called on to execute most often during a ballgame, and he must observe closely how quickly and how well each player masters the skills and techniques. The coach must objectively evaluate his players' skills rather than merely making the subjective judgment, "Boy, he's a pretty good player!" The problem with subjective evaluation of players is that often a coach will remember a dramatic play someone made (maybe only once) or a play that someone made recently. The player who made the play will occupy in the mind of his coach an elevated position, a plane higher than his skills warrant. The expectations for him to perform well will thus be higher than his skill level. By using objective evaluations of players, the coach can minimize the influence of dramatic plays and be realistic in judging what players can do consistently. With the objective approach, a coach looks at his stopwatch and says, "That kid is a 4.1 runner," rather than looking at a player and saying, "Boy, can that guy fly!"

Their Players

The head coach or a member of his coaching staff should keep hitting and pitching charts on all opponents as well as information on their base-running skills, defensive abilities (such as arm strength, release time, and accuracy), and in what situations they attempt stolen bases, hit-and-run plays, and other special offensive and defensive plays. Coaches should pay particular attention to the opposing pitcher and catcher because they are the heart of the team's defense and their skills will influence many of the offensive strategy decisions that the head coach makes during the game.

Coaches should note the catcher's ability to throw quickly and accurately, his skill in blocking balls in the dirt, and his ability to react quickly on balls bunted in front of the plate or that get past him toward the backstop. Coaches should also watch for particular patterns and tendencies of the catcher in calling pitches. Some catchers, especially younger ones, get into a habit of following one particular pitch with another pitch. If a pattern can be determined, the hitter and coach can make better strategy decisions.

Evaluating the opposing pitcher is especially important in planning strategy. One common evaluation method is simply to check the pitcher's statistics. Although statistics can be deceiving at times, if a guy is 10-0 with a 1.02 ERA you have to figure he has the ability to get people out consistently.

Coaches must realize that when their team is facing an outstanding pitcher, they must usually play aggressively to try to get one or two runs. That may be all they can get against that pitcher, and then they must hope that their pitcher can shut the other team out or hold them to one run. The obvious things coaches should look for would be the opposing pitcher's "stuff"—the speed, control, and movement of his fastball, his breaking ball (the sharpness of the break as well as his control of it), and his off-speed pitch. Coaches should also look for such things as how fast or how slowly a pitcher works during a game, whether he becomes irritated when hitters upset his preferred pace, how well he pitches with runners on base including his ability to hold runners close to bases and his skill in executing various pickoff moves, his body language on the mound (especially when he gets in trouble during an inning), and how well he controls his emotions under pressure.

Coaches will also find it helpful to evaluate the ability of the opposing third baseman in fielding bunts, both sacrifice bunts and bunts for a base hit. If he demonstrates a lack of skill in this area, players who can bunt well can take advantage of that flaw. Evaluation of the abilities of opposing infielders in turning the double play is also useful. If they are able to do that well, they have a weapon they can use to advantage in certain situations of the game. If the opponent does not execute the double play well, the offensive team can adjust their strategy to take advantage of that weakness. For example, the offense would have more strategy options with runners on first and third bases and one out in a close ballgame.

Coaches should also study the defensive abilities of the opposing team's outfielders, especially their throwing ability—the strength of their arms, the quickness of their releases, their accuracy, and their skill at getting into good throwing position on fly balls or ground balls. Some outfielders have such great throwing skill that teams will generally not challenge their arms except in do-or-die situations. Other outfielders might be challenged constantly because of their poor throwing ability.

Nature of Baseball Strategy

One of the problems in making both offensive and defensive strategy decisions is that people oriented to football, basketball, and soccer try to apply to baseball the same strategy that they would use in the other sports. The first thing coaches and players must understand is that general baseball strategy is exactly backward from the strategy of football, basketball, and soccer because the strategy of those sports depends on a clock and how much time is left in the game. In football, for example, a team behind late in the game is running out of time and thus must gamble aggressively, taking dangerous chances to try to score quickly. Conversely, a football team with a lead late in the game will become conservative in an effort to kill the clock and deny the other team the time it needs to catch up. Baseball, however, has no clock, so time is not a factor in strategy. The critical factor in baseball is the number of outs remaining in the game, so baseball strategy for the team that is behind centers on conserving those outs. On the other hand, a baseball team ahead late in the game can remain aggressive (unlike in football) because what it does on offense does not affect the number of outs the opposing team has remaining. This characteristic of baseball influences every offensive strategy decision made in baseball games. Understanding that principle can help a coach avoid making decisions that cause everybody watching the game to shake their heads in wonder.

In any given offensive situation, the coach must consider four factors in making his strategy decisions. He should analyze these factors in order of their importance. If a coach has a specific play in mind in a particular situation, or perhaps a couple of plays that he is considering, he should first consider the most important factor. If that coincides with what he wants to do, then he considers the second factor, then the third, and finally the fourth. If all four factors are in agreement with his idea, then his decision will be a sound one. Working through this process may appear to be time consuming, but it isn't really all that complicated because a couple of the factors will be obvious even before the play that sets up the game situation occurs. Much of the decision making is almost automatic.

The four factors the coach should consider, in order of importance, are

1. score,
2. inning,
3. number of outs, and
4. position in the batting order.

Score

In making any strategy decision in baseball, the most important factor is the score of the game. This should come as no surprise because the score affects the strategy decisions in every sport.

Leading in the Game

When a team is ahead in the score, it has the opportunity to become more aggressive on offense. It can gamble and take chances on the bases without affecting the other team's chances of scoring because the opposition will still have the same number of innings (or outs) to work with for the remainder of the game. A team ahead in a game may run itself out of an inning by having a base runner thrown out, but that will not keep the offensive team from winning the game if it keeps the other team from scoring during its turn at bat. On the other hand, if the team that is leading is aggressive on offense, it may end up scoring more runs (maybe many more runs) and win the game easily, or it may put itself in a position to weather a late-inning rally by the other team and hold on for the win.

Many coaches are unsure about how aggressive their team should be when they are ahead in the game. Sometimes a team may be criticized for playing aggressively with a big lead in a game. Critics may say they are piling it on or rubbing it in. Many coaches get irritated when a team continues to play aggressively with a big lead, but this attitude has changed somewhat in recent years, especially in amateur and youth baseball. For one thing, young players don't have enough emotional control to turn it off and then back on again if they ease up and the other team mounts a strong rally late in the game. A team that eases up with a 10-run lead may fall victim to a big rally by the other team and end up losing by a run! A second factor is the lack of a million-dollar relief pitcher in the bullpen (as major-league teams have) who can come in and shut off a late-inning rally with a 97-mile-per-hour fastball. The scarcity of good pitchers in youth and amateur baseball offers some justification for continuing to try to score throughout the game. The third factor is the implied message that the coach is giving his team: "Ease up fellows. These guys aren't good enough to come back and beat us." Engendering that attitude can be dangerous during a game.

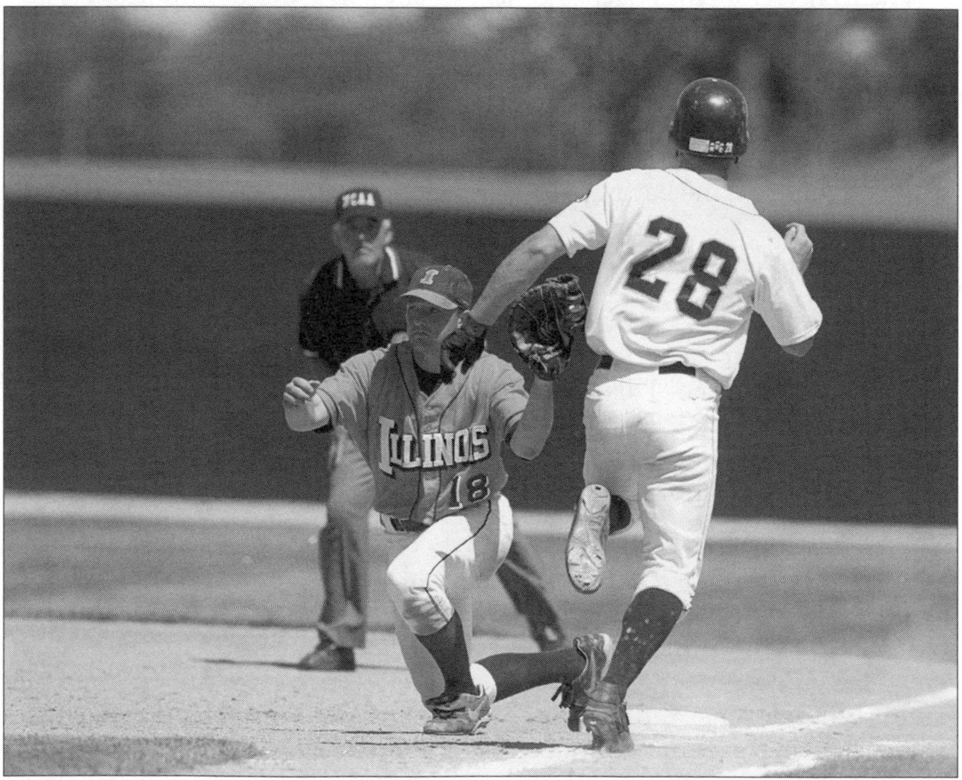

When a team is ahead in the score, it can afford to take more chances on offense.

The great collegiate coach, Gordie Gillespie, tells coaches at clinics, "Don't you dare ease up on my team! Don't you dare embarrass my team by easing up and implying we aren't good enough to come back and beat you!" A team with a lead should certainly continue to play aggressively early in the game and through the middle innings because offensive-minded teams can get a rally going and pile up many runs in a hurry. A coach who tells his team to ease up "because we already have enough runs" may live to regret it. In addition, the coach who through his actions implies that his team should ease up may cause his players to lose their competitive drive and end up just going through the motions. That behavior can cause real problems for a team, if not in that game then perhaps in a later one.

Trailing in the Game

When a team is behind in the score of the game, they should become more conservative to preserve the outs they have remaining in the game. The further behind a team is in the score, the more conservative they should become. If a team falls behind by two or three runs early in the game, they will probably stick to their normal game plan because many outs remain in the game and the team doesn't have to get all the runs back at one time. But it is foolish for a team to take a chance on wasting an out late in the game trying to score one run when they need five or six runs just to gain a tie! The inning in which a team begins to play conservative baseball should depend on how far behind they are, the type of skills the team has, and their ability to score runs. A team might continue to play aggressively if the best offensive skill they have is speed. They might play conservatively if their best skill is power.

The total number of runs in a game can influence the offensive strategy. For example, if in the middle of the game a team is trailing 3-0, it is clear that neither team is scoring much. Aggressive play may be necessary to scratch out a couple of runs to get in position to tie or win the game. On the other hand, if a team is behind 15-12, they are still behind by three runs, but both teams are scoring a lot of runs. Being aggressive to score one run may not be that important because the other team may score five or six more runs in their half of the inning!

Score Tied or One-Run Difference

With the score tied or with a one-run difference either ahead or behind, a coach should probably look at the way the game is developing and play accordingly. In a low-scoring, hard-fought pitching duel, a coach will probably lean toward playing more aggressively to score one or two runs because that may be all he can get and all he can expect to get. And one or two runs may be enough to win the game. On the other hand, if the game is developing into a slugfest with runs being scored in bunches like grapes, taking a big gamble to score one run may not help if the other team scores five runs in the next inning.

Inning

After the score, the next most important factor to consider when planning an effective offensive strategy is the inning. The decision to play more conservatively or aggressively often depends on whether the game is in its early, middle, or late innings.

Early Innings

Some youth teams seem to delight in scratching for an early run, perhaps to get the lead and put the other team at a psychological disadvantage. That strategy might be wise if their talent is best suited for one-run-at-a-time baseball, but a team must have good pitching and good defense to play that style of baseball. In addition, that approach ignores the fact that in most baseball games a big inning of three or four runs plays a big part in the outcome of the game.

According to major-league baseball statistics, in a little over 50 percent of all major-league games, the winning team scores more runs in one inning than the losing team scores in the entire game. A team should thus look for the opportunity to go for a big inning whenever possible. This approach may be especially successful early in the game when the starting pitcher may not be settled down or effective. Most teams will generally play more conservatively at the start of the game in hopes of getting several runs in an inning. Other teams often sacrifice bunt in the first inning to try to get one run and the lead. By doing so, they may rob themselves of a big inning and allow the opposing starting pitcher to settle down with only one run scored. Another interesting statistic from major-league baseball is that (on the average) teams score more runs in the first inning than they do in any other inning of the game. Teams may waste a potentially big first inning by sacrifice bunting and playing for one run to start the game. On occasion that approach may work and produce a 1-0 victory, but the percentages of baseball would argue against using that type of strategy in the first inning or early in the game.

Middle Innings

The middle innings often determine the character of the game. If the game has become a slugfest, the strategy of the coaches should reflect that circumstance. If the game has developed into a pitching duel, they should make strategy decisions accordingly. Of course, the character of a game may start out one way and then change as the game progresses. A 0-0 pitching duel with a lot of strikeouts may change in the middle innings if one or both pitchers suddenly can't find the plate with a roadmap or if they start to find the middle of the plate rather than the corners. Base runners begin to look like a blur going around the bases. On the other hand, after giving up four or five runs in the first inning and causing his coach to start pulling his hair out, a pitcher may suddenly settle down and begin to pitch like Pedro Martinez. Coaches should carefully evaluate the mood of the game in the middle innings and try to take advantage of any changes or mood swings that occur.

Late Innings

Late in the game a team's offensive strategy will, of necessity, revolve primarily around the score of the game. The team will play conservatively if it is behind to save outs, and it will play aggressively if it is ahead to try to add to the lead. By this time, the character of the game (low scoring or high scoring) will be established, and the coach can make decisions accordingly.

Coaches must understand that the decisions they make in the late innings of a close game are often important to the outcome. Coaches must keep their emotions under control during this time. Strategy decisions made under any circumstances must be well thought out and take into consideration all relevant aspects of the game, but decisions made in the late innings of a close game require even more emotional control. The coach should make a rational, intelligent decision rather than make a snap judgment in the heat of the moment. All too often, when a coach gets into a tight situation late in a close game, he begins worrying about winning the game rather than thinking about what decisions he can make to help the team perform to the best of its ability. Wanting to win is obviously important, but when a coach gets so wrapped up with the thought of winning that he can't think rationally about what his team should do in a close game, he will usually fail to think objectively and will make decisions based on a gut reaction rather than on sound strategy principles.

One of the factors that can radically change the way a coach uses strategy during the late innings of a game is the presence (or absence) of an outstanding relief pitcher. Teams having an outstanding relief pitcher will feel comfortable playing for one run late in the game because they are confident that their closer can hold the lead. On the other hand, the presence of an outstanding relief pitcher on the other club may cause the offensive team to change their strategy in the late innings of a game to try to avoid going into the last inning trailing by a run . The presence of a great relief pitcher in the bullpen will influence the strategy of the managers in both dugouts in the last two or three innings of a game.

Number of Outs

Following consideration of the score and the inning, the next factor the coach should consider is the number of outs in the inning. A coach must consider what the percentages are of scoring a run (or runs) in a particular inning. The number of outs remaining in the inning will significantly affect those percentages.

An inning comprises three portions (or three-thirds), and baseball percentages show, understandably, that a team's chances of scoring a lot of runs in an inning are better with none out, when it has all three of the thirds of the inning remaining. The percentages for a big inning are somewhat lower with one out and only two-thirds of the inning remaining and less still with two outs and only one of the thirds left. Of course, we all know that occasionally a team will erupt with two outs and nobody on base to score five or six runs, but a big inning like that occurs much more often with none out or one out. Coaches must consider the percentages in planning their strategy moves for each inning.

No Outs

With no outs, a team should play somewhat conservatively if the number of runs and the inning also make it practical because of the good possibility (in percentage terms) of getting a big inning going and scoring several runs. For example, if a runner is thrown out trying to stretch a long single into a double with none out, the team may have lost its chance of having a big inning. Certainly, having a runner thrown out at third base or home plate for the first out of the inning results from questionable strategy. The runner may be able to make it safely on a close play, but the runner at second base or third base with none out may have a greater probability of scoring than he does in an attempt to beat a close play at third base or home plate. The old cliche "Never make the first out of an inning at third base or home plate" makes a lot of sense from the standpoint of strategy and percentages.

One Out

With one out a team should be a bit more aggressive in trying to score one run. One-third of the inning is already spent, so the percentages for a big inning are somewhat lower. With one out a team will want to be very aggressive in attempting to reach third base if the score and the inning are in agreement because a runner at third can score on a fly ball or an infield grounder in addition to the other ways of scoring. Most high school and college coaches and major-league managers strongly emphasize getting base runners to third base with one out if the score is close.

Two Outs

With two outs and only one-third of the inning remaining, the percentages for a team to score many runs in the inning are greatly reduced, so (if the score and inning are in agreement) the team should aggressively try to score one run. A team should be especially aggressive in trying to reach second base with two outs because the probability of scoring from first base with two outs is low (14 percent). Taking the gamble to reach second base may be worth it because the scoring percentages are much better (26 percent).

In addition, a team should be extremely aggressive in trying to score with two outs if the chances of scoring are better than the next batter's chances of hitting safely. For example, if the third-base coach feels that the base runner has a 50-50 chance of scoring on a hit with two outs, he should send him in unless the on-deck hitter is hitting near .500 because the percentages for success are better. With two outs, holding up a runner with a 50 percent chance of scoring doesn't make sense when the on-deck hitter is batting .190!

Position in the Batting Order

The last factor to be considered in planning strategy is the sequence of upcoming batters. Although the batting order may be the last factor to consider, it is no less important than several of the others are. The hitters coming up and their skills (or lack of skills) will have a big effect on the coach's decisions.

Most batting orders are pretty standard (in spite of some far-out ideas generated at times by fans, TV announcers, and sportswriters) because a normal batting order makes sense and goes along with the percentages of baseball. The better hitters for average and on-base percentage and the better base runners usually bat 1-2-3 in the order, the power hitters usually bat in the 4-5-6 positions, and the weaker hitters generally bat in the 7-8-9 positions. At times a coach who is a so-called baseball expert will come out with a plan to improve baseball scoring percentages by having Barry Bonds, Sammy Sosa, or Mark McGwire hit in the leadoff spot, but within a short time he will usually go back to the standard batting order.

Offensive strategy should be planned according to the skills of the player at bat and the abilities of the players due to bat later in the inning. A team will normally play more conservatively with its stronger hitters coming to bat in an inning because they have a better chance to score a bunch of runs. A team will normally play a bit more aggressively with their weaker hitters due to bat because they may only get a chance to score one run.

A coach should not deliberately use his stronger hitters in such a way that he puts his weaker hitters in a position to have to drive in the important runs. A good example of this might be using the number 5 hitter to sacrifice bunt a runner to second base. The opposing team then walks the number 6 hitter, and now the number 7 or 8 hitter has to drive in the run. Upon reflection, the decision to bunt may have been unwise.

Speaking at a clinic, Bill Rigney, former manager of the Giants, told the story of having Willie Mays sacrifice bunt in the ninth inning of a one-run game. The other team then intentionally walked Willie McCovey (who was replaced by a pinch runner), and now he had two left-hand hitters facing a left-hand closer with the two best RBI men in the National League sitting beside him on the bench. Said Rigney, "I suddenly realized I wasn't too smart."

To devise a good strategic plan, you have to know the percentages. The scoring percentages in table 6.1 are based on more than 60 years and thousands of major-league baseball games, but they should be reasonably similar for youth, high school, collegiate, and minor league baseball. A study of these statistics reveals some interesting facts and conclusions.

The scoring percentage of a runner on first base with none out is 43 percent, and with a runner on second with one out it is 45 percent. That tiny 2 percent increase in scoring percentage makes the idea of using a sacrifice bunt with a good hitter at the plate suspect. The scoring percentage of a runner on second base with none out is 60 percent, and with a runner on third base and one out it is 54 percent. This decrease in scoring percentages makes sacrifice bunting the runner to third base extremely questionable if the batter is a decent hitter. Another look at the percentages shows that the improvement in scoring percentage by having a runner on third base instead of on second base is 10 percent with none out, 9 percent with one out, and 6 percent with two outs. Therefore, on a steal of third base (regardless of the number of outs) the runner must have a great jump on the pitcher and a chance of success up around 90 percent for it to be good strategy.

Base-Running Strategy

The choices that coaches make from among the dozens (or hundreds) of different tactics available for use in the various game situations can be a big factor in the outcome of some games. The coach should make strategy decisions based on the four factors of score, inning, outs, and position in the batting order already covered in this chapter, and he must be especially aware of the skills of the players involved, both his and the opponent's. In addition, the coach must work with his players to acquaint them with good strategy because he often does not have enough time or opportunity to relay to his players what he wants them to do if A happens, or B happens, or C happens, or if C and J happen at the same time! The wise coach will use

TABLE 6.1 Scoring Percentages

RUNNER ON FIRST	RUNNER ON SECOND	RUNNER ON THIRD
0 out = 43%	0 out = 60%	0 out = 70%
1 out = 29%	1 out = 45%	1 out = 54%
2 outs = 14%	2 outs = 26%	2 outs = 32%

intrasquad games and practice drills to set up various base-running tactical situations so that players can learn to react to them properly when they occur.

Runner on First, Less Than Two Outs, Questionable Fly-Ball Catch

With less than two outs a runner on first should go as far toward second base as possible while still being able to get back to first if the ball is caught. The runner should be on balance and standing still when the fly ball approaches the outfielder so that he can break for second base if the ball falls in or return to first if it is caught (see figure 6.1). Many runners go too far and then start leaning or moving back toward first base as the ball nears the outfielder. If the ball falls in safely, they may not be able to change directions quickly and may be forced out at second base.

On an ordinary fly ball, the runner on first can go farther toward second base on a ball hit to left field than he can on one hit to center field or right field because the throw from the left fielder to first base after the catch will be a long one (see figure 6.2). On a deep fly ball to left or left-center field, the runner from first base can go all the way to second base and stand on the base with his right foot on the bag and his left foot and his body facing toward third base. If the ball is not caught, he can break immediately toward third base and may be able to score if the ball is not returned to the infield quickly. If the ball is caught, the runner should first move his left foot toward first base, push off with his right foot that is on the base, and return to first base. In starting to return to first base the runner should take plenty of time and be deliberate in his movements because

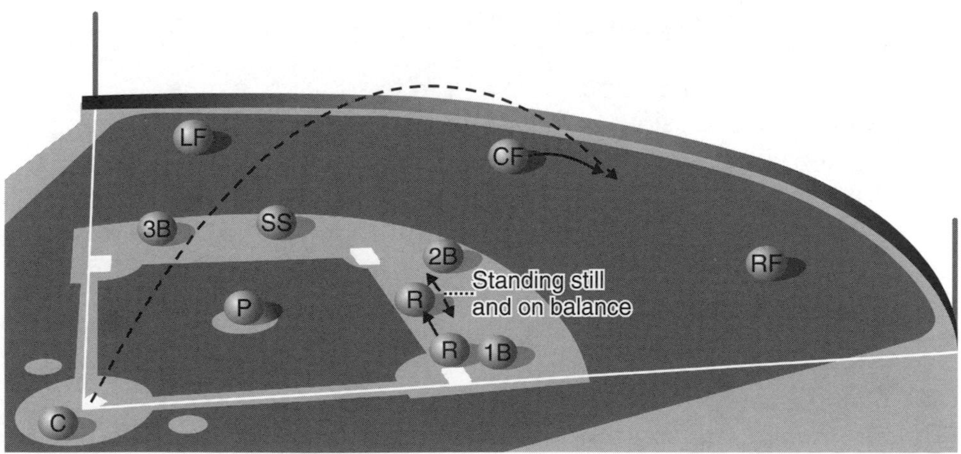

FIGURE 6.1 Runner on first, less than two outs, questionable fly-ball catch.

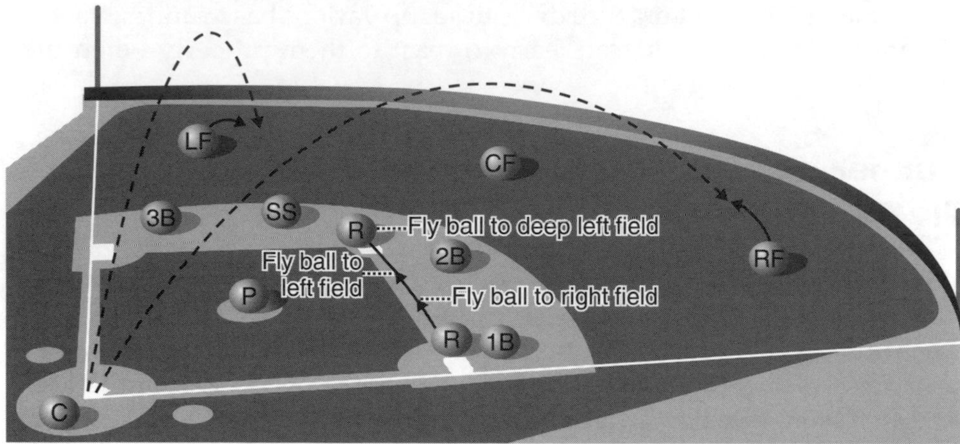

FIGURE 6.2 On a fly ball to left field, the runner on first can go farther toward second than on one to center or right field. On a deep fly ball to left field, the runner on first can go all the way to second.

1. he wants to make sure he doesn't step toward third base with the right foot *before* stepping toward first because doing so constitutes "starting for third base" and the runner could be called out on an appeal play for not retouching the base, and
2. most left fielders are not noted for strong throwing arms and wouldn't be able to get the ball from deep left field all the way to first base unless it goes by Federal Express.

Runner on Second, Less Than Two Outs, Questionable Fly-Ball Catch

The situation with a runner on second and less than two outs often causes indecision and confusion in the minds of base runners and sometimes coaches as well, but remembering a couple of basic strategy concepts can make matters clear. Two strategy principles already discussed in this chapter dictate what the runner should do in this situation, notably trying to reach third base with one out and not making the third out of the inning at third base. With a runner on second base and none out, the runner should tag up on second until it is obvious that the outfielder cannot catch the ball (see figure 6.3). By waiting to be sure, the runner may not be able to score if the ball falls in but is returned to the infield quickly, but even then he would be on third base with none out and a 70 percent chance of scoring. Once the runner is certain that the ball cannot be caught, he can break toward third base and should be able to score on the play, but as long as there is any chance that the outfielder will catch the ball, the runner should stay tagged up on the base.

With one out, the runner should come off the base as far as he can while still being able to get back to the base if the ball is caught in the outfield. He should be on balance and standing still when the ball is coming down so that he can react equally well back to second base or toward third base (see figure 6.4). As long as there is any chance that the ball will not be caught, he should remain off the base; if it becomes obvious early enough in the play that the ball will be caught, he should go back to second, tag up, and advance to third after the catch. The runner must clearly understand that it is

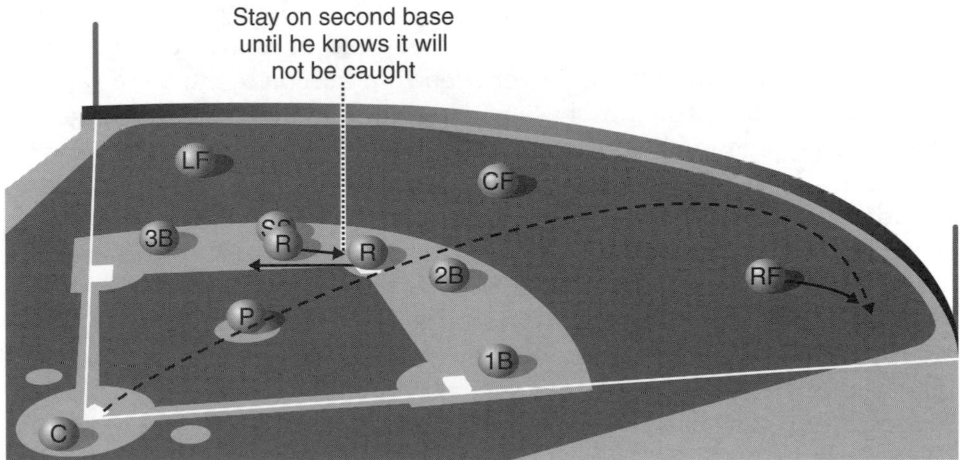

FIGURE 6.3 Runner on second, no outs, and a questionable fly-ball catch.

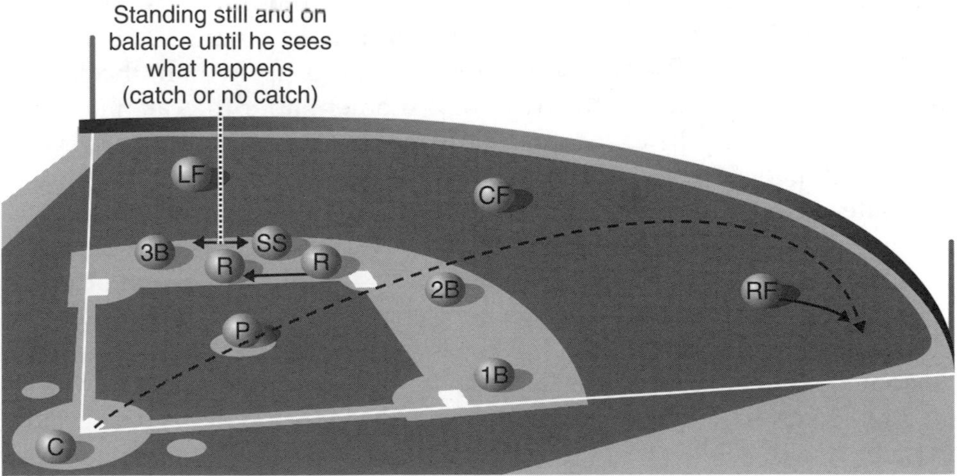

FIGURE 6.4 Runner on second, one out, and a questionable fly-ball catch.

not good strategy to try to advance to third if doing so might result in making the third out of the inning at third base. The runner should not try to advance unless he can do so with an excellent chance of success.

Runner on Third, Fly Ball With Less Than Two Outs

A runner on third base should go back to the base and tag up on all balls hit anywhere in the air. If a line drive is hit in the direction of the third baseman, the runner must immediately break back toward third base to avoid being doubled off if the third baseman catches the ball. If the ball gets past the infielder, the runner can change direction and score easily, but he must avoid being doubled off on a line drive toward third base. Bucky Harris, manager of the Washington Senators back in the good old days, was once asked to recall the greatest play he had ever seen in a baseball game. He replied, "Mickey Vernon was on third base with a right-hand hitter at the plate. The batter hit a screaming line drive that the third baseman caught moving toward third base—he took one step and tagged the bag, but Vernon was already back to it." "What's so great about that play?" he was asked. Harris said, "Because 99 out of 100 players would have hesitated before going back to third and would have been doubled off."

With none out the runner on third base should be conservative in his attempts to score on a short fly ball that might result in a close play at the plate, especially if the next batter is a fairly good hitter. The probability of scoring from third base with one out is 54 percent, so the runner should have better than a 50-50 chance of scoring with none out for tagging up to be a wise move.

With one out a runner at third base will be more aggressive in attempting to score on a short fly ball (if the other factors suggest being aggressive), because the probability that a runner will score from third base with two outs is only 32 percent. If the next hitter is hitting less than .320, being aggressive is probably the right thing to do. On a deep fly ball, the runner tagging up should stay on the base for a moment after the catch to make sure that he will not be called out on an appeal for leaving too early. On a short fly ball, however, that practice will probably result in a close play at the plate, so he must leave *exactly* with the catch of the ball (see figure 6.5).

Normally, a runner on third base with less than two outs will tag up on all fly balls and stay on the base until the ball is caught, but in one situation he should use a different tactic. On a very short fly ball to the outfield on which the runner would not be able to tag up and score if the ball is caught, he should come off the base as far as possible, but not so far that he would be doubled off if the ball is caught. If the ball hits the ground he may be able to score; if it is caught, he simply returns to third base (figure 6.5). If he stays tagged up on the base on a short fly ball and leaves the base when the ball hits the ground, the outfielder may be able to throw him out at the plate.

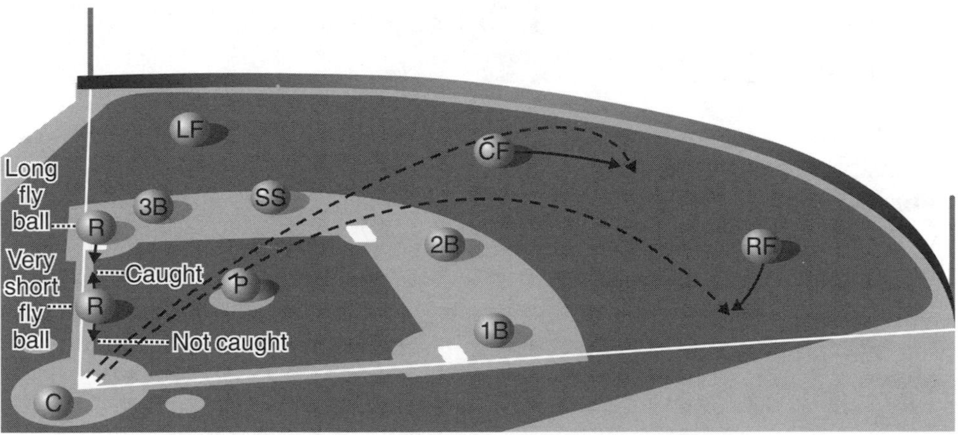

FIGURE 6.5 Runner on third, fly ball with less than two outs.

Runners on First and Third, Fly Ball With Less Than Two Outs

On a fairly deep fly ball with runners on first and third, both runners can tag up, but the runner at first or the first-base coach must alert the batter not to pass the runner tagged up at first base. When the ball is caught, both runners can break after the catch and watch the throw (see figure 6.6). If the throw is to home plate, especially if it is a high throw over the head of the cutoff man, the runner on first should be able to advance to second. If the throw is toward second and it appears it will beat the runner from first to the base, the runner can stop and return to first base as the runner from third base scores.

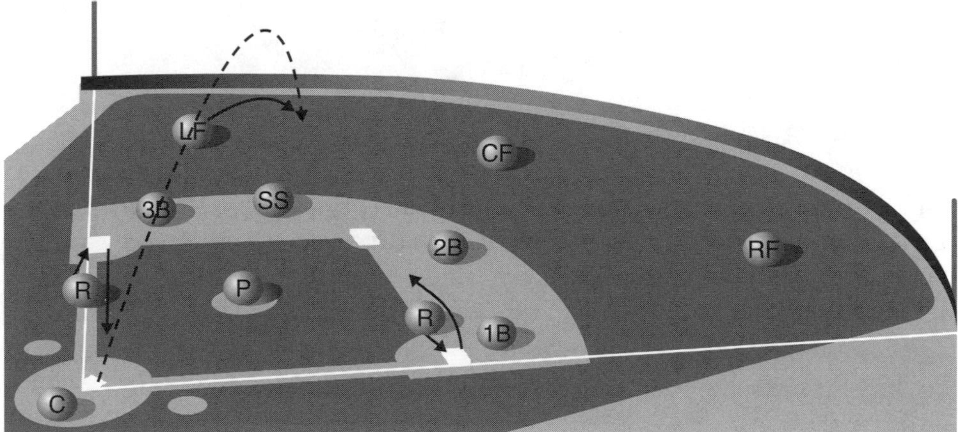

FIGURE 6.6 Runners on first and third, fly ball with less than two outs.

Runners on Second and Third, Fly Ball With Less Than Two Outs

With runners at second and third on a fly ball that will be caught without difficulty, both runners can tag up and break when the catch is made (see figure 6.7). The runner on second base must keep an eye on the runner ahead of him to make sure that he continues toward the plate. If the runner from third base believes the throw will beat him to the plate and he retreats to third base, the runner from second base must also stop and return to second. Otherwise, two runners will end up at third base, making for an easy tag out.

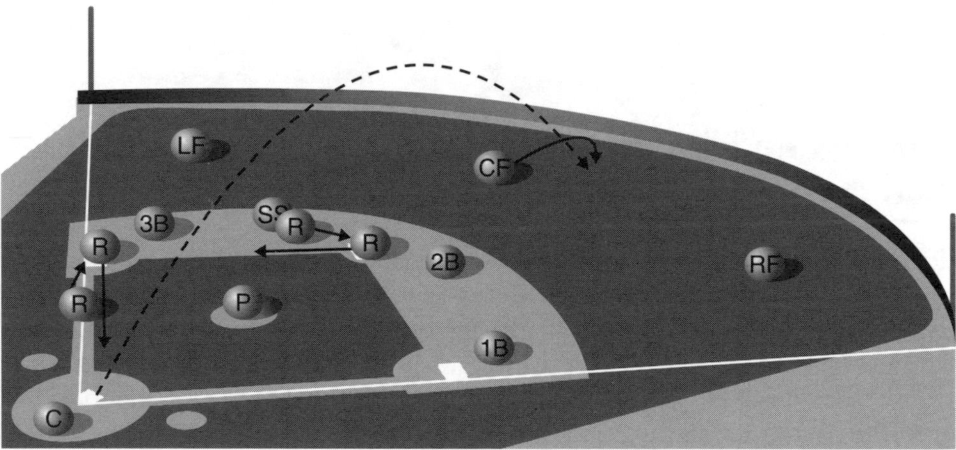

FIGURE 6.7 Runners on second and third, fly ball with less than two outs.

Foul Fly Ball With Less Than Two Outs

All runners should tag up on all foul fly balls, regardless of where they are hit. If a fielder does not make the catch, the runners can simply stay at their bases. If the ball is caught, they may have a chance to advance. The runner who wanders around the infield on a foul fly ball simply because he thinks it will not be caught is foolish. Occasionally a player will make a great catch of a foul fly ball, crash into the fence, and have trouble getting up. The base runner does not want to be standing 30 feet from the base watching with his mouth open in amazement. By tagging up on all foul fly balls, runners can react to a caught ball if there is a possibility of advancing (see figure 6.8).

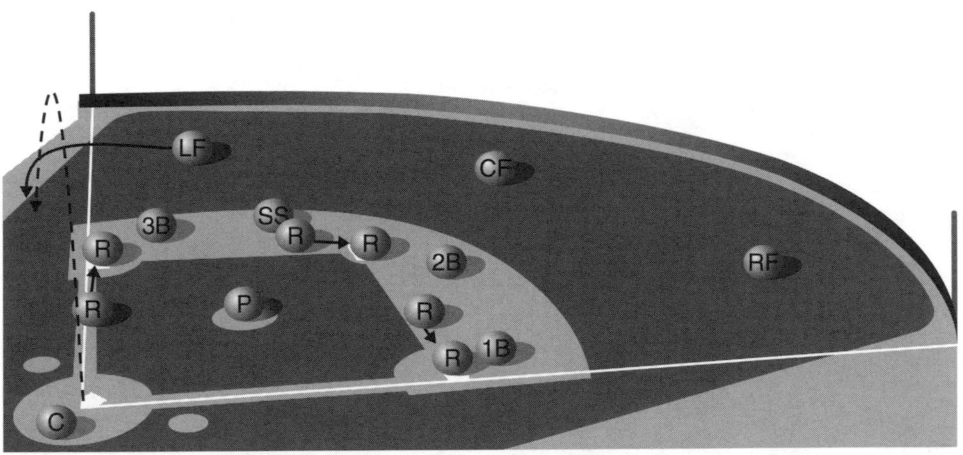

FIGURE 6.8 Foul fly ball with less than two outs.

Runner on Second, Ground Ball With Less Than Two Outs

A runner at second should try to advance to third base on all ground balls hit to his left unless the ball is hit near him and hit very hard. The shortstop must make a tough play to go to his left, field the ball, and then turn and make a good throw to third base. If the ball is a one-hop, hard-hit grounder directly to the shortstop, he may be able to make the play, but most of the time a runner at second base can advance and reach third safely on a ground ball hit to his left. If the ground ball is hit straight at the base runner and he has his weight leaning toward third base at the end of his secondary lead (as he should have), he should be able to reach third base most of the time. On a ground ball to his right, the base runner must freeze in place until the ball gets past the third baseman. If the ball goes into the outfield, he can then break for third base. Although his momentary delay may prevent him from scoring on a ground ball that goes into left field, he will not run into an easy out at third if the shortstop or third baseman fields it. If the batter hits a slow roller that the third baseman must charge, the base runner should be able to reach third base easily as the third baseman makes the play to first. Of course, a ground ball hit to the second baseman or first baseman should allow the runner on second to advance easily to third base (see figure 6.9).

Runner on Third, Ground Ball With Less Than Two Outs

A base runner at third with less than two outs should review the game situation with the third-base coach before the play develops so that he will be

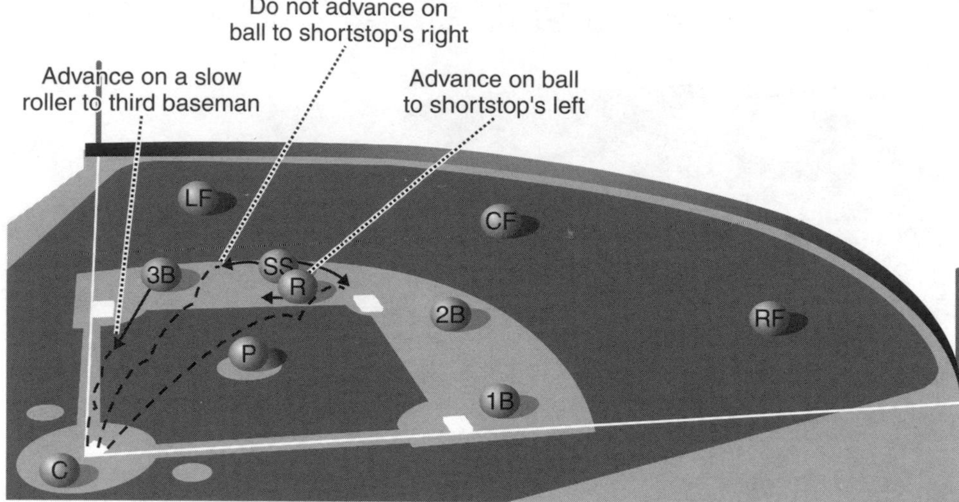

FIGURE 6.9 Runner on second, ground ball with less than two outs.

confident about what he needs to do. He should then check the positioning of the infielders to see if they are at normal depth or in close to cut off the run at the plate. Normally, base runners should not attempt to score with none out on a ground ball unless the infielders are back and the ball is a high bouncer that the infielders cannot field and throw to the plate quickly. The runner should remember not to make the first out of the inning at home plate. With one out the runner should discuss the appropriate strategy with the third-base coach and make sure they agree about the best percentage play to use at that time. If the infielders are playing in, base runners will often be told to try to score only if they get a good break on a high bouncing ball. If the infielders are halfway or in the deep position, the coach will instruct the runner either to go on contact or to read the bounce.

If the coach has decided that the situation of the game warrants aggressive baserunning, he will tell the runner to go on contact. On any ground ball the runner will immediately break for the plate and try to score. This action obviously has advantages and disadvantages. If the ball is hit straight at an infielder, the runner may be out at the plate by a big margin, but if the infielder has to move a step or two to field the ball, the runner has a chance to be safe at the plate.

If the coach decides to use the read-the-bounce play, the runner will break for the plate on any ball that bounces high or is not hit straight at an infielder. He will not break for the plate on a hard-hit ground ball until the ball passes the infielder and goes to the outfield. Obviously, this requires the base runner to delay momentarily the decision to go or not to go. That slight delay may give the infielders enough time to throw him out at the plate.

Runners on First and Third, Ground Ball With Less Than Two Outs

The situation with runners at first and third seems to cause confusion and indecision in many baseball games, especially at the youth and amateur level, and even in the major leagues! The defensive team may turn the double play in a first-and-third situation while the lead runner remains at third base. Even worse, the runner at third may hesitate for a moment, break for the plate when he finally hears the third-base coach screaming at him to go, and then get thrown out at home plate for a triple play. Applying a basic base-running principle simplifies the strategy for this play.

If the infield defense is at normal double-play depth, the runner on third must break for the plate on all ground balls hit sharply enough to the infield that they can be turned into double plays (see figure 6.10). If the runner does not break for the plate and the defense turns a double play with none out, the offensive team ends up with a runner at third base with two outs and only a 32 percent chance of scoring that inning. On the other hand, if the runner on third breaks for the plate and is thrown out, the offensive team now has one out, runners on first and second, and a 45 percent chance of scoring that inning. If the runner does not try to score with one out and the defense turns the double play, the inning is over. If the runner breaks for the plate and is thrown out, there are now two outs, runners are on first and second, and the inning is still going. In this situation a good base runner can sometimes break for home, glance back, see that the throw is going to the plate, stop, and get in a rundown long enough to allow the other two base runners to advance to second and third.

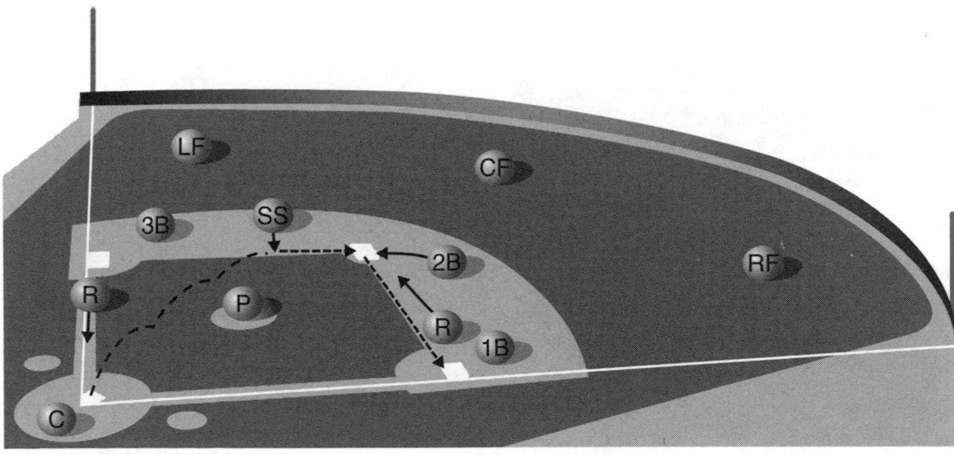

FIGURE 6.10 Runners on first and third, ground ball with less than two outs, and the infield at double-play depth.

With runners at first and third, less than two outs, and the infield in on the grass to cut off the run at the plate, the runner on third should normally not try to score on a ground ball because the middle infielders will find it extremely difficult to turn a double play from the in-on-the-grass position (see figure 6.11).

Tendencies of Opposing Coaches

Every baseball coach will tend to do certain things in certain situations with particular players. This tendency may not represent a failure to think creatively; it is more likely the result of having some success with certain offensive or defensive plays (and with the players involved) and feeling comfortable with them. A coach should constantly study the actions of opposing coaches so that he can remember (or better yet, write down!) what the opposition usually does in certain game situations. Just as a coach should develop a "book" on the skills and abilities of the players on all opposing teams, he should develop a book on the opposing coach so that he can anticipate what the opponent might do in particular situations based on what he has done in the past in similar situations.

Trying to guess what an opposing team will do in certain situations based only on a gut feeling isn't too smart. But if the coach knows that the opposing coach has attempted a particular strategy in the same game situation in the past, he can make an intelligent guess about the opponent's next move. Because memory can play tricks on all of us, coaches should keep notes on opposing coaches to have accurate knowledge of their tendencies.

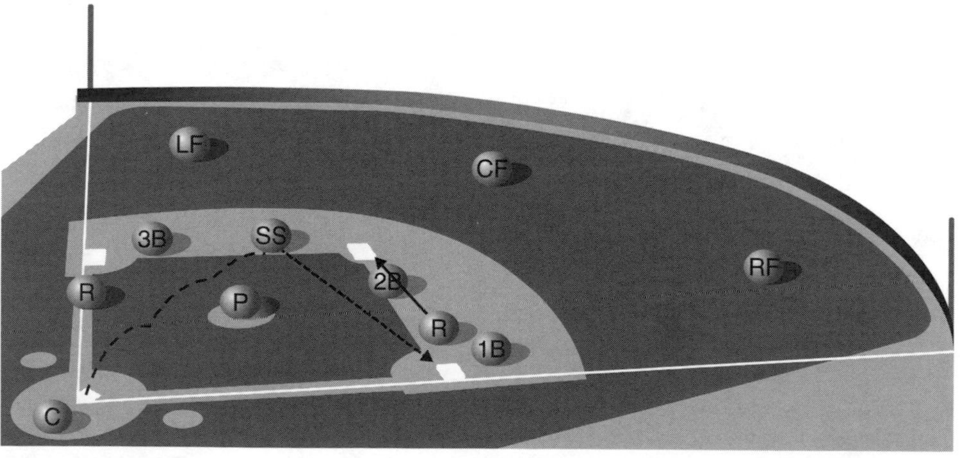

FIGURE 6.11 Runners on first and third, ground ball with less than two outs, and the infield in on the grass.

Another way to discover the tendencies of an opposing coach is to observe what he tries to do on defense when his team is in certain offensive situations. Those tendencies can provide a good indication of how he would react on offense in the same situation and vice versa from offense to defense. He thinks you are going to try a particular play right now because that is what *he* would do in that situation, so his actions can give you an insight on what he might do when the roles are reversed. For example, if your leadoff man gets on first base in the first inning and the opposing team puts on a special bunt-defense play, that should indicate to you that *he* would bunt in that situation. If the opposing coach brings his infield in with a runner on third base and less than two outs in the first inning, that should tell you that he believes that run is vital to winning the game, and thus he is probably not going to play for a big inning later in the game. A coach who allows his hitter to swing on a 3-0 pitch in a certain situation will probably expect you to let your hitter swing on a 3-0 pitch in the same situation.

I remember a Georgia Southern University game many years ago when Tom Kotchman (now a scout-manager in the Anaheim Angels organization) hit a bottom-of-the-9th, two-out, nobody-on, 3-0 batting-practice fastball out of the park (to the amazement of the other team) to tie the score. He came up with two outs and nobody on in the bottom of the 11th inning, and they threw him *another* 3-0 count batting-practice fastball. He won the game when that one also went out of the park—you have to wonder if the other team was watching the game at all!

If an opposing coach is consistent in his strategy moves and you remember them or write them down, you will have a good idea of what a coach might do in a particular situation. Although those predispositions are not carved in stone, knowing an opponent's tendencies can be a big help during any game.

A coach may disguise his tendencies by occasionally changing up in a particular situation of the game. Sometimes a coach will do something strategically out of character from what he would normally do in that situation simply to try to keep the other coach guessing and confused about his normal strategy decisions. Doing this often is unwise if it means doing something that is not a good percentage play. Normally a coach would not deviate from his standard best strategy in a crucial part of a game, but he may do so occasionally to confuse an opposing coach about his tendencies in certain game situations.

Matchups During a Game

Television announcers for major-league games seem to talk constantly about matchups during the game. They suggest that the two managers are playing a game of "If he does A, I will do B, and if I do C, then he will do D" throughout the entire game. In a major-league game, matchups are important, and the two managers will be constantly searching for an edge in a matchup of skills of opposing players. Trying to arrange good matchups at the minor-league, collegiate, high school, or youth level of baseball, however, is difficult simply because the level and consistency of skill is not as high. If a major-league manager does some deep thinking and crafty maneuvering to arrange for his left-handed pitcher to pitch to their left-handed batter, he should have some good reason to expect his left-hander to give their left-hander some tough pitches that he can't handle well. Much of the time this matchup will give one manager's team a slight advantage over the other team. The left-handed pitcher may face only that one hitter, and a side-arming right-hander may come in to face the next hitter (who hits from the right side of the plate) in yet another matchup. So it goes in the constant battle of wits between the two managers, each seeking favorable matchups in the game.

Contrast that sequence to a situation in a game involving players who are younger and less skilled than major leaguers. One coach will bring in his left-handed pitcher to pitch to their left-handed hitter in a "good matchup." The southpaw pitcher throws four balls into a different area code and wild pitches in two or three runs in the process. Or a coach sends up a right-handed pinch hitter to face a left-handed pitcher. The batter swings at three pitches that hit on the grass in front of home plate for an embarrassing strikeout.

Rather than trying to create matchups with young players, coaches will often alter their strategy because of the matchup already present between the pitcher and batter. For example, with a runner on second base (who is an important run) and none out, a coach may allow the hitter to swing away if he is able to hit the ball to the right side of the ballpark (either to the second baseman or to right field) because doing so will get the runner over to third base with one out. But if the hitter cannot consistently hit the ball to the right side of the field, then the coach will put on the sacrifice bunt to get the runner to third base. Of course, if the hitter can neither hit to right field nor bunt well, the coach has no matchup at all. He will have to use a pinch hitter or just grit his teeth and hope for the best.

Coaches who try to establish good matchups in amateur or youth baseball should avoid thinking their way into trouble, which sometimes happens when they try to copy major-league managers. Coaches at amateur levels may have problems not because their decisions are wrong, but because the consistency of skills at that level is not high enough to allow accurate prediction of the players' performance. An example of an amateur coach overplaying matchups might be using a .280 hitter to sacrifice bunt a runner to second base to bring up the next hitter, who is batting .340. Great move, coach, but not if the .340 hitter does not match up well with that particular pitcher and is hitting only .160 against him.

The number of specific offensive situations in a baseball season is virtually limitless. If a coach is going to make strategy decisions that will give his team their best chance to win, he must be able to make wise, sensible decisions in every one of those game situations. A coach cannot possibly catalog every possible offensive situation that might arise in a season and devise a good decision for each one. He would need a book 12 inches thick, cross-referenced for every possible factor. So what the coach must do is understand the skills of the players involved and the percentages of baseball. He must then be able to evaluate each situation in light of that knowledge to arrive at a good decision. In addition, the coach must have the fortitude to make his decision and stick with it rather than allow other people (such as loud-mouthed fans) to second-guess him and push him into making a hasty and poor decision.

Postgame Wrap-Up

Offensive strategy and tactics in baseball, to use an old line, "ain't rocket science," but they do have some aspects of science in them and require a coach to understand basic principles. Certainly, baseball has changed considerably over the years, and strategy and tactics have changed to reflect the various skills of players, the improvement in equipment, the way ballparks are constructed, changes in the entertainment demands of the fans, and even changes in society.

Any student of the game knows that baseball in the days of Ty Cobb, Honus Wagner, and Tris Speaker emphasized the sacrifice bunt, the hit-and-run, the stolen base, and one-run-at-a-time baseball much more than they are today. A player in that era who wanted to be in the starting lineup had to develop his skills in those techniques to a high level or the manager would not play him much. As a result, many players at that time could perform those skills well, and mangers commonly used strategies that called on those skills.

Current baseball strategy and tactics normally place greater emphasis on power hitting, the use of pinch hitters and pinch runners, selective use of the stolen base, and a more conservative offensive strategy that tries to avoid wasting outs in an effort to create the big inning. But effective application of both strategies—the old-fashioned one-run-at-a-time strategy of yesteryear and the modern big-inning strategy of today—requires consideration of the situation of the game, the percentages of baseball, and especially the abilities of the players. That part of baseball strategy and tactics has never changed because it makes sense, it is consistent, and it works!

PART II

Pitching

Shutting Down Hitters

Keith Madison

We often hear that practices belong to the coaches and games belong to the players. We also hear baseball gurus say that pitching is anywhere from 80 to 90 percent of the game. Consequently, coaches must spend quality time preparing pitchers mentally and physically for the challenge of shutting down hitters. Few pitchers have major-league talent, but if coaches can get the most out of each pitcher on the staff, they can be assured of a big-league experience.

Developing Mental Toughness

Yogi Berra once said, "Ninety percent of this game is half mental." Most pitchers on a staff have the God-given ability to pitch at that particular level or they wouldn't be on the team. In many cases the amount of success a pitcher enjoys depends on his mental condition, his mental toughness. Most coaches spend 95 percent of their time on the physical or mechanical aspect of coaching and 5 percent on the mental. Then coaches are amazed that their pitchers aren't mentally tough! If a pitcher lacks skill in the mental game, he will be less successful in what he is trying to do physically—get the hitter out.

Tough physical conditioning helps a pitcher's mentality. It gives him confidence. Competing against the hitter can be easy compared with doing physical conditioning in practice, so pitching becomes challenging and fun instead of physically draining.

Another way to strengthen a pitcher's mentality is through positive visualization. A pitcher's body will respond to the last thought he had. If his last thought was, "I hope I don't hang this curveball," his body responds to the subject of his last thought—hanging the curveball—and he will hang the curve. If his last thought before releasing the ball is, "This curve will break sharply and hit the target low and away in the strike zone," he will be much more likely to make the pitch.

During my junior year in high school, I was a hard thrower but averaged almost a walk per inning. A couple of months before my senior season began, my coach challenged me to visualize the best hitters in our district each night before I fell asleep. He encouraged me to see my fastball low and away in the zone with the hitter's bat swinging late and several inches over the ball. He asked me to visualize my curve breaking sharply and finishing low in the zone. Thankfully, I took him up on his challenge and cut my bases on balls dramatically.

For some pitchers, positive thoughts and positive visualizations come easily. Others must practice and condition themselves. Coaches should get the staff together, have them close their eyes, and ask them to visualize the ball doing exactly what they want it to with the result being an out for the team. This exercise can be an enjoyable, relaxing, and productive part of practice.

Mastering the Strike Zone

In any game or situation, especially a big game, the pitcher and catcher must know the zone. Keep in mind that there are four strike zones:

1. The pitcher's zone
2. The hitter's zone
3. The rulebook zone
4. The umpire's zone

A coach should have no sympathy for a pitcher who whines about the strike zone. The only zone that matters is the umpire's zone. As long as the umpire is consistent, a pitcher can use the umpire's zone to his advantage. If a pitcher is consistently near the umpire's zone, he will get calls on the borderline pitches. The pitcher's pitch should be from the top of the kneecap to the bottom of the kneecap. If a pitcher can live there, 99 percent of the umpires will call it a strike

Creating Deception

Deception is the most underrated tool in shutting down hitters. Many hitters have come back to the dugout wondering how that 84-mile-per-hour fastball got on their hands so quickly. An 84-mile-per-hour fastball with deception is just as effective against a good hitter as a 90-mile-per-hour fastball without deception. Some pitchers seem to be sneaky and have natural deception. Others must develop deception. Good extension (reaching toward the plate with a loose arm), keeping the front shoulder closed as long as possible, and breaking the hands with both thumbs down are all ways to help create deception and promote sound mechanics.

Photo courtesy of University of Kentucky Baseball

Pitcher Brandon Webb shows good deception by hiding the ball from the hitter.

Locating Pitches

Crucial to the art of shutting down hitters is the ability to locate pitches in the zone. At the advanced level of baseball, control is more than just throwing strikes. Control means being able to pitch to a scouting report and locate pitches.

Location is more important than stuff. No matter how a pitcher feels any certain day, location will win for him. Most of the time, a pitcher will not be able to improve velocity or "life" during a game, but he can always fix the location on his pitches with a good mental approach and sound mechanics.

God blessed each pitcher with a certain amount of ability to throw a ball. After a pitcher reaches a certain age, he will most likely not improve his velocity, but he can improve location, movement, and pitch selection. Not all pitchers were blessed with Roger Clemens' ability, but everyone has 24 hours in each day and seven days in each week to improve and strive to perfect his game. Greg Maddux, with his 86-mile-per-hour fastball, will have the same amount of space in the Hall of Fame as Roger Clemens and his 96-mile-per-hour fastball.

Locating the Fastball

Ninety percent of all pitchers use the fastball as their basic pitch or setup pitch. In professional baseball, pitchers throw more fastballs because of the wood bat and their ability to throw in the low to mid 90s. Even with the use of the aluminum bat at the high school and college level, a good fastball located properly in or near the strike zone can be a pitcher's bread and butter. A misconception many young pitchers have is that most hitters like to hit fastballs. Fastballs are straight and easier to hit, the pitchers believe, and therefore they are afraid to use their fastballs. Obviously, if a fastball is straight (no movement), then it becomes an inviting pitch for a hitter with good bat speed. But every hitter has a hole or a weakness in the strike zone that makes him vulnerable to a well-located fastball. The advantages of throwing a fastball are that it has more velocity than other pitches and is usually easier to control. In addition, despite what most hitters say, their biggest fear as hitters is getting a ball thrown *by* them or getting jammed and having their "manhood" taken away from them. The key is locating the fastball in the hitter's hole. If a pitcher can do this, his job becomes much easier because the located fastball sets up all other pitches. Location, not velocity, is the most important facet of throwing a fastball. Next is movement, and last in importance is velocity.

Pitchers can obtain movement by experimenting with grips and arm angles. The four-seam fastball (gripping the ball across the horseshoe, or wide seams) will give optimum control and velocity. The two-seam fastball (gripping the ball between the narrow seams) will in most cases give a sinking or boring movement with slightly less velocity. Actually, the four-seamer and the two-seamer can be like two completely separate pitches.

To establish the inside fastball, the four-seamer is best because it is less likely to tail in to the hitter and give him a free base. If a good hitter becomes too comfortable in the box, the four-seamer can be used to keep the hitter from diving in and owning the plate. The pitcher should always feel as though *he* owns the plate. The four-seamer will help the pitcher establish the fear factor and repossess the plate. With no fear, the .330 hitter becomes a .400 hitter. By establishing the fear factor, that .330 hitter becomes a .250 hitter. A good aggressive hitter, if he is allowed to own the plate, will dive in and be able to cover not only the outside portion of the plate but also be able to hit a good pitcher's pitch two to four inches off the outside of the plate. By coming in occasionally on the hands of the good hitter, the pitcher will keep the batter honest and prevent him from being able to hit the pitcher's pitch on the outside corner. A coach should never advocate head hunting or throwing at hitters, but he should teach his pitchers to establish the inside fastball and occasionally pitch under a hitter's hands. In that way, a pitcher can equalize the aluminum bat. Otherwise, the hitter could become the headhunter by hitting rockets up the middle.

Pitching inside and throwing the ball beneath a hitter's hands is an art that has been given a bad name by those that choose to head hunt and play the game in an unsportsmanlike fashion. Hitters in the new millennium have more protection (helmets with ear flaps, elbow guards, and so on) than hitters did in the past, and pitchers brush hitters off the plate less often than they did in the past. These developments are part of why offense has become more prominent in college and professional baseball.

The two-seam fastball is a great pitch to use to get the ground ball with a man on first for the double play. With a man on first the pitcher must think ground ball as opposed to strikeout. Isn't it more fun to get two outs with one pitch? The two-seamer on the knees or below the hands will most likely get that double-play ball for the pitcher.

Locating the Breaking Ball

One of the most effective pitches in any pitcher's repertoire is the curve or slider low and away. In most cases the pitcher wants the breaking ball in one location. For a right-hander, he should try to throw the breaker down and away from the right-handed hitter and down and in to the left-handed hitter. The pitcher should practice this one location repeatedly in his bullpen workouts. Some pitchers have the ability to throw the backdoor breaking ball (a right-handed pitcher throwing the ball to the outside corner to a left-handed hitter and a left-handed pitcher throwing the ball to the outside corner to a right-handed hitter). Few pitchers can master this pitch, but those that do have a great pitch to use against a pull-oriented hitter.

A pitcher should strive to achieve command of two different breaking balls—one to throw for a strike in any count (the control breaking ball) and one to use as a kill pitch that he can throw on or below the knees with a sharp downward break. The kill pitch is useful with two strikes against the aggressive hitter.

Locating the Change-Up

With the fastball, a pitcher can pitch in the L (up and in, low and inside, or low and away) with success. The curve or slider can be thrown low and away or backdoor to a hitter. The pitcher should always throw the change-up at knee level or below. Ideally, the change should be thrown low and away to coax the hitter into pulling off or thrown below the zone to get a groundball. The low inside change, although not an ideal location, can be effective because the batter will most likely pull the pitch foul for a strike.

While throwing the change, the pitcher must trust the grip and allow the grip to slow the pitch. He must try to maintain his fastball arm speed, delivery, and follow-through. Quality arm speed and a good follow-through increase deception. Again, location is crucial. An average change-up on or below the knees is much better than a great change-up that is up and out over the plate. A change-up that creates deception, changes planes, and is thrown to the proper location is a wonderful pitch for a hurler at any level. A good change-up is usually 10 to 12 miles per hour slower than the pitcher's fastball. The change-up is a great pitch in itself, but it also enhances the fastball, making it appear quicker than it really is.

Practicing Pitch Location

When I was growing up, my brother, Tom, and I spent hours each week throwing to each other and playing strikeout. He would catch me until I struck out three hitters, and then I would catch him until he struck out his three guys. The catcher was always the umpire, and as brothers we competed in everything. When my brother wasn't there to throw with me, I would draw a target on the side of the barn and throw my two or three baseballs toward my target, pick them up, and start over. These early sessions not only improved my arm strength but also enhanced my ability to concentrate, throw strikes, and locate my pitches. Locating the pitches in the zone is similar to shooting free throws, kicking field goals, or putting. One develops the feel for it by practice, practice, and more practice. This requirement is a big reason why a pitcher shouldn't have too many pitches in his repertoire. If a pitcher has a four-seam fastball, a two-seam fastball, a breaking ball, and a change-up and throws a 60-pitch bullpen, he will practice each pitch in his arsenal only 15 times. Add a split-finger and he throws each pitch 12 times. Instead of being a jack-of-all-trades and master of none, the pitcher should limit his repertoire to four pitches. He should perfect those four and learn to locate them.

A good drill for off-season bullpen work is for the pitcher to identify locations within the strike zone and orally call the zone where he wants to locate his pitch. To a hitter, the low and inside pitch is a one zone, the low middle pitch is a two zone, low and away is a three, middle is a four, middle-middle is a five, middle away is a six, up and in is a seven, up and over the middle of the plate is an eight, and up and outward is a nine zone. Figure 7.1 illustrates the nine zones.

An example of calling location would be for a pitcher to pick the target he wants to hit before his delivery, say "three," and then try to throw the pitch low and away. This drill holds the pitcher accountable to the coach and catcher and heightens his concentration and effort.

Calling out the location holds the pitcher more accountable. In goal setting, if you tell someone what your goal is, you will work harder to achieve it. If you keep it to yourself, it is easier to give in and fall short of your goal.

At times during the early phases of off-season workouts, the coach may want to challenge pitchers to succeed in locating 16 out of 20 fastballs before they throw any change-ups or breaking balls. Or perhaps, if a pitcher is having trouble locating his change-up, the coach could have him call his zone and locate his change 12 out of 15 times in the two and three zones before moving on to the next sequence.

During these bullpen workouts, the coach should make sure that the pitcher has a plan—a sequence of pitches thrown in the windup, out of the stretch, and to right-handed hitters and left-handed hitters.

Reading Swings

The pitcher should learn to identify whether or not a hitter is "on" a pitch. How can a pitcher tell? If a hitter fouls a pitch hard and straight back to the backstop or pulls a pitch foul and spins a base coach around, he is on the pitch. At this point the pitcher must change speed, location, or both. If a right-handed hitter facing a right-handed pitcher lines the fastball in the first-base dugout, the pitcher should be able to read the swing and know the hitter's barrel is not quite getting there. The pitcher should not speed up a slow bat; this is not the time to throw a breaking ball unless it is in the dirt. A hitter with a slow bat must start his swing earlier, so curveballs down below the zone can be effective. A good pitch would be another fastball, this time on the hitter's hands. If a hitter continues to pull the fastball foul, the pitcher should start working off-speed pitches and fastballs on the outside of the plate.

A left-handed hitter will often have a smooth, powerful, sweeping swing. The fastball up and in is typically a good pitch. Because his left hand is

One zone

Two zone

Three zone

Four zone

FIGURE 7.1 Locations within the strike zone against a right-handed hitter.
Photos courtesy of University of Kentucky Baseball.

Five zone

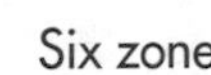

Six zone

Seven zone

Eight zone

FIGURE 7.1 *(continued)*

Nine zone

FIGURE 7.1 *(continued)*

dominant, his swing may have a loop in it, so a fastball down and in can be a dangerous pitch. When a right-hander throws breaking balls down and in, the pitch must break very low and in beneath his swing plane. Change-ups low and away and backdoor breaking balls can also be effective.

For the hitter who has success staying inside the ball, the pitcher should throw hard stuff in with breaking balls away. For the left-handed inside-out hitter, breaking balls down and in and fastballs in can be successful pitches for a right-handed pitcher.

Often, when a power pitcher has overpowering stuff on a particular day, a smart hitter will "cheat" by opening up his stance slightly and starting his swing early. Occasionally, an average big-league hitter will jerk a line-drive foul on the pull side against an exceptionally hard thrower like Randy Johnson or Roger Clemens. Most likely these hitters "cheat" and guess. The pitcher must be observant and read any change in a hitter's stance or body language.

With some hitters, especially aggressive high-fastball hitters, a pitcher can "climb the ladder." If a hitter swings and misses or fouls a high fastball straight back, a pitcher can throw the second fastball a little higher. If the hitter misses again, the pitcher should go even higher for strike three or completely change planes and throw a curveball below the strike zone.

The catcher and coaches can help the pitcher read the swing. The catcher knows how close the hitter is to the plate. He can more easily observe whether the hitter is covering the entire plate with the barrel. With any luck, the catcher will be in the rhythm of the game and know the confidence level of the pitcher and hitter.

Classifying Hitters

In reading swings and communicating with catchers and pitchers, coaches will find it helpful to identify and classify different types of hitters. These classifications and pitching strategies aren't foolproof, but they serve as a good starting point.

Classification	How to pitch
Dead pull hitters	Throw fastballs and off-speed pitches away. When ahead in the count, show the fastball in and off the plate to set up the pitch away as an out pitch.
Uppercut swing with power	Normally, this is a left-handed hitter using his dominant hand to create a slight loop in his swing. Throw hard stuff up and in and throw off-speed stuff low and away. Breaking balls from right-handers against a lefty with this style should be low and inside, below the zone.
Slow bat (slider bat speed)	Throw hard stuff in on hands and away (work fastballs in and out). Throw all off-speed pitches below the strike zone—in the dirt with two strikes. Any off-speed pitch up and out over the plate has a chance to be crushed. Don't muscle up on the fastball, causing it to flatten out and lose velocity.
Breaking-ball out	Obviously, throw a steady diet of breaking balls, but when ahead in the count, throw the fastball up and out of the zone. The hitter may swing at it because he finally sees a pitch he thinks he can hit. If he doesn't swing, the high fastball will set him up for the good breaker down in the zone. Make him put the ball in play.
Inside-out hitter	This hitter has a knack for hitting the ball to the opposite field. His hands will lead in his swing, and the barrel will stay on the ball slightly longer than it does with other hitters. The inside-out guy likes the outside pitch. The pitcher's approach should be to pour hard stuff inside below the hands. When ahead in the count, show off-speed pitches away off the plate and get him out with heat in.
"Mix" hitter	This is usually the hardest type of hitter to get out. Mix a repertoire of pitches down in the zone. He is normally the best hitter in the lineup and one of the best in

"Mix" hitter *(continued)*	the league. Keep the guys who hit in front of him off base. In crucial situations, pitch around this guy by mixing pitches six to eight inches off the plate and below the zone.

Getting Ahead in the Count

First-pitch strikes are crucial to a pitcher's success. With an 0-1 count the hitter must deal with a pitcher's pitch. The pitcher can throw any pitch in his repertoire in any location he wants. Most pitchers have better control of the fastball than they do any other pitch, but a pitcher can't afford to become too predicable. As stated previously, a pitcher must develop at least two or preferably three pitches he can throw for a strike in any situation. To keep a hitter defensive instead of offensive, a pitcher at an advanced level should be able to throw the fastball, a control breaking ball, or a change-up for a first-pitch strike.

The first time through the lineup, a pitcher should be able to challenge most hitters with a first-pitch fastball. During the first two or three innings, the pitcher's arm is live and fresh. The hitter's timing is normally not at peak performance on the first pitch he sees in the game. The second time through the lineup, the pitcher will need to mix his pitches more on the first pitch, especially against hitters who consistently like to swing at the first pitch.

On the first pitch a pitcher should not be as fine—that is, pitching for the corners or trying to nibble on the corners—as he would be on, say, an 0-1 count or a 1-2 count. The first pitch to a hitter in most cases should be a challenge pitch. A challenge pitch need not be a four-seam fastball. It can be a two-seamer with sinking movement, a control breaker, or even a change-up. Normally, a pitcher should not throw a change-up on the first pitch the first time through the batting order. In most cases a hitter must see a fastball before the change can achieve maximum effectiveness. A change disrupts the hitter's timing and is usually more effective after the hitter has already seen a fastball. The second or third time a pitcher faces a hitter, a first-pitch change may be very effective, especially against first-pitch swingers. But a pitcher shouldn't try to paint the black on the first pitch and risk getting behind to a 1-0 count. The 1-0 count, obviously, is a hitter's count instead of a pitcher's count.

According to a study by Spanky McFarland based on data gathered from five years of Division I baseball, the batting average on the first pitch, or 0-0 count, is .186. The batting average on the 0-1 count is .199. On a 1-0 count, hitters hit a robust .386. These statistics and those in table 7.1 show that pitchers should challenge hitters in the zone early and get ahead in the count!

TABLE 7.1 Batting Averages on Specific Counts

COUNT	BATTING AVERAGE
0-2	.118
1-2	.151
2-2	.169
0-0*	.186
3-2	.192
0-1	.199
3-0	.267
1-1	.269
2-1	.290
3-1	.329
2-0	.342
1-0	.386

*First-pitch hitter

Reprinted, by permission, from Joe 'Spanky' McFarland, 1990, *Coaching pitchers* (Champaign, IL: Human Kinetics), 77.

Once a pitcher gets ahead in the count, he can start expanding the zone. On pitcher's counts—especially two-strike counts—a pitcher should throw his pitches as close to the zone as possible without hitting it. In other words, he should get ahead in the count with strikes and then get the hitter out with balls. When a pitcher gets behind in the count, he too must expand the zone and risk hitting a pitch out of the zone without getting good wood. Most of the time, this results in an out. When the hitter is ahead in the count, a pitcher can sometimes use the hitter's strengths to get him out. For instance, if a hitter is a "dead red" fastball hitter, the pitcher may show him a fastball out of the zone. If the hitter thinks he won't get another fastball to hit, he may swing at one out of the zone and get himself out.

Practically all hitters have a weakness. The coach, catcher, and pitcher have the job of finding that weakness and exploiting it, especially when ahead in the count.

Pitching Behind in the Count

Counts such as 1-0, 2-0, 2-1, 3-1, and 3-0 are known as hitter's counts. Typically, these are challenge counts for the pitcher. A pitcher with an exceptional fastball with life and movement still has a good chance to win when he is behind in the count. The pitcher must trust his stuff and not muscle up or overthrow in these situations. When a pitcher muscles up and overthrows, he usually loses velocity and movement and has poorer control—a bad combination. A catcher or coach can help the pitcher by reminding him to pitch at 98 percent rather than throw at 110 percent.

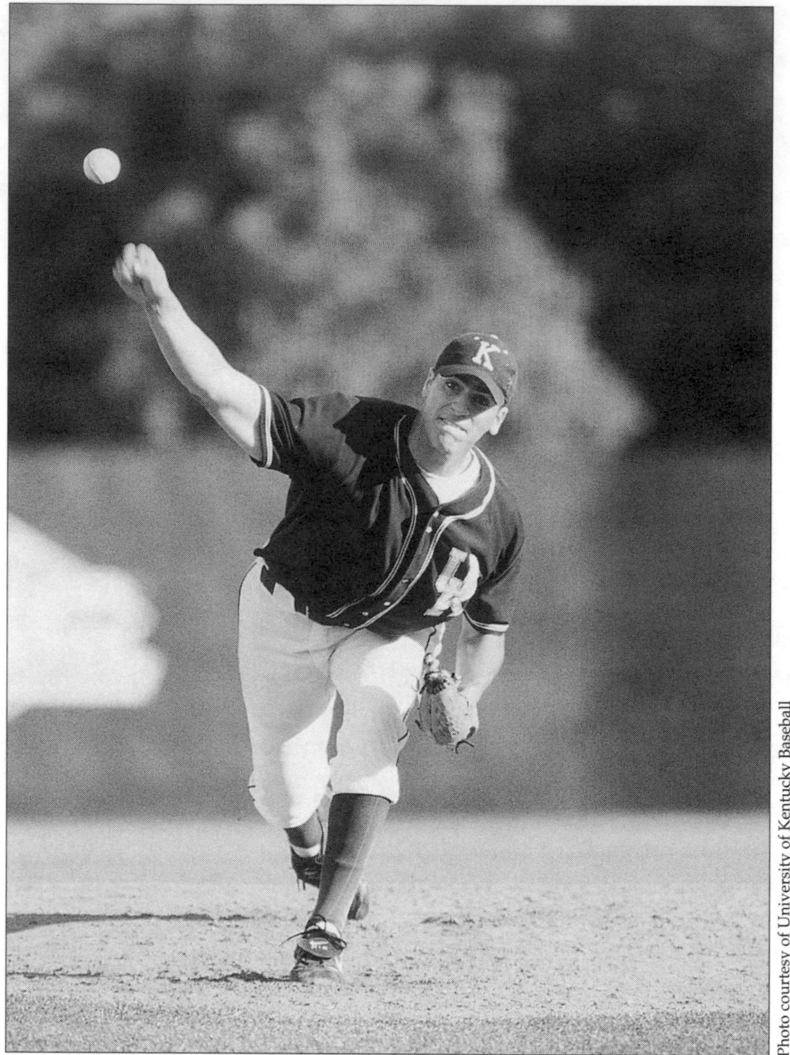

Photo courtesy of University of Kentucky Baseball

A pitcher with an exceptional fastball still has a good chance to win even when behind in the count. The key is to stay relaxed and avoid the tendency to muscle up and overthrow.

Ideally, a pitcher will have at least a couple of pitches he can throw for a strikc when behind in the count. A control breaking ball or change-up are both excellent pitches to throw when he finds himself in a fastball count.

The pitcher must exude confidence when behind in the count. The catcher and the seven guys behind him feed off the pitcher's confidence. When the pitcher is confident, the defense is more likely to make the big play. The pitcher may want to take a deep breath and remind himself that he is still in control. Pitchers who have the ability to relax know that the hitter will be coming out of his shoes in a hitter's count, so they throw a batting-practice (BP) fastball to coax the hitter into overswinging and popping up or pulling a ball foul to help even the count. A BP fastball is nothing more than a fastball thrown with a smooth delivery that is typically 6 to 8 miles per hour slower than the pitcher's normal fastball. Many confident pitchers have gotten out of big jams by throwing this gutsy pitch.

Repeating Pitches

Sometimes hitters think too much. A pitcher can have success against the thinking hitter by throwing the same pitch in a good location twice in a row. Many times after a hitter has been jammed or takes an inside fastball, he may look for a breaking ball away. Another aggressive fastball on the black on the inside of the plate may freeze the hitter.

A pitcher may miss with a curveball to a hitter, causing the hitter to assume that the pitcher can't get the breaker over and to look for a fastball. By repeating the curve, the pitcher will probably fool the hitter. The pitcher will also make an adjustment and throw a better curve on the second try. So, in repeating pitches, the pitcher not only outguesses the hitter but also makes adjustments on the pitch he repeats. Because the hitter usually is looking "dead red" fastball after a pitcher misses with a curve, a change-up is also a good pitch in that situation.

Pitching Backward

Controlling or having command of at least three pitches allows the advanced pitcher to pitch backward. Normally, pitchers are taught to throw fastballs to get ahead and breaking balls to get outs. Pitching backward simply means to get ahead with off-speed pitches and then throw fastballs in typical breaking-ball counts. Pitching backward has become more popular at the college level to counteract the effect of the ever-improving aluminum bats.

Controlling the Tempo

Several years ago, one of my assistants, Jim Hinerman (now head coach at Georgetown College), conducted a study on the most productive allotment of time for pitchers between pitches. He discovered, to no one's surprise, that pitchers who take a lot of time between pitches usually struggle more than pitchers who work fast. Jim found in his study that the ideal time between pitches (from the time the catcher catches the ball to the next pitch) is 11 seconds. Using a short interval between pitches provides the additional benefit of keeping teammates on their toes instead of their heels. An aggressive, confident pitcher not only controls the tempo but also keeps his teammates and his fans in the game. A composed, enthusiastic pitcher is more effective and more fun to watch. Umpires enjoy a fast-moving game and sometimes get in a rhythm with the pitcher and call more strikes. The pitcher should not change or rush his delivery, just take less time between pitches.

Another way for the pitcher to control the tempo is to prevent an aggressive hitter from rushing him. A smart pitcher can take an aggressive, hyper hitter out of his rhythm by simply stepping off the rubber, asking for a new ball, or making an extra trip for a rosin bag. A frustrated hitter loses concentration, making him an easier out.

Knowing Your Pitcher

The coach can sometimes help the pitcher avoid big innings by knowing his hurler's weaknesses. Most teams can survive giving up a run or even two during an inning, but a three-, four-, or five-run inning can be devastating even for a great offensive team.

Some pitchers have trouble getting out of the gate and have their worst inning in the first. For the slow starter, the coach should have a good plan for a pregame bullpen routine. The pitcher should throw a simulated first inning in the bullpen with a hitter standing in. He should face a minimum of three hitters—a leadoff hitter, an inside-out hitter, and a breaking-ball-out hitter. This preparation will force the pitcher to bear down and focus before going to the mound.

For the pitcher who has trouble getting the third out in the inning, the catcher and a leader in the infield should challenge and encourage him after two outs. An example may be for the third baseman to say, "All right, get a ground ball for me right here, and we'll go score a few runs for you." The pitcher must be encouraged to think positively and believe he can achieve a three-up, three-down inning.

For the pitcher who tires early or loses it after a certain number of pitches, the coach should have someone ready in the bullpen for relief as the maximum pitch count approaches. The coach may want to review this pitcher's conditioning, long-toss drills, and bullpen routines to improve his stamina and endurance.

Then there is the guy who loses focus and concentration in the middle of an inning. Perhaps the umpire squeezed him or an infielder made an error or his girlfriend is sitting in the stands with an old boyfriend. The catcher and infielders can have a huge effect on a pitcher who loses focus. The catcher can demand eye contact, place the ball in the pitcher's chest, and remind him that the team is depending on him. If that doesn't work, the catcher can signal the coach to get someone loose immediately.

Maintaining Composure

"You can't control the game if you can't control yourself" is a statement my pitchers have heard many times. A pitcher can't control the comments from the opposing dugout, the yelling of the fans, a bad call by the umpire, or an error by a teammate, but he can control how he handles those circumstances. To deal with those events, he needs discipline and concentration; anything less than total composure and positive body language will be harmful. Positive body language helps a pitcher exude confidence, which transfers to his teammates. Negative body language from the pitcher gives the hitter confidence, encourages bench jockeying and catcalls from the stands, and may even affect the umpire on a borderline pitch. The guys in blue are human, too! A baseball field can hold only so much confidence. With negative body language, the pitcher gives his portion to the hitter. With competitive, positive body language, the pitcher can rob the hitter of his confidence.

Working With the Catcher

After a pitcher throws a no-hitter or wins a big game with clutch pitching, I have always enjoyed observing that the catcher is just as jubilant as the pitcher. The catcher was just as into the game as the pitcher was. Seeing a catcher and pitcher working as one in a big game is a thing of beauty.

As a pitcher, I sometimes knew what sign the catcher would hang before he put his fingers down. Sometimes, I would go an entire inning, or even several innings, knowing what pitch he was calling before he called it. These dynamics improve the pitcher's rhythm and tempo, creating such positive momentum that a pitcher seemingly breezes through a long stretch of innings.

At other times the pitcher-catcher duo are completely out of sync. This may occur because of poor planning and the absence of communication between the coach, pitcher, and catcher. Although not always available, a scouting report on hitters can be extremely helpful. The help that a coach gives his pitchers and catchers in reading swings and discussing hitters and their tendencies between innings can make the difference between winning and losing.

At times a catcher will take his previous at-bat with him behind the plate. This mistake can allow the opposition to have a big inning, resulting in a loss. The catcher should be an extension of the pitcher. As much as possible, the battery should think as one and spend much time together in the dugout between innings.

The starting catcher should catch the starting pitcher as often as possible between starts. He should also catch the last part of his pregame warm-ups before the game. The catcher should know what is working for his starting pitcher and be in tune with the pitcher's level of confidence and concentration.

The pitcher should have complete confidence in his catcher's ability to block the curve, slider, split-finger, or change-up in the dirt with a runner on third base. This gives the pitcher the incentive to make the kill pitch with two strikes and get out of a jam.

The catcher's body language should build confidence in a pitcher. It is uncanny how a positive gesture from a respected catcher can help a pitcher pitch with a higher level of confidence and efficiency.

A catcher is more than a target with a mitt. While working with a pitcher, he challenges, encourages, informs, and sometimes even helps coach a pitcher. Only a special individual can handle a struggling, high-strung pitcher. When possible, an upperclassman should be behind the dish, even if his skill level may be slightly behind that of an underclassman. Maturity and leadership are key. When Bob Uecker was a rookie catcher for the Braves, he made a mound visit to help the successful veteran Lew Burdette. Lew was steaming mad by the time Bob reached the mound. He told Bob, "Turn right around and get your rear end back behind the plate. I don't want anyone in this stadium to think you know more about pitching than I do!"

Catching is more than catching a ball and trying to throw runners out. A catcher's gamesmanship and moxie will often help a pitcher and team register a W instead of an L.

Calling Pitches and Pitch Selection

Whoever calls the pitches—coach, catcher, or pitcher—must know the pitcher's strengths and weaknesses and, if possible, the hitter's strengths and weaknesses. Most baseball experts contend that good pitching will normally win over good hitting. Just because a particular hitter may be a good fastball hitter doesn't mean that a pitcher should abandon his fastball. If the coach or catcher calls the game, the pitcher should always have the option to shake off the pitch and throw what he believes is his best pitch at that time. Suppose that in a crucial bases-loaded situation the pitcher faces a hitter identified by the scouting report as a breaking-ball out. If the pitcher doesn't have confidence in his curve, he may walk in the winning run with the recommended pitch. The wrong pitch thrown with confidence is better than the right pitch thrown with little or no confidence.

When trying to shut down hitters, confidence and location are more important than pitch selection. Coaches, catchers, and pitchers get worked up over pitch selection. People second-guess them, and they second-guess themselves about throwing the wrong pitch. Remember that 90 percent of the time the wrong pitch and the right location thrown with confidence will get a hitter out.

Photo courtesy of University of Kentucky Baseball

If the coach or catcher calls the game, the pitcher should always have the option to shake off the pitch and throw what he believes to be his best pitch at that particular time. Here, Joseph Blanton chooses to throw a slider.

In the 1996 World Series, one of my former players, Jim Leyritz, hit a game-winning home run against Mark Wohlers. At that time Wohlers had one of the best fastballs in the major leagues. He consistently threw in the high 90s. Mark threw a slider and it hung a little out over the plate, and Jim crushed it. All I heard the next day was, "Why didn't Wohlers throw Leyritz a fastball in that situation?" The truth of the matter was that Jim was an excellent fastball hitter, and the slider was the right pitch in the wrong location.

Never say never concerning which pitch to throw in a certain situation. Most coaches list in their top three pet peeves 0-2 base hits. But Greg Maddux says, "Why waste a pitch? Go ahead and get the guy out on three pitches." Unfortunately, most of us don't have a pitcher with Greg's repertoire and command.

One of my peeves is to see a pitcher throw a ball two feet outside just so a coach won't yell at him. The 0-2 pitch, in most cases, should be a setup pitch, not a waste pitch. For instance, if a particular hitter is a breaking-ball out, the pitcher should throw him a fastball off the plate a few inches inside or perhaps well above his hands out over the plate to set up the breaking ball away. Or if a hitter has a slow bat, a pitcher may want to throw a fastball just off the plate on the outside. Then, on the 1-2 count, the pitcher can come hard in on the hands to jam the hitter with another good heater.

Pitchers from my era were taught never to throw two change-ups in a row and never to throw a change-up with two strikes. Shortly after my minor-league stint with the Reds, I watched Mario Soto pitch against the Mets at Riverfront Stadium. Mario struck out Darryl Strawberry with the change three times and on a couple of occasions threw *three* change-ups in a row. There are rules of thumb in pitch selection but no hard and fast rules.

To shut down hitters consistently, a pitcher must compete, pitch with confidence, and remember that location and movement are more important than velocity.

The competition between the hitter and the pitcher is one of the great matchups in all of sport. Getting a hitter to ground into a double play or strike out with a runner on third base with less than two outs makes a pitcher feel like a million bucks. This doesn't happen by chance; it takes preparation, poise, and a plan. As coaches, we can help pitchers prepare, guide them through a plan, and then help them develop poise and confidence by believing in them every day. An assistant coach several years ago was struggling with his relationships with our players. I asked him one day, "Why do you coach?" He responded immediately by saying, "I love the game." But it is not enough to love the game. Millions of fans love the game. We must love the players who play the game. We coach baseball players, not baseball. When we learn to love our players and can provide discipline and good coaching, then our players will have the poise and ammunition it takes to be champions.

Stopping Base Runners

Bob Bennett

Stopping an opponent from executing any offensive aggression requires two fundamental skills—catching and throwing. The more skilled the offensive opponent, the more refined these two fundamentals must be. Stopping the running game, particularly when the runners are highly skilled and well educated, is an extremely challenging endeavor. When both the offense and the defense are equally talented and educated, great moments occur.

For every great defensive strategy created, an equal offensive strategy may also be created. If the talent and education of both sides are equal, I believe that the defensive team has a slight, if not significant, advantage. In no other sport does the defense control the ball. Control of the ball allows the defense to determine whether to throw to the batter, attempt a pickoff play, vary the timing between pitches, throw a pitchout, or run a special play.

Good base runners are aware of the arsenal possessed by the defensive team. A good base runner attempts to gain the edge over the defense by taking command of that arsenal. So the job of putting together a method for stopping the running game is no easy task. Putting together a successful running game is equally difficult. There are no easy solutions. Hard work, concentration, determination, competitive drive, and repetition are the tools I would choose to assemble a method to stop the running game.

Some argue that base running wins or loses more games than any other aspect of baseball. Both the offense and defense must recognize and emphasize base running. This chapter deals with how to stop the base runners; therefore, a strategy for defense will be developed.

A basic defensive premise is to make base runners earn advancement to second base. The defense must not allow runners to advance to second because of negligence, sloppy play, lack of vigilance, or the inability to catch and throw. More singles are hit than extra-base hits. Generally, an error only allows the runner to reach first base, and a walk only places that runner on first base. If the defense consistently keeps the runners who reach first base from advancing to second, winning will likely result.

Developing Strong Catching and Throwing Skills

To stop any base runner, catching and throwing skills are essential. A good throw followed by a mishandled ball produces a failure. A weak or off-target throw followed by a good catch also usually results in an unsuccessful play. Even if every other part of the play is well done, these two basic skills are needed to stop the base-running game consistently. The pitcher's time to the plate with accuracy is a key component. The catcher's accuracy, strength of arm, and quickness of delivery to the base is another important ingredient. The final part of the play is for the infielder to be able to hold his ground (field his position), move to the base, make the catch, and tag the runner. Teamwork is fully in bloom when successfully defending against a base runner.

A first baseman's ability to hold the runner and give an alert call to the catcher when the runner attempts to steal second is crucial. Warnings by one of the middle infielders of an attempted steal of third base are equally crucial, as is the warning by the third baseman should the runner at third attempt to steal home.

Each infielder, the catcher, and the pitcher must perform specific duties well to stop a base runner. To develop the teamwork required to combat the attack of aggressive base stealers, players at each position must hone the skills to match the challenge. Prudent teaching methods call for diligent independent work with each position before coaches can expect perfection as a team. Coaches should strive to teach players at their respective positions the skills necessary to perform successfully. As each player develops, a coach can help refine a player's skills by connecting the various responsibilities. When the pitcher has learned various pickoff moves and understands that timing is important and the catcher has learned footwork and can consistently throw with accuracy to each base, the two positions are ready to work together. When the infielders have raised their level of skills to hold runners, move to the base, and quickly make a tag, the team is ready to defend against the steal. How they perform when they come together tells the coach and the players what skills need improvement and what skills shine.

In working with individual groups, I suggest that no times be kept and that no runners be used in the drills until each group is ready. When they are ready, runners should work only on leads and jumps. If all the parts appear to be working adequately, then go full speed. If the success rate for throwing out runners is poor, identify the problem or problems, go back to individual position work, and refine the skills before going live again. This may take a great deal of time, or it may occur relatively quickly. The skill level of the players and their commitment to the job will determine the speed and success ratio. In order for each position player and the pitcher to understand their roles, their positions must be clearly defined. Each player needs a clear understanding of how important his position is in containing the running game.

Understanding Each Player's Key Role

The pitcher and catcher are extremely important to stopping the running game. They depend on one another to be successful. A great deal of the responsibility for stopping base runners falls on the catcher and pitcher, but each of the other positions has an important role as well.

Infielders

Each infielder has specific duties that he must perform consistently and properly to defend against base runners. Base runners create problems for any defensive unit. Infielders must sacrifice some range to hold base runners close to the base, but the infielder responsible for holding the runner must also be able to field his position. In some situations, and with some runners, infielders give up a great deal of ground to hold the runner close. Other situations may call for the fielder to sacrifice little ground. The defensive team needs to be aware of each situation and make sure that they position themselves to match the situation.

First Baseman

With a runner on first base the first baseman is responsible for holding that runner close to the bag. Normally the first baseman places his right foot on the inside portion of first base and moves off the base to cover his area when the ball is delivered to home plate. This method greatly limits the range of the first baseman. If the runner is a threat to steal second base and the score is close, the first baseman has no choice but to go to the bag and hold the runner.

The first baseman has some other options. He can play behind the runner, approximately three steps toward second base and three steps toward right field, as shown in figure 8.1. (Note that all steps referred to in this and other illustrations in this chapter are three feet in length.) In this position the first baseman will be able to hold the runner. In addition, he will be able to move closer to his normal fielding position as the pitcher delivers the ball to the plate. In certain situations this positioning is sound. A slow runner will allow the first baseman to play in this position. If the score favors the defensive team in the late inning and the base runner at first is not a key run, then the first baseman may also wisely choose this position. The three-over and three-back position may also be used to set up a pickoff play.

The first baseman may also choose to play back even farther, even all the way back in his normal position (see figure 8.2), depending on the score, the inning, the runner, and the ability of the first baseman and the pitcher.

With a runner at first base and the bunt play imminent, the first baseman must hold the runner at first and then break in to field his position. The first baseman's duties increase with a runner at first base, but the possibility for him to shine and show his worth to the team also increases. From the charging position to cover the bunt, the first baseman and the pitcher can work a timed pickoff that creates an advantage and a weapon for the first baseman.

The first baseman also has the key role of notifying the pitcher and the catcher when the runner advances to second base. When the runner strays off first base and leaves himself vulnerable, the catcher and first baseman should be ever vigilant and use various pickoff plays.

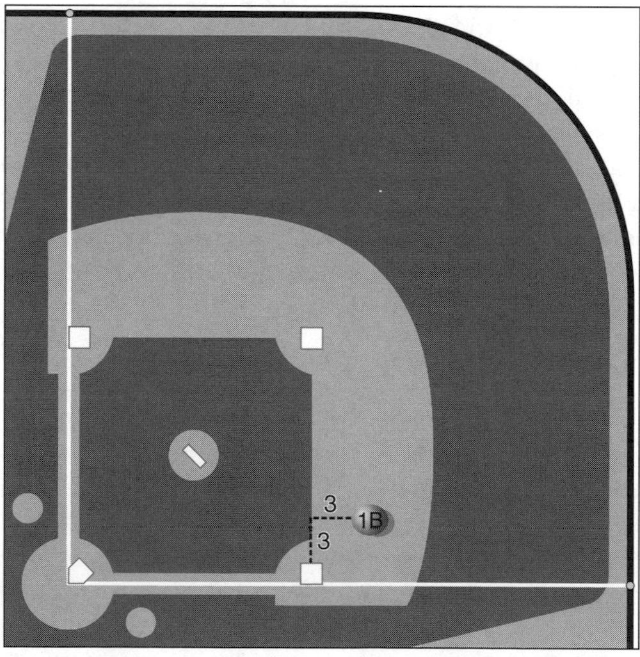

FIGURE 8.1 A position that allows the first baseman to hold the runner is the three-over and three-back position—three steps toward second and three steps toward right field.

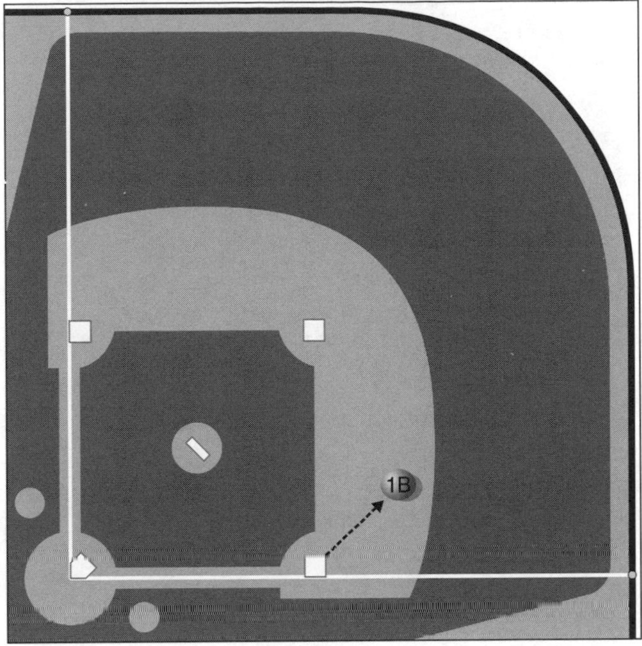

FIGURE 8.2 Alternate position for the first baseman.

Middle Infielders

One of the middle infielders will be responsible for covering second base if the runner attempts to steal that base. That infielder must move in a few steps so that he can both cover the base and field his position. Like the first baseman, the covering middle infielder has a more difficult job and gives up range because of the possibility of a stolen base.

The noncovering infielder can play in normal infield position (see figures 8.3 and 8.4). Some infield coaches have both infielders move in. In this case both middle infielders sacrifice range. A wiser method is to have one middle infielder play in a normal position and the other middle infielder move in to cover the bag. Generally, the second baseman covers the bag when a right-handed hitter is at the plate (see figure 8.5). The shortstop covers the bag when a left-handed hitter is at the plate (see figure 8.6). With skilled hitters at the plate, the middle infielders will be forced to switch coverage and alternate according to the pitcher, the pitch thrown, and the strategy they believe the opponent is trying to employ.

With a runner at second base one of the middle infielders will be primarily responsible to work with the pitcher to keep the runner from getting maximum leads. The other middle infielder will have secondary responsibility and may act as a decoy or even ad lib a pickoff with the pitcher or the catcher.

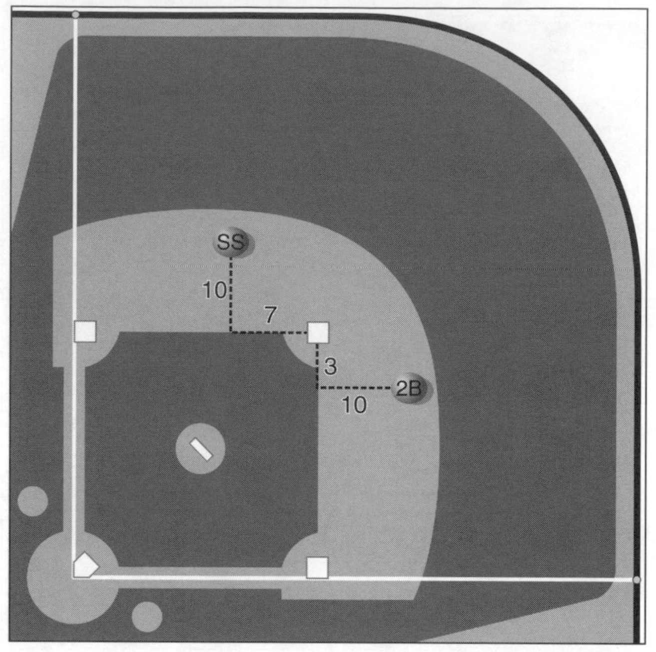

FIGURE 8.3 Normal position for middle infielders (right-handed batter).

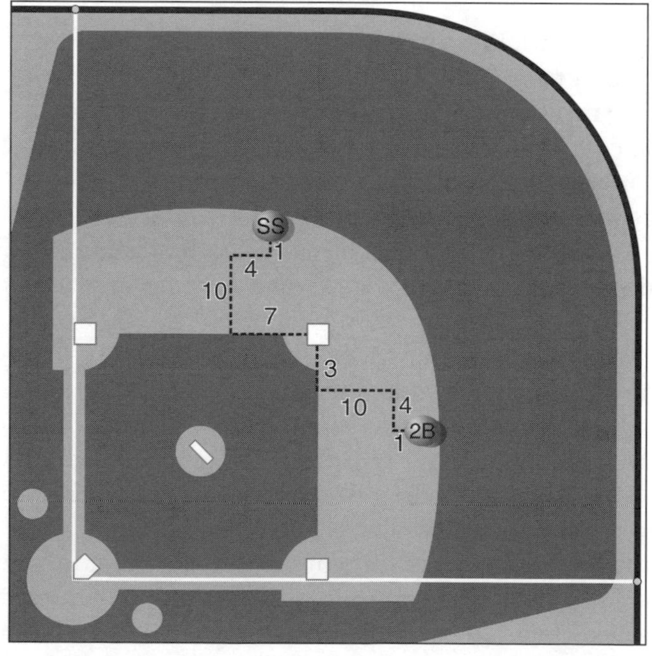

FIGURE 8.4 Normal position for middle infielders (left-handed batter).

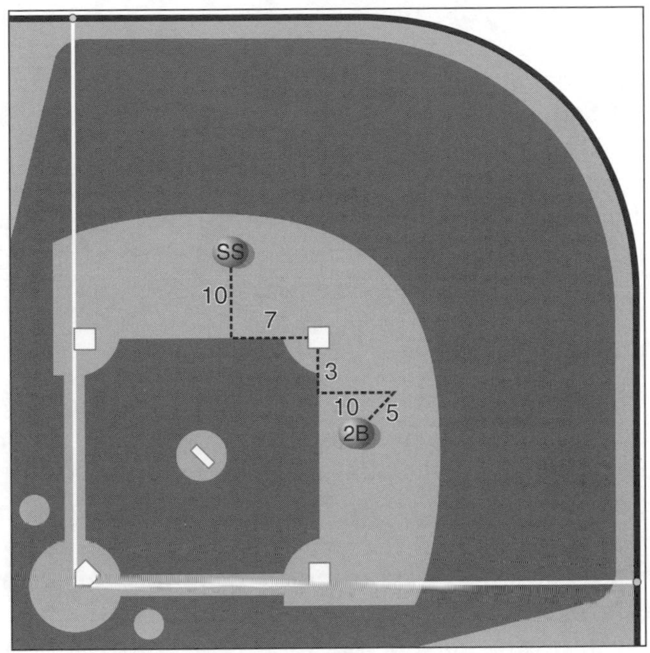

FIGURE 8.5 Middle infield coverage with runner on first base and right-handed batter.

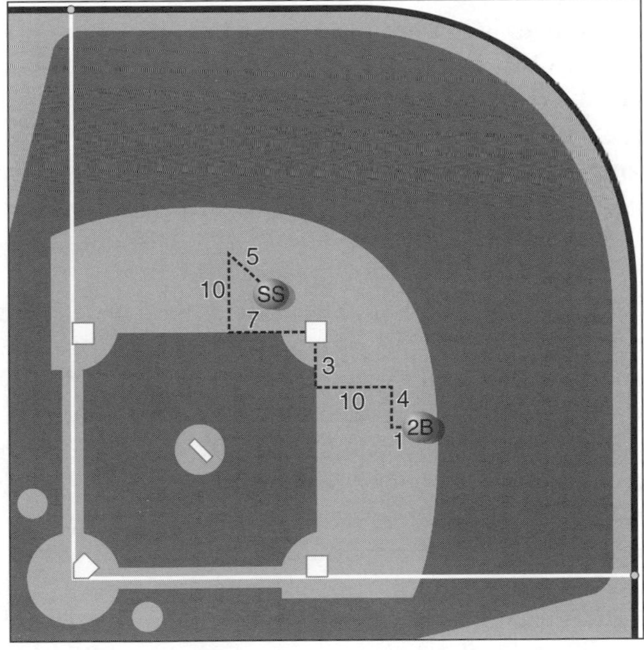

FIGURE 8.6 Middle infield coverage with left-handed batter.

Movement by the middle infielders helps drive the runner back toward second base. These two players have the job of shortening the lead of the runner or getting the runner to move back toward the base before the pitcher delivers the ball to the plate. The pitcher should work closely with the middle infielders. He is responsible for allowing the middle infielders to work with the runner and then be able to recover in time to field their respective positions properly. Timing and movement may be enough to minimize leads and jumps. If the runner maintains a long lead or is getting a good jump, several kinds of pickoff plays can be effective if done properly.

Third Baseman

A skilled, fast base runner who is able to maximize his leads often forces the third baseman to alter his position, especially if the third baseman likes to play extremely deep. Generally, the third baseman has time to play in a normal position and still get to third base to cover the bag on an attempted steal.

The third baseman is also responsible for making sure the runner at third is not allowed to expand his leads freely. The third baseman must force the runner to retreat toward third before the pitcher throws to the plate. The pitcher and third baseman should work out the same kind of timing that the pitcher uses at second base with the middle infielders.

Outfielders

Stopping base runners is not only the responsibility of the pitchers, catchers, and infielders. Outfielders also play an important role in reducing the effectiveness of the running game. An outfielder's negligence can negate a diligent effort to keep the base runner from stealing a base or getting a good jump. Throwing to the wrong base, not hitting the cutoff man, failing to charge the ball, and not getting into good fielding position to make a catch are some of the ways an outfielder allows base runners to take over the game.

Each outfielder should know the strength of his arm. Having this knowledge will help the outfielder cut down lead runners, prevent them from advancing, and stop the trailing runner or runners from advancing. For example, if his arm strength and accuracy is 220 feet, that is his maximum throwing range. At the 220-foot range or less, that outfielder should have a good chance of throwing out a lead runner under normal conditions. Making a throw of greater distance gives the advantage to the base runner. The outfielder's option in such a case should be to give up the run or lead runner and keep the trailing runner from advancing.

Game situation, score, speed of the base runner, the jump by the base runner, and the distance the outfielder ran to get into his throwing range must all be figured into the strategy of whether to throw to get the lead runner or keep the trailing runner or runners from advancing. Outfielders are keenly involved in minimizing the running game of the opposition.

Catcher

Receiving the ball properly, getting a proper grip, keeping the feet balanced, having a quick and consistent release, and throwing with accuracy are skills that the catcher must have to stop the base runner from advancing on him. To be considered a solid thrower, the catcher must transfer the ball from his mitt to the glove at second base in 1.9 to 2.1 seconds. This time must be consistent to be effective in stopping the steal. A lot of work and a good deal of talent are necessary to attain these marks consistently. If the catcher's times are slower than desired, the pitcher's quickness to the plate may be able to make up the difference and provide adequate time for the catcher to throw out the potential base stealer.

The catcher's stance has a great deal to do with his mobility. The manner in which he receives the ball has a lot to do with how he gets the ball into position to throw. A coach and the catcher should be committed to sound fundamentals in both positioning and receiving the ball.

A catcher willing to throw has some great opportunities to bail his team out of some crucial jams. He should develop one or more pickoffs with each infielder. Base runners become reluctant to take liberties with a catcher who has a quick pickoff move. An aggressive and vigilant catcher stops base runners from taking long leads and prevents those runners from casually returning to base after taking a lead.

An aggressive, prudent catcher will use the pitchout as an important tool to stop the base runner. The pickoff play emanating from the catcher is also an effective weapon.

Pitcher

The pitcher is in control of every play because the action starts with him, so he is the key figure in stopping base runners. His first opportunity to stop the base runner is to keep the runner from getting on base. That is the first line of defense. Obviously, fewer base runners create fewer challenges.

Control is a pitcher's ally when facing good base runners. Control and good stuff create an even stronger weapon against the running attack. These strengths give the infielders, outfielders, and catcher a chance to maximize their abilities. Add power to control and stuff, and the defensive team's advantages grow greater. When the pitcher strikes out a lot of batters, walks very few, and has the ability to minimize the strength of the batter, the infielders get better hops, can make more reliable decisions, and simply face fewer tough situations. Outfielders can position themselves more efficiently and get more reliable jumps on both fly balls and ground balls.

Unfortunately, some pitchers with superior talent grow up relying only on that talent. They don't pay much attention to base runners, give little attention to getting the ball to the catcher quickly, and have little concern about holding runners close to the base. To have an effective defense against a good running team, a good bunting team, or a good hit-and-run team, the pitcher must realize that he is the key to stopping those kinds of offensive teams. The pitcher can develop many tools that will serve him well against such teams.

Vigilance is a word the pitcher should attach to any base-running situation. He must be alert and aware. He must prepare for any situation, avoid surprises, take charge of the game, and be ready to use all available tools. For example, in an average game six or seven runners will reach base by way of base hits. Two of the hits will probably be for extra bases. The pitcher will walk three or four batters, and the defense will make one error. In an average game then, 12 to 14 batters will get on base. The pitcher should hold runners on base, stay vigilant, operate with sound fundamentals, and not allow runners to reach a base they have not earned.

Without a concerted and competitive effort from the pitcher, the defense cannot stop base runners. The pitcher must seek and expect to succeed on every pitch.

Holding Runners

The pitcher has many weapons in his arsenal to battle aggressive and clever base runners, but he too must be willing to be aggressive and clever. Being quick to the plate, varying the kinds of looks to the base runner, varying the timing before he throws to the plate, using different kinds of pickoff moves, stepping off the rubber, and using a glide step are some of the useful techniques and movements he has at his disposal.

Quickness to the Plate

A quick delivery to the plate is the best way to keep a runner from stealing a base. If the pitcher delivers the pitch to the plate in 1.3 seconds or less, only an exceptionally fast runner will be able to steal. Even the fast base runner will be greatly challenged if the pitcher is quick to the plate. He is even more challenged when that pitcher uses the rest of his weapons. The pitcher that commits to getting the throw to the plate quickly enhances all of the other tools and methods for stopping the base runner. A pitch that gets to the plate in 1.3 seconds or less is the primary weapon to use against fast base runners.

Glide Step

By using a lower leg lift, known as a glide step, the delivery to the plate can be quicker. The glide step gets the stride foot down more quickly and should cause a quicker delivery to the plate. The glide step is a good secondary way to defend against a potential base stealer. Good base runners often abort an attempt to steal because they are able to see the change in delivery. When that happens the glide step has served its purpose.

The reason the glide step is not a good primary way to throw from the stretch is that the throwing arm has trouble catching up with the quick stride. The pitcher finds it difficult to get on top of the ball and keep the ball down. When he rushes the arm to get into throwing position, the curveball flattens out.

The move is a useful extra weapon or a supplement to the regular stretch move. The glide step should allow the pitcher to cut 1 to 2 tenths of a second off his normal stretch time. By using it occasionally, the pitcher plants a seed in the base runner's mind that he may use it at any time.

Varying the Timing From the Set Position to the Delivery of the Pitch

The pitcher must come to a definite stop in his stretch position. He can stop and then quickly throw to the plate. He may also choose to hold in the set position before delivering the pitch. Changing the interval between the set position and delivery of the pitch disrupts the timing of the base runner. By controlling the tempo the pitcher destroys tactics like walking leads and makes it difficult for the runner to time the delivery.

The pitcher should know what kind of lead each runner has taken. If the lead is too big, the pitcher should step off the rubber, throw to force the runner back to the base, or throw to pick the runner off that base. Upsetting the timing of the base runner can effectively prevent him from getting a good jump. A smart pitcher appears to change the timing before each delivery to the plate. On one pitch he may choose to stop and then quickly start his delivery. On succeeding pitches he may stop and wait for a count of three before beginning the delivery to the plate. His goal is to keep the base runner guessing and prevent him from timing the delivery.

Varying the Looks to the Base Runner

Before delivering each pitch to the plate, the pitcher must look at the lead of the base runner. After coming to a set position, he may look at the runner once and then throw to the batter. Base runners often read the pitcher's look and get their jump, or start, based on the pattern the pitcher establishes. If the pitcher varies his looks to the runner, he does not establish a pattern.

The pitcher can vary the looks in many ways. The look can be once, twice, or three times. It can be a quick look or a long look. To avoid creating a pattern of where he looks before delivering the pitch, the pitcher should always look home before throwing home or before throwing to any base.

Another way to vary looks at the runner is to use different techniques in head movement. One technique is to move the head from shoulder to shoulder in a parallel direction. Moving the chin up and down is another technique. A combination of both movements is a third way to disrupt the timing of the base runner.

Stepping Off the Rubber and Throwing Over

Simply stepping off the rubber can disrupt some runners by forcing them to retreat and at least rethink the issue. This technique can defuse the runner who takes a walking, or running, lead. Combining the step-off with a throw to the base is also a deterrent to a base stealer. By varying the interval between the step-off and the throw over, the pitcher creates yet another method of forcing the runner to shorten his lead. A well-organized and prudent use of the step-off, timing, and a throw over can also result in a good pickoff play.

The pitcher essentially becomes an infielder when he steps back and clears from the rubber. After stepping off the rubber, the pitcher may also develop one or more methods to deter the base runner from straying off base or from stealing the next base easily. The Barr move is such a pickoff play. Jim Barr, a former major-league pitcher, made this move famous. When Barr, a right-handed pitcher, stepped off the rubber, he stepped back and toward third base. This movement essentially placed his body in a better position to make a quick throw to first base without stepping with his stride foot. After clearing from the rubber, he was legally in a position to throw to first base without using a stride. He spun on his left heel and threw to first base. When variation in timing is added to this move, it becomes an excellent pickoff move (see figure 8.7).

Pitchout and Pickoff Plays

Other effective weapons for controlling the running game include the pitchout and pickoff.

Pitchout

A vigilant, smart catcher prudently uses the pitchout to throw out runners and control the running game. If the pitchout is properly executed, the runner should be thrown out. Both the pitcher and catcher have major responsibilities in executing the play.

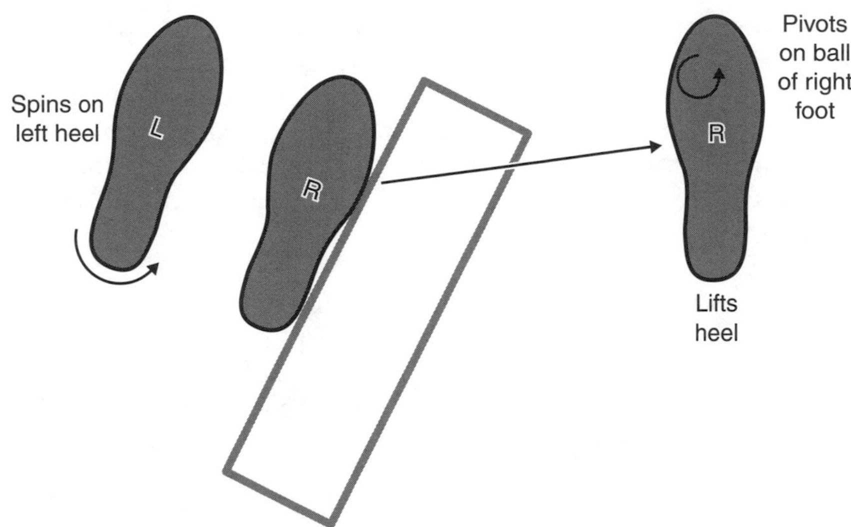

FIGURE 8.7 Barr pickoff move.

The pitcher should bring up his lift leg in normal fashion. To quicken the release, the pitcher shortens his arm arc. This action will get his arm in throwing position much faster than would occur in his normal throwing action. The pitchout is similar to the throw of the catcher. The start of the pitch should look as though it is a regular delivery to the plate. Shortening the arc of the backswing and striding quickly after lifting the leg to its normal height should reduce the pitcher's delivery time to the catcher by 1 to 2 tenths of a second. The pitch must be thrown far enough outside the strike zone so that the batter is unable to reach it.

When properly executed, the pitchout controls the base stealer and virtually destroys the hit-and-run. The pitchout can successfully defuse the aggressive offense in bunt situations. A pitchout combined with a pickoff play by the catcher often cools the hot feet of a base runner.

The catcher should assume his natural stance. When the pitcher lifts his stride leg, the catcher should slide his left foot to a position even with and touching his right foot (right-handed batter). He uses the same technique with a left-handed hitter except that he moves the right foot to a position even with the left foot to get into a good position to receive the pitchout. This movement places his feet in position to achieve good balance when moving to get in front of the pitchout. The catcher has the responsibility of getting his body into a balanced position to throw.

Pickoff Plays

To maximize use of the pickoff, the pitcher should first use the previous information. We often hear that a pitcher attempted a pickoff and that the play was unsuccessful. But a successful pickoff play need not produce an out. Of course, if an out occurs, the play is successful, but success also comes if the pickoff play forces the runner to shorten his lead or disrupts his ability to get a good jump. Among the several different kinds of pickoff plays are spin turns, jump turns, timed pickoff plays, daylight-method pickoff plays, and count-method pickoff plays. Pickoff plays between the catcher and each infielder are also important in defending effectively against the base runner.

A well-timed pickoff is a beautiful sight for the defensive team and a devastating one for the offensive team. Pickoff plays are difficult to perfect because they require teamwork. Perfecting a pickoff play takes more than two or three group practice sessions. Many kinds of pickoff plays at each base can be effective, but perfecting just one is better than running several sporadically. The team should thus work to excel at one before trying to do several.

Pickoff Plays Between the Pitcher and First Baseman

The pitcher can throw over to first base not only after he comes to a set position but also as his hands move up or down while getting ready to come to a set position, as long as the first baseman is at the bag holding the runner. As the pitcher, particularly a right-handed pitcher, is starting his hands up to get into a set position, he may choose to turn and throw over to first base. He may also turn to throw over as his hands move downward to assume the set position. This move is particularly effective if the base runner tries to get an early lead or if the base runner tries suddenly to extend his lead. The left-handed pitcher is facing the runner. He may also throw to first base before coming to the set position, but he can create more deception by using balance and timing after he has come to a set position.

After the pitcher comes to a set position, he should have a quick, effective way to turn and throw to the first baseman. He can use two basic maneuvers. One is to lift the heel of the push-off foot to clear the rubber, turn on the ball of the push-off foot, step toward first base, and throw. He should bring the ball above the glove as he is making the turn. This will get him into a throwing position quickly. He should work on this standard move until he perfects it.

Another standard maneuver is a jump turn. This move requires the pitcher to jump without balking or bending either leg dramatically, land on his push-off foot, and throw as he strides toward first base. He should lift the ball above the glove as he is spinning in the air. He clearly lifts both feet and must make sure that his stride foot lands in an angle toward first base. Some pitchers are adept at this pickoff maneuver, which is a legal move. Umpires do insist that the heel of the stride foot gain ground toward first base. A spin on the stride-foot heel is illegal. The stride foot must move toward first base.

Either pickoff move can be effective. Whether one move is better than the other depends on the pitcher. A pitcher effective with both moves has two valuable weapons to use against an aggressive base runner. If he perfects one move but not the other, he can use the move not yet perfected as a setup move.

When the first baseman plays behind the runner, the pitcher and the first baseman will have to work out some sort of signal to execute the play. The pitcher must ascertain the intention of the first baseman. If he knows that the first baseman will move to the bag, a timed pickoff can be effective. This can be done by counting or by having the pitcher visually time the movement of the first baseman.

When the first baseman is deep, a count-method pickoff is effective and may surprise the base runner. Generally, on a count-method pickoff, the movement toward first base by the first baseman begins when the pitcher turns his head to look toward home plate. The pitcher begins to count one thousand one, one thousand two, and when he reaches the one-thousand-three count, he turns and throws to the first baseman, who should just be reaching the bag to make a tag.

If the first baseman holds the runner at first, he must move off the bag and charge toward home plate when a bunt is possible or when the batter squares to bunt. A useful planned play calls for the first baseman to leave early. The pitcher waits until the first baseman and the third baseman are strategically located before throwing to the batter. After the pitcher releases the ball, the first baseman charges directly toward the potential bunter. This is one way to defend against the bunt and a good way to set up a pickoff at first base. To run the pickoff play, the first baseman charges off the bag and moves in toward the batter. After taking three steps toward the bunter, he retreats quickly to first base and takes the throw from the pitcher, who has timed the movement of the first baseman. Ideally, the ball and the first baseman arrive at first base at the same time.

A good first baseman is always looking for ways to hold runners close to the bag and still gain as much range as the situation allows. To stop the running game, the pitcher must be vigilant and ready to use any or all of the techniques and plays at his disposal.

Pickoff Plays Between the Pitcher and Middle Infielders

The techniques and strategies used at first base can also be employed at second base. Varying the timing and number of looks, stepping off the rubber, and a using a variety of pickoff plays give the pitcher and middle infielders a slight, if not significant, advantage. The pitcher and the middle infielder who has primary base coverage must coordinate their jobs. A steal of third base or failed bunt coverage usually occurs when the players at the two positions fail to work closely with one another. The shortstop or second baseman is responsible for keeping the runner close to the bag. The pitcher should not throw to home plate until the runner at second base is stabilized or forced back toward the bag.

If the infielder is unable to stabilize the runner or minimize his lead, the pitcher should step off. On particularly troublesome runners, the pitcher and one or both of the middle infielders can initiate one of many pickoff plays. The count method, the daylight method, the fake and go, and the Z-out method are the most common pickoff plays.

Count Method After the middle infielder, usually the shortstop, gives a signal, the pitcher turns his head toward the hitter. That starts the count for the pitcher and tells the infielder to start moving to the bag. The pitcher counts one thousand one, one thousand two, and on the count of one thousand three, he turns and throws to the infielder. The ideal timing calls for the ball and the infielder to arrive at the same time. To add more deception to the play, the infielder giving the signal may signal to the pitcher to look back at the plate more than once. The action should begin on the look indicated by the infielder.

Daylight Method When the shortstop is covering the bag and gets closer to the bag than the runner so that the pitcher can see daylight between the two, the pitcher should turn and throw to the bag. When the shortstop gets far enough ahead of the runner to show daylight to the pitcher, he should always continue to the bag. The pitcher must throw to him or step off. The pitcher should never throw to the plate under these conditions. To offer more security to the pitcher, the shortstop may extend his glove toward the bag to indicate that he is definitely going all the way to the bag. That signals to the pitcher that a pickoff play is on. If the second baseman is covering the bag, his bare hand should extend toward the bag to tell the pitcher that a pickoff play is on.

Fake-and-Go Method Both middle infielders and the pitcher are involved in the fake-and-go pickoff play. After the signal is given, one middle infielder moves quickly to the bag. This action should force the runner back toward the base. After drawing the runner back, the covering middle infielder moves quickly back to his position, inducing the runner to move toward third base and renegotiate his lead. As the covering middle infielder starts back to regain his fielding ground, the other middle infielder moves quickly to the base to receive the throw from the pitcher. The pitcher times the second infielder. His throw ideally arrives at second base as the second infielder gets to the bag.

Either middle infielder may break first and retreat from the base, leaving the other middle infielder responsible to time the action, move in to receive the throw, and make the tag on the runner. A carefully designed signal system indicates to the pitcher which infielder is to take the throw. The middle infielders signal each other to determine who is responsible for the fake and who is responsible for receiving the throw. One of them then signals that information to the pitcher.

Z-Out Method The Z-out move is an effective pickoff play. The move can be created in the process of driving the runner back to the bag. As the shortstop moves toward the bag, he can read the base runner's reaction. If the runner immediately moves back to take a lead as the shortstop regains his fielding position, the Z may be effective. In such a case the shortstop moves off the bag in a different angle than normal. The pitcher will be able to recognize the difference in the angles. The shortstop moves off the bag but drifts enough toward center field so that the pitcher can recognize that a pickoff play is on. Besides setting the angle, the shortstop can indicate that the pickoff play is on by opening his glove to the pitcher. This pickoff is somewhat like the daylight method in that it can be done spontaneously. The major difference is the angle taken by the shortstop. The second baseman can use the Z-out as well.

Pickoff Play at Third Base

Prearranged pickoff plays can be used at third base. The pitcher and third baseman can use the count method, or the third baseman can break for the bag when the right-handed pitcher is at the top of his leg lift. The third baseman can also work an effective pickoff with the pitcher by pointing with his bare hand toward the base, indicating to the pitcher that he is going to the bag. The pitcher should visually time the third baseman and get the ball to the bag as the third baseman arrives.

Not as many pickoff attempts are made at third as are made at other bases. Both vigilance and prudence are necessary to defend properly against the base runner at third base. Timely throws to the base are important in preventing the runner from stealing home or advancing on a pitch that gets a few feet away from the catcher. If the runner is taking a reasonable lead and not forcing the third baseman to alter his position, then attempting a pickoff is unwise.

Bases-Loaded Pickoff

The catcher should always be looking for ways to help his pitcher when he gets into a jam. A successful pickoff play does that. The catcher initiates the bases-loaded pickoff play, which is most effective when the shortstop covers second base. This planned play requires a signal to the shortstop. A prearranged signal alerts the pitcher to pitch from the windup position. The signal indicates that on another signal from the catcher, the catcher will indicate to the pitcher when to step off the rubber with his push-off foot, pivot, and throw to the shortstop, who is covering second base. The catcher is responsible for the timing between the shortstop and the pitcher. This pickoff can be used when second and third base are occupied.

First-and-Third Pickoff

With runners on first and third, the pitcher has control of the situation if he uses his defensive arsenal. Besides the normal pickoff move, the first-and-third pickoff play can put some fear and caution into the mind of the base runner. To say that this play never works is to admit that one has not been observant. Remember that a pickoff play does not have to result in an out to be successful. If it freezes the base runner, causes the base runner anxiety, or creates doubt in the base runner's mind about the kind of lead or jump he can get, the play is successful. When run correctly, the first-and-third pickoff not only creates anxiety and freezes the base runner but also often results in an out.

The right-handed pitcher should make the start of his delivery look normal by lifting his stride leg to its normal height. He should look home before and during the leg lift. Because this is prearranged, he can use balance to make it look as though he is going to deliver the pitch to home plate. But instead of striding toward the plate, he sets his stride foot down by using a shorter stride and directing the stride foot toward third base. After a short stride toward third base, the pitcher releases his push-off foot from the rubber and then quickly pivots and throws to first base. At the least, this move causes the runner at first to hold his ground. If the runner at first base starts to steal as the pitcher lifts his stride leg, the runner will be picked off. The reverse of this play can also be used. The right-handed pitcher should quickly step back off the rubber, fake throw to first base, and then quickly use a full pivot and attempt to pick off the runner at third base.

The left-handed pitcher can step back off the rubber, fake a throw to first base, and then pivot to attempt a pickoff at third base. The left-hander may also fake a throw to third base, disengage from the rubber by stepping back, pivot quickly, and throw to first base.

Defending Leads and Special Plays

To contain the running game, a defensive team should develop specific strategies for defending against leads and special plays like the delayed steal, the double steal, the bunt, the hit-and-run, and the run-and-hit.

Running or Walking Leads

The remedy for defending against the walking lead or the running lead is to destroy the base runner's timing. This type of runner takes a short lead and starts his movement as the pitcher delivers the ball. An inexperienced pitcher, or a pitcher who refuses to pay attention to what the base runner is doing, can be run out of the ballgame. On the other hand, a vigilant pitcher who varies his looks and changes his timing between the set position and the beginning of the throw to the plate will stay in control of the game. The pitcher should throw to the base more often to break the rhythm of the base runner. Mixing in a glide step with the regular leg lift moves is also a good maneuver.

© Rob Tringali Jr./SportsChrome USA

A vigilant pitcher who varies his looks and changes his timing between the set position and the beginning of the throw to the plate will stay in control of the game.

Delayed Steal

A team should always guard against the delayed steal. Generally, this steal is effective only when one or more defensive players become sloppy or are negligent. The delayed steal is usually effective because a middle infielder fails to drift toward the bag after the pitch passes the batter. The delayed steal is even more inviting for the runner when the middle infielders take their eyes off the ball after it passes the batter. A delayed steal may be successful if the catcher gets in a habit of lobbing the ball back to the pitcher. If the defensive players play each pitch with intensity, the delayed steal is less likely to be successful.

First-and-Third Situation

The double steal is always a threat and can be a nightmare for a team that is unprepared. It is hard to defend if the defensive team is unable to play catch. This situation requires the ultimate in teamwork. Each player has important responsibilities in defending successfully against the double steal.

Again, the defensive team has several weapons available, and they have the advantage of knowing which weapons they will use. The catcher has four basic ways to attack the runners:

1. He can look the runner back at third base and throw to second base.
2. He can look the runner back at third base, arm fake to second base, and throw to third base.
3. He can look the runner back at third base and throw high to the pitcher. If the runner bites on the high throw, the pitcher will be able to throw him out at third or get him in rundown between home and third base. This play requires a signal from the catcher to the pitcher before the signal for the pitch is given.
4. He can look the runner back at third and throw to either the shortstop or the second baseman. When the catcher uses this option, he must signal to the middle infielder that this special play is on should the runner attempt to steal second base.

The catcher must look the runner back on each of these options. Should the runner take too big a lead on any of these plays, the catcher should abort the planned play and simply throw the runner out at third base or get him in a rundown. If the runner at third breaks toward the plate as the catcher is looking him back, the catcher aborts the planned play, runs at the runner, and makes a tag or throws him out at third base.

This play requires discipline and aggressiveness on the part of the defensive team. The catcher must be well schooled in footwork and rhythm in throwing. The pitcher and each of the infielders must also be aggressive and disciplined.

The pitcher has control of the ball. His timing and ability to hold runners close are key components. In addition, the pitcher can use one of several pickoff plays. He must alert himself before each pitch of the potential double-steal attempt. Other weapons available to the pitcher are several kinds of pickoffs and the pitchout.

The middle infielders work as a team on this play. One of the middle infielders will receive the ball, and the other serves as the eyes for the receiver.

The Bunt

Most teams that use base stealing as a key component in their offense also include the bunt, the drag bunt, the squeeze bunt, and the push bunt to augment the running game. Again, catching and throwing are critical here. Unless the bunt is placed perfectly, an out should result. Often the defensive unit that is extremely good at playing catch can turn the bunt into a double play or get the lead runner. In that case the offense has failed to execute effectively.

A good bunting team is a formidable foe because they force the defense to execute. If the defensive team is aggressive, is able to play catch, and uses the arsenal they have at their disposal, they will prevail.

Regular bunt defenses, special bunt defenses, the pitchout, the pickoff play, holding runners close, and pitching high fastballs up and in all help defuse the bunting game. A well-disciplined and aggressive defensive team invites the opponent to bunt. A bunt should result in an out.

Hit-and-Run and Run-and-Hit

Stopping the running game also includes successfully defending the hit-and-run and the run-and-hit. Running teams invariably use the two plays to aid base runners. Both plays are difficult to defuse.

The pitcher who stays tuned in to the tendencies of his opponent, is aware of game situations, uses the pitchout and pickoff, and is able to execute good pitch selection and pitch placement makes these plays difficult for the offensive team to execute.

These plays place demands on the middle infielders. Both middle infielders must hold their ground until the hitter misses the pitch or until they determine the direction of the hit ball.

Knowing the Opponent's Offensive Tendencies

A key part of defusing an explosive base-running onslaught is knowing the opponent's past tendencies. Careful study of a team will reveal some patterns. Gaining knowledge of these tendencies is the first step toward developing a way to defend against them.

Base Runners' Tendencies

The defensive team should study the opposition and learn the tendencies of each base runner. Some runners will present a threat on every pitch, whereas others will apply pressure only in certain situations. To defend properly against the opposition, the defensive team should carefully consider this information.

A runner who takes a minimal lead should not draw many throws, particularly if he is cautious and eager to get back to the base after each pitch. The defensive team should watch for any change in the runner's body language or the size of the lead he takes. Any runner is a potential threat to attempt a steal.

Runners with a history of aggressive base running require a good deal more attention. Almost every base runner does something when he attempts to steal a base that is different from what he does when he is just getting a good lead. Only careful observation can pick up these little details.

Coaches and players should examine the opposition closely. Some teams and individual base runners attempt to steal on curveball counts or in counts when the pitchout is less probable. Some are more aggressive in certain situations. Those who seek to excel defensively will try to learn about these tendencies.

Counts favorable to the runner are 3-2, 3-1, 2-0, and 2-1. The pitchout is less apt to be called on these counts. These counts are also favorable for the hit-and-run and the run-and-hit. Because these counts are favorable to the base runner, the pitcher and catcher should be alert and at their best.

Some base runners are good at picking breaking pitches or off-speed pitches for steal attempts. A 1-2 or 2-2 pitch is considered a breaking-ball count. A 2-0 or 3-1 count is considered an ideal situation for a change-up. Some pitchers, however, regularly use the breaking ball and change-up on other counts. To stop the base stealer from gaining an advantage, the pitcher should avoid patterns. A good pickoff move, intelligent pitch selection, pitchouts, and a quick move to the plate are all methods to neutralize the base stealer. When the pitcher uses these weapons to contend with the base runner, he must simultaneously maintain focus on competing with the hitter.

Coaches' Tendencies

Every coach develops a unique base-running strategy, and each has tendencies, ranging from very conservative to extremely daring. Some coaches play by the book more than others do. Some coaches are guided by hunches, whereas others lean more strictly to the dictates of strategy. Some are predictable; others are not. Knowledge of the opposing coach's tendencies may be more valuable than knowledge of the tendencies of the base runner.

The following list serves as a quick review of the most effective strategies for stopping the running game. Keep in mind that total teamwork is necessary to stop base runners. All of the entities must be coordinated to be effective. As stated earlier in this chapter, a strong desire to keep base runners from advancing without their earning the trip is paramount in stopping aggressive base runners.

- Take control of the game.
- The pitcher must be quick to home plate.
- Pay close attention to each base runner.
- Be aware of the situation.
- Know the tendencies of the opponent.
- Develop and be able to execute one or more pickoff plays at each base.
- Vary the looks at the base runner.
- Vary the time between the set position and the beginning of each pitch.
- Use the glide step in key situations.
- Use the pitchout.
- Hold runners close, especially on steal situations, bunt situations, and hit-and-run situations.
- Outfielders should throw to get lead runners only when the percentages are on their side.
- Keep trailing runners off second base.
- Each position must assume responsibility.
- Compete fully.

A well-orchestrated defense with desire and sound fundamentals can often shut down a good running team. A sound defensive unit may even make it appear that the offensive team is running itself out of potential rallies. Making this happen requires hard work and hours of correct repetition. Without hard work and effort, a defensive unit will be overmatched by a running team.

The runner will have an advantage if only one part of the defensive team misfires. Each player of the defensive unit must take pride in his job. Without teamwork, the defensive team forfeits the advantage of controlling the ball.

Although no formula can stop base runners entirely, the defensive unit has ways to compete and come out on top. As stated at the beginning of this chapter, the team with the ball has the advantage because they initiate the play. They control the tempo unless the opposition is good enough to take control of the situation. Never lose sight of, or fail to respect, the opponent. The opponent also has maneuvers, plays, and the ability to formulate plans and compete effectively against defensive strategies. A good base runner is difficult to stop, but a defensive unit with a well-organized plan, teamwork, vigilance, and good execution can slow him to a crawl.

Fielding the Position

Geoff Zahn

Back in 1995 I was the pitching coach for Pepperdine University. We were ahead 1-0 in the ninth inning at Santa Clara University, needing a victory to have any shot at the conference championship. Our starting pitcher, freshman Randy Wolf, had just walked the leadoff hitter. I visited the mound to see whether he was too tired to continue. Before I got there he asked, "You're not going to take me out are you? I've got the next guy and I am going to finish this game." I had my answer before I asked the question. I reminded him that this next hitter would be bunting and headed back to the dugout. The next hitter put a perfect sacrifice bunt down the first-base line. I immediately yelled for the ball to be thrown to "One, one!" Randy was already charging for the ball. He picked it up and in one motion while falling across the line, jumped and fired the ball toward second. My voice went from "Oh no!" to "Great play!" as the throw beat the runner at second base. I had just witnessed the greatest fielding play by a pitcher that I had ever seen or have seen since in my 30 years of playing and coaching. Pepperdine and Randy Wolf went on to win that game 1-0.

Randy could never have made that play except that he believed he could make it. In his mind, nothing could stop him from making that play on that bunt. He had decided that the runner was not getting to second base by way of a bunt if he had anything to do with it. He didn't have to wait for the catcher to tell him where to throw. He had already made the play in his head, and he only had to react to where the ball was bunted.

How did Randy, or any pitcher, attain that mind-set of utter aggressiveness that allows him to make good, and sometimes great, fielding plays? If a pitcher wants to be a good fielder, he must start with his thought process. He can practice all he wants. He can do drills all he wants. He can strategize all he wants. In the end it comes down to having an aggressive thought process that wills him to make the play. How many times have you seen players make plays that you didn't see in drills or that ran contrary to the strategy you had in mind for a particular situation? I have seen it happen many times. As coaches, we often think we have a drill for everything, and we forget to reinforce the very thing that will make great plays happen.

The key to everything I am about to discuss about fielding the position is that pitchers must have a tremendous will, a mind-set that they are going to win the game. You must reinforce that goal repeatedly so that it permeates everything they do. You ask them, "Why are you out there on that mound?" The answer they must offer is, "Someway, somehow, I am going to win this game." It goes from getting strike one, to getting the first batter out each inning, to saying, "I am going to get three outs before this team scores." Only then will fielding occupy as large a place in the pitcher's mind as throwing strikes. Fielding the position then becomes as important as any other facet of the game, a vital part of getting three outs before the other team scores. Thus, when you discuss and drill them on covering first, picking up bunts, backing up bases, and so forth, they approach it with a mind-set that fielding will help them win.

This may sound elementary, but it isn't. Players today subconsciously put other concerns above winning. How hard am I throwing? Are my mechanics good today? Is my curve breaking correctly? Are the scouts in the stands? What do I have to do to make the right impression? Will these guys score enough for me today? Will my team make the plays behind me? These are just a few of the things that can take first place in a pitcher's mind unless he is a born winner or unless his coach keeps winning in the front of his pitcher's mind. The winning mind-set sets the stage for the thinking and strategy of the different plays.

Covering First

No batter-runner can beat the pitcher to first base. In baseball lingo we hear, "There ain't a runner alive who can beat me to first." On any ball hit to the left side of his left shoe, the pitcher must explode with his first few strides toward the first-base line about 10 feet in front of the first-base bag (see figure 9.1). The pitcher should run to the line rather than directly to the bag for three reasons:

1. By running to the line and then up the line, the pitcher will be in line to hit the bag even if his attention is focused on catching the ball.
2. By running up the line and tagging the inside of the bag, the pitcher will avoid being spiked by the runner on a close play.

3. By getting to the line the pitcher creates a better angle to receive the ball from the first baseman. The only time the pitcher goes to the outside of the bag is when the first baseman fields a ball that takes him into foul territory and calls for the pitcher to go to the outside of the bag.

Once the pitcher gets to the line, he starts to get his body under control by taking short, choppy steps. This action gets him ready to become a first baseman and stretch for the ball in case the first baseman bobbles the ball and is not ready to feed it to him. The pitcher, like all other fielders, should always expect a bad throw. If he expects a good throw, he will not be ready to adjust to a bad one. If he always expects a bad throw, however, he will be prepared for the good throw as well as ready to make that extraordinary play on the bad throw.

A pitcher should go directly to the bag only if he gets a late start off the mound for some reason or if a runner is on first in a double-play situation. With a double-play ball hit to the first baseman, the pitcher heads directly to the first-base bag and yells to the first baseman that he has the bag. If the pitcher has time he gets to the bag under control and turns to stretch as a first baseman. This play is difficult for a left-handed pitcher because the ball is often on its way toward first from the shortstop before the lefty reaches first. Ideally, the left-handed pitcher should turn to stretch for the thrown ball with his left foot on the bag. As a left-handed pitcher, I found that I often didn't have time to get turned around, and I learned that it was more efficient just to put my right foot on the bag and stretch for the throw with my left foot.

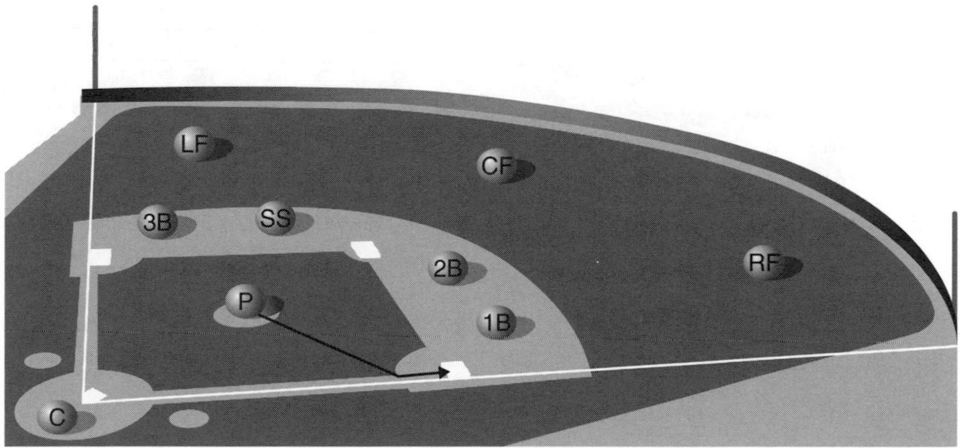

FIGURE 9.1 If the ball is hit to the left side of the pitcher's left shoe, the pitcher should cover first by running to the line about 10 feet in front of the first-base bag and then up the line to the bag.

Gene Mauch, my manager with both the Minnesota Twins and the California Angels, employed the best strategy for balls hit to the right side. The first baseman's mind-set is that he will come to get every ball he can unless he hears the pitcher call for the ball. The first baseman does not need to call for the ball because the pitcher assumes that he is coming after everything. The first baseman also knows that if he cannot get the ball to the pitcher before the pitcher gets to the line, the pitcher will slow down and stop at the bag to receive the throw. Ideally, the first baseman gets the ball to the pitcher early so that the pitcher has time to find the bag and step on the inside of it.

The pitcher's mind-set is that he will field every ball he can get that is in line with his path toward the first-base line and every ball that is in front of that line. He will only call for the batted ball that he is positive he can field. If he just *thinks* he can field it, he should let it go and let the first baseman take it. With any ball that the pitcher fields on his way to first base or any ball that he is late in calling for, he should be prepared to beat the batter-runner to first base because the first baseman may have committed too far toward fielding the ball. If, on a ground ball, the pitcher has to deviate toward second base from his path to the first-base line, he should definitely let the first baseman take the ball. This strategy works well because both the first baseman and the pitcher can remain aggressive within their areas of responsibility and there is no confusion about who is calling for the ball. This strategy is also successful when a batter pushes a bunt toward the right side.

With a runner on second base at the time of the pitch, the pitcher must prepare himself to throw home after he catches the ball and touches the first-base bag. He does this by pushing off the bag to the inside of the base line and moving his feet and arm into a position to throw home. By doing this, he protects himself from being hit by the runner crossing first base. By getting his body ready to throw, the pitcher is ready for the call from the catcher to throw home.

When we did our pitcher's drill at Michigan, we always simulated having a runner on second, and we had the pitchers throw home so that they were comfortable with making that throw. We also hit a number of ground balls that the pitcher had to read and decide whether to field the ball or let the first baseman handle it. When any fielders communicate I want them to use their "big-boy voice," the voice that everyone in the stadium can hear. By using that voice the players become accustomed to being decisive in calling for the ball.

Fielding Bunts

Again, the mind-set of the pitcher is that he will field everything and throw out the lead runner. He must have the attitude that the offense must execute perfectly to make a sacrifice or drag bunt successful. Some coaches designate areas in front of the plate and the pitcher's mound that players use to decide whether the throw goes to second or safely to first. I believe the situation of the game and the ability and attitude of the pitcher dictate where the throw goes. Usually, if you are way up in runs or way down, you will make sure to get an out. Or, if you are up by two in the eighth or ninth inning, you will make sure to get an out. If you believe that runs are going to be hard to come by because of inclement weather or a developing pitchers' duel, even if it is early in the game, you want to be aggressive.

Again, attitude plays a big role in where the throw goes. Some players in the big leagues, even when they fielded balls in plenty of time to get the lead runner, always opted to make the safe play. The pitcher must be confident that he can make the play. Here is where a coach can make a big difference in a player's confidence. I will never forget a situation that occurred when I was in high school during basketball practice. I took a crazy jump hook shot that careened high off the backboard. My coach blew his whistle to stop practice. I was sure he was going to chastise me for taking such a low-percentage shot. Instead, he asked me if I thought I was going to make that shot. Inside I thought I could, but I thought he wanted me to say no. He then chastised me to take only the shots I thought I could make. He said there was nothing wrong with the shot as long as I thought it was going in. He taught me a valuable lesson. He was allowing for my individuality within my ability, and he was giving me the freedom to break out of the routine play. I ask my players if they think all those crazy shots that Michael Jordan or Magic Johnson made were the first time they ever took those shots. Of course not: those players practiced those outlandish shots repeatedly so that they just happened in the game. For that reason you should encourage your players to stretch themselves in practice to perform and practice the extraordinary play. They have fun with it, and you can applaud with them when they have the confidence to execute it in a game.

The key to fielding bunts efficiently is the footwork. Whenever possible the pitcher should get his footwork out of the way and be in a position to throw the ball before he fields the bunt. An aggressive pitcher will get his feet in a position to get the lead runner. Then, if he doesn't have a play at the lead base, he makes the adjustment to get the out at first. He should be in a position to take a crow hop toward the base he is throwing as he picks up the ball. For the left-handed pitcher that often means getting around the ball and turning toward the glove side. The pitcher must use his feet. I tell them often, "You didn't make a bad throw. You had bad footwork." When the pitcher picks up the ball he should use both hands, although he should also practice picking up a stopped ball with his bare hand. Pitchers should also practice throwing like an infielder without having to stand up all the way. They must learn this skill because often they do not have time to straighten up and crow hop toward the bag to make a good overhand throw.

Getting the body in position to throw before fielding the ball and then throwing from a lower fielder's position is more efficient. Figure 9.2, a and b show the pitcher throwing from a lower position with knees and back bent from picking up the ball. This throwing action resembles that of an infielder. The pitcher can perform it more quickly than he can the action of fielding the ball and then straightening up to make an overhand throw, as shown in figure 9.2, c and d. In the time the pitcher takes to straighten up to throw, the runner has made two or three steps toward first base. When the pitcher throws to a base, he should make a good, firm throw, but he should not throw all out using his best moving fastball. If possible, he should grip the ball with four seams.

Participating in a Double Play

When a runner gets on first base with less than two outs, the pitcher should be thinking double play. Before he ever gets on the rubber to look in for the pitch sign, he must check with his middle infielders to see who is covering on a ball hit back to the pitcher. The shortstop is generally the one who will let him know by pointing to the pitcher and either back to himself or toward the second baseman. I believe it is best to have the shortstop take as many throws as possible because it is an easier play for him coming across the bag. The only time the second baseman should take the throw is when a right-handed dead-pull hitter is at the plate and the shortstop needs to shade to the hole between third and short.

Next, the pitcher should think of what pitch he could throw this particular hitter to get him to hit the ball on the ground in the middle of the field. Obviously, in most situations, the pitcher wants to keep the ball down or have it moving downward underneath the bat to produce a ground ball. If the hitter is right-handed and looking for the ball away to hit behind the runner, then the pitcher can jam him with low fastballs or throw him low off-speed pitches to speed up his bat and cause him to hit toward the middle of the field. An inside change-up and a left-hander's slow curveball are not the best pitches in this situation because the batter can pull either pitch through the hole at short. Remember that I am speaking in generalities, not absolutes. If a pitcher has a devastating pitch that can strike out a hitter at any time, then he needs to have the confidence to throw it. If the hitter is a right-handed pull hitter, the pitcher should make him hit something hard, low, and away.

If the hitter is left-handed, the pitcher should first assume that the batter is looking for a pitch he can pull. He wants to hit the ball on the right side of the diamond in the hole created by the first baseman holding the runner on and the second baseman playing close enough to second base to turn the double play. Generally, the pitcher should throw the typical lefty pitches that are down hard and away.

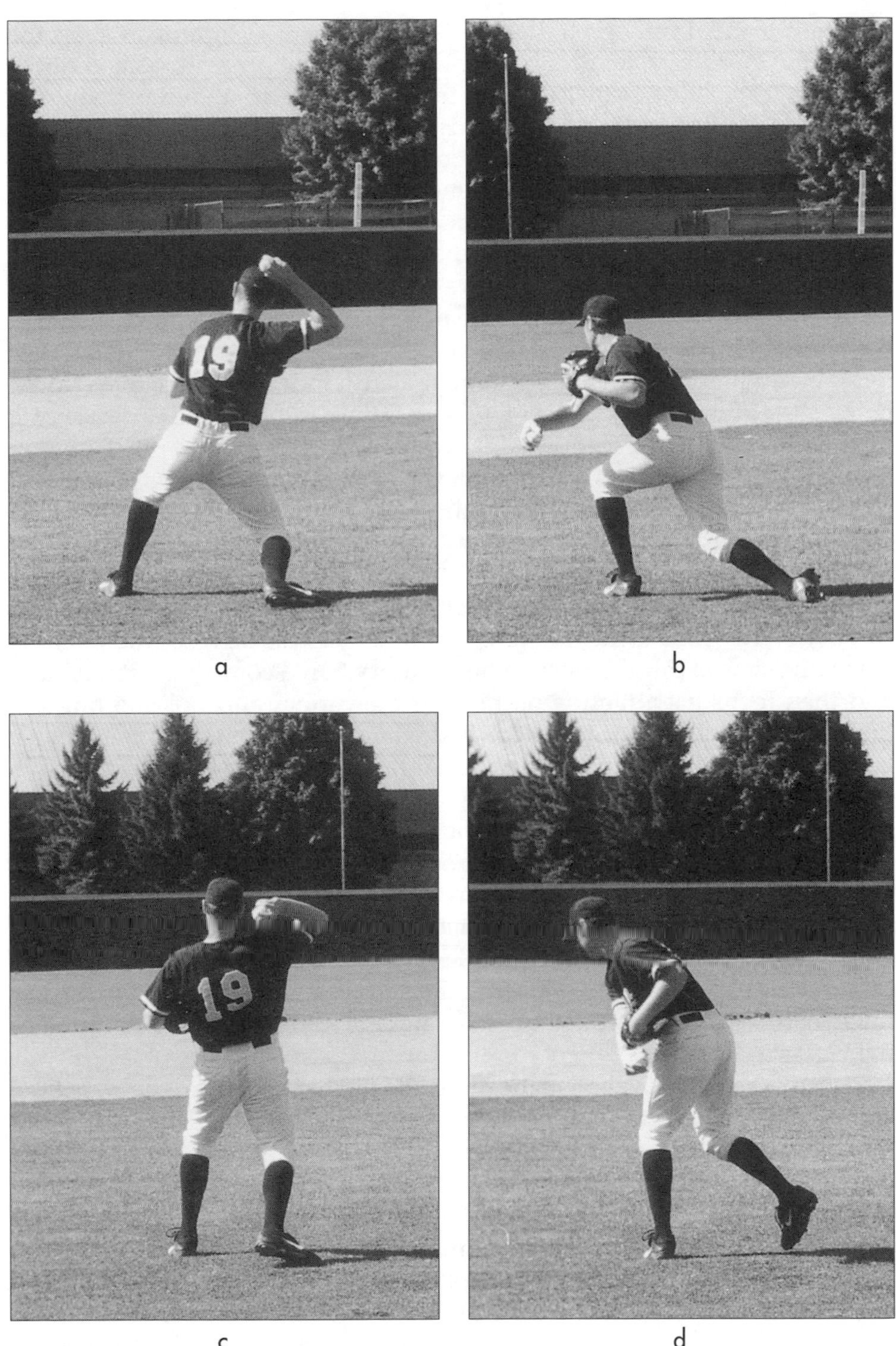

a b c d

FIGURE 9.2 Throwing from a low position, as shown in *(a)* and *(b)*, is much quicker than taking the time to stand up to make an overhand throw, as in *(c)* and *(d)*.
Photos courtesy of Bob Kalmbach—University of Michigan.

A left-handed pitcher facing a typical left-handed hitter can keep the ball in the middle of the field by throwing his regular or cut fastball down and away. One year early in spring training, I, a left-handed pitcher, was scheduled to pitch batting practice. My manager, Gene Mauch, had me face left-handed hitters Rod Carew, Reggie Jackson, and Fred Lynn. He got behind me, behind a screen, and told me to throw them fastballs down and away. He bet me that if I would get the fastball down and away, they would hit the ball on the ground in the middle of the field. On top of that, he made me tell them what was coming. Sure enough, every ball I got down and away ended up on the ground in the middle of the field. Granted, some of them were hit hard, but Gene's theory worked. He reasoned that because left-handed hitters did not see that many left-handed pitchers, they would give a little at the plate and pull the front shoulder out a little early, leaving them vulnerable to the low outside pitch. I figured that if that pitch worked against three future Hall of Fame players who knew what was coming, I had better use it in the game. Of course, Mauch was also telling me that I was going to use it. I didn't need any further discussion with Gene. I got out of many a jam with that pitch for the rest of my career.

Once the pitcher has his plan about how he wants to pitch the hitter, he can get on the rubber for the sign. When he gets the sign for the pitch he wants, he should put the pitch in his memory bank, come to a set position, and then focus his attention on reading the runner and holding him on. Before he decides to throw to the plate, he must go back to his memory bank and refocus on the pitch before he starts his delivery.

I do not encourage left-handed pitchers to raise their legs to start their delivery to the plate and then read the runner. I believe this method causes them to divide their focus, which ultimately affects their control of the pitch. Against a lefty who practices that move, we instructed our runners to make an early false break to divert the pitcher's attention or cause confusion. I believe in keeping everything simple and in the pitcher's favor. I would rather see the lefty learn to be quick to the plate just as a right-handed pitcher must learn to get the ball to the catcher in time for him to throw out potential base stealers.

After he releases the ball to the plate, the pitcher becomes a fielder. If the ball is hit hard back to him, he should know that he has plenty of time to make the double play. He should catch the ball and then turn his feet toward second while his eyes are picking up the fielder who is covering the bag. He should then take a crow hop and lead the fielder so that he can catch the ball, step on the bag, and throw to first. If the ball is hit softly or a little to the side, the pitcher should get his footwork out of the way by turning his body in a line toward second before he catches the ball. That way he can be moving toward second the instant he catches the ball. He visually picks up the fielder and then makes a quick throw to the fielder covering the bag. This method is much faster and gives him a greater chance of completing the double play or at least getting the ball to the infielder quickly so that the incoming runner isn't on top of him as he catches the ball (see figure 9.3).

Again, the pitcher should make a firm throw, not a moving fastball. If the runner is moving on the pitch, the pitcher should plan to throw to second, especially on a hard-hit ball. He should get the throw off to second

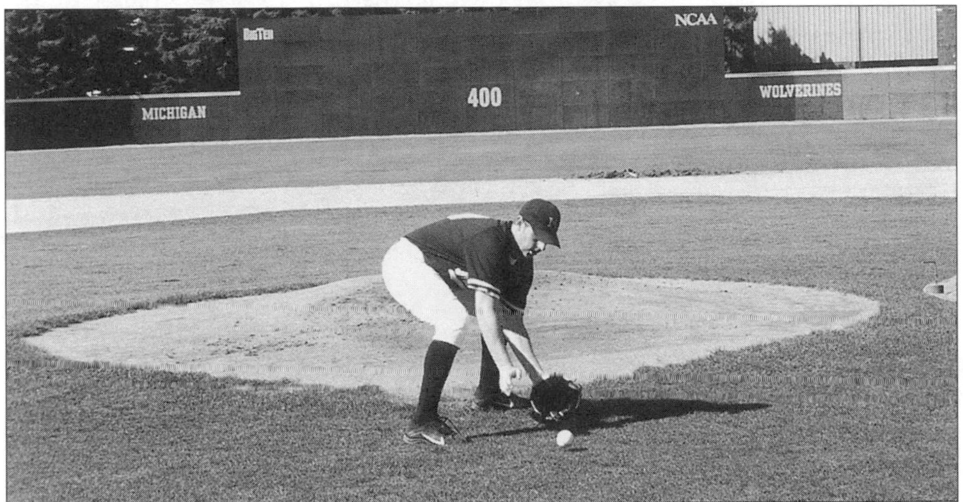

a

b

FIGURE 9.3 *(a)* The pitcher is already turned toward second as he fields the ball and is in great position to pick up his target and make the throw to the fielder covering second. *(b)* The pitcher is incorrectly facing home plate as he fields the slowly hit ball. He has not gotten his footwork out of the way, and he must turn to pick up the target of the fielder covering the bag. This method takes more time and lessens the chance of completing the double play.
Photos courtesy of Bob Kalmbach—University of Michigan.

quickly. If the fielder knows he cannot get the incoming runner out, he should come off the bag toward the pitcher, receive the ball, and relay to first in time to get the batter-runner. But if the fielder is yelling "One, one," the pitcher should adjust and throw to first to retire the batter-runner.

If the ball is hit to the first baseman, the pitcher explodes toward first to receive the return throw from the fielder. He must communicate with his first baseman to let him know that he will cover the first-base bag.

During pitchers' drills we often had a runner at first during the double-play situation. We told the runner to try to get a jump on the pitcher if he could. In this way we made the drill more gamelike because we required the pitcher to hold the runner on and then throw a strike to the plate. Sometimes, if the runner stole, we let the pitch go through and allowed the catcher to throw to second. This told us whether the pitcher was adequately holding runners on first base and allowed our catcher to throw to second in game situations.

First-and-Second Bunt Situation

A bunt situation occurs in late innings of tight ballgames with runners on first and second and no one out. The offensive objective is to move the runners into scoring position at second and third. The general offensive strategy is to bunt the ball hard down the third-base line to force the third baseman to field the ball and thus have no play on the lead runner at third base. I have seen many defensive plays designed to try to stop this play, but I will discuss only one of those plays.

Why am I choosing to focus on one play? When I was coming up through the Dodger organization, we were taught just a few defensive plays. The Dodgers reasoned that they would much rather we execute a few plays well than run a myriad of plays that we performed with mediocrity. Throughout the minor leagues, we had four bunt and pickoff plays that our opposition knew we ran. We got many outs with those plays, even though the opponents' coaches warned their players of the plays we were about to run. I believe the play I am about to discuss is the best defensive play in this situation because over the years it has had the most success.

Usually the first baseman gives the play to the pitcher orally. The first baseman may say something like, "Bunt play number 1 is on. You have the third-base line." Once the pitcher understands that the play is on, he can get on the mound to take the pitch selection sign from the catcher. (I choose to give the plays to the pitcher orally because many pitchers are so wrapped up in the pitches that they do not get bunt-play signs.)

I should mention here two points of strategy:

1. If the pitcher wants to know whether the offense has put the bunt play on, he should perform a spin move pickoff toward second base.

If the batter is going to bunt, he must make a move to get into the bunting position when the pitcher picks up his lead leg. If he makes no move to get ready to bunt, the coach may want to take off the bunt play.

2. If the pitcher suspects that the bunt is on, he should make sure he throws strike one. In addition, the hardest pitch to bunt down the third-base line is something hard, low, and away. A fastball, cut fastball, or hard slider, serves that purpose. If he can throw strike one, hard low and away, the pitcher will make it difficult for the offense to execute the bunt.

After the pitcher gets the sign, he should come to a set position and then look back to check the runner at second. The shortstop will be holding the runner on and may even give up his defensive position to do that. The pitcher's responsibility is to focus on the runner to make sure he does not get too big a lead or start moving toward third when he turns to deliver the ball to the plate. He does not need to worry about the shortstop being out of position for this play. The pitcher only needs to make sure that the runner at second does not get a good jump toward third.

Once the pitcher has determined that the runner is under control, he devotes all his attention to the pitch. He must turn his head and deliver quickly to the plate, not giving the runners time to get a large secondary lead. As soon as the ball leaves his hand, the pitcher must start toward the third-base line. This movement is the key to this play. Before the pitch gets to home plate, the pitcher should be on his way to the third-base line in the direction of a little less than halfway toward third base (see figure 9.4). His fielding responsibility is to get any ball bunted to the left side of the mound.

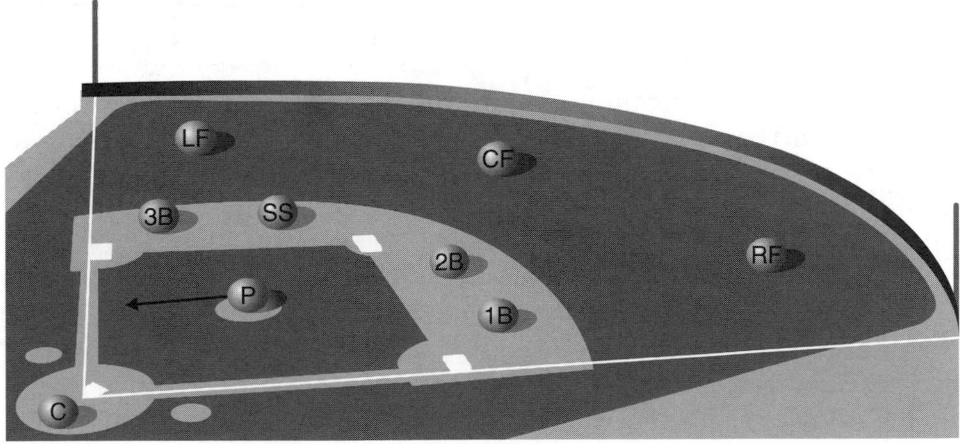

FIGURE 9.4 Immediately after he releases the ball to the plate, the pitcher should take a path a little less than halfway toward third base to cover the third-base area for bunts.

The first baseman's responsibility is to cover the area from the mound to the first-base line. (He can do that by reading the angle of the bat before the ball is bunted.) If the ball is bunted down the third-base line, the third baseman must either go get the bunt or let the pitcher field the ball and get the out at third. Making this judgment requires the third baseman to know his pitcher's ability to get off the mound, make the play, and then make a good throw to third.

To help the third baseman learn his pitcher's ability, we often had the outfielders bunt and run the bases when we practiced this play. The pitchers run the play the same way they would in a game, other players get some practice bunting and running in a game situation, and the third baseman and pitcher develop the necessary coordination and timing.

I can't stress enough the need for the pitcher to have an aggressive mental attitude to make this play successful. He must fix in his mind that he will get the out at third. He must come off the mound aggressively with the intention of being the one to make the play. He must make the offense execute the bunt perfectly to advance the runners. With that in mind, he should make the play at first base only when

- he bobbles the ball and loses the play at third,
- he hears the catcher and third baseman yelling, "One, one," or
- he hears the third baseman calling for the ball. (Even if the pitcher is already over the ball ready to make the fielding play when he hears the third baseman calling for the ball, he should know that the play has to be at first base because the third baseman has left his position to make the play. When he hears the third baseman call for the ball, he should allow the third baseman to make the play. The third baseman usually has an easier play because he is moving somewhat toward first base.)

As with all plays, communication plays a key role in the success of the play. The third baseman has the most responsibility on this play to communicate with the pitcher, although the catcher must also see the play and call for the throw to go to the correct base. The situation of the game will determine how aggressive the third baseman is in taking the play. With a safe lead late in the game, a coach may say to his third baseman, "Make sure you get an out." On any bunt on which he has any question about whether the pitcher will make the play, the third baseman should call for the ball and get the out at first. In this situation, the defensive team is willing to give up the advancement of the runners in turn for the out because they want to make sure they stay away from a big inning for the offense. None of this strategy should change the pitcher's aggressiveness in making the play. He just always needs to be ready to listen to the third baseman.

This play is easier for the left-handed pitcher because he can field the ball and easily get his feet ready to make the play at third. The right-handed pitcher should try to get around the ball, turning to his glove side, so that he can get his feet ready to make the throw to third base (see figures 9.5 and 9.6.). If he must redirect the throw to first base, quick feet are the key to making a good throw.

Backing Up Bases

For the pitcher, the key in backing up bases is to anticipate where the play is going to end up and where he can perform the role of being the last safety valve. For instance, on a base hit to left field, the pitcher should position himself between first and second in line with the throw to second and out of the way of the base runner. He becomes the safety valve if an overthrow occurs at second or the ball gets away from the infielder. If the pitcher will end up in foul territory when backing up a base, he should get as deep as the field will allow. Coming up to get a bad throw is always easier than having to go back to get a throw.

With a runner on first base and a routine base hit to the outfield, the pitcher should back up the most forward bag, third base in this situation. If, in this situation, the ball gets by the outfielder or is an extra-base hit, the pitcher should back up home plate and be ready to adjust to back up third base in case the play shifts to third.

When an extra-base hit occurs with runners on first and second, the pitcher should hustle to a position between home and third base where, as he sees the play develop, he can adjust to where the throw ultimately goes. If the ball is hit to right field in this situation, he usually will have taken a step or two toward first base to cover the bag in case an infielder stops the ball. Once the ball gets through the infield, he must hustle to a position between home and third to be ready to back up either base (see figure 9.7). I like the pitcher to shade toward home plate on this play because if the play does go to third base, the left fielder should have moved in to position to help back up third base. If the ball is hit to left field in this situation, the play is much easier for the pitcher. He should position himself behind home plate in line with the throw from the outfield. He should be ready to cover home plate as well as get any errant throw.

As a rule, the catcher should be calling the base to which the throw will be going, but the pitcher should not just blindly go to back up that base. The catcher may often start by calling a particular base but change his call as the play develops. The pitcher should therefore put himself in a position where he can adjust.

Pitchers are generally taught to follow their throws during pickoff attempts and back up that base. I think it is important to consider the

a

b

c

FIGURE 9.5 The pitcher-fielder correctly gets around the ball by *(a)* moving toward the ball, *(b)* getting his body in line with where he is going to throw the ball as he fields it, and *(c)* throwing the ball from that position. This technique is much faster and more accurate than the one shown in figure 9.6.

Photos courtesy of Bob Kalmbach—University of Michigan.

FIGURE 9.6 In *(a)* the pitcher-fielder fields the ball while still facing home plate. His back is to his intended target. In *(b)* he has had to turn around to pick up his target and make the throw. This technique is much slower and less accurate than the method shown in figure 9.5.
Photos courtesy of Bob Kalmbach—University of Michigan.

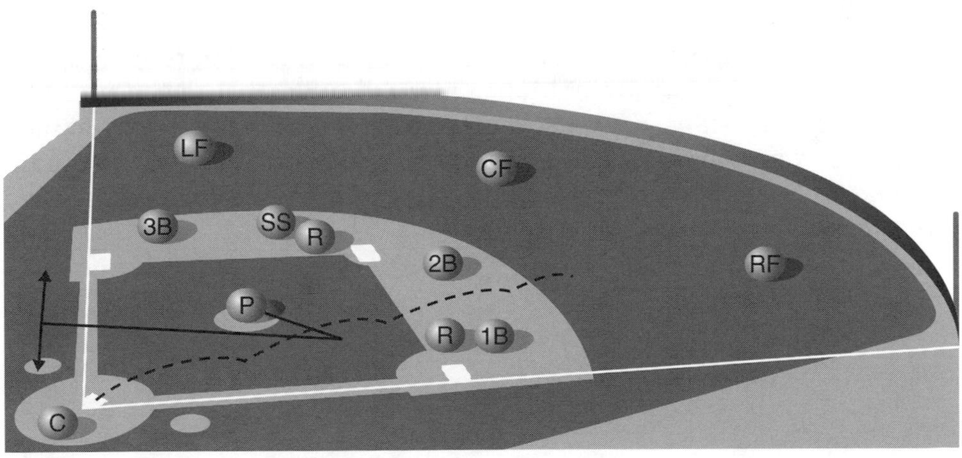

FIGURE 9.7 With runners on first and second and a ground ball hit through the right side of the infield, the pitcher must start to cover first base. After the ball gets through, he must hustle back between third and home to back up those bases. This is one of the hardest defensive plays to execute properly.

opponent's strategy and back up accordingly. With runners on first and third and two outs, the pitcher should expect some kind of play to be run to try to score the runner on third. If he picks off the runner at first base in this situation, it is usually because the opponent wanted the runner picked off. With that in mind, the pitcher must figure that the play will ultimately end up at home plate, with the opponent trying to score the runner from third, so he should back up home plate.

Although coaches can use many different drills and ways to develop these defensive skills in their players, much of the success that players have comes back to their attitude of aggressiveness. Those who have a perfectionist attitude will usually need some time before they feel free to make that tremendous aggressive play. Perfectionists will spend hours honing their skills before they ever try them in a game. They don't want to stretch out of their mold until they are extremely confident they can pull it off without making a mistake. They aren't opposed to being aggressive; they just want to practice and perfect all aspects of a move before they exhibit it. Patience and practice are the keys for these players. The coach should provide constant reinforcement that it is OK to stretch oneself and fail. With time, perfectionists can become extremely aggressive.

All types of individuals need to be positively motivated to stretch themselves in the joy of competition. Tommy Lasorda, my coach in the minor leagues and with the Dodgers, was and still is a great motivator. When a player would not hustle to first base on a hit that could have been a double had he been aggressive, Lasorda would let the player know clearly that he was wrong. He would shout, "A truck driver could have gotten a single on that ball! A *ballplayer* would have had two on that hit! We're looking for *ballplayers*." That was his straight-talking way of saying that aggressive players win championships. They also enjoy the game more and know that they are doing everything they can to be the best they can be. I hope you are inspired to help your players become outstanding, aggressive defensive *ballplayers*.

10

Working a Game

John Winkin

The strategy involved in working a game centers completely on the pitching capabilities of each pitcher, especially on several key factors. First, and perhaps most important, are the pitcher's individual talents, his strengths and weaknesses, his mental toughness and mound composure, and his game and mound experience.

Few coaches are fortunate enough to have entire pitching staffs made up of players possessing outstanding pitching talent, good mound composure, and the kind of mound experience that allows planning a strategy for working a game. Coaches must usually center strategy for working a game on each individual pitcher's capabilities.

A second key factor in working a game centers on pitching mechanics. All of the things a pitcher wishes to accomplish in delivering each pitch revolve around his pitching mechanics. Many pitching coaches stress that success stems from the delivery of the pitch from an appropriate balance point with a lift-and-throw action to the determined location. Good pitching mechanics greatly increase the chances of successfully accomplishing the determined mission of each pitch.

The third vital factor in working a game is the ability to locate a pitch consistently in and out and up and down in the strike zone. Consistently locating each pitch plays heavily in the ability to work a game.

Of course, the ability to deliver each pitch in the desired location affects game-planning adjustments involving pitching strategy. These include

- all matters relating to pitch count—number of pitchers, pitching endurance in a game, and so on;
- planning any strategy about how to pitch to individual hitters, let alone an entire batting order; and

- looking and plotting to keep key hitters from exploiting the extension of their hands and the fat part of the bat.

The ability to pitch to location and do it on a consistent basis weighs heavily in any strategy for working a game and planning pitching changes.

The fourth key element in working a game is the ability to change speeds. Coaches working with pitchers emphasize the need to have command of a fastball, a breaking ball, and a change-up. Having the ability to call on this kind of an arsenal certainly arms a pitcher with a greater ability to work the game.

Pedro Martinez is considered the most dominating pitcher of his time. He has the reputation of having the best fastball, the best breaking ball, and the best change-up among his pitching peers. That certainly explains a lot about his ability to work his game and dominate hitters. Perhaps his greatest weapon is his ability to change speeds. Greg Maddux, with perhaps a lesser fastball, breaking ball, and change-up than Pedro, accomplishes the same kind of exceptional success with his great ability to locate each pitch and change speeds.

The fifth key factor is self-esteem, a paramount requisite to having the ability to work the game. Self-esteem encompasses several important facets:

- What does a pitcher believe he does well and does the best?
- What is a pitcher good at?
- What gives a pitcher the confidence and composure to overcome whatever adversity arises?

Those qualities are all part of self-esteem as a pitcher; one can't succeed and survive without it.

Those five factors serve as the foundation for working a game, and they establish the basis for strategy involved in any game experience.

Establishing a Strong Foundation

In my coaching experience at the high school level, in American Legion, at the college level NCAA Division III, NCAA Division I, and NAIA, I've counted on a six-step warm-up or pregame routine as the first move toward establishing the foundation for working a particular game. This pregame experience is designed to establish and practice the five key factors for a successful game experience:

1. Mastering proper pitching mechanics, from the balance point in the delivery, to the windup, to the stretch

2. Locating pitches in and out and up and down in the strike zone
3. Changing speeds
4. Establishing at least two pitches that will be strengths
5. Building self-esteem for the game experience at hand

This six-step routine allows a pitcher to warm up while slowly increasing the distance between steps. Each step is a new drill that focuses on an aspect of pitching mechanics, making the pitcher's delivery more consistent. The drill also serves as a starting point in building endurance. These are the five goals of the six-step routine:

1. To allow the pitcher to stretch out safely while concentrating on specific mechanics
2. To develop a routine for the pitcher to warm up properly
3. To practice and make a habit of using proper pitching mechanics
4. To allow 10 repetitions in each step that focus on certain aspects of the pitcher's delivery (with each step in the progression relying on each of the earlier steps)
5. To complete, in 15 to 20 minutes, the progression in which the pitcher gradually works back to the full distance of 60 feet, 6 inches, from a beginning distance of 15 feet between pitcher and catcher

Step 1: Two-Knee Drill

The pitcher kneels about 15 feet from and squared to the catcher. With the ball in his throwing hand, the pitcher rotates his upper body so that his nonthrowing shoulder and elbow point to the catcher as he brings his throwing arm and the ball up to the cocked position.

Once the arm and hand are in the cocked position, the pitcher gains momentum by uncoiling his upper body. He then spins the ball at half speed to a location as he stretches out. As the pitcher releases the ball, he protects his arm and shoulder with the proper follow-through—armpit over the knee, elbow by the knee, and a complete sweep of the fingers. For steps 1, 2, and 3, the best location is low and inside to the opposite hitter—right-handed pitchers to left-handed hitters and vice versa.

Step 2: One-Knee Drill

The pitcher and catcher position themselves about 20 feet apart. The pitcher kneels on his drive-leg knee with his stride leg bent toward the catcher. The stride leg (or landing leg) is in the ideal landing position.

While in the cocked position, the pitcher focuses on location. As he throws he transfers his weight from the back leg to the front leg by pushing off the back foot, rising from a kneeling to standing position while uncoiling his upper body to allow for the explosion and travel of the arm, elbow, shoulder, and hip. Again, as the pitcher releases the ball, he must concentrate on the proper follow-through—armpit over the knee, elbow by the knee, sweep of the fingers, and rotation of the hips.

Step 3: Hip or Chair Drill

Hip Drill

The pitcher stands on the mound about 30 feet from the catcher. The pitcher needs to measure off his stride line, ensuring that his toe and knee are pointing toward the catcher.

Once the pitcher is at cocked position, he will simultaneously transfer his weight from the drive leg to the front leg, begin rotation of the hips toward the catcher, and bring the arm and shoulder through the proper throwing path, ending with the correct follow-through.

This drill develops powerful hip rotation. On the follow-through the pitcher should not bring his drive foot forward. He merely turns the foot over so that the outside part of the ankle points toward the ground and the inside of the knee points toward the opposite knee.

Chair Drill

The chair drill uses the same ideas and concepts as the hip drill, but it may be used when a mound is unavailable. Use the chair to simulate the downward slope of the mound. Follow the procedure used for the hip drill. The pivot foot rests on the chair and rotates on the chair as the pitcher executes drill.

The push-off foot does not leave the chair. The pitcher should concentrate on turning the foot over and rotating the hip. His weight should not shift forward until his arm is up and in the cocked position.

Step 4: Balance-Point Drill

This step, along with steps 5 and 6, should be done from the pitcher's mound. The catcher positions himself about 45 feet away from the pitcher. The pitcher marks the point at which his stride foot should land, making it easier to verify a correct landing spot.

With all his weight over his drive leg, the pitcher raises his stride leg until his thigh is parallel to the ground. The stride toe should be pointed down to allow the pitcher to land on the front half of his foot. The glove and throwing hand should be at break point. The pitcher focuses on the catcher's mitt, breaks his throwing hand down and out of the glove, and brings it quickly to the cocked position. At the same time, he strides toward the plate, transferring his weight from the back to the front leg, begins hip rotation, and brings his drive foot off the ground and forward as he moves his arm and shoulder through the proper throwing path. He should end with the correct follow-through.

This being the most important step, the stress must be on being in balance before the pitching explosion. We use the expressions "Lift and throw" and "Throw up-down."

Step 5: One, Two, Three Drill

The purpose of this drill is (a) to bring together steps 1 through 4 and (b) to break the delivery into three stages, stopping after each stage to ensure that the pitcher is in the correct position. Stage 1 focuses on addressing the rubber and beginning the delivery. Stage 2 emphasizes the balance point. Stage 3 concentrates on the release of the ball.

The catcher positions himself about 50 feet from the pitcher. In stage 1 of this drill, the pitcher addresses the rubber, gaining momentum by stepping back with his stride leg and turning his pivot foot in front of the rubber. As he begins this rocking step, he must keep both his wrist and the ball completely hidden in his glove. At this point, the pitcher should stop and check his position.

Stage 2 concentrates on the balance point and cocked position. As the pitcher reaches the balance point, he must conceal his wrist and the ball from the batter's view. The coach should stop at this phase to check that the pitcher is in proper balance, with hands breaking from the middle of his body to go to the cocked position.

Stage 3 is the throwing and follow-through stage. With the arm in the cocked position and weight over his back leg, the pitcher aims his hip and front shoulder toward the target. He drives with the back leg and strides toward the plate. As the stride foot lands, he transfers his weight from the back leg to the front leg, rotates his upper body so that the throwing shoulder replaces the nonthrowing shoulder, opens his hip toward the catcher, brings his arm and shoulder through the proper throwing path, and ends with the correct follow-through.

Step 6: Stretch Drill

The stretch is from full distance, 60 feet, 6 inches. In developing the slide step, the pitcher quickens his delivery home while changing his proper pitching mechanics as little as possible. From the stretch the pitcher comes to the set position.

Once he completes step 6, the pitcher should be adequately warm and stretched. He is now ready for the rest of his throwing experience, whether it is his long or short throwing day. At this point the pitcher should gradually add other pitches to the fastball, such as the curve, slider, or change. Once he is comfortable with his pitches, he can complete his throwing for that day. We do this by throwing three sets of spins, or "2-2-2" (two fastball spins; two breaking-ball spins; two change-up spins).

This pregame warm-up goes a long way toward establishing the foundation for working a game. The warm-up is a vital experience for setting the tone for any strategy that might be involved in working that game. An important part of this experience is the supervision provided during this warm-up period. At the college level a pitching coach is probably available to guide the warm-up. At most other amateur levels a coach may not be available. In that case the pitcher and catcher must be knowledgeable about the steps practiced in the warm-up and the key guidelines for concentration in each step. The pitcher must also be able to correct himself.

Coaches must find time to provide coaching support sometime during the pregame warm-up period. Skip Bertman, the legendary LSU head coach, always made time to get to the bullpen area to observe, counsel, and check on the warm-up of his starting pitcher. During my head coaching experience at all amateur levels, I've tried to follow that same procedure. For most college programs with a good pitching coach on the staff, one can expect careful monitoring of that warm-up experience.

In monitoring at least part of the warm-up experience, the coach should offer encouragement to the pitcher to provide that all-important building of confidence, self-esteem, and appropriate frame of mind for the game.

Jay Kemble, who served as a pitching coach for the University of Maine for quite some time and who in recent years has been a successful high school and legion coach, puts it this way: "To me, building pitchers' confidence is the most important thing; you have to get pitchers to think they're better than they really are." The pitcher's frame of mind going in is vitally important. Coach Kemble also says, "No matter what the level, I've told the pitcher, 'Don't leave the bullpen until you have two pitches going for you.'"

Each step in the six-step warm-up has 10 warm-up pitches. In each step the pitcher works on location in the strike zone. The pitcher practices 5 pitches in and 5 pitches out or 5 pitches up and 5 pitches down. Similarly, in working on change of speeds the pitcher throws 5 fastballs and 5 change-ups in each sequence. The warm-up should emphasize the balance point, the windup, and the stretch. The pitcher must follow and practice proper pitching guidelines.

After completing the six steps of the warm-up period, the pitcher concentrates on his strengths—practicing the fastball, the breaking ball, and the change-up. We've found it useful to have him practice pitches in sets of two pitches each (2-2-2)—two fastballs, two breaking balls, two change-ups. Normally, we've begun with three sets of 2-2-2 as the starting point. The pitcher then focuses on having his top two pitches going for him before he leaves the bullpen.

During the many years I've coached, few players have had natural pro-prospect talent, so building that foundation has been crucial. I've counted on the supervised six-step approach to get a pitcher ready to work the game. The success of that preparation usually sets the tone for any strategy involved in working a game.

At the amateur level of baseball competition another important factor is the pitcher-catcher relationship. A key starting point in this relationship is having the catcher handle the pitcher in as many pitching-catching experiences as possible. An important time in developing this relationship is the warm-up period, especially the closing portion when the concentration is on mastering strengths. The feel each gets for what is going well—knowing what the strong pitches are, what the pitcher can do well—creates the appropriate starting point for working the game. The pitcher and catcher must work together at least during the ending of the warm-up period. Obviously, this all sets the tone for any strategy considerations involved for the start of the game.

Maximizing the Pitcher's Strengths

Our overall philosophical approach has for many years centered on maximizing the use of each pitcher's strengths. We go with what each pitcher can do the best, what each can do with confidence and poise, and what each can do consistently! This approach obviously offers the best percentage chance for success. The old adage "Don't get beat with your third best or weakest pitch" certainly fits most amateur-level pitching choices. You have to go with what you can do best, what you can locate best, and what you have confidence in. It's hard to succeed with what you can't do well just for the sake of what might be good strategy. You must capitalize on a pitcher's strengths, whatever they might be.

As pitchers accumulate game experience, their strengths broaden and grow. I've long counted on the maturation that each pitcher gains with game experience and appropriate guidance. Good coaches and catchers recognize this maturation and broadening of strengths. Accordingly, the ability to work a game and apply strategic pitching combinations grows with this maturation, but having success still goes back to going with a pitcher's strengths game by game.

The key to pitching success centers on consistent use of what produces the needed strike or needed out. Several times in my coaching experience, I've won key in-season games, postseason tournaments, and even a College World Series game by pitching to one location. I often used only two pitches

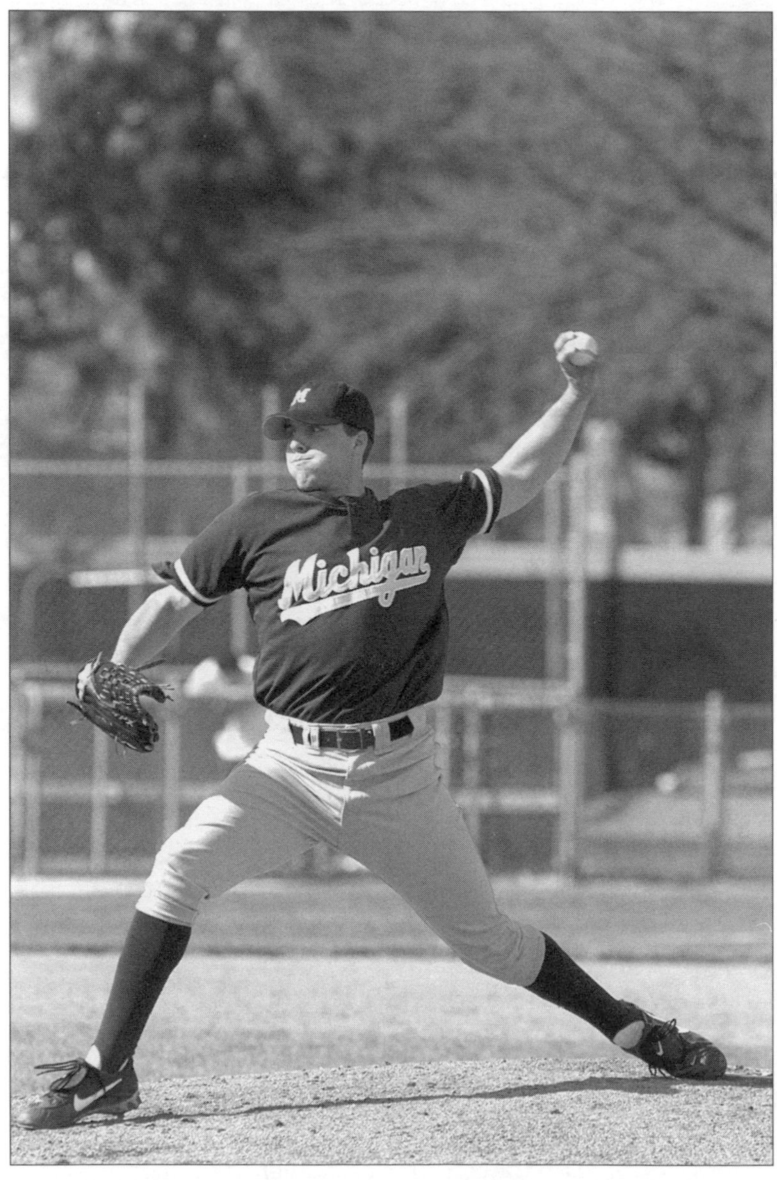

Pitching success centers on consistent use of what produces the needed strike or needed out. The key is to capitalize on each pitcher's strengths.

because that's what the pitcher on that day could perform with consistency and confidence. We always feel that it's important to capitalize on the pitcher's strengths.

Getting the First Strike

Having success all starts with getting first-pitch strikes. What are the two pitches the pitcher can throw for strikes? What can the pitcher get over for the first strike? Most important, on that day what is the pitcher's best pitch to get over for a first-pitch strike to each hitter?

Hall of Fame coach Charlie Greene has had many years of experience as a pitching coach in professional baseball. When asked about the importance of getting the first-pitch strike, he said, "Getting the first-pitch strike is the key to any success in working a game. You've got to go with what the pitcher can throw the best to get a strike." Charlie says that the slider may be the easiest pitch to get in for a strike and that the two-seam fastball is next.

Greene says, "You can't aim for the corners when you can't throw strikes; you may have to go for the middle of the plate and hope the movement on the pitch will keep the ball from going in the middle of the plate." The pitcher must work to get first-pitch strikes on each batter. I've always liked the two approaches that Charlie emphasized:

1. When you're behind in the count, go back toward the middle of the plate.
2. When you're ahead in the count, go away from the middle of the plate.

These are excellent guidelines for working the count. Pitching starts, however, with working with the one or two pitches that the pitcher can throw for a first-pitch strike.

Mike D'Andrea, a former pitcher at the University of Maine and in the Atlanta Braves organization, is now a highly successful coach at the high school and legion level. As of this writing, he has had three consecutive state high school championships and two state legion championships. Standout pitching and defense have been the key to his success. Mike says, "You have to throw strikes; if you can't throw strikes, you're not good enough to pitch in my program. I want my pitchers getting the first-pitch strikes to over 50 percent of our hitters."

Mike D'Andrea said that as an Atlanta Braves organization pitcher, he was fined accordingly if he didn't get first-pitch strikes to over 50 percent of the hitters. D'Andrea uses these goals for his high school and legion pitchers:

- Aim to achieve 50 percent first-pitch strikes in the game.
- Keep 3-and-2 counts to fewer than five per game.

- Move around the strike zone on the opponent's number three, four, and five hitters.
- Never walk the opponent's number seven, eight, and nine hitters; attack them down the middle.

How does a coach get young pitchers to achieve first-pitch strikes to over 50 percent of the hitters? D'Andrea suggests starting by having pitchers master throwing pitches down the middle of the plate. Next, pitchers divide the plate in half and work each half of the plate. Finally, they divide the plate into thirds—in, out, middle—and work the thirds. In essence the six-step warm-up routine suggested earlier is the perfect routine for following this method.

D'Andrea works toward getting his pitchers to throw strikes—over 50 percent first strikes, no walks, no long counts—by thinking that way from day one of practice. Let me emphasize again that a crucial point in achieving first-pitch strikes is the tail end of the pregame warm-up in the bullpen.

Bill Swift, a former University of Maine pitcher, started in four consecutive College World Series, pitched for the U.S. Olympic team in 1984, and rose to become a 20-game winner with the San Francisco Giants. He currently coaches at the amateur level in Arizona. He stresses that at all levels he wants his starting catcher to catch at least the last 10 or 12 pitches in the pen. Both the pitcher and the catcher must know what's working well before they start the game.

The pitcher has to go into the game focused, prepared, and confident in his ability to throw first-pitch strikes. The head coach, pitching coach, catcher, and pitcher all have roles in achieving that success. Constant work by all parties starts on the first day, becomes an ongoing process up to the first game, and continues game by game all season long.

Several other important factors are involved in getting strikes. First, emphasis must be placed on pitching mechanics and mastering and grooving the pitching explosion for the delivery of each pitch to location. Someone on the staff with the necessary pitching knowledge (comparable to a pitching coach) must supply constant supervision to each pitcher. He must carefully monitor focus and concentration, proper grips, and the facets of pitching that affect control. If a head coach doesn't have the proper help available, he must find time to monitor and work with those who will do the job for him.

Second, the pitcher must focus on location, that is, the target, usually the glove. We've found it important for the pitcher to focus his eyes on the target when he gets to the balance point and separates the pitching hand from the glove. Charlie Greene agrees that the "look at the target must take place when the hands separate. The focus on the glove and the quality of concentration are extremely important!"

Third, pitch selection depends on what the pitcher can get over for a strike. Valuable here, of course, are the two pitches the pitcher can throw for strikes. Normally, the slider is the easiest to throw for a strike, and the two-seam sinker is probably next. Greene notes that "anytime you can 'cut' the ball, it's easier to throw for a strike." He also points out that the curveball is toughest to throw for a strike. As for strategy, Greene says that "you can't aim for corners if there's inconsistency; it is better to go for the middle and hope movement will take it away from the middle."

Mike D'Andrea likes his pitchers throwing a lot of fastballs. He feels that pitching fastballs sets the tone and that, at the high school level, the fastball is the easiest pitch to control. By practicing throwing the fastball often (as suggested earlier by dividing the plate), I'm not afraid to go with that pitch to get strikes.

As for grips at that level, right-handed pitchers should use the two-seam fastball throwing to the right side of the plate and the four-seam fastball to the left side. Left-handers should throw two seams to the left side of the plate and four seams to the right side. Some coaches suggest using two seams all the time. By the way, D'Andrea makes an important suggestion: "Don't take movement away from a pitcher by forcing him to use a grip." In other words, go with what is comfortable and works well for the pitcher.

Best Pitch

The pitcher should always use the best pitch on certain counts, and the catcher and pitcher must be in tune about what the best pitch is for each point of the game.

Obviously, if you can count on two pitches (a la Pedro Martinez), you are that much better off. Two critical counts that call for using the best pitch are 1-1 and 2-2. As Greene points out, "You're advancing the count. You have to try to get ahead." Greene likes a sinker as a best pitch. My experience has been that the best pitch most times is the one that's going the best for you at that point in the game. The catcher and pitcher have to be on top of this all the time. Bill Swift says, "I always depended on what was going best for me at that point. If I was on a good roll and in a good rhythm, I could depend on that strength that was going good."

I believe in that approach and would again add that in these situations the pitcher should never get beat by his third-best pitch. The head coach or pitching coach should always make sure that the pitcher and catcher are on the same page.

Out Pitch

The out pitch comes, of course, on a 3-2 count or on the 1-2 or 0-2 count when it is not used for waste, batting practice, and change-of-speed strategies. The out pitch should be a best pitch, but more appropriately it should be the pitcher's most effective out pitch. Often a best pitch is a fastball in a certain location, but that pitcher's out pitch might be a particular breaking ball or change-up. Again, the pitcher and catcher should be in tune on this and use the out pitch accordingly.

I like the philosophy Charlie Greene suggests: "For the location of the out pitch, the further ahead you are in the count, the farther you can go away from the middle of the plate—for the 3-2 count, you need accuracy, not full effort."

Changing Speeds

Pitchers must be able to change speeds on the good hitters to keep them off balance. The outstanding pitchers are masterful in changing speeds. One marvels at the greats in professional baseball and the success they enjoy by using change-of-speed strategy. Skip Bertman for years had his pitchers use a BP (batting-practice speed) pitch, always located away from the middle—even low and outside the zone. This strategy gives pitchers a three-speed arsenal. The success of this strategy depends on getting ahead of the count with strikes. Pitchers have a powerful weapon when they can throw strikes, have a good change-up, and can effectively locate a BP pitch when ahead in the count.

As indicated earlier, we've always spent time having pitchers throw change-ups in these workouts. The focus is first on mastering a comfortable grip, then developing the appropriate release, and finally improving pitch location.

Changing speeds is a valuable part of strategy in handling and pitching to the good hitter—the hot hitter.

Mastering Pitch Location

The ability to use the width of the plate aids any strategy involved in working the game. Atlanta Braves pitchers Greg Maddux and Tom Glavine epitomize how successful one can be by mastering location of pitches in and out. I've marveled at their level of accomplishment for years and spent a great deal of my time with pitchers having them work to achieve a good level of consistency in pitching to the direction desired. Location wins games for pitchers who can't always count on overpowering hitters, and it obviously makes the talented pitcher that much more effective. Working on direction and location with a high degree of concentration can do wonders in improving the effectiveness of any staff. Pitchers who can place the ball with accuracy can use strategies that involve use of location in working a game.

Mental Approach of the Starter

Bill Swift, who currently coaches amateur baseball in Arizona, says it best: "You have to have confidence going into a game. You have to think positive. You have to stay positive." That to me implies one thing: pitchers need to have great self-esteem. A pitcher going into a game has to know what he can throw for strikes; he has to know what he can do well to accomplish the goal. A pitcher has to believe in what he can do well and capitalize on it.

Swift goes on to say, "You know the good hitters are going to get their 3 hits, but that you're going to get 7 outs out of their 10 at-bats; you hope the good hitters don't get them against you. I've always concerned myself with the hot hitters that pop into your head." Swift continues, "You can't be intimidated by any pressures. There are a lot of different pressures—fans,

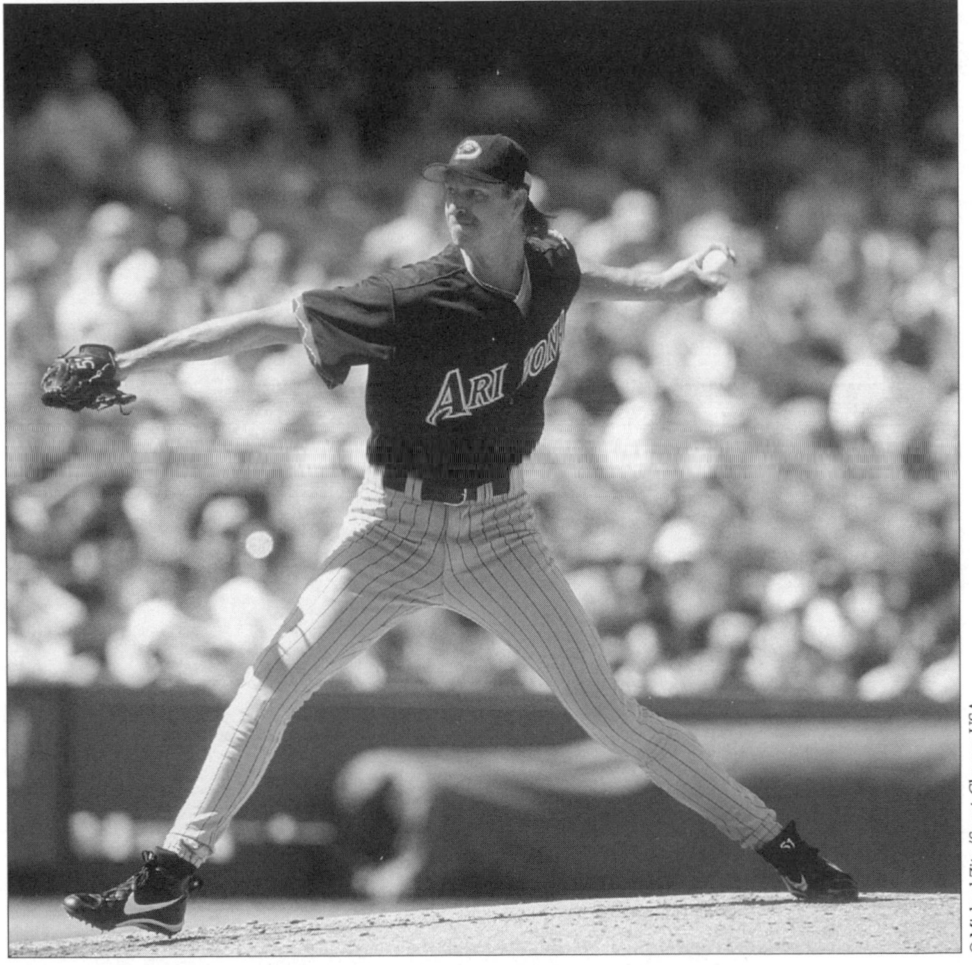

© Michael Zito/SportsChrome USA

A great pitcher stays focused despite the many pressures of the game.

press, the crowd on top of you, and so on. You have to prepare to be focused and make yourself stay focused—you've got to go for it."

Jay Kemble believes that the mental approach of the starter going into a game at the high school and amateur level is key: "It's the most important thing. You have to build his confidence in any one-on-one opportunity you have with the pitcher."

Improving a pitcher's mental approach really starts with the preparation from the first day—the setting of goals and the focus on achieving those goals. Careful monitoring and one-on-one communication between the pitching coach, the coach, and the catcher are vital stepping-stones toward the establishment of the needed self-esteem and confidence. Every throw is an opportunity to work toward a positive mental approach.

Nothing is better than a game-day approach to preparing for the season. Gamelike experiences offer the best ground for building and establishing confidence in what a pitcher can do well. Live pitching to hitters with a specific purpose provides key opportunities for establishing confidence.

Using a game-day approach for each starter in a rotation scheme serves as ideal preparation for getting starters ready for a season, particularly as you build up the endurance of pitchers with each game-day outing. By setting goals for each game-day experience, coaches have a great opportunity to work with pitchers one-on-one and build their confidence.

D'Andrea sets individual goals with each pitcher. In working with a pitcher's mental approach, he says, "You have to battle yourself to stay positive and always think 'I'm good enough.'"

I've always tried to plan opportunities in practice and game situations for each starter to succeed doing what he does best. Nothing is more important than self-esteem. By providing opportunities to succeed, the coach makes it possible for the pitcher to reach agreed-upon goals for each outing. Each pitcher should be hungry for success.

The game-day approach is a great way to provide pitchers the opportunity to be on top of what they can always do well—being positive, staying focused, and charging ahead. The real key to it all is self-esteem. Providing your starters the chances to do what they do well in live hitting circumstances is the best vehicle for gaining that positive self-esteem.

Effective Preparation Methods

Most coaches and pitchers count on the work they do between starts as key preparation for game pitching experience. Bill Swift says, "It's getting ready for the job you've got to do in the game; at each level of competition you're in, the level of work increases." Mike D'Andrea claims that as a professional, "I never felt the workouts at the park were near enough to get me ready. I had to do things on my own to be sure I would be ready for my start."

Both Swift and D'Andrea emphasize that conditioning was the biggest concern, especially running. Both also acknowledge having to be careful about eating. For Swift, it was important to get enough rest before each start and to pay attention to proper nutrition—a healthy diet, the use of vitamins, and so forth. Rest and diet are especially important for professionals because of the traveling and night games involved.

We've always stressed running as a vital part of conditioning. Many approaches have been developed recently to accomplish desired conditioning. The proper mix of endurance running and interval running spaced between starts needs to be planned. We've made the day following a start a conditioning day, one that calls for both hard running and a throwing routine that's comfortable and appropriate for each pitcher. Many pitching coaches recommend long toss for this conditioning day.

We've always favored what we've called a short-throwing day two days before a scheduled start. This workout allows for working on mechanics, direction and location, changing speeds, and fine tuning the best pitch and the out pitch. It is a stretch-out day in our six-step warm-up routine, centered on perfecting pitching mechanics while stretching out through the six-step routine. This workout provides an excellent opportunity for one-on-one monitoring and coaching. The greatest gains in fine tuning often happen in these workouts, which are a key part of the preparation ritual.

The game-day six-step warm-up ritual is a key period of the pregame preparation. The warm-up should begin with some running and stretching exercises with a light weight. (We use a tennis can with sand.) A long-toss routine before the six steps is often part of this ritual. Ideally, the pitching coach will monitor this routine. Jay Kemble suggests, "If you don't have a coach, give the kids something to coach themselves. In the six-step warm-ups, they get to know the guidelines for getting ready."

Swift advises pitchers in the pregame warm-up to "work to develop a rhythm; get a flow to get yourself going; try to work towards getting everything in sync." As suggested earlier, the pitcher should be sure to come out of the pen with at least two pitches ready to go.

Getting the Book on the Opponent

At the professional level, the book on opposing hitters is highly sophisticated. What's more, the professional pitcher has the talent, the tools, and the command of pitches to execute a strategic plan. At the college level a fairly high degree of sophistication is involved in accumulating the same kind of information. Some college pitchers are also capable of executing a carefully planned strategic approach to handling opposing hitters. At all other amateur levels the book on opposing hitters is less comprehensive, and the ability to execute a desired plan is more modest.

Swift and D'Andrea acknowledge that as professional pitchers, a big part of getting ready was meeting to go over all the accumulated information. Swift reports, "What was most important to me was knowing who was hot with the bat, who was getting the hits, who was driving in the runs, who I do not give into, who I pitch around." Swift goes on to say, "It was important to me that my catcher and I agreed on each guy's strengths and how we were going to handle the lineup." D'Andrea counted on a notebook he kept and game charts he charted the day before a start for knowing where the holes for each hitter were, what each hitter was hitting well, and in what count he hit well. Then, like Swift, he would meet with his catcher about handling the batting order.

Information gathered by whatever means can provide valuable insight for forming a strategic plan. Pitching and hitting charts are especially valuable if the pitchers facing the hitters have some similarity to the pitcher who will start.

Observing batting practice, keeping charts, and watching games is useful for discovering

- who the hot hitters are,
- where and how hard the good hitters are hitting the ball,
- what pitchers are being hit hard, and
- on what count the hitters are hitting the ball hard.

Kemble cautions, "At my level, I really can't count on the book; I'm more concerned with my pitchers' strengths. We have to use what they do best. Of course, it helps if the pitcher who will start has the tools."

Getting the book on opposing hitters is helpful in achieving the goal of handling the opposing lineup. Of course, the book needs to be applied according to the talent, ability, and success probabilities of the pitcher involved.

Pitch Count and Number of Pitches

I learned the importance of pitch count and the number of pitches from my college coach at Duke University, Jack Coombs. Jack was a great major-league pitcher with the Philadelphia Athletics. He won 31 games in a season and won five World Series games without a loss. He was the master college coach on pitching during his time, and much of my pitching background comes from what I learned from him during my college career. Coombs kept the scorebook himself, noting every pitch—a practice I have always used in my coaching career. The pitcher designated to be the next starter now commonly handles this job. This view of the pitch count on each hitter and the running total of the number of pitches thrown is valuable information for pitching decisions that the coach must make during the game.

First, with prior knowledge of the likely total number of pitches the starter can handle, the signs of when to remove the pitcher begin to develop. For most in-season starts, 100 pitches is a key point of consideration.

The endurance of starters differs, but even for a properly conditioned and experienced pitcher, 100 pitches thrown in a contest is a key juncture in deciding when to remove the pitcher. If a lesser number of pitches has been established as the limit before the game, that limit becomes a guiding point. The pitch count is especially important when pitching injuries or arm difficulties are a factor.

At the amateur level, it is particularly important to avoid overuse. Too many pitchers face the consequence of severe arm problems because of overuse. Going too far with the number of pitches thrown in an outing will hurt the pitcher.

The inning-by-inning pitch count gives managers and coaches a good picture of the pitching trends in a game. The manager or coach knows the number of first-pitch strikes, the number of high pitch counts (2-2, 3-1, 3-2), what pitches are being thrown for strikes and what pitches are not, and what pitches are being hit hard. The combined indications can help in making a pitching decision.

The key to being a successful manager or coach is making pitching decisions at the right juncture in games. Many major-league managers have lost their jobs because of their inability to make the right pitching decisions. The ability to make the correct decisions is an instinct, a feel that one acquires through experience. The most helpful guide for making such decisions is the number of pitches in a game and the picture of that pitch count to opposing hitters game by game.

Finally, pitch count should serve as the guideline for the amount of rest a pitcher should have between outings. If the pitch count accumulates to 60 or more pitches at the amateur level, one might suggest a minimum of at least three days of rest between starts. For outings that total between 30 and 60 pitches, at least two days of rest is recommended between outings. For outings of 15 to 30 pitches, at least one day of rest is needed. Remember, exceeding such guidelines too often can bring about arm difficulties that lead to serious consequences.

Analyzing the Pitcher's Stuff As the Game Proceeds

Knowing what's going well—what the pitcher can throw for strikes, what the best pitch is at each juncture of the game, what the out pitch is for each such situation—is a key factor in the success of any outing. A cooperative relationship between the pitcher, catcher, and pitching coach is invaluable in determining this as a game goes forward.

Before the game, a pitching plan for handling the batter order should be developed based on information previously gathered and studied. At the college and high school levels, observation of batting practice serves as an ideal point for analyzing such factors as

- batting stance,
- position of the hands,
- concentration of the head,
- stride,
- quickness of the hands (bat speed),
- opening of the hips and front shoulder, and
- telltale signs that suggest use of certain pitches.

Any game plan devised for handling the batting order in the pregame meeting must be based on each hitter's strengths and weaknesses and the strengths and weaknesses of the starting pitcher.

The pregame warm-up serves as a first juncture for analyzing what's going well, what can be thrown for strikes, and so on. The pitching coach should help with this analysis and be alert for the telltale signs. The game catcher observing his part of the warm-up concentrates on what's going to be ready for use at the start of the game.

I always wanted to know, either by personal observation or from the pitching coach, what is working well for the pitcher, what he is throwing for strikes, and the availability of the pitcher's strengths. This breakdown sometimes calls for adjustments to the agreed upon strategy.

An important period for analyzing the pitcher's stuff is between innings. To make adjustments to game strategy, the coaches can go over the charts kept, the observations of hitters reacting to the pitcher's strengths and weaknesses, and the inning-by-inning analysis of what is or isn't working well.

On some days a pitcher will not have success with his customary strengths. In these cases, it is smart to stay with what has made that pitcher a starter. The coach or manager should remember that opposing hitters have good and bad spells. Analyzing the pitcher-batter matchups as the game moves along can dictate the strategy for handling each at-bat.

I cannot stress enough the importance of having the right catcher handling the pitching staff. The catcher must have the instinct, flare, and ability to use each pitcher's strengths, to know what's going well for the pitcher, and to know what in the pitcher's arsenal can fit the pitch count. The catcher has always been a key for any championship team. Great catchers get the most out of a pitcher by analyzing the pitcher's stuff and the hitters he will face as the game proceeds.

A coach should work to establish an ongoing examination of this kind with each opportunity for communication, whether it's between innings or on that important trip to the mound. The discussion on the trip to the mound should usually center on the adjustments needed to handle what is or isn't going well. Most pitching coaches are responsible for this.

Sometimes a trip to the mound involves a specific pitching situation—that of challenging a hitter, pitching tough to a hitter, or pitching around a hitter. In my experience as a head coach, I usually used a trip to the mound either for that type of pitching situation or to make a pitching change.

The ongoing analysis of a pitcher's stuff and what the opposing hitters are hitting hard determine how one plans to challenge a hitter—to pitch tough to a hitter or pitch around him. One wins or loses on this critical choice at a particular situational pitching juncture.

It comes down to these choices:

- Do you take a chance on letting the hot hitter beat you by challenging him?
- If you don't, do you want to take the chance that you can either pitch tough to him by pitching him away from the middle of the plate, mixing the fastball with a change-up or breaking-ball out pitch?
- Or do you want to pitch around him with pitches designed to prevent him from putting the fat of the bat on the ball?

If you determine that your starter is still capable of beating the hot hitter with his strengths, you challenge the hitter by going after him with your two best pitches or perhaps only your best. Keeping abreast of the pitcher's ongoing strengths obviously goes a long way toward making this choice. Good catchers—ones who have a good feel for this—are often the key persons in making this choice.

Communication With the Catcher

No player in the game is more important than the catcher. The catcher's position has always been the first one I determine in my lineup. You need someone capable of getting the most out of your pitchers. Championship teams have catchers who capitalize on each pitcher's strengths. I've always felt that the coach is responsible for training and developing catchers to handle pitchers and get the most out of them.

Many coaches have recently taken this a step further and assumed the responsibility for calling all pitches—the pitch to be used, its grip, and its location—especially at the high school and college level. At the professional level it's more common for the bench to focus on controlling the runner or runners on base by calling for throws to a base and pickoff plays. To call pitches to the catcher, the coach must have a finely tuned communication system. The system must be quick, easy to understand, and indecipherable by the opponent. The system must use a clear indicator to relay the pitch to

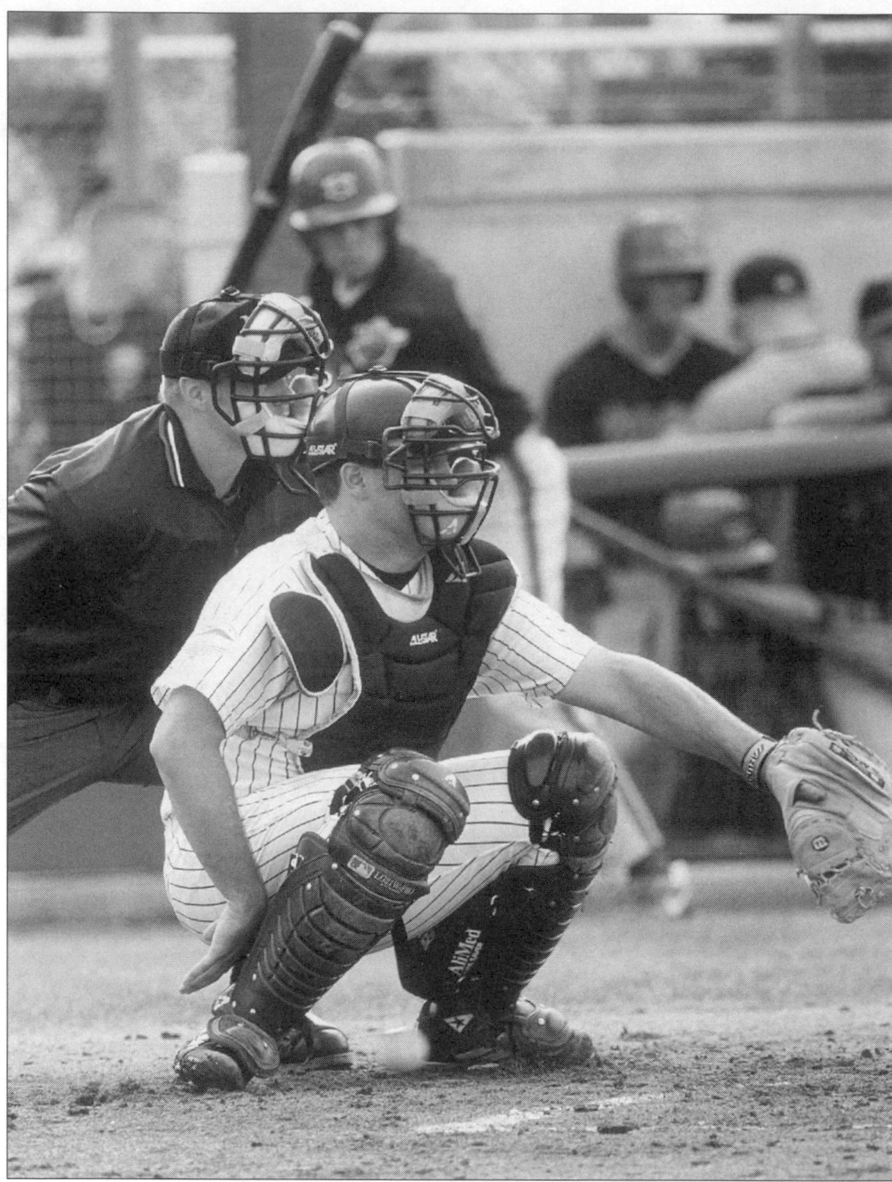

A good catcher knows how to get the most out of his pitcher.

be used, including its location. Similarly, with a runner on second, signs between the pitcher and catcher must use an indicator that keys the needed call.

Coaches use varying philosophies about calling the game. Legendary coaches like LSU's Skip Bertman and Southern California's Mike Gillespie, each of whom has won national championships, completely controlled calling this part of the game. University of Miami coach Jim Morris, with two recent national championships, has his pitching coach handle it.

Mike D'Andrea, at the high school and legion level, has used a mix of systems. He calls everything for a new catcher until he feels that the catcher is ready. Then he turns it over to the catcher and calls pitches only when the catcher looks to him for help.

Mike puts it this way: "You need to feel comfortable that the pitcher is throwing the ball you want for that count. Pitchers don't have time to think—they just have to learn to pitch." Mike feels that his catchers eventually learn what he wants pitchers to throw in all situations. Mike can then feel comfortable about having the catcher call the game.

Many others, including me, are uncomfortable calling the game from the dugout. I never felt that I had the same feel that the catcher had for what was happening—the bite on the curveball, the movement on the fastball, the spin on each pitch. Thus training the catcher to handle calling the game for the pitcher has been a priority for me. I reserve my participation for the occasional situational call, key pitch call, or for making the decision to change pitchers.

Unquestionably, communication between the pitcher and catcher is required if the catcher is to call the game. Again, the pregame meeting largely determines how the game will be handled and how each hitter will be pitched to. The coach involved should ensure that a clear strategy has been planned and agreed upon.

With the unfolding of the game, I've always favored having the catcher call the game, though with ongoing communication between the pitcher and catcher. The experienced pitcher should take advantage of his feel about his strengths. He should not hesitate to communicate his opinion by occasionally shaking off a call, expressing himself in a timeout in a crucial moment, or talking with the coach and catcher between innings. A good battery learns to communicate through game experience and appropriate encouragement and monitoring from coaches.

The coach must feel comfortable with the system he uses to call the game. He must make sure that each person involved understands his role in the communication process. The coach should establish definite guidelines for

- who makes the call,
- how it's communicated,
- the pitcher's prerogatives for changing the call, and
- what determines the ultimate call.

Coaches who favor controlling all calls must ensure that the communication of the battery follows specific guidelines regarding the call. Coaches who favor having the catcher call the game must ensure that the players clearly understand how the calling of the game is to be controlled and adjusted. An effective relationship must exist between pitcher and catcher.

A coach must be comfortable with the system and believe that it gets the best out of his pitching staff. I favor having the catcher call the game. I felt that it was my responsibility to help the catcher develop the feel and instinct for calling the game, but at key junctures I made situational calls.

Developing a Rhythm

Of all the pitchers I coached over the years, Bill Swift best epitomized the pitcher who always pitched with a rhythm. Swift himself points out that as a coach he now works "to get my pitcher on a good roll. You've got to get him in a rhythm—everything has to feel in sync."

Mike D'Andrea likes to get this flow going by having his pitchers "pitching fastballs down the middle, then to halves, then the thirds of the plate." D'Andrea reasons, "Not many high school pitchers have control, so I use this system not only to get them going but also to get them throwing to location. When they get to hitting the thirds of the plate it becomes a reward."

Jay Kemble counts on the six-step warm-up system we used for so long, which helps to develop the rhythm for the game for his pitchers. Finding a rhythm is a point of emphasis in the process and "especially for establishing and meeting the goal of coming out of the bullpen into the game with two pitches going for you."

Having a rhythm in a delivery reflects confidence, appropriate concentration on the target, and smooth execution of pitching mechanics and pitching flow for each pitch. The pitcher can't work a game the way it's been planned or throw a pitch where he wants to throw it without developing pitching flow or rhythm.

The ultimate test of the success of any rhythm is related to the degree to which a hitter can disrupt it. A pitcher with self-esteem, mound poise, and maturity counters the hitter's attempts to unsettle him with the appropriate handling of such tactics from the balance point in the delivery. We tell our pitchers to "get to the balance point, lift, and throw!" Experience in such situations helps the pitcher keep his poise and flow.

Mental Approach of Relievers

Like starters, relievers must have a positive mental approach. Relievers need to go into the game thinking positively and being unaffected by the pressure of the situation or a hot hitter. The key is to stay positive.

If the relief pitcher starts the inning, Swift suggests, "You come into the inning to get three outs—it's like the first inning." He adds, "The worst pressure is coming in with one or more men on. You have to be prepared. Above all, know your role when you come."

Again, the key for the pitcher is coming in ready to go with his real strengths—what will go well for him—throwing strikes. Swift reports that the key difference between getting ready as a starter and a reliever is "getting loose fast—starting to throw harder earlier, perhaps earlier than five minutes." He further emphasizes, "You've got to get your strengths ready fast and go out there with your best pitch."

How does one know when a pitcher is ready to come in? Even the bullpen coach or pitching coach has difficulty with that call. Swift says he observed many relievers saying they're ready before they really are. They need to learn to develop a rhythm faster, to get everything to feel in sync faster. Experience will help a pitcher learn how to do that. I've always asked that a pitcher indicate his readiness when he can at least come in with his best pitch.

Certainly at the amateur level, the reliever can be effective coming in from the bullpen with only his best pitch. The ideal is having the time to come in with his two best pitches in readiness.

Pitching strategy in working a game, particularly at the amateur level, depends on many factors: what the pitcher does best, the consistency with which he can do it, and the talent he has for getting it done. These considerations will determine the strategy involved.

The greater the tools, talent, and self-esteem for getting it done consistently, the more weapons and strategy can be involved. Most of us have to work with the strengths at hand and the confidence involved and then get the most we can to accomplish each victory.

We have lived with this philosophy for each game situation: "Have your pitchers, whether starters or relievers, as prepared as possible. Don't mess around with things that are not going well. Go with what's going well and with what will be good for you!"

Handling Pitchers

Steve Hertz

I would first like to say what an honor it is to be asked to contribute to this book and share some of my experiences and methods. I remember attending my first national baseball convention 25 years ago as if it were yesterday. I had the overwhelming feeling that I didn't know anything or anybody. I was intimidated, and I remember asking myself after every terrific presentation, "Why aren't we doing that?" Oh, what a feeling of inadequacy I had.

But as the years and conventions rolled by, I began to realize how this amazing body of knowledge worked. Baseball people share, they teach, they borrow, they learn, they give, and they care about the game, their teams, and the future of the game. What a wonderful environment! What I've learned and shared during those early conventions are a huge part of our program. The convention is the vehicle that each of us has relied on for support and growth.

Well, now my hair is gray, and the colleagues that I am proud to call my friends are too numerous to count. What I have learned from those battle-tested generals is who I am. So, in that realization I have settled my anxiety and insecurities, and, with their help, I feel centered enough to share on this grand stage.

Monitoring Pitchers' Arms

I've heard about, seen, and read about pitching systems, programs, structured workouts, and plans. This one. That one. Throw in a game, then do this on day one, this on day two, throw this many pitches on day three. Or, throw, throw, throw, more, more, more. But I've never seen a rigid system that's right for every pitcher.

All arms are different. All pitchers are different. All bodies are different. What works for one won't necessarily work, or work as well, for another. It seems to me that the health and recovery of an arm and body are extremely important, along with the strategic plan used to get hitters out. Success in these areas is driven by an individual's mental approach. A pitcher must be mentally tough enough to handle the adversity inherent in the position.

Coaches should teach their pitchers to learn their bodies and their arms. Among the many questions that should be answered are these:

- What is my best way to recover?
- How many days of rest do I need?
- Should I ice my arm?
- How much should I run?
- What kind of conditioning should I do?

Every pitcher and pitching coach should search for, learn, study, refine, and settle on a total-body workout involving prestretching, circulation through conditioning, a strength program that not only builds strength and muscle tone but also maintains it through a long season, and a poststretching routine.

I want our pitchers to be in complete control of their arms. I want them to make the decisions about their arms. I want our pitchers to rate their arms daily because they are the only ones that truly know how their arms feel. To create that self-knowledge, we have set up a rating system. I am so tired of asking pitchers, "How do you feel?" and hearing them reply, "I am fine." That kind of communication between a pitcher and a pitching coach is not precise. I want to know exactly how his arm feels. Moreover, I want him to know and learn how to evaluate and measure where his arm is on a day-to-day basis. Only then will he begin to make quality decisions for the health of his arm, and only then will the coach be sufficiently informed to manage each pitcher's ability.

Our rating system works this way. Every day after the pitching staff plays catch to their tolerance at the beginning of practice, my pitching coach, Chris Sheehan, will ask each of them to rate his arm on a scale of 1 to 10. (*Tolerance* refers to a personal feel for feeling loose and warmed up along with a sense of any degree of pain, discomfort, or fatigue.) On a scale of 1 to 10, 1 means he's lying on the ground unconscious and we're calling 911, and 10 means his arm feels perfect—no pain, maximum strength, and in midseason condition. If a pitcher is feeling OK, he'll usually give a 7 to 8 1/2 rating. In that case Coach Sheehan says nothing. If the rating is communicated as a 6 1/2 or lower, Coach will ask why and adjustments may be made. We list these ratings every day on a sheet with every pitcher's name on it so that we can learn and monitor how our activity taxes their arms.

With this data over an extended period, we get a great feel for who can do what. We can then make quality, healthful decisions about our pitchers' arms. This really helps us when we come to deciding our staff's different roles. Each pitcher must follow two rules with this rating system. The first is to be honest. The second is to be consistent. One pitcher's 8 may be different from another pitcher's 8, but the key for us is to learn each pitcher's arm and to manage it wisely. A daily rating determines what degree of throwing each pitcher will do on that particular day.

Overcoming the Velocity Complex

We try to sell our pitchers on embracing the craft of pitching—getting hitters out. Too often young pitchers equate velocity, strikeouts, and stuff with pitching. And all too often we run into young pitchers who have developed a velocity complex, which compels them to throw harder and harder in situations when adding effort to pitches only makes things worse. We try to have each pitcher find his tempo—a tempo that through evaluation and practice we have determined to be his proper physical effort. That tempo aids his mechanics and facilitates his repeating of those mechanics, thus promoting a pitching mentality rather than a throwing mentality.

A pitcher must be in touch with his tempo at three times—during practice and bullpens, during fatigue in a game, and under pressure in a game. If a pitcher has the ability to find his tempo at those three times and not add effort to his pitches, then he creates poise and proper thinking on the mound. Coaches and players should often discuss this pitching-versus-velocity approach to develop understanding, and pitchers should practice it daily for feel.

Determining Rotation

The following topics are considerations for choosing your starters and making quality rotation decisions.

Starter's Arsenal

Before the coach can see the complexion of his staff, he must allow enough time for the entire pitching staff to get in proper shape and then throw enough innings in enough outings. A coach has to be able to decide who his starters are. An important criterion in this decision is the pitcher's ability to get different types of hitters out. You have contact hitters, pure hitters, big power hitters, slap hitters, poor hitters, outstanding hitters, and you have to remember that the pitcher will see hitters from both sides of the plate. To sustain success as a starting pitcher throughout a diverse lineup, a pitcher must have command and must throw strikes. He must have three pitches:

1. a fastball that he can locate with accuracy,
2. a breaking ball that he can throw over the plate, and
3. a change-up so that he can change speeds.

Without those three pieces of the puzzle, a starting pitcher will have difficulty getting different kinds of hitters out during a five- to seven-inning outing. Other attributes that a starting pitcher must have include the right psychological makeup, the ability to pitch tough in tough situations, the ability to keep pitching, and the ability to be competitive.

Lead With Your Ace

If your pitching staff is fortunate enough to have a pitcher with at least three pitches, command of those pitches, and great competitiveness and mental makeup, then you have the luxury of having a true ace. I have always believed that you lead with your ace in the first game of every series. This does many things to help your ballclub. First, when your best pitcher is on the mound, your entire ballclub plays with more confidence. If you play with confidence in the initial game of the series, you'll have a better chance of establishing some momentum going through the series. Also, if you win the first game of the series, you have a better chance to win the series, which could lead to a championship. If you do not lead with your ace, you run the risk of sending an awkward, possibly negative message to your pitching staff and your entire team. To manage in a positive and successful way, coaches need to send solid, positive messages to their ballclubs.

Show Contrast with Your Starting Rotation

When determining a starting rotation, I feel it is important to keep in mind the differences between your pitchers. If you have a hard thrower, a soft lefty, and a guy who throws a split-finger fastball at midlevel velocity, you have the advantage of being able to show contrast to your opponent. For example, in the first game you lead with your ace, who has the best stuff, possibly a hard fastball. The second game you come back with a pitcher whose abilities contrast with the hard-throwing ace by going with your soft-throwing, crafty lefty. Then, in the third game, you show contrast again by throwing your hard-velocity right-hander. This sequence will tend to disrupt the timing of your opponent's hitters and quite possibly give you advantage.

Photo courtesy of Gonzaga University Baseball

Leading with your ace in the first game will help establish momentum going into the series.

Establish Roles

As a pitcher, I always wanted to know when I was going to pitch. Not knowing is difficult. So, having experienced that myself, I have made it a rule to let every pitcher on my staff know what his job was going to be for each game, but I always let them know that it could change if the situation changed. To know what their roles were going to be each day was helpful mentally to my pitchers. Over the years, pitchers have told me that they have appreciated knowing. We don't have anything to hide from them on that subject. I think that having this communication with your pitching staff is important.

Establishing roles is an extremely important part of the development of your pitching staff. A pitcher needs to know what his role is—starter, long reliever, middle reliever, setup guy, or closer. All those roles require different skills and different skill levels; establishing roles allows a pitching staff to create an identity, have a regimen, and develop a consistent work ethic to help each pitcher fill his particular role. Each of those roles has a different workload with respect to the daily routine. Your staff must embrace those roles mentally. A pitcher must not be disappointed if he is not a starter. He should perform the role he has to the best of his ability with an intellectual understanding that every championship ballclub has outstanding starting pitchers, outstanding long relievers, outstanding middle relievers, outstanding setup men, and an outstanding closer. The realization of that by your staff and their acceptance of their individual roles are vital to the success of your team and your pitching staff.

Advice on the Lineup

The following is a concise discussion regarding a coach's considerations in making out a starting lineup. You must consider this information in concert with your decision on the starting rotation and consequent moves in the bullpen.

Use What You Know

I like a set lineup so that my players begin to learn about themselves and the subtleties, the little characteristics, and the tiny ways in which the game changes. I like my players to know those things about one another. I think that shaking up a lineup is tough on a ballclub. I also believe that you pick your lineup based on the personnel you have. If you happen to have a team with a lot of power rather than a team with speed and contact hitters, you work with that situation to choose your starters and pick what type of offense you create. Out of that decision you make out your lineup.

The phrase I like to use is "You know what you know." You know if a particular hitter is a good contact hitter. You know if he has speed or not. You know if he is your best hitter. You know if he has power. You know if he is not a good contact hitter or if he strikes out a lot. You can't be duped into hoping that a player will do what you know he can't do or has not been able to do. Go with what you know he can do. Use what you know.

A good rule to follow in deciding who plays and when they play is to start your best all-around players and then make defensive replacements when ahead in the game and offensive replacements when behind. In developing a starting lineup, you can choose from among the following three philosophies:

1. Pitching-staff driven. If you have an outstanding pitching staff you may be well served by starting the best defensive lineup. If your pitching staff has shown a tendency to give up a lot of runs, you may be tempted to start a lineup that produces more runs.
2. Defense- or offense-oriented. In this case you always have an offense-oriented lineup and a defense-oriented lineup. It's your choice.
3. Best combo players, "baseball players." You choose the best all-around players, guys with the best combination of speed, hitting, and defense.

Put your players in situations where they can be successful. Ask them to do only what they are skilled enough to do. Let the complexion of your players' skills determine your offensive style and make your decisions in concert with those skills. Again, ask your players to do what they are good at.

Characteristics of One Through Nine Hitters

Your leadoff hitter is your offensive catalyst—not necessarily your fastest guy, but the guy who gets on base the most. Finding this guy and allowing him to do what he does best will be huge for your ballclub. He is the guy you hate to see come to bat against you. Give him your most at-bats and hit him leadoff.

To me, the number two guy is my second leadoff hitter. He should have many of the same characteristics because if your leadoff guy doesn't get on, you have a second chance to get things started. I want this guy up a lot and on base often.

Your number three hitter is your best offensive player. He is your pure hitter, the guy you want up when the game is on the line. He is your toughest out. He is the guy who is going to throw everybody on his back and carry you when it gets tough. He is Mr. Clutch.

Number four is your scariest guy. I like this guy to be big, strong, and imposing. I want the pitcher and catcher to see this guy come to the plate and say, "Oh, no. Be careful," because when a pitcher and a catcher think that way, I can't see how good things come of it. This guy should be your second best all-around offensive player and an aggressive swinger.

The number five hitter is a big swinger too, with imposing size. He should have excellent power so that the opponent pitches to the four hitter. It will help if this guy can run. Usually your four hitter doesn't possess much speed, and you don't want to bunch up a lot of guys who can't run. So if you have an imposing guy with good speed, hit him fifth.

At six and seven, I like to hit guys who can really run. I like to save one of my better hitters for the seven spot because this spot, for some reason, seems to come up in clutch situations often.

A good fastball hitter should be in the number eight hole because pitchers want to get that hitter out, especially with two outs so that the nine hitter leads off the next inning. So the eight hitter faces a lot of challenge situations. And I think pitchers and catchers tend to challenge with a fastball. I think the guy in the eight hole can be productive as a good fastball hitter.

The nine spot is where I put my best speed—a drag bunter, a base stealer, and also a fastball hitter who can take a pitch and walk. Some of the best innings I can recall had the nine hitter leading off the inning with a base on balls. Then here comes the top of your order.

Several other considerations are worthy in deciding whether players should start or where they should hit in the order:

- Good contact hitter
- Good speed
- Hitter who can make two-strike adjustments
- Power
- Mentally tough competitor
- Guy who is better with people on base
- Good bunters (drag or sacrifice)

When you platoon, you don't have a clear winner at a position, but you may have a left-handed hitter who hits right-handed pitchers pretty well, a right handed-hitter who hits left-handed pitchers pretty well, and both struggle in the opposite situation. The combination of these two can create one good starter.

Scouting Your Opponent and Implementing Data

To give your team an edge in a game, you should gather scouting data about the opponent and execute it effectively.

Anticipate Plays and Relay Information

I believe in scouting reports and knowing our opponent. We want to respect our opponent, do our homework, and know what task is in front of us. We spend an enormous amount of time gathering data on our opponents—their tendencies, their speed, their power, what plays they like to run, how they run the bases, and whether they bunt. All this data helps us anticipate what they are going to try to do. The hitters' tendencies, what they might do against particular pitchers, how we are going to play them, and how we are going to pitch them is all included in a scouting report that we hand to each player in a meeting before every series. We then try to execute that plan. As the series progresses, we may modify the plan from game to game or even from at-bat to at-bat. But the information gathered over a few games tends to repeat itself because players, pitchers, teams, and coaches tend to follow patterns. They may put the ball in the same place, struggle against the same pitch, be successful against the same pitch, and call the same plays in the same situations. Knowing this information going into a game is vital. I believe that anticipation is one step quicker than reaction. This whole process is anticipation, an educated anticipation.

Figures 11.1 and 11.2 are examples of how we acquire data that goes into our scouting report for an opponent. These and other reports are carefully kept and closely monitored so that we gain valuable information regarding that particular opponent. The compilation of this information in like situations prepares our players and, better yet, allows them to anticipate what the opponent will do. Incorporating this data into our alignments and decision making has won many games for us over the years.

Figure 11.1 is a chart kept by one of our pitchers who is probably not slated to pitch that day. He has a notebook with sheets titled "Opponent's Offensive Plays." He must carefully watch and accurately record all offensive plays put on by the opponent and fill in all the categories listed. Coaches tend to do the same things in the same situations with the same people. Coaches like to steal in certain situations and in certain counts. This data gives us a good feel for each coach's tendencies so that we can employ the proper defense against it.

Figure 11.2 is a composite that we have for each hitter we will face on a given day. As you can see, we have watched Mr. Miller for at least 16 at-bats and many pitches. In watching him and recording anything we see that is listed on the sheet, he has given us a lot of data with which to combat him.

The information gathered won't be useful unless we have a system to relay it. The following is an example of what we do with our center fielder, shortstop, second baseman, and catcher in communicating our information on each batter. Each of the four players has a piece of tape on his glove with our scouting information on it, one through nine. As each hitter comes to the plate, our catcher can refer to the scouting report on his glove about how to pitch the hitter. The second baseman and shortstop relay the appropriate information (tendency and speed) to their respective corners. The center fielder does likewise to his flanks in left and right field. The following is a system we have used to communicate this information:

Gonzaga University Baseball
Opponent's Offensive Plays

Opponent *Fresno State*
Date *1-14-02*

	Hitter	Runner(s)	Count	Outs	Score	Inning	Hit where
Hit-and-run	*Jones*	*Smith 1B*	*0-0*	*0*	*1-0*	*2*	*Right side*
	Bishop	*Harper 1B* *Evans 3B*	*2-1*	*1*	*2-0*	*4*	*Left side*
Steal	Runners	Base(s)	Count	Outs	Score	Inning	Steal type
	Smith	*1B*	*1-0*	*2*	*2-0*	*3*	*Straight*
	Rollins	*1B*	*2-2*	*2*	*3-2*	*6*	*Delay*
Bunt	Hitter	Runner	Count	Outs	Score	Inning	Where
	Harper	*Bishop 1B*	*0-0*	*0*	*4-2*	*5*	*Sac. right side*
	Bishop	*None*	*1-0*	*0*	*4-3*	*7*	*Drag left side*
	Edwards	*None*	*2-1*	*1*	*5-3*	*8*	*Drag left side*
	Jones	*Rollins 2B*	*2-0*	*0*	*5-3*	*8*	*Push right side*
1st and 3rd	Runner 1B steal?	Runner 3B steal?	Count	Outs	Score	Inning	What happened
	Smith-delay	*Evans on throw*	*2-2*	*2*	*3-2*	*6*	*Scored bad throw*
	Bishop-3/4	*Jones on C's throw*	*1-2*	*2*	*5-3*	*8*	*Out at plate SS-C*

FIGURE 11.1 Chart used to record the opponent's offensive plays. This data goes into a scouting report for an opponent.

Opponent Scouting Report – Hitter

Team *UC Irvine* Date *1-28-02*

Number *14* Player *Miller*

Bats: R / (L) / S Runs: A- / A / (A+) / A++ Steals: (Yes) / No

Tendancy: *PM-5* Power: *Ave* Contact: *Good*

Sac: (Yes) / No Push: Yes / (No) Drag: (Yes) / No Hit-and-run: (Yes) / No

Hitter Strengths and Weaknesses

Strengths	Weaknesses
Pitch strength: *FB*	Pitch weakness: *LH-breaking ball and change*
Location strength: *Middle-in*	Location weakness: *Away, up*
First-pitch hitter: (Yes) / No *6/16*	Pitches swung through: *LH-BB, RH-change*
Two-strike adjustments: (Yes) / No	Pitches chased: *FB, LH-BB, RH-CH*
Hit-by-pitch: (Yes) / No	Locations chased: *Up, down and away*
Box location: *Up and on dish*	

	At-bat	Count	
Vs RHP	1. *1B*	*0-0*	*FB in*
	2. *2B*	*1-0*	*FB mid*
	3. *K*	*3-2*	*FB up*
	4. *F-8*	*1-2*	*BB mid*
	5. *3U*	*0-0*	*CH mid*
	6. *HR*	*0-0*	*FB mid*
	7. *4-3*	*2-0*	*CH away*
	8. *1B*	*0-0*	*FB in*
	9. *1B*	*3-1*	*FB mid*
	10. *F-6*	*1-0*	*CH away*
	11. *HBP*	*1-1*	*FB in*
	12. *F-8*	*0-0*	*CH mid*
Vs LHP	13. *5-3 drag*	*0-0*	*CH away*
	14. *4-3*	*2-2*	*BB away*
	15. *K*	*1-2*	*BB away*
	16. *BB*	*3-2*	*FB up*

FIGURE 11.2 Sample scouting report on opposing hitter.

	Right-handed hitters	Left-handed hitters
P = pull	1. below-average power	4. below-average power
M = middle	2. average power	5. average power
O = opposite	3. good power	6. good power

If a guy is a P-3, he pulls everything with good power. If a guy is a PM-2, he is pull on the ground and middle in the air with average power.

We also want to communicate each hitter's speed, which is a significant variable in solid infield play. We communicate the information by the following:

A++	Great speed
A+	Good speed
A	Average speed
A–	Poor speed

The last factor we need to communicate on each hitter is how we are going to pitch him and where his location weakness is.

Reg.	Pitch this hitter "regular" (get ahead and go with pitcher's strength)
Chal.	Pitching challenge (go right at him with mostly fastballs)
Back	Pitch him backward (fastballs when ahead, other pitches when behind)
Jam	Location weakness is inside
Away	Location weakness is outside
Up	Location weakness is up in the zone

Putting all this information together, here is an example of what the tape on our fielders' gloves looks like for the opponent's first hitter indicated by uniform number:

MO-5 A++ Reg. A

This means that the hitter hits middle on the ground and opposite in the air, is left-handed with average power, and has great speed. We will pitch him regular, and his location weakness is away.

Calling pitches when you're sitting with the scouting report in front of you tells you that a hitter likes a certain pitch, has a weakness in a specific location, a strength in another location, chases a particular pitch, and hits another pitch well. Having all that data is a powerful advantage, but it can also be dangerous.

The pitcher can make two kinds of mistakes. A physical mistake is simply missing the intended location. A decision mistake is throwing the wrong pitch in the wrong area. We as coaches tend to want the responsibility of calling the type of pitch and its location to reduce the frequency of decision mistakes. When we call the pitches, however, we eliminate one of the most natural exchanges and workings in the game, the pitcher-catcher relationship. We take away the catcher's feeling and understanding for how to get a particular hitter out by recalling what he did the last two times at bat and remembering the general scouting report on the hitter's weaknesses and strengths.

But we often have catchers who do not have the experience to couple the pitcher's strengths with the feel for getting the hitter out in a given situation. In those circumstances we call key pitches or even every pitch.

All of us have had a veteran catcher who has a great feel for getting hitters out. In that case we like to spoon-feed the pitcher and catcher before the ballgame and between innings with our scouting reports. Then we let them go with it and make the calls.

Be Careful Not to Tip Pitches

Programs and coaches are becoming increasingly adept at picking up pitches or signs from the coach as he relays them to the catcher, from the catcher as he relays them to the pitcher, or from the pitcher who makes some change in mechanics as or before he delivers the pitch. My teams have lost games because the coach, catcher, or pitcher has tipped our pitches or the location. That occurrence has led to a breakdown in our pitching effectiveness or our ability to get hitters out consistently.

How do you know when your opponent has your pitches or location? One way is to listen to the talk that comes from first-base coach, third-base coach, or on-deck hitter, or some consistent name, number, first name, last name, or phrase from the dugout. Usually the catcher is most able to pick up that kind of oral sign. This occurrence would cause you to look closely at where you are tipping and change your signs and signals.

Another way to figure out if the opponent is intercepting signs is to watch how their hitters swing at certain pitches. Do they seem to be taking great swings on every fastball? You can tell this is happening when hitters make a total physical commitment to the swing. Are they letting all the off-speed and breaking balls go? Do they seem to have great balance and take those pitches as though they know what's coming? What do their swings look like? If you add these things up, you will have an indication of whether a team has your pitches or signs.

Therefore, when deciding whether to call pitches or to call just a few key pitches, you should test your ability to give signs without interception. Have someone try to pick up your signs before you initiate a system and call pitches in games. Imagine how devastating it could be when you think you are doing something to promote getting hitters out but instead you are allowing the hitters to know exactly what's coming. Again, more programs are making sign stealing a large part of their offensive approach and are good at picking up opponents' pitches and locations.

To help your pitchers learn not to tip pitches, have a number of your players not in the game try to pick pitches from each of your pitchers. A teammate may spot something that the pitcher should correct to prevent tipping his pitches from the mound.

Opponents also try to pick pitches from your catcher. Be sure that your catcher is clean from both sides when giving pitches. Be sure his arm does not move when giving signals to the pitcher. Also, have two or three pitch routines that you can use with runners at second base. To make sure that your catcher is clean from tipping, use your intrasquad scrimmages to try to pick up signs from your catcher.

When calling pitches from the dugout, we like to use at least two people giving signs at the same time, thereby causing twice the work if someone wants to try to pick up our pitches. We will also do that even if the catcher is calling his own game to cause a little confusion on the other side of the field.

Some teams will act as though they have your pitches even if they don't in an effort to confuse you and cause your pitcher, catcher, and coaches to get away from their natural thinking process, disrupt your pitcher's tempo, and create a little paranoia. This ploy can be effective in disrupting what the pitcher, catcher, and coach are trying to do to get a hitter out.

Control Misses

In every ballgame a pitcher throws pitches that he did not intend to throw. He misses the location or the strike zone. A pitcher must recognize that he will often miss during a ballgame. We strongly believe that pitchers should work to refine their pitching to the point where they control their misses. Their failure to do this may be a major factor in winning or losing ballgames. Missing out of the zone at the right time and missing toward the middle of the plate at the right time can be the key to winning.

To increase concentration on good misses and controlled misses, we have a touch system that the catcher uses before each pitch or each set of pitches. This system is determined by each situation and more specifically by the count. For instance, on the first pitch to a hitter the catcher will touch the front of his mask. This tells the pitcher to miss toward the center of the plate if he misses the glove. He still may go for the outer half or inner half of the plate and throw to the glove, but should he miss the glove he'll miss toward the center of the plate for a strike. He will then be ahead in the count. He wants to avoid throwing an 0-0 pitch on the outer half and miss away to make the count 1-0.

The miss toward the center of the plate will remain the goal until the count becomes either 0-2 or 1-2. At that point the catcher will change the focus to miss outside the location or glove. The touch by the catcher will be on the side of the mask to tell the pitcher to miss outside if he misses the glove. The goal is to expand the plate and induce the hitter who is down in the count to swing at a pitcher's pitch. We work on this technique during bullpens and then apply it in ballgames. This system is a way of showing command with both strikes and misses. The pitcher who controls his misses limits the potential damage when he misses the target.

Three Plans for Getting a Hitter Out

The pitcher must have a plan to get the hitter out as he steps to the plate. We ask our pitcher to focus on three such plans:

1. Get ahead and expand the plate.
2. Get behind and pitch backward.
3. Challenge him, go right after him, and invite contact.

As I mentioned earlier, the situation may dictate which of these plans a pitcher will use. But going after a hitter without a plan is dangerous. Too often a pitcher's plan will be to get ahead of the hitter with a first-pitch strike, stay ahead, and then get the hitter out. When that plan blows up and the pitcher finds himself behind, he must realize that an equally powerful and productive way to get the hitter out is to pitch backward, which is simply to throw pitches other than fastballs in fastball counts.

Getting ahead of a hitter is powerful because the pitcher is able to throw pitches out of the zone and induce the hitter to chase them while maintaining control of the count. Challenging hitters, going right after them, can be as powerful as the other two because just getting base hits is difficult. Any pitcher who can throw strikes will induce his opponents to put the ball in play, which will produce many outs. In the right situation, under the right score, challenging hitters is an outstanding plan.

Three Things Every Pitcher Should Know

The last time the ABCA convention was in Atlanta I had the chance to listen to Kevin Brown give a wonderful clinic on some of the things that he uses. I must give credit to him. He said that every pitcher should know three things before going up against an opponent:

1. Know who in a ballclub is hot and is swinging the bat well so that he can pitch them a little bit differently than he does the other hitters.

2. Know who runs, has good speed, and will steal bases. This knowledge is key to setting his break time when he is in his stretch and holding certain runners close. He should know who to hold close and who is less of a concern.
3. Know who the first-pitch swingers are. The pitcher can be hurt by a hitter who makes his living by swinging at first pitches in the strike zone. If the hitter picks the right pitch and the pitcher is simply trying to get ahead, the result can be disastrous. So every pitcher should know who the first-pitch swingers are.

Maximizing the Stuff Available

Each of our pitchers has accepted and employed the following components to maximize his stuff as part of his plan for getting a hitter out. I believe that every great pitcher possesses these elements.

Two-Against-One Mentality

In every team sport in which a double team may occur, such as in basketball when two players guard a player with the ball, one side has an obvious physical and mental advantage. In football when two players decide to double team a lineman or double cover a receiver, they have the same obvious physical and mental advantage. We like to turn that two-against-one mentality over to our pitcher and catcher to get the hitter out. In a sense we have that same mental and physical advantage. We want our pitchers to use that mental advantage by hooking up with the catcher to get a hitter out.

The catcher and pitcher decide what pitch they will use. They also decide where the pitcher will throw the pitch. They have the advantage of deciding to deceive through different speeds, pitch selection, and approach. What a decided advantage that is. And when the catcher makes his pitcher's success his own, you truly have a two-against-one advantage on every hitter. Your pitcher and catcher must understand this advantage. When you have this, you can have that specially pitched game. Without question, we are remiss as coaches if we fail to sell our pitching staff and catchers on this obvious advantage.

Chart BP for Confidence

Every year coaches have pitchers who lack confidence. Lack of self-assurance will be a constant enemy. If a pitcher pitches with confidence, he will pitch better. He will execute better. As in hitting, confidence might be the most vital factor for success. In that regard, pitchers need to remember and recognize how difficult it is to get base hits and what a great advantage they have by having eight players behind them making plays.

Pitchers have a great advantage even if they don't have their great stuff. If a pitcher invites contact he has a great chance to get many hitters out. To make sure that our pitchers realize how difficult it is to get hits, we have them chart batting practice. We give the pitcher a clipboard, and they list the at-bats, the number of balls put in play, and how many hits and outs occur. What they find is that even with a batting-practice pitcher throwing all fastballs right down the can at 70 to 75 miles per hour, with no pressure on the batter, the pitcher is seeing 50 to 60 percent outs. When the pitcher adds breaking balls and off-speed pitches and knows the hitter's weaknesses, that percentage increases dramatically. When pitchers see that, they can regain the confidence they may have lost. When we have someone struggling, my pitching coach might go to the mound and simply remind the pitcher how difficult it is to get base hits even in batting practice.

Power of the Count

The count is a powerful entity in getting the hitter out. The count itself can destroy the hitter's confidence. The hitter thinks much differently at 2-0 than he does at 0-2. Studies of how the count affects hitting show overwhelmingly how low batting averages are at 0-1, 0-2, 1-2, and even 2-2 as opposed to 1-0, 2-0, 2-1, and 3-1. The pitcher need not rely on just surviving the hitter or waiting for the hitter to make an out. A pitcher's mental ability to use the power of the count can be a powerful, even devastating, tool in his success.

First-Pitch Strike

I have often heard knowledgeable pitching coaches ask the question, "What is the best pitch in baseball?" And they answer, "The strike." We would like to go one step further and say that the best pitch in getting the hitter out is the first-pitch strike. By getting the first-pitch strike, the pitcher has many ways to go about getting the hitter out. The pitcher becomes the boss in getting the count further in his favor and putting the hitter at a decisive disadvantage.

We feel that when everything in pitching boils down, the most important factor in winning a baseball game is the pitcher's ability to throw first-pitch strikes and get first-pitch outs. But the pitcher cannot acquire this skill simply by the coach's suggesting it or demanding it. The coach must emphasize it and have the pitcher work on in it in his daily routine. We have built charting of first-pitch strikes into our flat-ground work, our pitcher catch, and our bullpens. Throwing first-pitch strikes is as much a mental skill as a physical skill. We work on it daily. We even have a catcher signal that the catcher gives to the pitcher before the pitch signal to get the pitcher's mind focused on the first-pitch strike.

When working at this skill, pitchers often become tight. They want to execute it so badly that they go backward for a time. I believe we must accept this phase. Eventually the pitcher will learn the skill and improve upon it. I believe that the first-pitch strike percentage is directly correlated with ERA and winning percentage.

Maintain Mental Focus in Three Key Situations

Years ago I had the pleasure of listening to Coach Skip Bertman at LSU talk about catching. In that presentation he talked about patterns that his catcher would give their pitchers, and I thought his plan was outstanding. We employed it in our program with some modifications. We want our catcher to communicate three patterns to our pitchers with a simple touch.

The first pattern is to signify to our pitcher that the leadoff hitter is the most important hitter of the inning. All mental effort must go into retiring this hitter. We feel that the ability to get leadoff hitters out is a key factor in limiting the opponent's runs. An offense will have difficulty scoring with one out and no one on. We believe that focusing on the leadoff hitter is a mental skill attained through emphasis and practice daily. So we try to eliminate the laziness or passiveness of pitchers who start an inning without complete, dialed-in focus.

We use a second pattern when runners are on base or things are not going well. We feel that how the pitcher pitches in this situation is one of the keys to success. When bad things are happening, I want my pitchers to pitch at their best. The pitcher may have to deal with a bad call or two, an error, or the disappointment of having given up hits and runs, but at this time he must have great focus, concentration, and resolve. Otherwise, the game can unwind quickly and fall apart. But should he pitch at his best when times are tough, you have a pitcher who can prevail in difficult situations.

We call the third pattern two-out dial-in. In this pattern we recognize that after we attain the second out, we become this incredible, huge force. We envision this bigger-than-life entity shoving the door closed. If the pitcher can achieve this kind of mental focus, he has a powerful tool. After they get that second out, pitchers all too often become lazy, lose their focus, and allow an inning to get started. Instead, they should imagine a huge, powerful entity slamming the door on the inning.

Work 75 Percent From the Stretch

When working in the bullpen we have our pitchers work 75 percent from the stretch. We do this because the most important pitches of the game of-

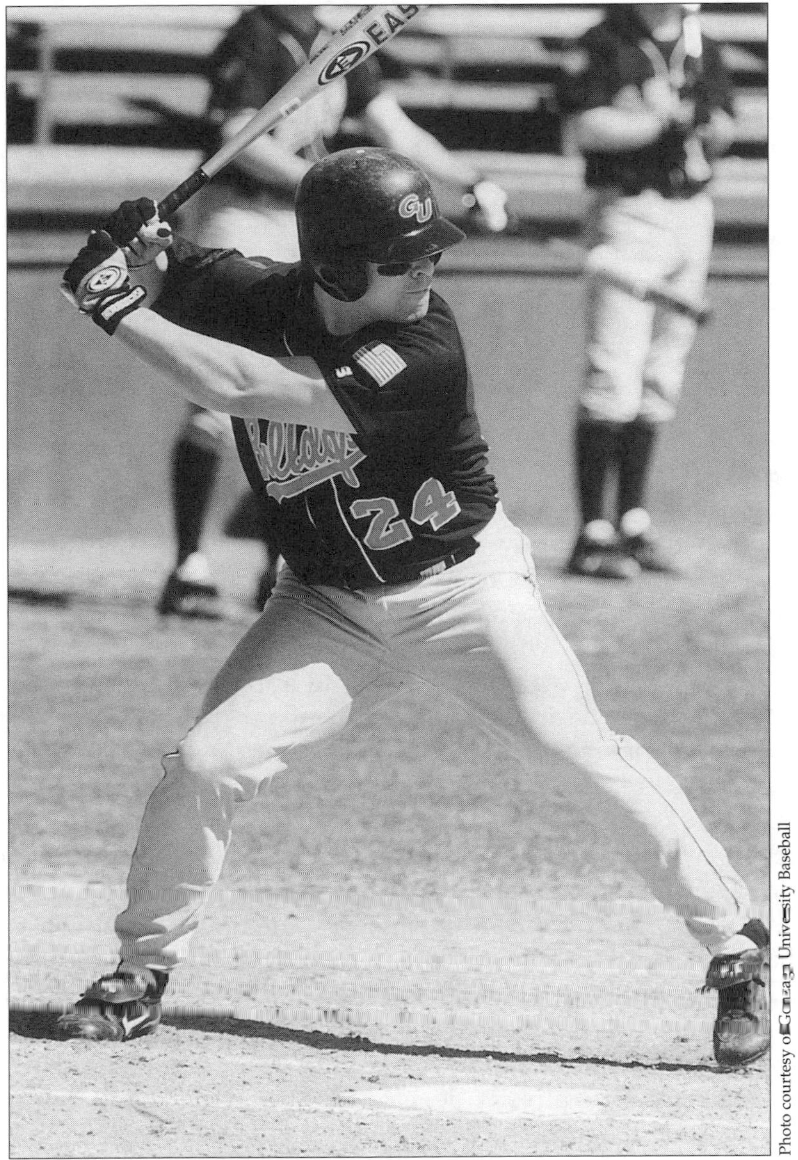

Photo courtesy of Gonzaga University Baseball

The ability to get leadoff hitters out is a key factor in limiting the opponent's runs.

ten occur from the stretch position. Many pitchers work more from the windup than they do from the stretch because they start an inning from the windup. But a pitcher could throw one pitch from the windup to start an inning, have the hitter get on base, and then throw the rest of the inning from the stretch. So we use our 75 percent rule not only in practice and bullpens but also between innings. The pitcher is then confident of his preparation for those tough situations with runners on base.

Never Compromise Your Stuff

One of the most common negative situations for a pitcher is temporary loss of control or command. We believe in allowing the body to do what it knows how to do, so the right response for the pitcher in those situations is to step off the mound, allow his mind to get right, and then not compromise his stuff to throw a strike. When control problems arise, the pitcher's first reaction is often to aim or guide the ball. He thus becomes tentative with the arm, loses command altogether, and loses his stuff. Instead, we want the pitcher to get out of the way and allow his body to do what it knows how to do by staying free, easy, and loose. He should get right mentally, dial up, lock on to his target, and let it rip.

Three-Ball Level

Have you ever noticed how many strikes a pitcher throws after he gets behind 2-0, 3-0, 3-1, or 3-2? On any three-ball count an enormous number of strikes occur. What's happening here, I believe, is a lack of focus at the beginning of an at-bat. Then, when the pitcher gets behind, he shifts into a have-to mode, which is a powerful mental approach. But when a pitcher gets behind 3-1 or 3-2 and then starts pouring on strikes that get fouled off, he has no room for error and is simply surviving, just throwing strikes, and the hitter is at a great advantage. In addition, ball four on a close pitch often ensues.

Pitchers who throw strikes have this mentality flipped around the opposite way. They shift into a have-to mode at 0-0. They are at their best at the front end of an at-bat and find themselves ahead of almost every hitter. I once had a player who showed me after a couple outings that he had lazy focus early. He would get behind and then throw an enormous number of strikes when he got to three balls. It was uncanny. So I just sat down with him and said, "You know, if you can flip that around and use that survival technique that you've already developed at three balls and get three-ball level focus at the beginning of every hitter, you could turn your pitching completely around." Well, eight consecutive complete games followed, and this young pitcher had obviously turned his fortunes around. Since then we've had marked success with proposing that three-ball level mentality to some pitchers. They understand it and are able to use it to great advantage.

Using the Bullpen

Few successful baseball teams, especially at the college level and above, do not possess a varied and productive bullpen. I have often felt that having a solid middle guy, a good setup man, and a dominant closer are three pieces of the championship puzzle. One might argue that those three roles have more effect on the outcome of games than the three starters. Regardless, everything revolves around your pitching, and a huge part of that has to do with your bullpen organization and how efficiently your relievers pitch when they enter the game.

What You Emphasize Is What You Will Be Good At

I feel that the reliever's approach as he enters the game will dictate his initial effectiveness. We key on the first hitter. If your reliever, whether middle man, setup man, or closer, retires the first batter, you're in business. So we practice that.

I believe that you will be good at whatever you emphasize, teach, and practice routinely. The points in a game when you make pitching changes are critical. So being outstanding at getting that first hitter out is huge. We must have an extremely organized bullpen routine—no nonsense, with tremendous mental preparation and energy. At first it is just a great act, but with success it quickly turns to a genuine big-time approach. I tell our relievers that they are the cavalry coming to save the day, William Wallace from *Braveheart* storming across the Highlands, or Maximus from *Gladiator* upholding his family's pride. I think they like that image, and it helps them embrace their roles. We all know that most pitchers want to be starters. Somehow, we need to create an environment in which they relish their roles. Let's face it; they will go out there and pitch whenever and wherever we tell them to, and they will salute. But I believe that saluting will get you second place. When they embrace pitching with their hearts, you will get first place.

It's a Serious Place

We always have a pitching coach in the bullpen directing the plan, the routine, and the approach. Probably the most important ingredient in the bullpen process is the catcher. In our program we create a great bullpen catcher. He must have tremendous character, great energy, be a powerful motivator, and genuinely care for each pitcher and how he gets ready for his first hitter. If we have a bullpen catcher of that quality, we are bound to pitch well all year.

Know Your Pitchers and Manage

As a head coach, I will put in my two cents on a pitching change, but I leave the ultimate decisions to my pitching coach because he knows the pitchers best. He works with them daily and is in touch with their strengths and weaknesses, both physically and mentally. He is the boss, and I want all the pitchers to know that. Only then will he have the power to influence them as he needs to.

Focus 12 and Scripted 2

I am adamant about that first hitter, or in a starter's case, that first inning, which is often an ugly monster to our starters. I want them to get ready, take a two-minute break, and then come back and throw what we call our focus 12. In a sense, we want them to throw that first inning in the pen. We have a hitter stand in for each of the first three hitters on the appropriate side of the plate (for example, left, right, right). Our starter throws all four of his pitches to each hitter, locations and all. Staying with our 75 percent rule, the pitcher throws to the first hitter from the windup and the next two from the stretch. He finishes by going back to the first hitter from the windup to throw his scripted 2, the first two pitches and locations that he is going to throw to that first and most important hitter.

Pitching is a craft, and in handling pitchers we must be craftsmen. Search, research, learn, adjust, modify, and be willing to change and improve. Work hard to learn each of your pitchers, remembering that each of them is different. How you handle your pitchers, how you manage them, can be the most important factor to their improvement and success.

One last piece of advice: don't miss the richness and pride of striving to get there. The bullpens, the daily work, the anticipation of getting better are the true joys of the craft. Working hard with young pitchers, whether the dreams come true or not, is beautiful and just might be the real enjoyment of the game. Don't miss that process. Value and execute the process, and let the outcome take care of itself. Let *them* pitch.

PART III

Defense

12

Setting the Lineup: Positions 2 Through 9

Jim Morris

This chapter describes my philosophy behind establishing an optimum lineup. Setting a defensive lineup in positions 2 through 9 is a matter of putting together position players who will give you the best chance to get three outs each inning without giving the other team any extra outs by making errors or mistakes. If you do that, you are going to get back in the dugout quickly so that you can try to score some runs, which is the only way you can win the game.

You must have infielders who are successful defensively. Having quick, acrobatic infielders who make phenomenal plays is great, but it is more important to have infielders who can consistently make the routine plays, who are in the right position for *this* pitcher, *this* hitter, and *this* situation, and who then know what to do when the ball is hit.

The one thing that really carries over defensively and offensively is speed and quickness. People say that speed never goes into a slump. Speed can also make up for mistakes you make defensively. As always, I feel the number-one thing is to be strong up the middle.

Keep in mind that you need to get offense out of your infielders, especially at first and third base. I want my defense on the corners to be as good as possible, but the first and third basemen must drive in runs. You cannot be a starter for me without offensive production, although I may make late-inning defensive replacements. Earl Weaver, the great manager of the Baltimore Orioles, was a strong advocate of having as many strong hitters in the lineup as possible, and this philosophy gave him several championships.

This is not to say that the "Earl of Baltimore" did not believe in having good defensive players, but he did feel that one couldn't sacrifice offensive strength too much to have defensive strength. "After all," said Earl, "a player may only get one or two tough plays a game on defense, but he is going to get four at-bats every day." Of course, in a perfect world, we would have great defense and great offense at all eight positions.

Good infielders are developed through hard work. I want our infielders to take 100 ground balls daily and, just as important, make 100 throws daily. Few infielders carry out this plan, but I want that to be their goal. If their arms become tired after a lot of throws and the throws to first base feel too long, they can throw to second base or field slow rollers. Although hard work is vital for infielders to develop the skills they need, hard work alone is not enough. They must work hard at specific skills to develop defensive skills properly. One often sees infielders taking a lot of ground balls in practice, but a careful examination of their work habits might show that they are just going through the motions and not accomplishing anything of substance. To develop good skills, a player must work at a specific skill! I have never had a great infielder who did not take great pride in his defense and work ethic.

Coaches always talk about players working hard in practice, and certainly that is a major factor in the development of a baseball player's skills. But just working hard is not the answer to skill development. Many players will work hard for two or three hours in a practice session and not improve their skills at all. A player may come in after practice covered with sweat and with his head down on his chest with fatigue, but if you ask him what he accomplished during practice, he'll shrug and say, "I worked hard out there! Just look at how tired I am!" That is an example of a player working hard but not working to improve on a specific skill!

For example, if a middle infielder has trouble turning the double play because his steps around the bag are too long, causing him to take too much time to throw the ball, he can work on double plays for hours, but he won't improve his skill unless he works specifically on shortening his steps around the base. Another example might be an infielder who has problems catching ground balls because he holds his glove too high. He may field ground balls for a month, but he will not improve his fielding skills until he makes the specific correction in his execution by getting his glove lower.

Positioning Infielders

All infielders should know where to line up in any situation. Under normal conditions, infielders should move as a group, no matter if the batter is a pull hitter or a hitter who hits the opposite way. One (or more) of the infielders should take charge and make sure that all the infielders are alert to the signals from the dugout about positioning. Good defensive players should constantly talk to one another about the various aspects of the game that relate to good positioning. They should make sure that everyone is aware of the proper positioning for the particular situation, and all four infielders must constantly keep an eye on the coach in the dugout who is responsible for their positioning.

One of the first things the coach should consider in establishing the positioning of his infielders is the type of pitcher he has going for him in that game. If he has a hard-throwing pitcher on the mound, a higher percentage of balls should be hit to the opposite field than would be the case with a pitcher who does not throw with as much velocity. With a hard thrower pitching, the coach might want to adjust his infield (and outfield) positioning a bit more toward the opposite field than normal.

Another factor that can affect general positioning is the condition of the playing field. If the infield is damp and somewhat soft, or if the grass is high, the infielders might need to be a bit closer to the plate than normal because more slow ground balls will probably be hit in that game. Conversely, if the infield is dry and hard, infielders might play a bit deeper than normal because the ball will reach them more quickly than normal and thus affect their range.

The coach must establish a system that can have the players in a consistent position, depending on the hitter, the pitcher, the playing conditions, and the situation of the game. There are four depths in infield positioning, with variations that depend on factors that develop in the game and the abilities of the players involved, on both offense and defense. The coaches in the dugout need to control the positioning of infielders, and players must constantly look into the dugout for signals for positioning. The coach responsible for positioning should devise a series of signals that make it easy for the players to understand what position is called for in any situation. Coaches can use any number of gestures or movements to direct their players, and although you want signals that will not be too obvious to your opponent, the system must be simple enough that your players can easily understand positioning changes you make from one hitter to the next, or even from one pitch to the next.

One-Depth Infield Positioning

The following is the procedure for what I refer to as one-depth infield positioning when no one is on base and the infielders are back (figure 12.1). This could be called the standard or starting infield defensive position. Every variation of infield positioning works off this one, so it is vital that all the infielders pay careful attention to it to make sure they are well aware of where they should be in this situation.

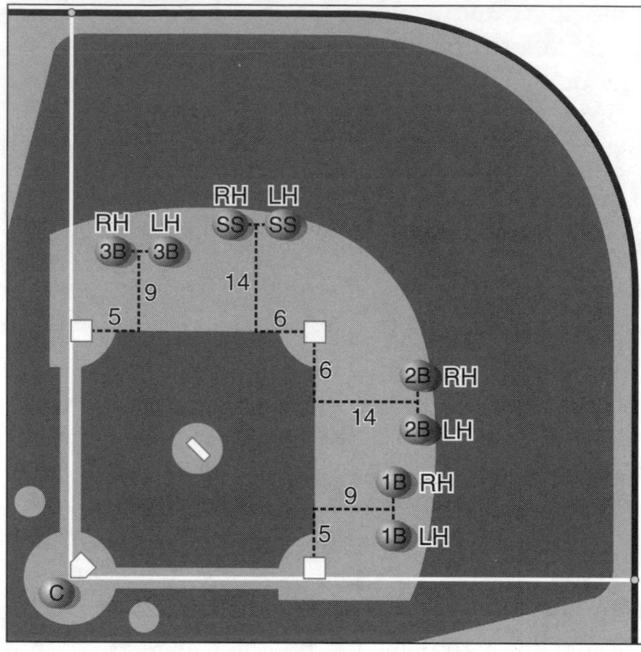

FIGURE 12.1 One-depth infield positioning.

- The first baseman and third baseman are 5 steps off the base toward second base and 9 steps deep.
- The shortstop is 6 steps off second base toward third base and 14 steps deep.
- The second baseman is 6 steps off second base toward first base and 14 steps deep.
- For a left-handed hitter, the infielders move 2 steps to their left, and for a right-handed hitter they move 2 steps to the right. This movement of 2 steps is consistent for one-, two-, three-, and four-depth positioning.

Two-Depth Infield Positioning

Two-depth infield positioning (figure 12.2) is double-play depth, so it will require some shortening up by all the infielders, especially the middle infielders. In a double-play situation, the middle infielder must break hard to get to the base under control so that he can pivot smoothly and according to the location of the throw. To do this he must be closer to the base in the starting position.

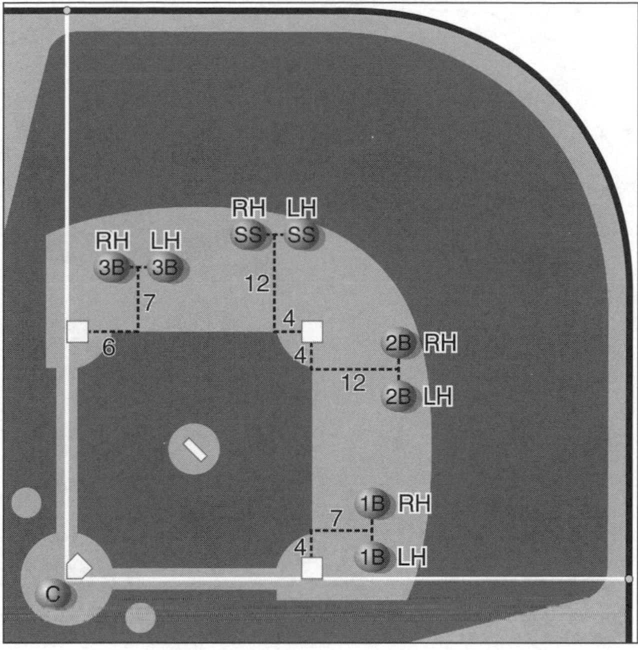

FIGURE 12.2 Two-depth infield positioning.

- Double-play depth for the first baseman and third baseman is up two steps and over one step from the one-depth starting position.
- The middle infielders are up two steps and over two steps toward second base from the one-depth position.

Three-Depth Infield Positioning

When a runner is on third base with no outs and the coach of the defensive team is confident that the other coach will play conservatively on a ground ball to the infield (following one of the unwritten rules of baseball strategy: don't make the first out of the inning at home plate), the defense should come in enough so that the runner will not try to score on a ground ball. At the same time they must understand that the farther in they are, the less range they have on a ground ball. In this situation the infielders should simply position themselves back two or three steps from the base line where they can accomplish the twin goals of keeping the runner from scoring on a ground ball yet have decent range on a ground ball. This is referred to as the three-depth position (figure 12.3).

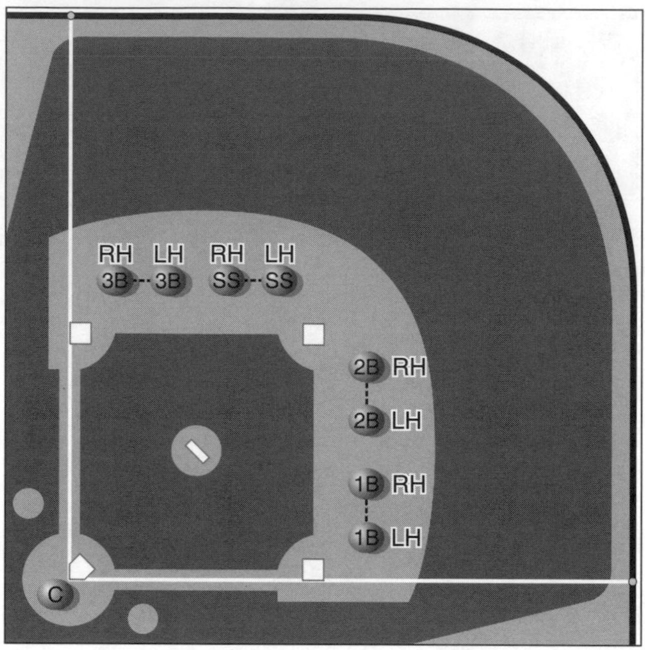

FIGURE 12.3 Three-depth infield positioning.

Four-Depth Infield Positioning

When a runner is on third base with one out and the game situation suggests that the base runner will try to score on any ground ball to the infield, all the infielders should be about even with the base line so that they can throw out a base runner at the plate trying to score. The infielders would walk forward from the one-depth position to a position even with the base line to reach the four-depth position (figure 12.4).

Some coaches like to add a little wrinkle to the four-depth position. Doing this is acceptable if it does not get too far away from the normal four-depth position. In this method, each infielder comes in toward the base line, but not all play at the same depth. They position themselves according to arm strength. For example, if the second baseman and first baseman each has just an adequate arm, they would be even with the baseline. If the third baseman has good arm strength, he might be a step behind the base line, and if the shortstop has a great arm, he might be a step and a half or two steps behind the base line. This method of using the four-depth position allows all four infielders to be able to throw out the runner at the plate on a normal ground ball, and it allows the infielders with stronger throwing arms to cover a little more ground. We must caution, however, that infielders should not position themselves anywhere they want; some players have an

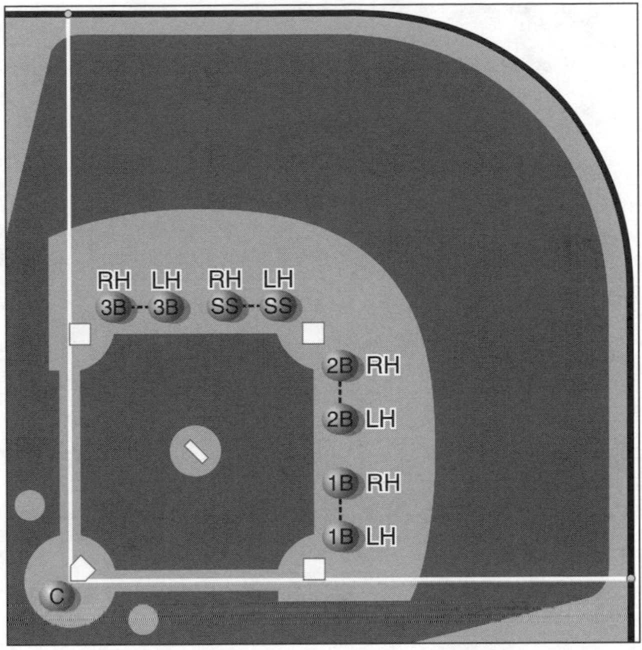

FIGURE 12.4 Four-depth infield positioning.

exaggerated opinion of their arm strength and may want to play deeper than advisable, so the coach must continue to control the positioning of the infielders.

The coach can simply signal one, two, three, or four depth, and the infielders will know where to play. The coach also needs to be able to move the infielders from pull to opposite way with a signal from the bench:

- Slight pull from the initial starting position is two steps, and dead pull is four steps. All infielders move as a group.
- Slight opposite is two steps, and dead opposite is four steps for the entire infield. Infielders should remember that the starting position for a right-hand hitter is different from the starting position for a left-hand hitter.

Scouting opponents and having a good idea where they are most likely to hit the ball is a tremendous advantage for any baseball team. Almost every baseball team will do some scouting of their opponents, with the extent of scouting generally dependent on the travel budget and the number of coaches available to watch games. But doing a good job of scouting and having good information about your opponents will pay off only if you have your defense aligned properly. Knowing the types of hitters on the opposing team can be helpful in a general way in the positioning of your

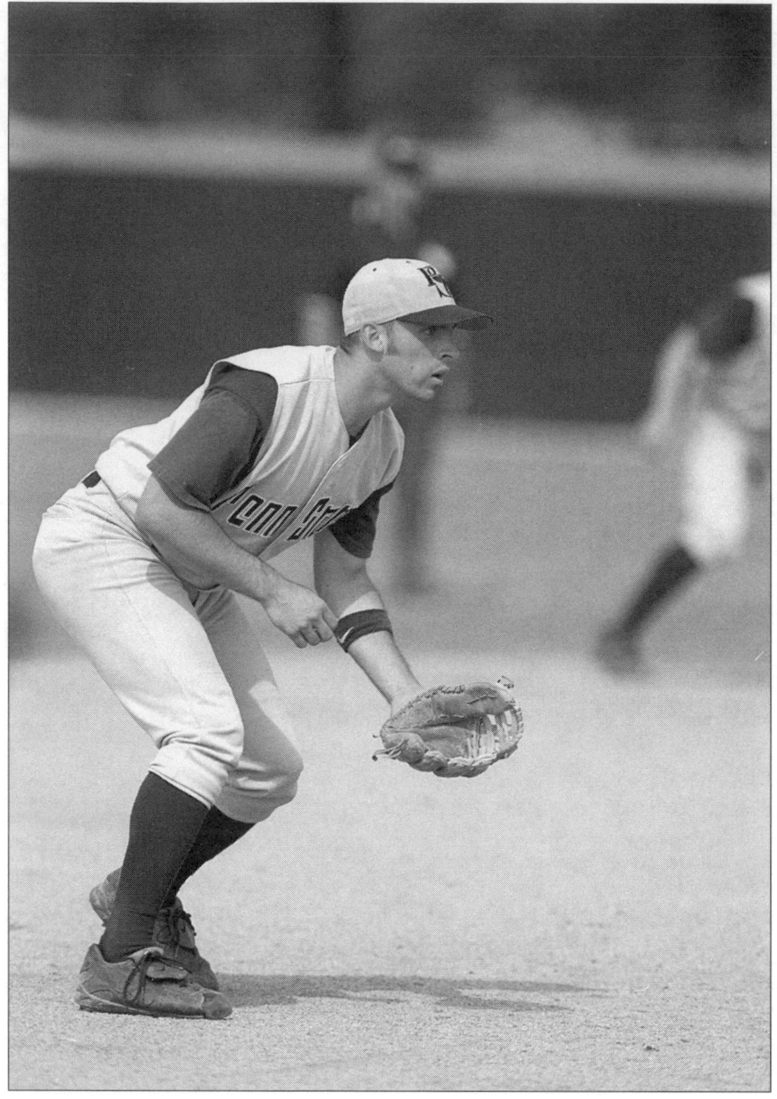

Infielders should never make a physical adjustment before the pitch or they risk tipping off the pitch to the hitter.

fielders, and, of course, specific information on each hitter in the opposing lineup is invaluable in planning your defense. Obviously, this scouting information can be used in pregame meetings with the starting pitcher and catcher as well as with the infielders and outfielders. The information should be catalogued for easy recall when each hitter comes to the plate during the game.

Discussing scouting information with your players is certainly valuable, but we believe the positioning of fielders should mainly be in the control of the coach in the dugout. Good positioning of infielders cannot be left to chance or to the whims of a particular player, nor can the coach assume that the players know what they are supposed to do without any instruction or attention from the coaching staff. Proper positioning of infielders (as well as outfielders) is something that must be done consistently well if the defense is to make the best use of their skills in various situations. Coaches can use various movements and gestures to relay the information from the dugout to the infielders. They should be simple enough that you can get the message to your players and change them from one hitter to the next or even from one pitch to the next without being so obvious that your opponent can easily read them.

Coverage of Second Base

Middle infielders should look at the catcher when he is giving signs for the type and location of the pitch. This information will give infielders an indication of where the ball is most likely to be hit if the hitter makes contact. The infielders are thus alert for the possibility that the ball will be hit in a certain direction, but they should not make a physical adjustment before the pitch. An infielder who moves early could tip off the pitch to the hitter.

Knowing the pitch and the abilities of the hitter is also important in deciding who covers second base on a steal or hit-and-run. A simple sign of open mouth or closed mouth between the shortstop and second baseman has been used for many years to indicate who is covering second base. This coverage signal can be changed on every pitch by the middle infielders if need be, depending on the pitch, the hitter, or the situation. An obvious situation to switch coverage of second base occurs when the base runner on first base is not a normal base stealer. Because he has little chance of stealing the base successfully, the opposing coach may want to put him in motion on a hit-and-run play. This is a good time to switch who covers second base. A simple sign from the coach on the bench to the middle infielders on whom he wants to cover second base will work.

Positioning Outfielders

The positioning of the outfielders should follow along the lines of the principles of positioning infielders. The three outfielders should be aware of the importance of shifting their positions constantly during a game, during each at-bat, and pitch by pitch. Because of the distance from the players, the coach responsible for positioning outfielders will often wave a towel or some similar object to signal correct positioning. Often the coach will appoint the center fielder to be the leader. He makes sure that the other outfielders are looking for the signal and moving as directed by the coach.

The coach should have signals to indicate the standard or starting position for the outfielders for both right-handed hitters and left-handed hitters and signals to indicate outfield depth and pull or opposite field. The system is similar to that used for positioning infielders, discussed earlier in the chapter.

The positions of the outfielders will depend on many things, such as the tendencies of the hitter, the wind speed and direction, the pitcher on the mound and his style of pitching, the pitch being thrown, the ball-strike count, and the game situation. All three outfielders should shift as a group to present a balanced alignment. For example, if the center fielder and right fielder move several steps toward the right-field foul line and the left fielder remains in place, a huge gap will appear in left-center field, weakening the outfield coverage of the team. Let's look at some of the major factors that should be considered in positioning outfielders:

- *The hitter.* Although amateur outfielders do not see opposing teams enough to learn all the tendencies of their hitters, team scouting reports, some close observation, and a little common sense can go a long way toward helping outfielders play hitters properly. If, for example, a right-handed hitter fouls off a fastball into the right-field bleachers, the outfielders may think, "Gosh, he didn't get around on that one very well," and let it go at that. But if the hitter is constantly late on fastballs, the outfielders should shift in that direction until the hitter proves he can get around on the fastball.
- *The count.* Outfielders must be aware of the tendencies of hitters according to the ball-strike count and shift accordingly during the game. Numerous studies conducted over the years have determined where hitters are most likely to hit the ball according to the ball-strike count, all the way from Little League to the major leagues, and all of them have shown the same thing—when a hitter is ahead in the count, he is more likely to pull the ball and hit with a bit more power, and when he is behind in the count, he is more likely to hit the ball toward the opposite field with a bit less power. Many coaches have their outfielders take two steps over and two steps up or back after every pitch. For example, the center fielder would get in his standard starting position for a particular hitter at the start of the at-bat. If the first pitch is a ball he would take two steps toward left field (the pull field) and two steps back (to account for added power). If the first pitch is a strike, he would take two steps toward right field (the opposite field) and two steps in (to account for less power). This would continue on every pitch (figure 12.5).

  I don't think we can expect our outfielders to move two steps here and two steps there on every pitch as if doing a dance step, but they should move after every pitch in the proper direction to adjust to the

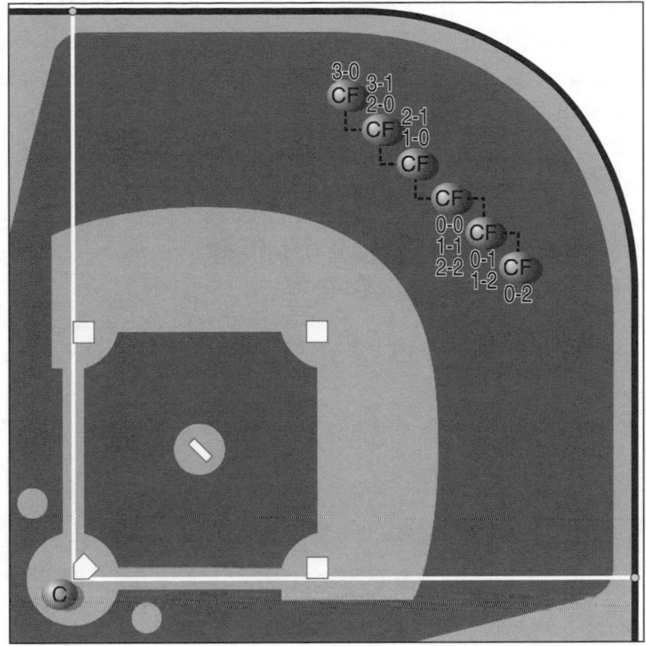

FIGURE 12.5 To adjust to the change in the ball-strike count, many coaches have outfielders take two steps over and two steps up or back.

change in the ball-strike count. An outfielder who stands in the same spot for nine innings is not alert to what is going to happen in the game!

- *The wind.* Outfielders should be aware of the direction and force of the wind throughout the game. The wind may not cause much change in the positioning of the outfielders, but they must be prepared to adjust to the wind when going after a fly ball. If the wind is blowing briskly, the outfielders should overcompensate for the effect the wind will have on the flight of the ball.

Developing a Priority System for Fly Balls

Good communication on fly balls is a tremendously important aspect of team defense, and a team should spend considerable time developing this skill. Good communication on fly balls is important in eliminating collisions, minimizing confusion and indecision, and ensuring that the player with the best skills and the best angle to catch the ball has the priority over less-skilled players. The frustration is enormous when a team mishandles a routine fly ball and allows it to fall to the ground safely. Poor communication or no communication at all is usually the cause, so coaches must develop and install a system that allows their players to understand and have confidence in a priority system for fly balls.

Simple terminology for fly-ball communication is always the best. For example, we have our players call, "Ball, ball, ball," when they want to make the catch. The other players call, "Take it, take it, take it," to reassure the priority player that he is in charge to make the catch. The player making the call should yell loudly three times because the crowd can be noisy and two (or more) players may call for the ball at the same time. Similarly, the other players should loudly call, "Take it," three times to eliminate confusion.

The following priority system should be in place:

1. All players have priority over pitchers.
2. The first and third basemen have priority over the catcher.
3. The middle infielders have priority over the first and third basemen.
4. The shortstop has priority over the second baseman.
5. The outfielders have priority over the infielders, with the center fielder having priority over the right fielder and left fielder.

This priority system works well because it gives the main priority to the player who should be the most skilled at catching fly balls and should have the best angle to the ball. For example, let's consider a short fly ball hit in the triangle near the foul line in short right field. The player with first priority to make the catch would be the right fielder, who is supposed to be highly skilled at catching fly balls and has a good angle because he is coming in on the ball. The player with second priority to make the catch would be the second baseman, who is generally a good glove man and in this case has an angle on the ball because he is going slightly backward and toward the foul line, catching the ball from the side. The player with third priority would be the first baseman, who would be in the lineup more to catch thrown balls and drive in runs than to catch fly balls. In addition, he has the worst angle of the three players because he is running straight back and will probably have to make the catch over the shoulder (figure 12.6).

The same principles for the priority system would hold for a fly ball hit in short left field near the foul line; a fly ball hit in foul territory between the first baseman, catcher, and pitcher; or for a fly ball hit anywhere in the ballpark!

Three additional suggestions for implementing the priority system on fly balls will help minimize or eliminate confusion and indecision.

1. The first is to limit the people who call for the ball to those who have a chance to make the catch. The right fielder doesn't need to be yell-

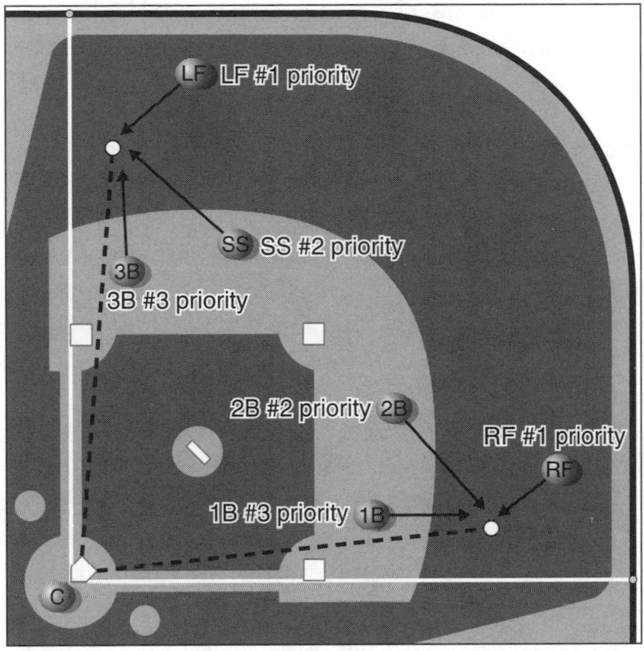

FIGURE 12.6 Priority system for catching a short fly ball hit in the triangle near the foul lines in right and left fields.

ing advice on a fly ball hit between the shortstop and the third baseman.

2. The second suggestion is for everyone to wait until the ball starts down to say anything. Calling for the ball when it first leaves the bat and is on its way up leads to players saying, "I've got it, no you take it!" Confusion and mistakes result. Calling for the ball too quickly is probably the most common mistake players make on fly balls. Teams must correct this tendency, especially on those in-between fly balls that can cause so much trouble.
3. The third suggestion feeds off the second—wait, wait, wait to call for the ball, and then call it loudly and with authority! If players practice and improve on the first two suggestions, they will begin to make these plays with increased confidence, which will lead to greater aggressiveness in calling for fly balls loudly and with authority.

Game-Situation Substitutions

The coach should build an attitude among his players that each has a job important to the success of the team, regardless of whether that job is as a member of the starting lineup or as a defensive replacement, pinch hitter, or pinch runner. If a coach has a good roster of players, some with better offensive skills and some with better defensive skills, he can use them to advantage by making intelligent game-situation substitutions. We prefer to have the strongest possible offensive players in our starting lineup, so many of our game-situation substitutions are to put in a superior defensive player late in the game when our team is leading. This action not only puts a better defensive team on the field late in the game when we have a lead but also ensures that many players get playing time during the season in crucial parts of the game. This approach can have a big effect on winning the game and is a great morale builder for the team.

On the other side of the coin, a team may have in the starting lineup an outstanding defensive player at a key position who is not a strong hitter. In this type of situation the coach may need to pinch hit for this player late in a game when his team is behind or tied. This type of move requires using two players, the starter and a pinch hitter who can play adequate defense at that position. At times, the move may require the use of three players—the starter, the pinch hitter (who is not an adequate defensive player), and a defensive replacement for the pinch hitter. If the pinch hitter does not run well, the move may require four players if a pinch runner comes in to run the bases. The coach must organize his thinking about the possible use of all his roster players in various situations so that he will be prepared to act when substitutions are needed. The coach should try to alert players ahead of time that they might be used "if this happens or if that happens" so that they can be preparing mentally and physically to go into the game.

A pinch hitter can be used during a game to substitute for a less skilled hitter who is in the starting lineup or to create a more favorable matchup between the pitcher and hitter. If a coach has an outstanding hitter who is not a regular player (something not often seen in amateur baseball), he may use that player to pinch hit regardless of how he matches up with the opposing pitcher. More often the coach will have several possible pinch hitters for a particular situation and will want to consider how well each of them matches up with the opposing pitcher. The coach can consider such things as sending up a right-handed hitter against a left-handed pitcher or vice-versa, inserting a good fastball hitter against a fastball pitcher (and the same against an off-speed or breaking-ball pitcher), or putting in a good low-ball hitter against a low-ball pitcher. A coach also needs to consider what type of hitter the situation calls for if he has several pinch hitters available. For example, if he needs a pinch hitter to lead off the inning, he might prefer to have a hitter who has a good eye at the plate, makes good contact, and can run the bases. On the other hand, if he has a runner on third base and less than two outs, he might prefer to use a hitter who can get the ball in the air to drive in the run.

Using team personnel to take advantage of the players' varied skills and abilities is a vital part of managing a baseball game. Coaches should study their personnel carefully to make the best use of their players and help the team perform to the best of its ability. A coach who uses his team wisely will be successful not only in winning games but also in developing a roster of skilled players who all feel important to the team's success.

13

Defensive Positioning

George Horton

When Abner Doubleday invented the game of baseball, I'm not sure anyone really knew how far ahead of his time he was. I find it fascinating that our game remains little changed from its inception more than a century ago. The height of the mound has been changed, the fences have been moved in and back, the bats and balls are different, but the baseball diamond itself has remained intact. It is amazing that the diamond dimensions have withstood the sands of time. The baseball diamond has to be the crown jewel of all sports.

Coaches and players have at times adjusted the standard positioning locations. In my career I have seen schemes with four outfielders and five infielders. I have seen the depths of outfielders and infielders fluctuate from program to program and philosophy to philosophy. But most teams continue to use the basic positions with only slight adjustments. Mr. Doubleday must have had incredible insight into the speed and timing of our game to create diamond dimensions that would stay intact forever.

The concept of positioning is simple, but the subtle adjustments can be complex in the total defensive scheme. I believe that you must have a system and philosophy and be consistent with execution. First, I believe that you must convince your players to buy into the system, and you must stress the importance of the team defensive philosophy. I try to make this statement with both a discussion and a physical exercise. Every year I do this session as the first baseball activity. I use a long discussion and physical practice period to get this point across. This session emphasizes to everyone the importance of this part of the game. They recognize that if I commit so much time and effort to team defense, it must be an important ingredient. Over the years this philosophy has proved successful. It definitely sends a strong message to my players, and I seem to get their commitment in return. The players always try hard to work together and within the system.

The athletic ability of your athletes will make a difference in the quality of the defensive coverage. Obviously, if you are loaded with quick, fast athletes, they will be able to get to more balls than a less athletic team can. This chapter covers concepts that maximize the defensive coverage, regardless of the athleticism of your team. Although we all must make the most out of what we have on our team each year, successfully recruiting outstanding athletes obviously makes any system more productive.

Team Defensive Philosophy

The team defensive philosophy that I like to use is detailed in the following paragraphs. In my 26 years of coaching I have adjusted and changed my philosophy many times. I use a combination of scouting information and a positioning scheme that covers the highest percentage of fair ground on the field of play. Over the years I have found this to be the most effective team defensive philosophy.

Playing a Zone Defense

The first point I make with my players is that they are going to learn how to play a zone defense. As in some other sports, the defensive scheme would be ineffective if we had some of the players playing a man-to-man scheme while the others were playing a zone. I realize that in basketball and sometimes in football, this mingling of concepts can be an effective defensive scheme. But in baseball, the goal is to cover as much fair territory as possible. I stress with them that most balls put in play go toward the middle of the field. I want them to understand the importance of the middle of the field so that they do not overplay the lines. We want to have a chance on balls hit in the seams of the infield or in the alleys in the outfield. I will discuss exceptions to this philosophy later in this chapter. The ultimate goal is to have a defensive player in the area where the ball is hit. The key points here are that we need only one player in that area and we need to defend only against the fair ball. Proper orchestration between players will minimize their overlapping of each other and their covering of foul ground.

I emphasize the importance of proper spacing to each defensive player. Predicting exactly where on the field the ball is going to be hit is extremely difficult. Certainly, we have scouting information that makes our predictions more accurate, but we're not always right. Because we cannot always be accurate with our defensive positioning, we want to use proper spacing to maximize our fair-ball coverage. I like to have a system that gets information to the players from the dugout so that they have time to interact with the other defensive players and commit to their responsibility. I don't want our players to be robots who rely totally on the coaches. We try to get information to them early so that they can make their own adjustments and use their own ideas. If we are too insistent on having accurate information, we eliminate the players' instincts and feel for the game. Forcing your players to do it your way can be counterproductive. I want them to be able to discuss their ideas with the coaches. Their instincts and information are often valuable to the team effort.

Establishing a Quick Tempo

One of our commitments on the defensive side is to establish a quick tempo. I believe that it is easier to play defense if a minimum amount of time passes between pitches. The defensive players will be on their toes. I like the pitcher to sprint to the mound between innings. I want him to do his warm-up pitches quickly without sacrificing quality. I want him to spend little time off the rubber. Obviously, if he is throwing strikes, this theory works better. At times, however, he should slow things down when the other team has created some momentum.

Using a Consistent Approach

Teams and coaches vary in how they position their defenses. The computer has made it possible to obtain and analyze a lot of information. This information can be customized into specific areas of emphasis. Many software programs on the market can be of great help in putting together a defensive plan. Some coaches like to position the defense based on where the hitter most often hits the ball. Others emphasize how they are going to pitch to each hitter. Another theory is to look solely at where all hitters tend to hit the ball off each individual pitcher. Baseball people have argued about these priorities as long as our game has been played, and they will continue to do so. I believe that you must stick by whatever priority you establish. By being consistent with your approach the percentages of being correct and incorrect will even out over the season. If you tend to switch around or go with gut feelings, you may find that your predictions are inconsistent. Our system emphasizes two main areas—how we pitch to a particular hitter and the opposing hitters' chart we keep for each individual pitcher (see figures 13.1 and 13.2). This system can only be effective if two things happen:

1. You must be coaching at a level at which the pitchers have consistent control, which means that the ball goes consistently to the called location.

2. You have a system that you run from the dugout or you have coordinated the pitcher's game plan with the positioning game plan and both the pitcher and the fielders stick with the plan.

Over the years we have found this system to be an effective way to set up our positioning. Obviously, any system includes variables because of situations and priorities based on the inning and score of the game. Situations and adjustments will be discussed later in this chapter.

Keeping It Simple

I like to keep our system simple. I think that many coaches put too many things in their playbooks. Doing this makes the game more difficult to play and accounts for the mental lapses caused by confusion. What happens is that the players tend to perform the fundamentals of catch in a mediocre manner when they have too much to think about. Your system will only be effective if your team can play sound catch within the system. I prefer to do fewer things and try to do them extremely well. This philosophy can apply to any defensive scheme. Keep the positioning system simple. Do not put in too many pickoffs, bunt defenses, or first-and-third defenses. I believe in having the fundamental plays and repeatedly working on them. This approach will maintain each player's confidence and efficiency in his part of the total goal and will slow down the game in your players' minds.

Another point of discussion is whether a coach calls pitches from the dugout. I have always believed in calling pitches and running the defense from the dugout. I know many coaches and analysts disagree with this approach. I believe that in the college game, the coaches have the most experience, knowledge, and information. But that doesn't mean that we are always right. Controlling the games allows us to put the entire defensive scheme together from the dugout. We do not use this method to prevent players from having input or thinking for themselves. We want them to have input and be able to discuss what they see or pick up on. Another knock against this approach is that from the dugout we are not able to see little adjustments that hitters make. To help solve this problem, we have adjustment signs from the catcher on the field. This contribution gives us valuable information that we can put in the formula to predict the outcome. Within our system we also allow the pitcher to shake off the pitch that we call from the bench. We understand that he must feel committed and good about the pitch selected. The pitcher must trust and commit to each pitch. Some people may argue that no teaching occurs if the coaches control everything. We work hard to communicate with and explain to our players the reasons for everything we do. This approach serves the purpose of educating them on the finer points of playing defense and prepares them for the time when they are calling things for themselves. This system has been extremely successful for me over the years.

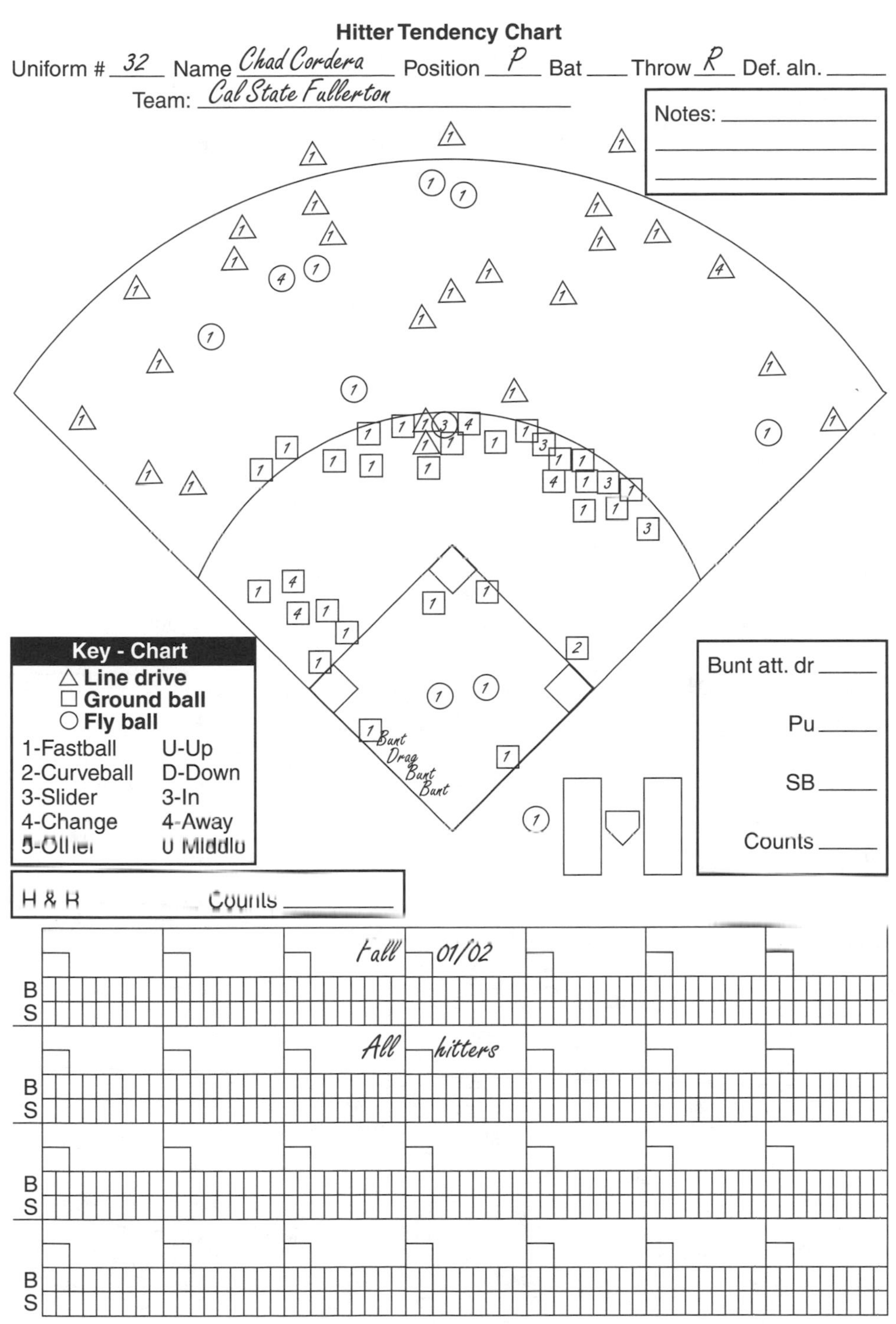

FIGURE 13.1 Opposing hitters' chart that we keep for each pitcher. The chart includes all hitters, both left-handers and right-handers, and indicates where they hit each type of pitch.

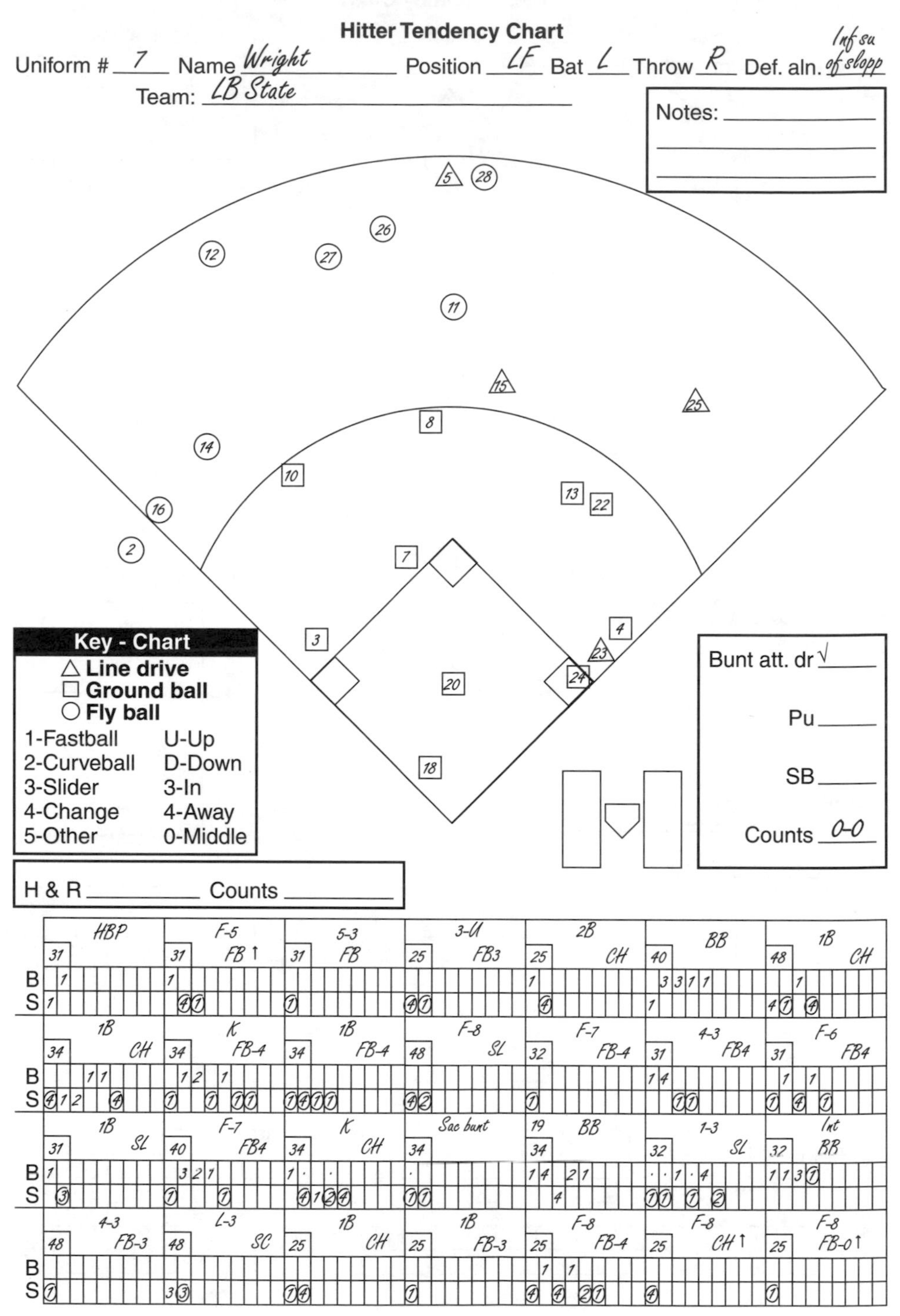

FIGURE 13.2 One hitter versus all pitchers.

Goals of an Effective Defense

An effective defense accomplishes many things. The defense uses a middle-of-the-field priority system, as discussed earlier. Quality defense eliminates free bases or free base runners and forces the opposition to earn everything they get. We try hard to limit the opportunity for extra outs in an inning. We try to get every out available within an inning or play. We try to be perfect mentally, but we realize that on occasion we are going to break down physically. We recognize that momentum is part of the game, so we try to capture or obtain that momentum from the defensive side. The three biggest defensive momentum builders or breakers are the double play, the successful extra-base-hit alignment, and the bunt defense. These defensive plays, when executed properly, are killers for the offensive effort. Failure to execute these plays is usually devastating.

A goal that I have in the learning phase of the defensive concepts is to teach enough complexity in defensive schemes that the players will simultaneously learn how to execute on offense. I believe that if you can successfully break down the difficulty in covering certain offensive plays, you can motivate your players to try certain things on offense. If a player believes that he can be successful with a certain play or skill, his chances of executing that play or skill go way up. Your players will be more likely to try

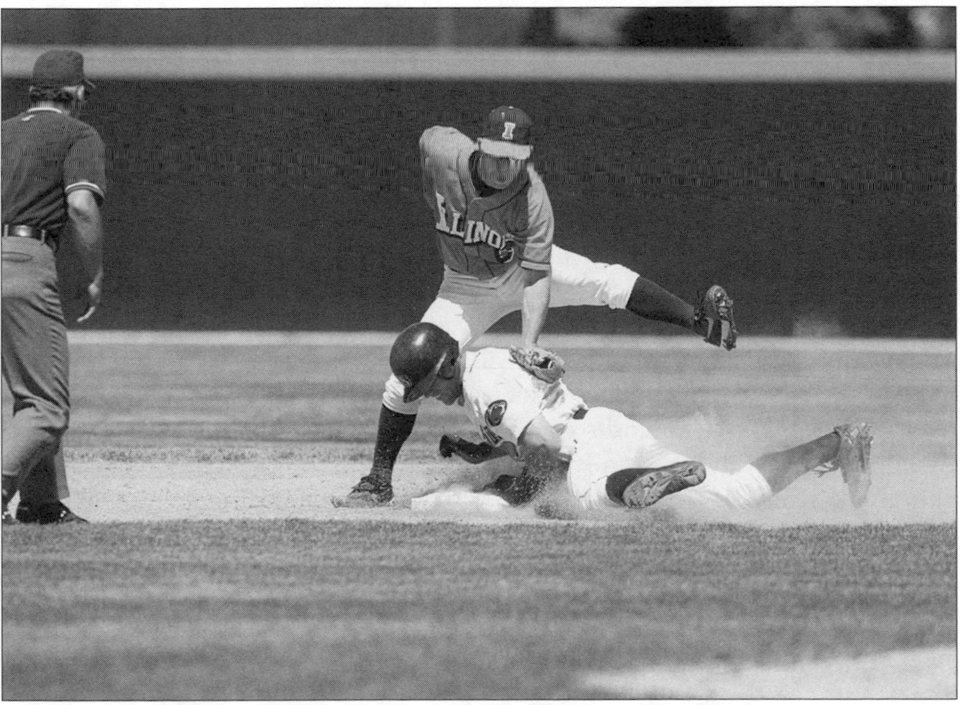

Quality defense makes the opposition earn everything they get.

things on their own. In simple terms, defense teaches offense and offense teaches defense.

Another huge goal that I have is to get my players to commit to the defensive effort. Accomplishing this task is sometimes difficult, perhaps because so much of the credit for the success of a baseball team goes to the players who do well offensively. The media is notorious for recognizing the top offensive players and saying nothing about the defensive effort of the team or individual players. Year-end awards and honors are based mostly on offensive success. In most cases, this fails to recognize the commitment that we tend to get from our players on defense. I believe that games and championships are won on the defensive side of the ball. Within a game a player performs defense much more often than he hits. My mission is to convince my players of the importance of their defensive commitment to the outcome of the game. One of the biggest challenges for most players is to play defense immediately after having had a poor at-bat. I want them to put that poor at-bat behind them and totally commit to the defensive effort, mentally and physically. This is much easier said than done. Teams and individuals must have discipline to adhere to this principle. They must be patient and wait for their next opportunity to release their offensive frustration. I just do not want them to be thinking about offense when they are on defense. I want them to leave their offensive frustration in the dugout.

Practice Format

The tricky part of my job is to create the right learning environment for my team to progress defensively. I try to accomplish this mission using the whole-part-whole system. In other words, I try to teach everyone what the team is trying to accomplish in whatever defensive system they are learning. After introducing the concept to the team, I address the individual fundamentals necessary to accomplish the system. I then like to go back to the team interaction and hope that it all comes together with quality execution. This philosophy usually holds up well with all defensive goals that my program uses. My team cannot be effective in executing a team defensive concept until they have a handle on the defensive fundamentals individually. Even the most fundamentally competent individual, however, cannot be effective within the team unless he has total understanding about the interaction with his teammates. Competency with both individual and team fundamentals is crucial for consistency in performance. I have found with this type of lesson plan that we end up with confident players.

Whenever possible and when time allows, I try to design my practices so that we work on the individual position fundamentals first. I like each player to go through some routine or session designed to help him with his physical mastery of defense at his particular position. Each position is unique as to the type of routine that players might go through. I then like to bring them all together for a quality catch session. Then we would do a session designed to work on a fundamental that is position specific. The fundamental for that day is usually consistent with the team session that follows. This allows the individual player to work on and, we hope, to master his part of the total picture. With this system, the individual's chances of controlling his part of the team interaction go way up. This system has been productive in leading to a positive practice session, and it applies to the confidence level I discussed previously. Most important, it paves the way for the team to compete with confidence in their capabilities.

Timing and Signals

In using signals we always try to keep in mind our goal of establishing a quick defensive tempo. We want our system to be simple and efficient. We want our system to work when the noise level is such that hand signs are the only way to communicate effectively. We use three coaches to signal the defense. One coach signals the outfielders, one coach signals the infielders, and the pitching coach signals the catcher and pitcher. We use three coaches because we want to save time and because a single coach cannot effectively handle all three areas. This system gives each coach a maximum of four players to manage and communicate with at any given time. In our system we give the information to our players early so that they have ample time to communicate and adjust with their teammates and go through their own mental routines before each pitch.

When the first hitter or a new hitter is coming to take his at bat, our system calls for all defensive players to pick up the appropriate coach with their eyes, just as the hitter reaches the dirt surrounding home plate. After each pitch, we teach the defensive players to get eye contact with the appropriate coach, just as the return throw from the catcher hits the pitcher's glove. This timing allows players to make any required adjustments and still allows them ample time to interact. We have to practice this routine. As I indicated earlier, it is our first lesson plan every year. The players work constantly on this system when we scrimmage so that they become comfortable with the routine and the sign system. We like to get all the tension or distractions out of the way so that they can get comfortable and commit to the baseball.

Positioning Basics

One of our first missions in the teaching sequence is to teach the defensive players the proper place to position themselves. We like to start with a session to show them where their home base should be with a right-handed hitter when playing him straight up with nobody on base. Once we have shown them where we think this position should be, we ask them to step off the distance from the bases. A good example would be the shortstop and second baseman's positions. In his right-handed straight-up position with no one on base, the shortstop would be approximately 7 steps from the second-base bag down the line toward third base and approximately 15 steps back from the base line. With the same hitter, the second baseman would be 5 steps from the second-base bag down the line toward first base and 15 steps back from the base line. As you might have noticed, the difference in the two positions is 2 steps in a lateral direction. The difference in the lateral direction is a reflection of the side the hitter is batting from. We use this 2-step difference with positioning adjustments for infielders, which I will explain later in the chapter. Stepping off the positioning spots is useful when we travel to different fields where the cuts of the grass vary from those in our home park. The bases will always be the same distance apart. Using this step system prevents distortions in the positioning plan that could come from unusual cuts of the infield grass and from outfield fences that are not symmetrical or have a short porch. Many infielders position themselves on the back edge of the infield dirt. If they use the dirt as a guide, they might be too deep or too shallow for our system. The outfielders sometimes base their depth on their distance from the fences. With some fields the depth of the outfield fence could distort the desired depths of the outfielders. The most accurate way to ensure consistency from field to field is for all players to judge their depths on distances from the bases.

Adjusting to Different Signs and Hitters

Once we have established the proper spots for right-handed straight-up for all positions, we have the players practice the adjustments to different signs and types of hitters. We use rules to ensure that we maintain the proper spacing when we make hitter adjustments. Our rule of thumb is that when an infielder makes an adjustment to slight pull or slight opposite, he moves two steps in the proper direction. The exception to this is that we have our corner infielders move only one step when moving toward the foul line, once they have reached the seven-step position, to avoid overlapping the foul line. If the plan were to play a particular hitter to pull, then all infielders except the corner infielder on the pull side of the field would move four steps in the proper direction. That corner infielder would move two steps. This system allows us to move and position the infielders with a specific sign. In addition, with this system we know they will be coordinating their movements, unless we choose to make a special positioning adjustment. This system also explains the two-step lateral difference between the shortstop and second baseman in our right-handed straight-up example discussed previously. As you can see, if the hitter at the plate was left-handed, the second baseman would be seven steps off the base and the shortstop would be five steps off the base.

In the outfield, our rule for every slight pull or slight opposite adjustment is for the outfielders to move three steps in the proper lateral direction. If the adjustment were from straight up to pull, then the outfielders would all move six steps in the proper lateral direction. Again, this approach allows us to have the outfielders coordinate their movements and spacing. Situations often occur when we do not want all three outfielders to move together. We accomplish this special alignment with a different set of signs.

This entire system allows a coach to give one sign to the entire defense and be able to count on the players to move to specific defensive spots. Countless variables in the objective of the defense would call for a few adjustments from this basic positioning system. Individuals could be moved with a sign specifically for each player. The infield might play the hitter one way while the outfield plays the hitter a different way. In some cases one side of the field may play one way while the other side plays another. This is one reason that we like to have two coaches giving the positioning signs. The main point to keep in mind is that within this system we can communicate accurately with every player on the field. Players should know exactly where to play with a hand signal.

Let's break this down with an example of the basic positioning for the infielders. Let's assume that we have to defense an average-running, right-handed hitter who is no threat to bunt. No one is on base, and it's early in the ballgame. Let's say we are going to play this particular hitter straight up. Here is how we would like our infielders to set up (figure 13.3).

First baseman—9 steps off first-base bag, 12 steps from base line

Second baseman—5 steps off second-base bag, 15 steps from base line

Shortstop—7 steps off second-base bag, 15 steps from base line

Third baseman—7 steps off third-base bag, 12 steps from base line

Now let's take the same game situation and put a left-handed hitter at the plate. We are still going to play this hitter straight up. Let's see how this differs from our positioning for a right-handed hitter and see if our adjustment rules would apply (figure 13.4).

First baseman—7 steps off first-base bag, 12 steps from base line

Second baseman—7 steps off second-base bag, 15 steps from base line

Shortstop—5 steps off second-base bag, 15 steps from base line

Third baseman—9 steps off third-base bag, 12 steps from base line

If we were going to adjust to the same left-handed hitter and go to a slight pull defense in the infield, here is how that would translate (figure 13.5).

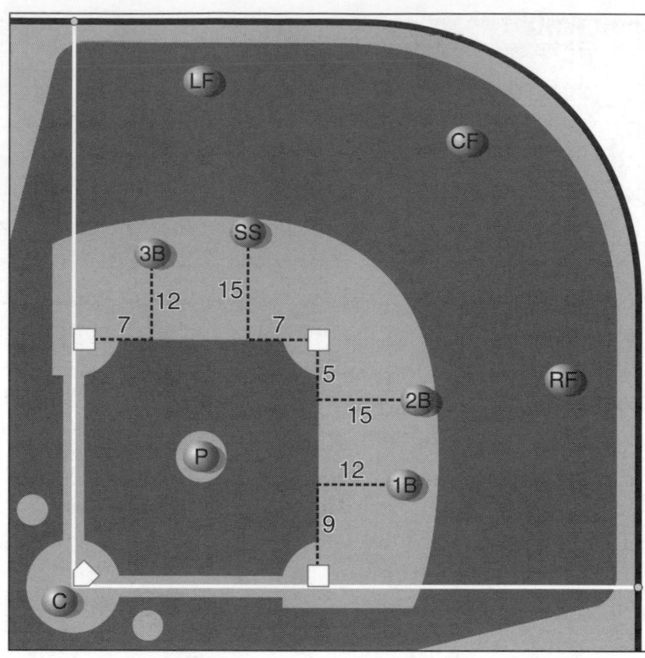

FIGURE 13.3 Straight-up positioning for defending against a right-handed hitter with average running speed, no bunt threat.

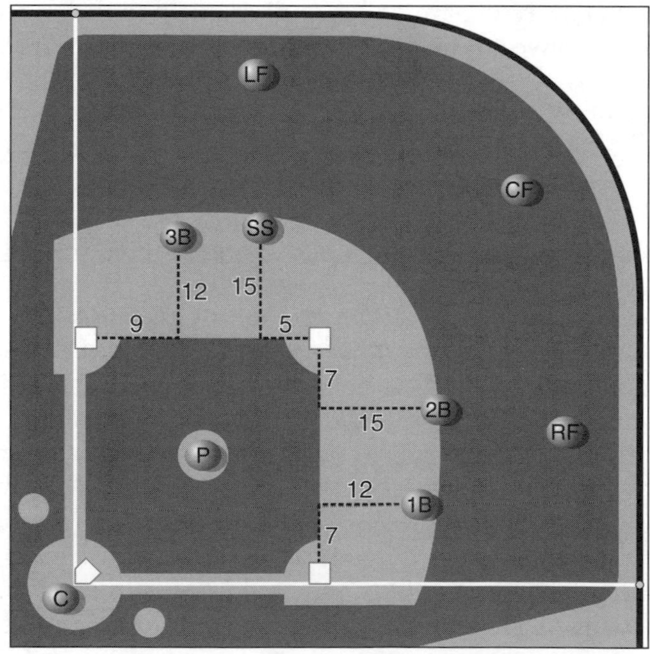

FIGURE 13.4 Straight-up positioning for defending against a left-handed hitter with average running speed, no bunt threat.

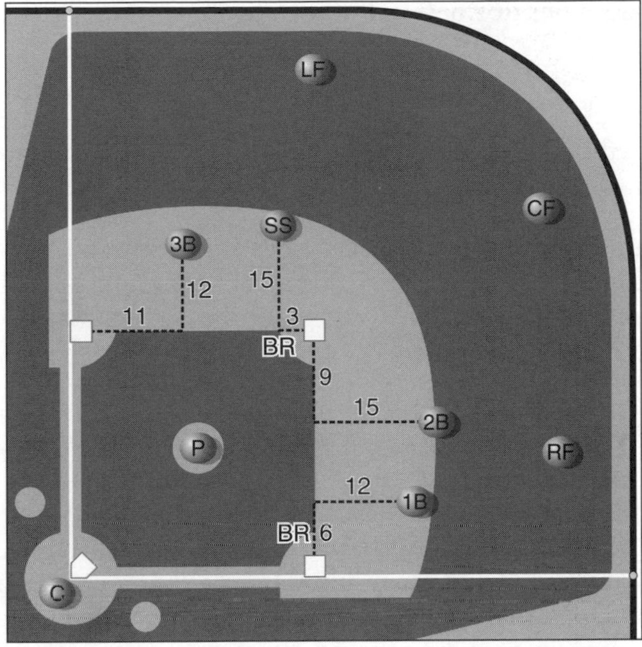

FIGURE 13.5 Slight pull positioning to defend against a left-handed hitter with average running speed, no bunt threat.

First baseman—6 steps off first-base bag, 12 steps from base line

Second baseman—9 steps off second-base bag, 15 steps from base line

Shortstop—3 steps off second-base bag, 15 steps from base line

Third baseman—11 steps off third base bag, 12 steps from base line

I hope this gives you a good understanding of the system we use. Obviously, this system does not account for all the variables in positioning that game situations or particular hitters call for, but we find it a useful basic system to work from in making more adjustments when necessary.

Now we have the decision-making process in front of us about how we are going to defend a particular hitter given the situation. As I mentioned earlier, you can choose what to emphasize in the scouting information that you have accumulated. When we put the plan into action, we always keep in mind that we cannot accurately predict where the ball is going to be hit all the time. No matter what our information tells us, we realize that the hitter could hit the ball anywhere on the field. So we must avoid overloading one part of the field and weakening the less likely part of the field. Our philosophy is to play to the scouting information collectively, without totally giving up the least likely areas for that particular hitter. In other words, we avoid extreme defensive alignments.

The two areas of information that we emphasize most heavily in deciding how to align our defense are

1. the way we plan to pitch to the hitter and
2. where the hitter has hit the ball off our pitcher or where similar hitters have hit the ball off our pitcher.

Over the years we have found these the best criteria to follow in developing a defensive plan. We can never be 100 percent accurate, but we try to boost the chances of being correct by having a solid plan. No matter what system you use, you must be consistent.

Establishing Priorities

I believe that it is important to convince young defensive players that they must establish and understand their priorities in positioning alignments and decision making. They must know their alignments for many special defenses and situations, such as the double play, base coverages for stealing, holding runners at first base and at second base, bunt defenses, first-and-third defenses, playing the infield in with a runner on third base, and taking away the chance for an extra-base hit. I have found that young players try to accomplish too much. When they play double-play depth, they tend to play too deep. The middle infielders get too far away from the second-base bag, trying to cover the hole between them and the corner infielder. When they have base coverage for steals, they try to hold their ground too long and are unsuccessful at beating the catcher's throw to the bag. When they play in to attempt to throw a runner at third base out at the plate on a ground ball, they play halfway in, in what I call no-man's land. In bunt defenses they do not commit to their responsibility well enough because they try to do too much. When guarding the line they play too far away from it, and inevitably a ball goes between them and the line.

Coaches must teach players that they cannot accomplish everything with their alignment scheme. In most cases they must sacrifice some coverage to position themselves for their individual responsibilities. As a coach you must make it acceptable for a player to get beat by a ball hit in an area that is priority three or four. You must make it acceptable for a ball to go through a hole created when a player leaves his spot to cover a base. Players must understand that sometimes we just have to give the hitter some credit. I like to use the phrase, "You must give up something to get something." This philosophy will make your defense more efficient when the batter hits the ball where you are trying to get him to hit it or bunt it.

The priority system can apply to decisions made by the players on defense. Young players often get things out of sequence because they are trying to trick the offensive players. They tend to think and prepare for the special play or trick play instead of committing their thought process to the most probable play. During my coaching career I've had some difficulty in this area with some of the more cerebral players. When this occurs, I try to get those players to understand why I don't want them to operate that way. I want them to keep the game simple in their minds.

Double-Play Depth

The priority for infielders is the double play. When they position themselves for the hitter, the infielders must understand that they have to give up some coverage to have a chance at the double play. This priority also applies to the middle infielders concerning playing the hole instead of being close enough to the base to have a chance to turn a double play. When we are playing a hitter to pull, the middle infielder on the pull side would not allow his lateral adjustment to take him so far from the base that he would not be able to beat the throw to the second-base bag. Therefore, we put hole coverage second to the priority of being at the base.

Here are some of the rules that we use for our infielders:

- The first baseman is no deeper than 7 steps behind the base line if he is playing behind the runner (figure 13.6). This rule would always apply with runners on first and second or with the bases loaded. This positioning is 5 steps farther in than the positioning he uses with nobody on base or in a two-out situation. The tendencies involving the hitter and pitcher would determine his lateral positioning.
- The third baseman is no deeper than 4 steps behind the base line (figure 13.6) whenever the double play is in order. This is 8 steps farther in than the positioning he uses with nobody on base or in a two-out situation. The tendencies involving the hitter and pitcher would determine his lateral positioning.
- The shortstop and second baseman are no deeper than 12 steps behind the base line (figure 13.6) whenever the double play is in order. This is 3 steps farther in than the positioning they use with nobody on base or in a two-out situation. The tendencies involving the hitter and pitcher would determine their lateral positioning. We do not allow them to move so much laterally that they are unable to turn the double play. The exception to this rule occurs when we put on a special defense that releases them from that responsibility. Occasionally we decide to commit to defending the hitter and how we are going to pitch to him. This option requires a special defense in which only one middle infielder will be in position to turn the double play. We seldom do this and try to avoid these exaggerated defenses.

Ideally, we are trying to get a ground ball hit in the middle of the diamond. When we accomplish that, we would like to have a defensive player in that area to get the double play that we worked so hard to set up.

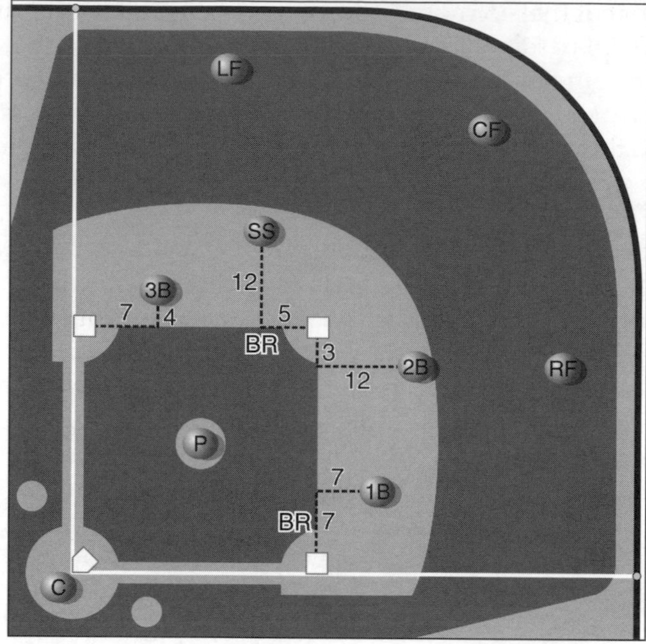

FIGURE 13.6 Double-play depth: runners at first and second, right-handed hitter, straight-up positioning. Defending against hitter with average running speed. No bunt threat and no sacrifice-bunt defense.

Special Coverage

Three situations require special positioning schemes:

1. Defending against the extra-base hit
2. Playing the infield in to attempt to throw out a runner trying to score from third base
3. Defending with what we call our flight-of-the-ball defense

We normally go into what we call our no-doubles defense beginning with the eighth inning of a one-run game. Several variables might change the timing of when we defend against the extra-base hit. The key is the percentage or chance that the opponent will get an extra-base hit and what that would mean to our team's chance of winning or losing a ballgame.

In defending against the extra-base hit, we make adjustments with the outfielders and the corner infielders. We generally like our outfielders to play four steps deeper. The only thing that would prevent them from taking the four steps back would be the depth of the outfield fence. If moving four steps back takes them too close to the fence, they would go back only far enough so that they do not overlap a home run ball. Keep in mind that if all three outfielders move four steps back, their spacing in the gaps will be distorted. Consequently, the corner outfielders should pinch the gaps by taking two steps closer to the center fielder (figure 13.7). The outfielders must also put this defensive plan into their decision-making process. When we are in the no-doubles defense, they are not to dive to catch a ball unless they are 100 percent sure that they can catch the ball or keep it in front of them. They must talk about this before the ball is hit.

The corner infielder's adjustment is to play close enough to the foul line that no hit ball could possibly go between him and the foul line. This means that the farther back they play, the farther off the line they can play. If they are shallow, they should be very close to the foul line. If the first baseman is holding a runner on first base, he should not move very far off the line on the pitcher's delivery to the plate.

When we defend with the infielders so that we can throw out a runner from third base at the plate, we make the following depth adjustments. The first baseman and third baseman align themselves three steps behind the base line (see figure 13.8). The exception to positioning at this depth would be to defend a potential bunt play or when an exceptionally fast runner is at third base. The lateral adjustments would be based on how we have decided to play the particular hitter. The middle infielder's depth would be

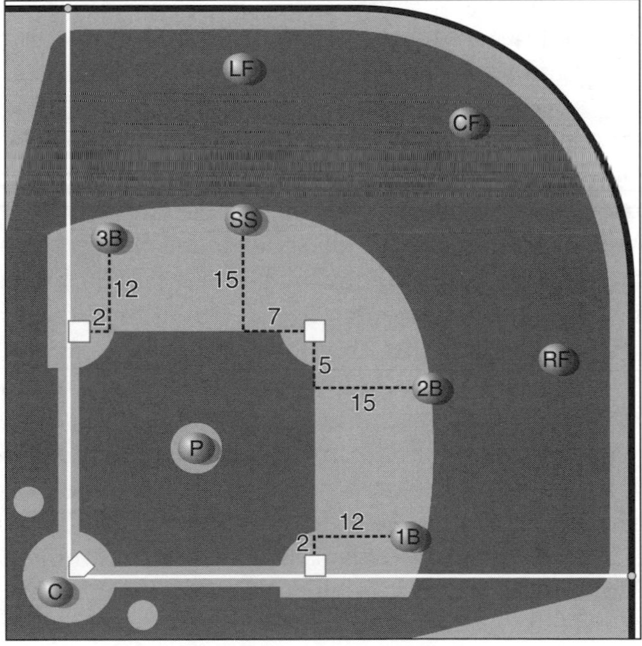

FIGURE 13.7 No-doubles defense: right-handed hitter, straight-up positioning. Defending against hitter with average running speed, no bunt threat.

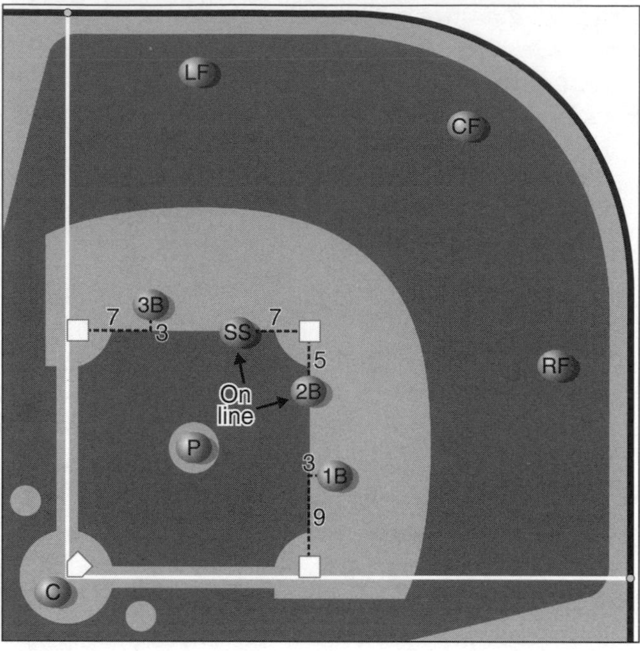

FIGURE 13.8 Defending with the infielders in: right-handed hitter, straight-up positioning, no bunt threat.

even with the base line. If there were an exceptionally fast runner at third base, the middle infielders would move in two steps. Their lateral alignment would be based on how we are playing the hitter.

We have an alignment that we call our flight-of-the-ball defense. In this defensive situation, there is one out and the double play is in order. A runner at third base is the game-winning or game-tying run. The goal of the infielders would be to get the double play if the ball is hit hard enough (flight of the ball) or, if not, to get the out at the plate. The speed of the hitter becomes a huge factor in the prepitch decision-making process, but the positioning is crucial as well. In this flight-of-the-ball defense (figure 13.9), the infielders make the following alignment adjustments. The third baseman plays two steps behind the base line and determines where to throw the ball based on how hard it is hit. The first baseman either holds the runner at first base in a first-and-third situation or plays two steps behind the base line. In our scheme the first baseman always throws a ball hit to him to the plate. We feel it is too difficult to turn a 3-6-3 or 3-6-1 double play with the game on the line. The middle infielders align themselves no deeper than four steps behind the base line. They base their throw on how hard the ball is hit. Their lateral adjustment is based on how we are playing the hitter. They stay close enough to the second-base bag to allow them to turn a double play, as we discussed in the paragraph on double-play depth.

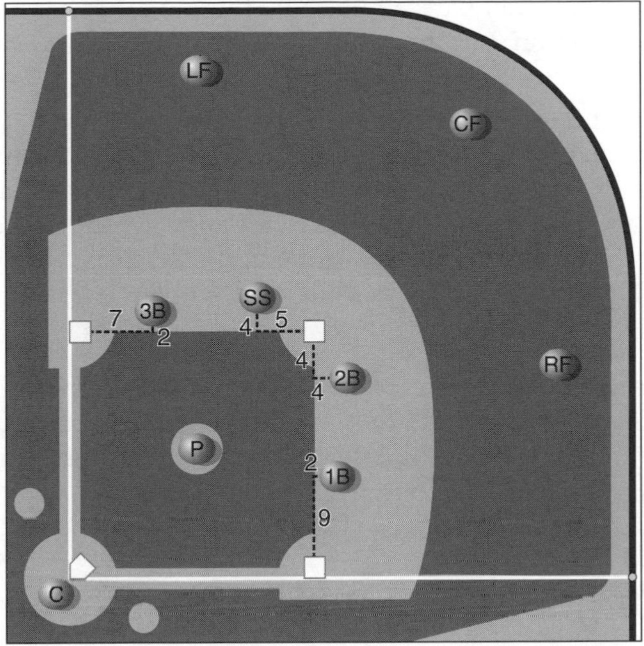

FIGURE 13.9 Flight-of-the-ball defense (bases loaded): right-handed hitter, straight-up positioning. Defending against hitter with average running speed, no bunt threat.

Late Adjustments

Many programs teach and believe that the infielders and sometimes the outfielders should make alignment adjustments according to the pitch being thrown. This can be accomplished by having the middle infielders relay the pitch orally or with a hand sign. We have gone away from this system because it allows a smart team or player to recognize the pitch being thrown by the pitcher. What happens is that the defensive player moves in one direction or another, which indicates what type of pitch is being delivered. We believe in relaying the pitch information to the infielders, but we do not move physically in any direction. Instead, we ask the infielders to anticipate in the proper direction. This method prevents the smart team or player from knowing what we are throwing.

Another form of late adjustment is what we call cat and mouse. In this adjustment an infielder shows one depth and moves in or back while the pitcher is in his delivery. We do this in three circumstances:

1. A corner infielder shows the hitter that he is taking away the bunt, but he then plays deeper for better coverage.

2. A corner infielder baits a hitter into thinking that he can easily bunt in his direction, but the infielder moves in to get an easy out on a bunted ball.
3. With a runner at third base and less than two outs, the idea is to show one depth and end up in another depth to confuse the decision-making process of the runner at third base. If the infielders start back and end up in, they might get an easy out at the plate on a ground ball hit to them. If the infielders start in and move back, they might induce the runner at third base to hold on a ground ball hit to them.

Our philosophy includes the cat and mouse with the corner infielders, but we don't believe in the cat and mouse with the runner at third. We like to keep things simple, and we think that the cat and mouse with a runner at third creates complexity that outweighs the benefits.

Dugout Communication System

As we discussed earlier in this chapter, we use two types of communication with the defensive players on the field. We use physical signs and oral signs. During most games, we can use both interchangeably and effectively. In the most important games, however, oral signs are typically useless because players cannot hear them coming from the dugout area. Therefore, we have found it essential to develop our physical signs to a point where we can communicate almost everything to the defense. This approach has served us well when we have participated in regionals and the College World Series. Although this chapter is about defensive positioning, we have both types of signs for all of our defensive systems, including bunt defenses, first-and-third defenses, base coverages, pickoff plays, pitching around hitters, walking hitters intentionally, and game-winning situations. We also have quite a few signs that allow the catcher and our pitching coach to communicate information back and forth and work together to get the hitter out.

Here is some of the information that we find necessary to get to our defensive players:

- Positioning alignment
- Individual defensive player adjustments
- Power or lack of power
- Slice
- Pinch
- Two-strike adjustment

These are just a few examples of the signals we use to relay information to defensive players.

Photos courtesy of Cal-State Fullerton.

- No doubles
- Hit cutoff man
- Throw directly to second base on a base hit (for outfielders)
- Nothing over your head
- Nothing between you and the line
- Shade the line
- First baseman plays behind the runner
- No-throw sign to any infielder and catcher
- Infielders must go the long way on ground ball on a full count
- Back-side runner on double steal
- Cat and mouse with corner infielders or base-hit bunt coverages
- Infield depths
- Speed of hitter
- Type of base-stealing threat
- Coverages for stealing between middle infielders
- Stall for time
- Pitch the hitter fine
- First-and-third defenses (identifying the fastest runner on base)
- Bunt defenses

As you can see, we have the ability to communicate a vast amount of important information to the defensive players. As I indicated earlier in this chapter, to be effective it is crucial to use this system properly. The information must be relayed at the proper time. The players must be trained to make eye contact at the proper time. They must have time to interact with their teammates and still be able to commit mentally to their individual responsibilities.

Although teams have played successfully with many different systems, not much has changed over the years. Some have fiddled around with exaggerated defensive alignments for certain situations or hitters, but most of us go back to an alignment that is virtually identical to the one used in the days when players left their gloves on the field. The more the game progresses with modern technology, the more it stays the same. The most athletic and best defensive players are likely to end up in the middle of the field. The players who are defensive liabilities are going to end up on the corners of the outfield. The slow, heavy kid with a good arm will end up behind the plate. If a player can hit, the coach will find a way to get him in the lineup, even if the designated hitter position is already taken. Abner Doubleday must have known what he was doing.

14

Defensive Tactics

Bob Morgan

Baseball games are lost, not won. A breakdown in team defense gives the opposition a chance to score. Good defense allows the offense only what they earn and nothing more.

The defense must be heads up and alert. Every player must be in the ballgame at all times. Every defensive player has a role on every play. Defense is the key to a sound and solid baseball team. The team that makes the fewest number of errors or mistakes in fielding and throwing will usually be the team that wins the game. Defensively, the focus should be on making the average or routine play. The reasons for failure in defense are that players hurry their throws, throw off balance, are out of position, or do not know what to do. Coaches need to teach players to be under control to make the routine play. Defensive teams that can consistently make the average play will be efficient and thus have a good opportunity to win games.

First-and-Third Defense

The most important aspect of a first-and-third defense is understanding the game situation. The number of outs, the score, the speed of the runners, and the arm strength of the players involved are the elements that the coach should evaluate before the pitch. If the defense executes properly, the offense will seldom score. After getting the defensive sign from the coach, the catcher puts on the specific first-and-third defense.

The shortstop is usually assigned to cover second base because he normally has the best arm. The second baseman covers second base in certain situations if his arm is strong enough to make the play.

Second Baseman As Cutoff Man

In the first-and-third defense illustrated in figure 14.1, the shortstop covers the bag and the second baseman becomes the cutoff man (10 feet in front of the base). When the runner from first breaks, the catcher checks third base to see if the third baseman has his hands up. If the third baseman sees the runner off the base too far, he should raise both hands over his head as he breaks to the base to signal the catcher to throw the ball to third. The third baseman uses this signal because the catcher cannot accurately judge the runner's distance from third base. If the third baseman's hands aren't up, the catcher should throw through to second base.

The second baseman must read the runner at third base. If the runner breaks, he should cut the ball and throw home; if the runner hasn't broken for home by the time the ball is in the cutoff position, the second baseman should fake a cut by slamming his fist into his glove to freeze the runner at third base. The shortstop covers second base and prepares to tag the runner if the ball goes through to the base. If the runner at third base breaks late, the shortstop can relay the ball home.

The pitcher fakes a cut on the catcher's throw to second base in an attempt to confuse the runner at third base. After a fake cut the pitcher breaks to back up home plate via the first-base line. The left fielder backs up a possible throw to third base from the catcher, the center fielder backs up the possible throw to second base from the catcher, and the right fielder backs up a possible rundown between first and second. The first baseman trails the runner to second base.

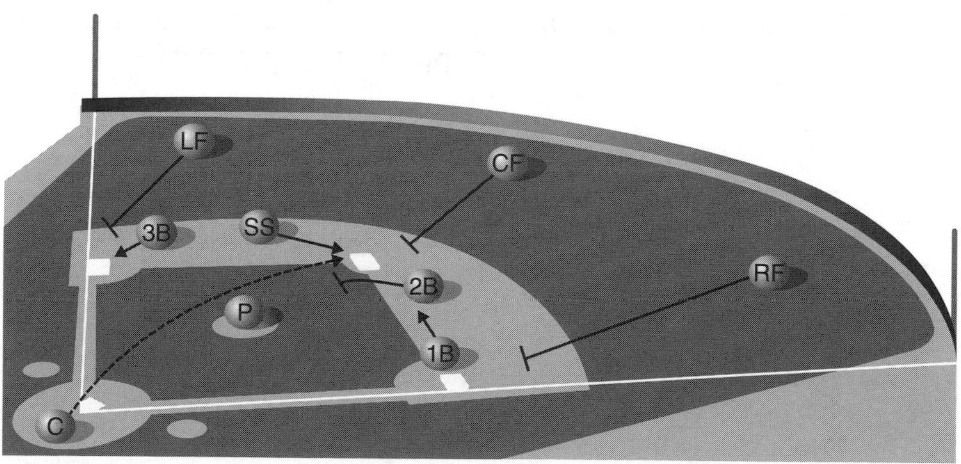

FIGURE 14.1 First-and-third defense: second baseman as cutoff man.

Throw Through to Second Base

In this defense the catcher again tries to freeze the runner at third base by checking the third baseman to see if his hands are up. If they are up, he throws to third; if not, he throws to the shortstop covering second base, who is one step in front of the bag squared to home plate (figure 14.2). The second baseman backs up second base. If the runner on third breaks for the plate, the shortstop charges hard, straight toward the plate, to cut the ball off. After chopping his feet for a couple of steps to get on balance, he catches the ball and throws to the catcher. If the runner on third doesn't break for the plate, the shortstop stays at the bag and tags the runner out coming from first base. If the runner on first base has the base stolen, the shortstop should charge in and cut the ball off to avoid a collision with the sliding runner.

The pitcher fakes a cut on the catcher's throw to second base to confuse the runner at third base. After a fake cut, the pitcher breaks to back up home plate via the first-base line. The left fielder backs up a possible throw to third base from the catcher, the center fielder backs up the possible throw to second base from the catcher, and the right fielder backs up a possible rundown between first and second. The first baseman trails the runner to second base.

Straight to Shortstop

This defense is designed to keep the runner on third base from scoring after the ball passes the batter. The shortstop takes two hard steps toward second

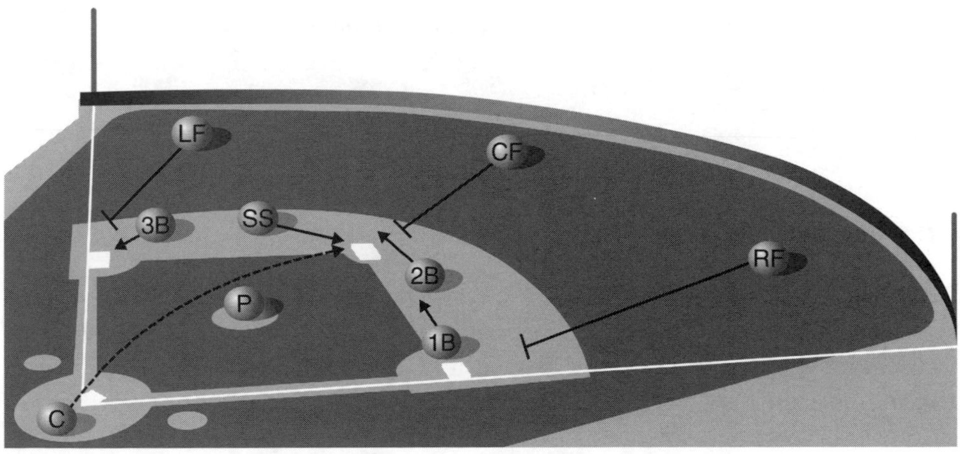

FIGURE 14.2 First-and-third defense: throw through to second base.

base then comes straight up toward home plate (figure 14.3). The catcher throws straight to the shortstop without looking the runner back at third base. The second baseman covers second base after the ball passes the batter, while the first baseman trails the runner from first base to a position midway between first base and second base. The third baseman covers third base and lets the shortstop and catcher know when the runner breaks for home plate. He does this by yelling "Four, four!"

The shortstop throws the ball back to home plate after he catches it, or he may possibly back door the runner at third base. The pitcher should back up home via the first-base line after he pitches to the plate. The left fielder backs up third base for a possible throw from the catcher, the center fielder backs up the shortstop from a throw from the catcher, and the right fielder backs up a possible rundown between second base and third base. The defense concedes second base to the offensive team.

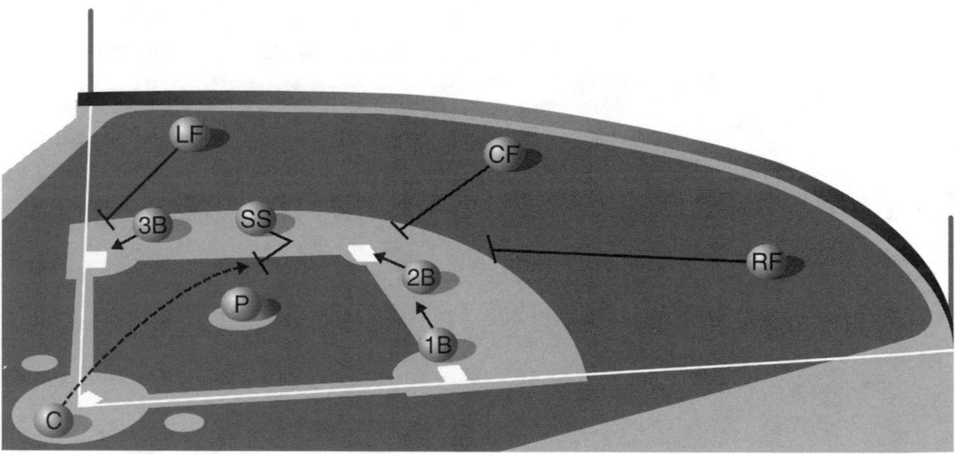

FIGURE 14.3 First-and-third defense: straight to shortstop.

Throw to Pitcher

The shortstop covers second base, and the second baseman goes to a cutoff position 10 feet in front of second base, as shown in figure 14.4. Without glancing at the runner at third base, the catcher throws the ball high over the pitcher as if he were throwing to second base. The pitcher cuts the ball off and checks the runner at third base. If he has no play at third base, he looks at second base. If the runner is caught between first and second, he gives the ball up to the shortstop covering second base or the second baseman, who is 15 feet up the base line depending on the runner's position. The shortstop or second baseman yells "Ball," indicating to the pitcher who should receive the ball. The other infielder drops to a knee and points to his teammate. Once the infielder checks the runner at third base, he shuffles (not sprints) the runner back to first base. He listens for a call from the third baseman should the runner from third base break for the plate. The pitcher covers first base once he gives up the ball, the left fielder backs up third base in foul territory, the center fielder backs up second base, and the right fielder backs up the second baseman's position.

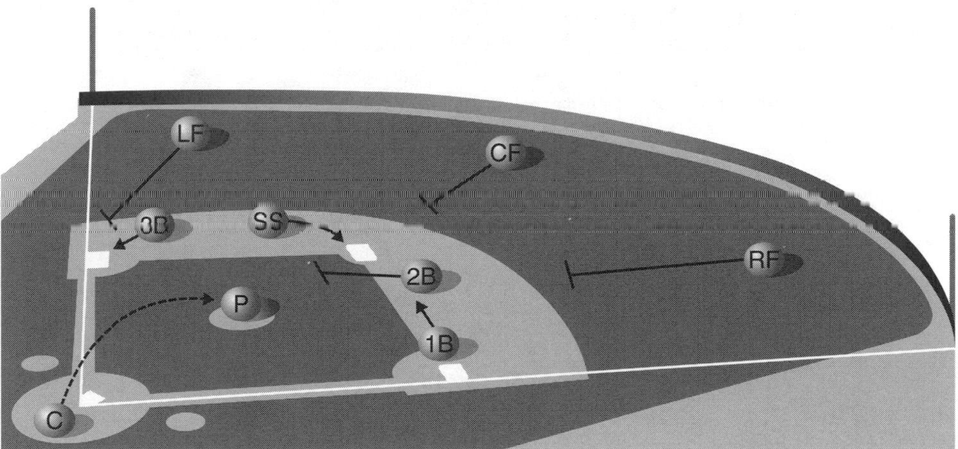

FIGURE 14.4 First-and-third defense: throw to pitcher.

Ball Fake and Throw to Third

In preventing the runner at third base from scoring, this defense concedes second base to the runner. After the pitch passes the hitter, the third baseman covers third base, the shortstop backs up third base, the second baseman covers second base, and the first baseman trails the runner to second base (figure 14.5). The catcher comes out and gives a good arm fake to second base, making sure he clears and goes beyond home plate, and then throws directly to third base. The pitcher backs up home via the first-base line after he pitches to the plate. The left fielder backs up the catcher's throw to third base, the center fielder backs up a possible throw from the catcher to second base, and the right fielder backs up a possible throw to second base from third base.

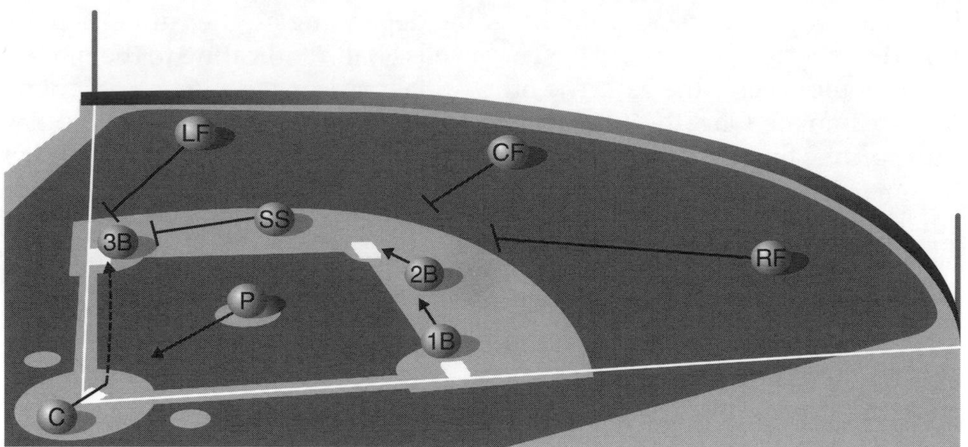

FIGURE 14.5 First-and-third defense: ball fake and throw to third.

Forced Balk Defense

The forced balk defense is the only first-and-third defense not put on by the catcher. The defense is a reaction to the offensive team's sending the runner from first base to second base before the pitch to the plate. The pitcher steps off the rubber and freezes the runner at third base by turning directly to third and checking the runner at the bag. If the runner is too far off, he throws to the third baseman. If he isn't far enough off, the pitcher throws the ball to the second baseman, who comes straight up to the inside of the base line approximately 15 feet from second base. The pitcher then goes to back up home by way of the third-base line. The third baseman covers third base and alerts the infielders if the runner breaks to home by yelling "Four, four!" The shortstop covers second base, the second baseman comes straight up into the base line to receive the throw from the pitcher, and the first baseman trails the runner to second base (figure 14.6).

When the second baseman receives the throw from the pitcher, he checks the runner at third base and begins to shuffle the base runner back to first base. If the base runner at third breaks to the plate, the third baseman yells "Four, four!" and the second baseman turns and throws to the catcher. The first baseman should call for the ball when he knows he can catch the ball and tag the runner out. He is then ready to throw home should the runner at third base break for the plate. The first baseman should avoid running with the ball toward second base.

If the pitcher is late stepping off the mound, the second baseman goes to a knee and points to second base. This signals the pitcher to throw the ball to the shortstop, who is covering second base. The left fielder backs up third base for a possible rundown, the center fielder backs up second base for a

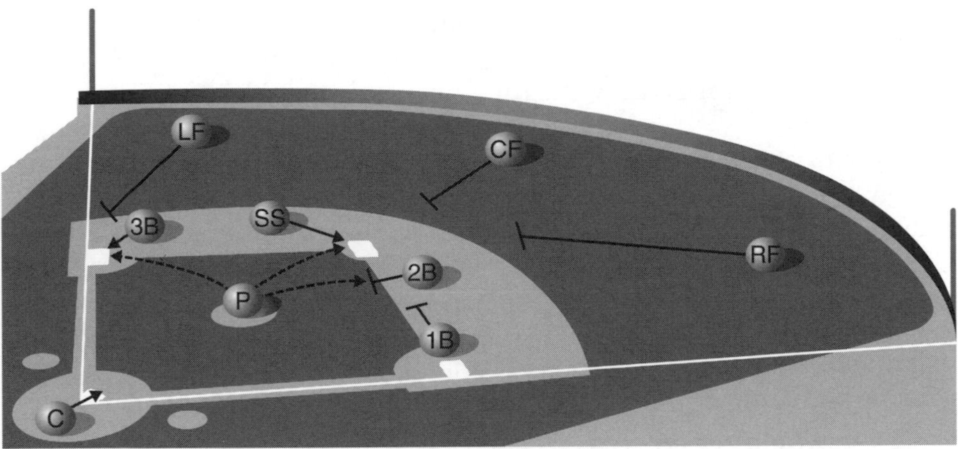

FIGURE 14.6 First-and-third defense: forced balk.

possible rundown between second and third, and the right fielder backs up the throw to second base from the pitcher.

Cutoff and Relay System

The purpose of your cutoff and relay system is to keep runners from taking an extra base if no play occurs at home or third. Relays and cutoffs are team plays that require a great deal of practice and teamwork to be executed properly. Too often, missed cutoffs and relay plays have given opponents the extra base that led to a run that decided the game. The throw from the outfielder must be low enough for the cutoff man to handle. If the throw is too high, the runner can react immediately and advance a base. We teach our outfielders to hit the cutoff man in the head. Many factors on a batted ball will help the outfielder determine where to throw the ball including

- the speed of the runner,
- the game situation,
- the outfielder's arm strength,
- how hard the ball is hit, and
- the distance the outfielder must move left or right to field the ball.

The outfielder can evaluate many of those factors before the pitch, which will limit the amount of information he needs to process after the ball is hit.

We want our relay or cutoff man to catch the ball on the fly, so if necessary he should move in or out to do so. Also, we want him to catch the ball on the throwing side and to catch it from the heel to the palm of the glove. To catch the ball on his throwing side, he steps forward with his right foot in the direction of the throw. Holding his hands letter high, he provides a good target.

The shortstop acts as the cutoff man on all throws to third base. On throws to home plate, the third baseman will line up home on all throws to the right of the shortstop. The first baseman will line up home on all balls to the left of the shortstop. The reason for using different cutoff men at home plate is the distance the first or third baseman would have to run to get in cutoff position. If the third baseman is playing deep and dives on the ground for a ball in left field, the first baseman should read this and handle the cutoff to home because the third baseman is out of position. The third baseman and shortstop would just crisscross; the third baseman would cover second and the shortstop would cover third. The same would hold true if the ball were hit into right field and the first baseman dove for a ball. If this happens, the first and third basemen would crisscross. The first baseman would go to cover second, and the second baseman would cover first. The third baseman would become the cutoff man to home.

The cutoff man's alignment will depend on the strength of the outfielder's arm, so the alignment will vary. The closer the cutoff man can be to the bag (40 feet), the harder it is for the runner to recognize whether to attempt to advance to the next base. The runner must delay his decision until the ball passes the cutoff man, which is an advantage for the defense. Also, from a spot closer to the base the cutoff man can more easily cut off poor throws, and he has more range in handling high throws. We want good, hard throws through the cutoff man's eyes.

To let a ball go through to the base, the receiver should yell "Go, go!" He should yell it loudly and in time to let the cutoff man react. If the receiver yells "Go!" the cutoff man should pop his mitt and fake a cut to keep the trailing runner from advancing. For the receiver to indicate that he wants the ball cut off, he should call out the number of the base where the ball should go. If there is no play at any of the bases, he would yell "Cut!" meaning for the cutoff man to catch and hold the ball. After catching the ball, the cutoff man should look for a possible play at any of the bases. If the throw is off alignment or dying and a play at the lead base is possible, the receiver should yell "Relay!" at which point the cutoff man would catch the ball and throw to the lead base. Also, the cutoff man can automatically cut the ball if he reads a ball that is dying or off alignment.

Tables 14.1 through 14.8 describe specific game situations and illustrate the most effective defensive strategies for each circumstance. Again, these relays and cutoffs require a lot of practice and exceptional teamwork to be successful. Strong, confident communication is necessary. Players must make decisions based on the likelihood of tagging the runner out and not allowing other runners to advance to better scoring positions.

TABLE 14.1 Single With No Runners On

BALL HIT TO LEFT

P	Moves toward 1B
C	Trails runner to 1B
1B	Backs up 2B, yells if runner goes to 2B
2B	Covers 2B
3B	Moves toward mound for deflected ball
SS	Lines up throw to 2B and throws
LF	Fields grounder to 2B
CF	Backs up left fielder
RF	Moves to backup 2B in line with throw

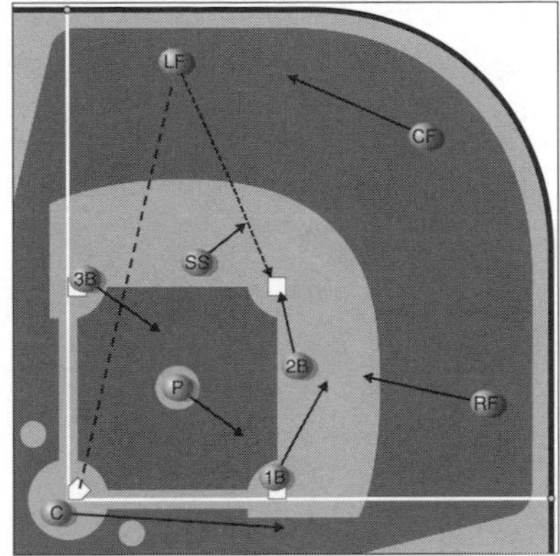

BALL HIT TO CENTER

P	Backs up 2B
C	Trails runner to 1B
1B	Makes sure runner touches base and then covers 1B
2B	Covers 2B
3B	Backs up 2B for deflected throw
SS	Lines up throw to 2B
LF	Backs up CF
CF	Fields grounder and throws to 2B
RF	Backs up CF and will cover 2B if ball is hit to CF's right

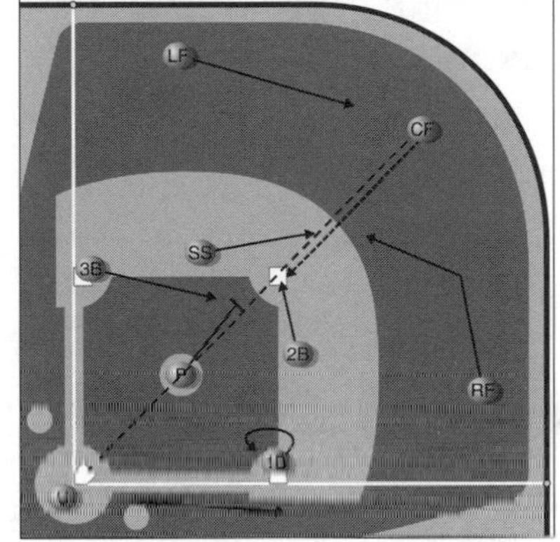

BALL HIT TO RIGHT

P	Breaks for 1B, backs up catcher if outfielder throws behind runner
C	Follows runner to 1B
1B	Goes after ball and stays away from 1B so that runner rounds bag
2B	Short cuts position and lines up throw to 2B
3B	Backs up 2B
SS	Covers 2B
LF	Backs up throw to 2B
CF	Backs up RF
RF	Throws to 2B, looks for possible play at 1B

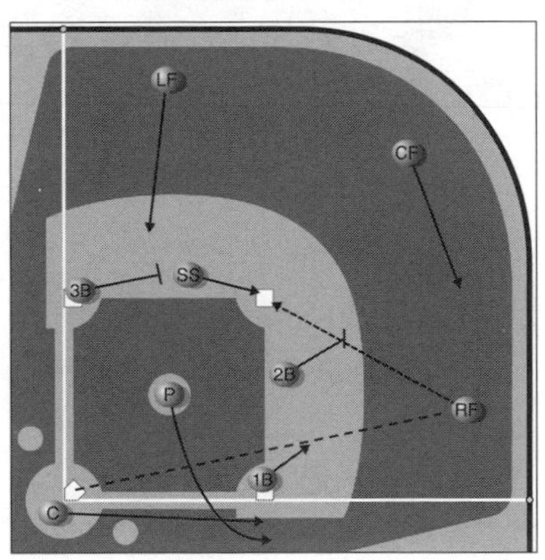

TABLE 14.2 Single With a Runner on First Base

BALL HIT TO LEFT

P	Backs up 3B
C	Backs up pitcher on play
1B	Makes sure runner touches 1B, backs up 2B
2B	Covers 2B
3B	Covers 3B
SS	Lines up throw to 3B
LF	Fields ball and throws to SS in cutoff position
CF	Backs up LF
RF	Goes toward 1B area

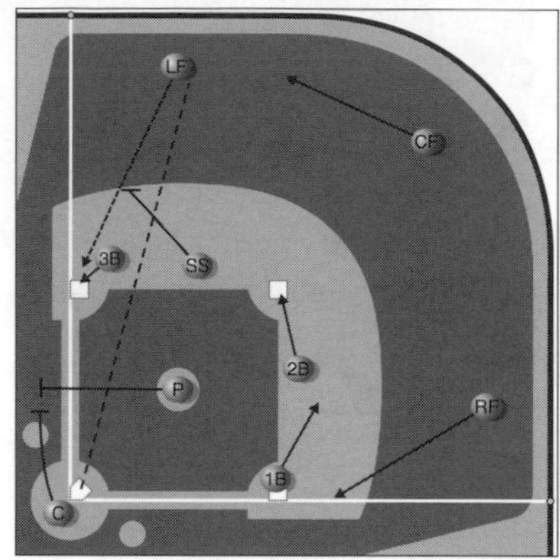

BALL HIT TO CENTER

P	Backs up 3B
C	Covers home
1B	Watches runner touch base, stays near bag
2B	Covers 2B
3B	Covers 3B
SS	Lines up throw to 3B
LF	Backs up CF
CF	Fields ball and throws to 3B
RF	Backs up CF

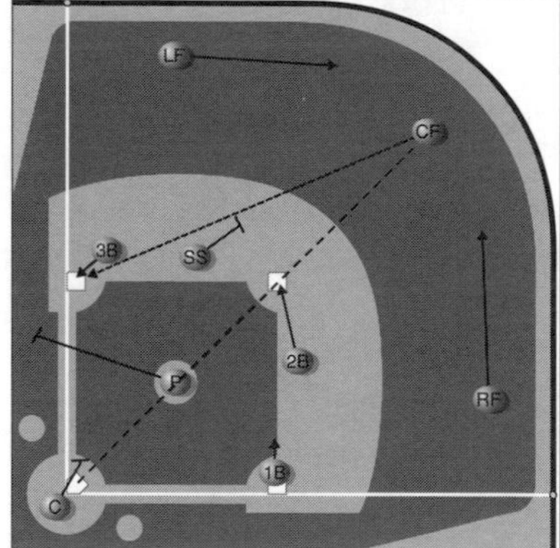

BALL HIT TO RIGHT

P	Backs up 3B
C	Backs up pitcher, covers home
1B	Watches runner tag 1B
2B	Covers 2B
3B	Covers 3B
SS	Cutoff man for throw to 3B
LF	Backs up 3B
CF	Backs up RF
RF	Fields ball and throws to 3B

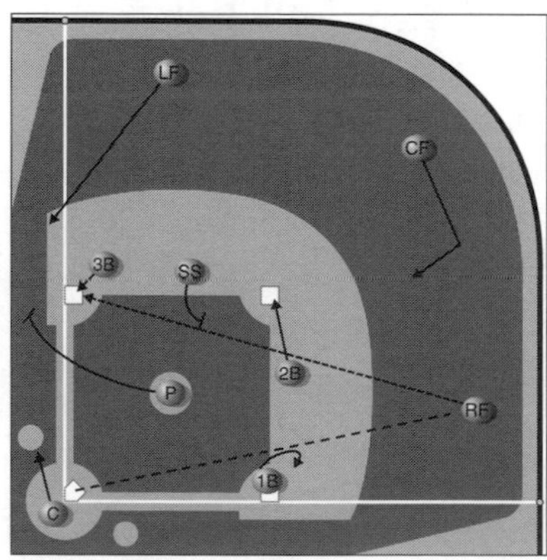

TABLE 14.3 Single With a Runner on Second Base

BALL HIT TO LEFT

P	Backs up home
C	Covers home
1B	Covers 1B, moves to cutoff position if to left of SS
2B	Covers 2B
3B	Lines up throw home
SS	Covers 3B
LF	Fields ball and throws home
CF	Backs up LF
RF	Moves to infield area

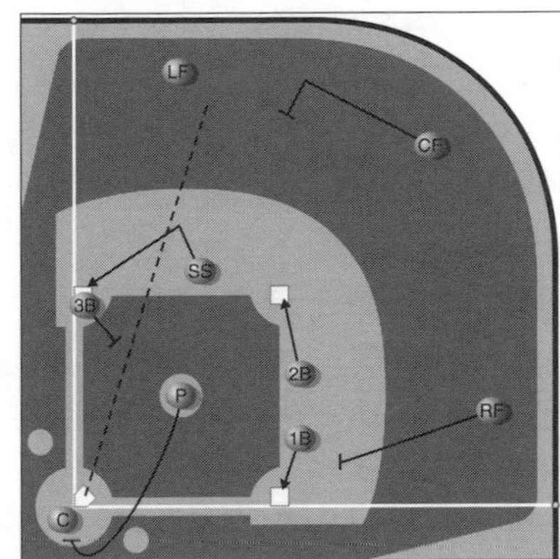

BALL HIT TO CENTER

P	Backs up home
C	Covers home
1B	Cutoff man behind the mound area
2B	Covers 1B
3B	Makes sure runner touches 3B, covers 3B
SS	Covers 2B
LF	Backs up 3B
CF	Fields ball and throws home
RF	Backs up CF

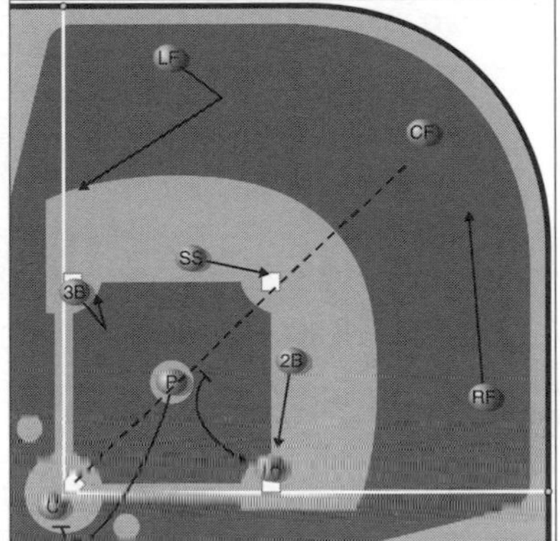

BALL HIT TO RIGHT

P	Backs up home
C	Covers home
1B	Cutoff man for throw home
2B	Covers 1B
3B	Covers 3B
SS	Covers 2B
LF	Backs up 2B area
CF	Backs up RF
RF	Throws to 1B in cutoff position

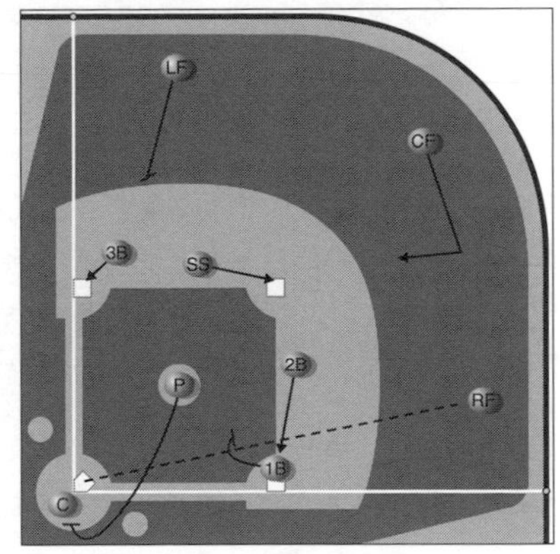

TABLE 14.4 Single With Runners on First and Second Base

BALL HIT TO LEFT

P	Goes between third and home and reacts accordingly
C	Covers home
1B	Covers 1B and makes sure runner tags it
2B	Covers 2B
3B	Cutoff man near home
SS	Covers 3B
LF	Fields ball and throws home
CF	Backs up LF
RF	Moves in toward infield

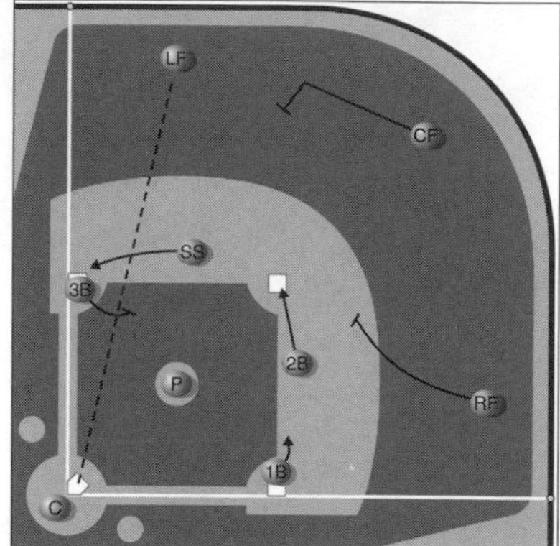

BALL HIT TO CENTER

P	Goes between third and home and reacts accordingly
C	Covers home
1B	Cutoff man for throw home
2B	Covers 2B
3B	Covers 3B
SS	Lines up throw to 3B
LF	Backs up CF
CF	Throws to cutoff man near home
RF	Backs up CF

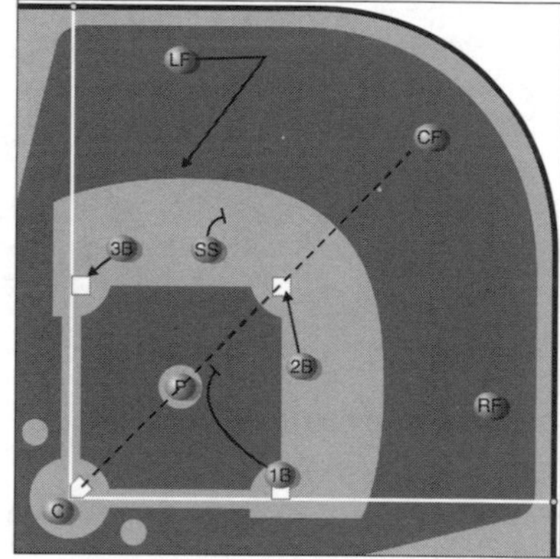

BALL HIT TO RIGHT

P	Goes between third and home and reacts accordingly
C	Covers home
1B	Cutoff man for throw home
2B	Covers 2B
3B	Covers 3B
SS	Lines up throw to 3B
LF	Moves in toward infield
CF	Backs up RF
RF	Throws to cutoff man near home

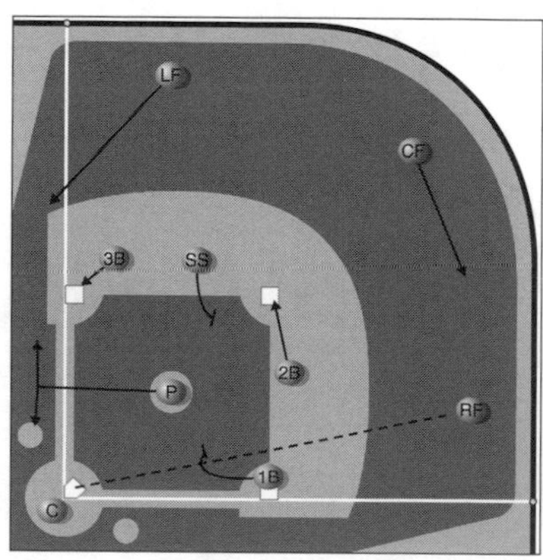

TABLE 14.5 Sure Double

BALL HIT TO LEFT

P	Backs up 3B
C	Covers home
1B	Watches runner touch base, trails him to 2B
2B	Covers 3B
3B	Backup man on tandem relay
SS	Front man on tandem relay
LF	Fields ball and throws to front man on tandem relay
CF	Backs up 2B
RF	Moves toward 1B area

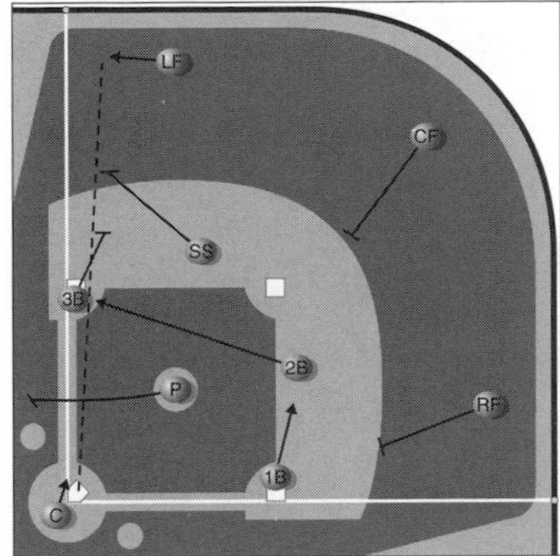

BALL HIT TO RIGHT CENTER

P	Backs up 3B
C	Covers home
1B	Watches runner touch base, trails him to 2B
2B	Front man on tandem relay
3B	Covers 3B
SS	Backup man on tandem relay
LF	Backs up 3B
CF	Goes for ball, hits front man on tandem relay
RF	Goes for ball, hits front man on tandem relay

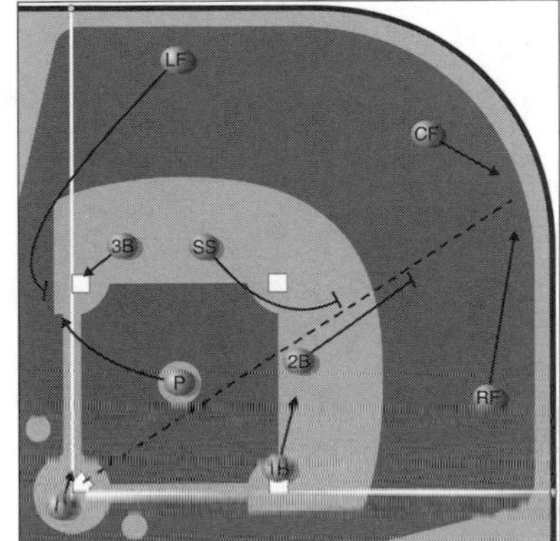

BALL HIT TO RIGHT

P	Backs up 3B
C	Covers home
1B	Cutoff man for throw home
2B	Front man on tandem relay
3B	Covers 3B
SS	Second man on tandem relay
LF	Backs up 3B area
CF	Moves to 2B area
RF	Goes for ball, hits front man on tandem relay

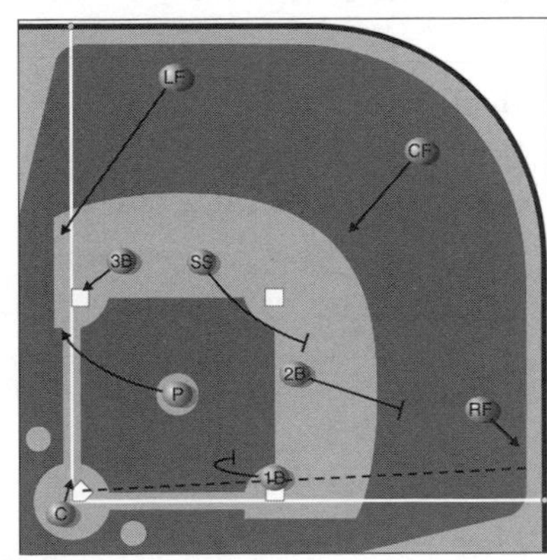

TABLE 14.6 Pop Foul, Runners on First and Third

POP-UP TO THIRD-BASE LINE

P	Covers 3B
C	Covers home
1B	Cutoff man for throw home
2B	Covers 2B
3B	Goes for ball
SS	Goes for ball
LF	Goes for ball
CF	Comes to 2B area
RF	Covers 1B

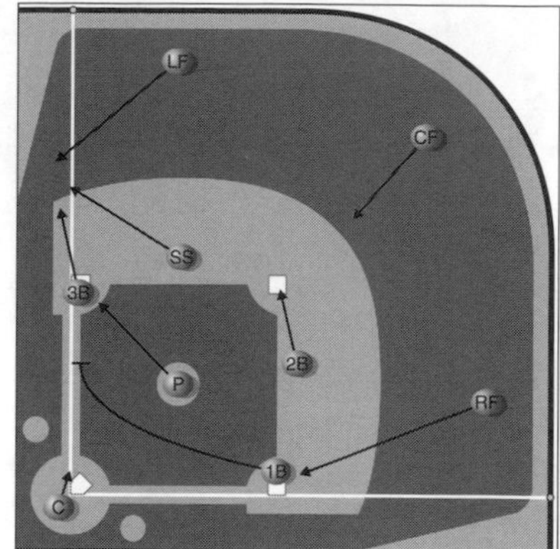

POP-UP STRAIGHT BACK

P	Covers home
C	Goes for ball
1B	Goes for ball
2B	Cutoff man for throw to 2B
3B	Goes for ball
SS	Covers 2B
LF	Goes to 3B area
CF	Backs up 2B
RF	Covers 1B area

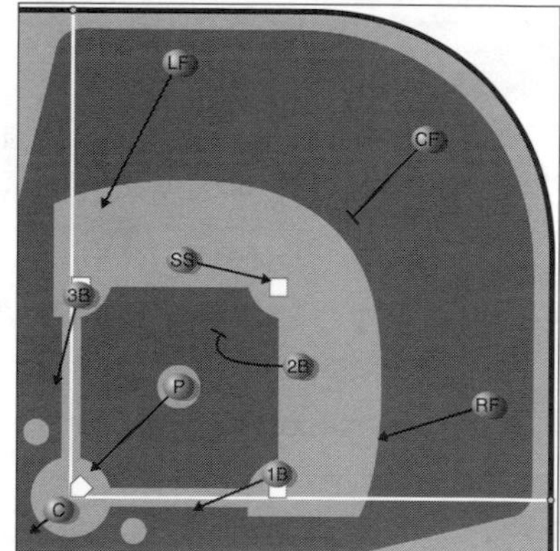

POP-UP TO FIRST-BASE LINE

P	Covers 1B
C	Covers home
1B	Goes for ball
2B	Goes for ball
3B	Cutoff man for throw home
SS	Covers 2B
LF	Covers 3B
CF	Comes to 2B area
RF	Goes for ball

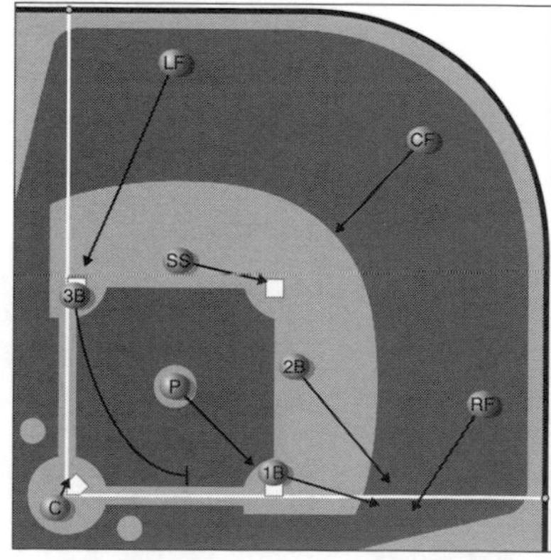

TABLE 14.7 Passed Ball or Wild Pitch With Bases Loaded

P	Covers home
C	Gets ball and throws to pitcher
1B	Goes to mound area to back up throw from pitcher
2B	Breaks in front of mound to back up throw from catcher
3B	Covers 3B
SS	Covers 2B
LF	Backs up 3B
CF	Backs up 2B
RF	Backs up 1B

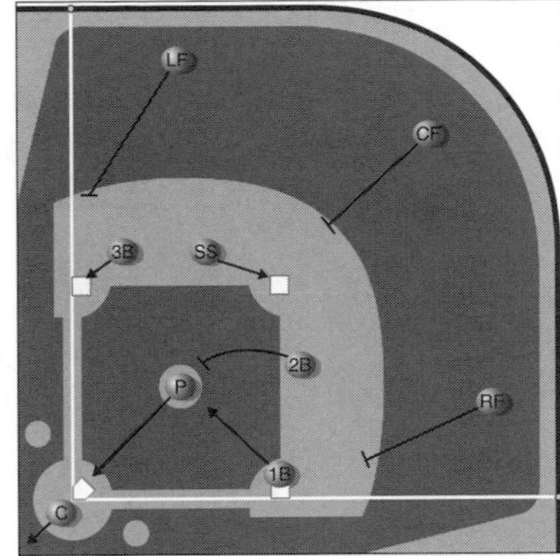

TABLE 14.8 Runner at Second Base, Ball Four or Strike Three, Ball Gets by Catcher

P	Covers home
C	Gets ball and throws home; if runner not coming throws to SS
1B	Covers 1B
2B	Cutoff position behind mound, reads runners
3B	Covers 3B
SS	Covers 2B
LF	Backs up 3B
CF	Backs up 2B
RF	Backs up 1B

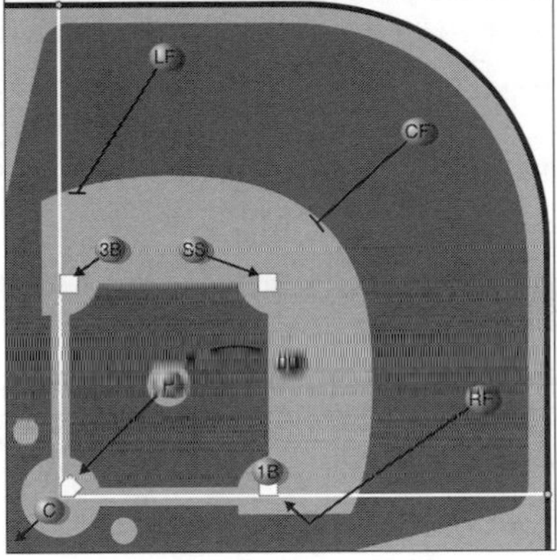

Rundowns

Rundowns are an integral part of the game of baseball, and thus the defensive team must practice them even though they occur less frequently than other defensive situations do. Handled properly by the defense, rundowns can be a pivotal point in the outcome of a ballgame. Rundowns may help your team out of a tough situation by foiling a rally by the opposition and should be an automatic out for the defense.

We observe some general rules in our rundown system. First, we want to make the runner commit himself and run at full speed in either direction. When a base runner is able to stop and change direction easily in a rundown, it is generally because he is able to stay under control while running and has not been forced to run full speed. When the defense forces a runner to run at full speed, he cannot easily stop and change direction. So the infielders can control a base runner running at full speed.

Another rule is to make at most one or two throws. With this method we would chase the runner in the direction he is going initially, usually forward. This technique requires the defense to make one throw. Trying to run him back to the base he last touched often requires an extra throw with additional chance for error. The one exception to this method is when we catch a runner between third base and home plate. If the runner goes beyond the halfway point in this situation, the third baseman will unload the ball to home plate, and we execute the rundown going back toward third base. That way, a mistake does not occur at the plate that allows the runner to score.

We have several general rules for the infielder with the ball. If the runner breaks hard and reaches the point of no return, the infielder unloads the ball. If the runner does not commit, then the infielder sprints the runner as hard as he can and anticipates a call for the ball. The infielder with the ball should run with the ball in the throwing position. If the runner is going away from his original base, the throw should be on the outside of the base line. When running a man back to his original base, the throw should be on the inside of the base line; the man catching the throw will be moved over, and the ball will be on his glove side. For left-handed throwers, the opposite is true, so an infielder receiving the throw moves over and lines up to receive the throw on the opposite side. The infielder without the ball should set up, go to the base if necessary, or close the gap. He should give the throwing infielder three keys about when to throw the ball:

1. He moves both his hands to a position head high.
2. He takes his first aggressive step forward off the base.
3. He yells "Ball."

He does all of this at the same time, which tells the throwing infielder to deliver him the ball head high. We want the throw from the head on up because this is an easy ball to handle when running.

In a typical rundown, you have a runner caught and you must get him with one throw. The infielders should get either outside or inside the base line. The fielder with the ball must go full speed at the runner to get him going full speed to the next base. The fielder with the ball will have his arm up in a throwing position as he runs, never faking the throw. When he does throw the ball on command from the receiving infielder, he throws the ball not with a normal motion but as if he were throwing a dart. If he throws it with full arm motion, he will have difficulty controlling the flight of the ball.

The key to the timing of the play is the receiving infielder, who positions himself on or beside the base the runner is running toward. If the fielder with the ball is doing his job, he should have the runner running toward the receiving infielder at close to full speed. The receiving infielder will then give the three keys about when to throw the ball: (1) both hands head high, (2) an aggressive step in, and (3) a yell of "ball." If the timing is good, the runner has no chance to avoid a tag.

The infielder should make the tag with the ball in the glove and the free hand on the ball to prevent it from falling out of the glove on the tag itself. The infielder throwing the ball should always lean away from the path of the runner after throwing the ball. If he is over halfway down the base line when he delivers the ball, he continues to the forward base. If he is less than halfway, he turns back and covers the back base. Backup people are at the bases in case two throws are needed. They use the same fundamentals on the second throw. On any pickoff at first base, the pitcher backs up first base. On a pickoff at second base, the pitcher backs up third base. On a rundown between third and home, the pitcher has the plate until the first baseman relieves him. The pitcher then backs up the play at home plate. Players should always continue a rundown until the umpire signals "Out." They must not assume that a runner is out because he ran out of the baseline or they tagged him out.

Bunt Defense

The main goal of any bunt defense is to get an out. Each of your bunt defenses is designed to get an out at a certain base. If getting that out is not possible, you must get the batter out. Many big innings occur when a defensive team does not get an out in a sacrifice-bunt situation.

The key to running a good bunt defense is having the fielder make the correct decision about where to throw the ball. The bunted ball will dictate which base to throw the ball to. All bunt defenses should be put on by the catcher, who gets the play from the coach.

Bunt defenses start with the pitcher throwing a strike on the lower part of the plate, a pitch that is hard to bunt. A large percentage of pitches thrown up in the strike zone are called balls, so pitching high tends to lead to walks in bunting situations. In addition, a ball up is more vulnerable to be hit hard. That becomes a factor if the bunter pulls back to hit. A strike is important in this situation because if the bunter takes the pitch, the offense will see your defense. They may then change the direction of the bunt, execute a hit-and-run, fake bunt and slash, or do any number of things.

A missed bunt is a great opportunity to pick off a base runner. Many base runners tend to overextend their secondary leads in bunt situations. Catchers should look for those opportunities.

You can try several maneuvers to see if a team is bunting or not. You can have your pitcher go to a long count and step back, use the inside move at second base, or try a pickoff attempt because many hitters will give the play away with their hands.

To confuse the offense, all bunt defenses should look the same. You can and should use pickoffs at each base off your bunt defenses.

Tables 14.9 through 14.14 describe and illustrate the most effective bunt defenses in specific game situations.

TABLE 14.9 Normal Bunt Defense, Runner at First Base

P	Holds runner close at first base, throws a mid-low fastball for a strike, and has front and left-side responsibilities
1B	Holds runner on until pitcher delivers the pitch, then charges the plate
2B	Cheats up and over and covers first base
SS	Covers second base
3B	Starts 15 feet in on grass and charges the plate, has priority over everyone on bunted ball
C	Covers in front of plate, calls where to throw the ball, has priority over pitcher and first baseman

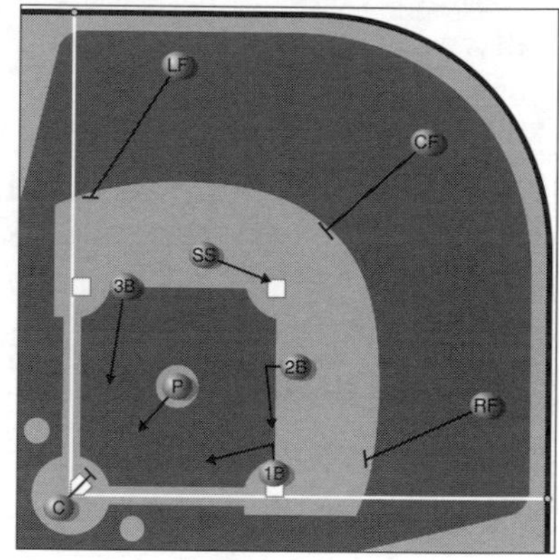

TABLE 14.10 Bunt Defense, Runner at First Base Breaks Early

P	Throws mid-low strike, covers areas in front of the mound, covers third if third baseman fields bunt
1B	Breaks to home plate when pitcher reaches top of stretch
2B	Cheats up and over, covers first base
SS	Covers second
3B	Starts 10 feet in front of grass, charges when pitcher reaches top of stretch
C	Covers in front of plate, makes call to infielders, has priority over pitcher and first baseman, covers third if pitcher isn't there

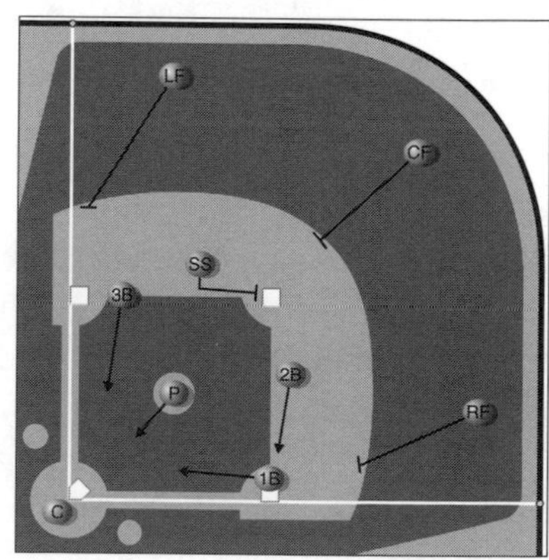

TABLE 14.11 Bunt Defense, Runner at First Base, Second Baseman Charges

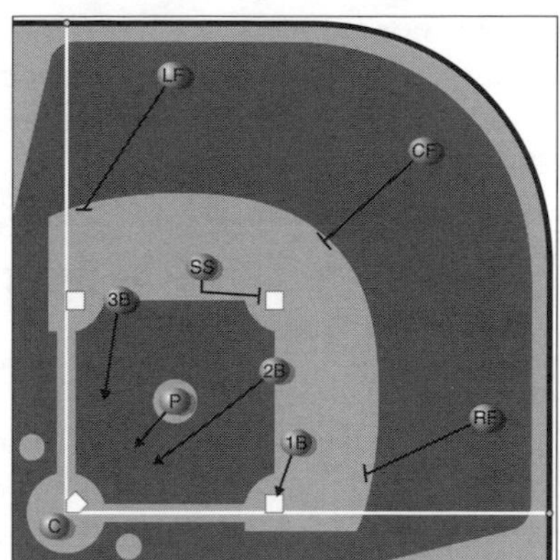

P Throws mid-low strike and breaks straight in, has coverage in front of mound, delivers to plate when sees second baseman out of corner of his eye

1B Holds runner on first

2B Starts on infield grass and breaks hard to plate when pitcher comes set, covers first-base side of mound

SS Covers second base

3B Starts 15 feet in front of grass and breaks hard when pitcher comes set, has third-base line

C Short front, calls where to throw the ball

LF Backs up third

CF Backs up second

RF Backs up first

TABLE 14.12 Normal Bunt Defense, Runners on First and Second

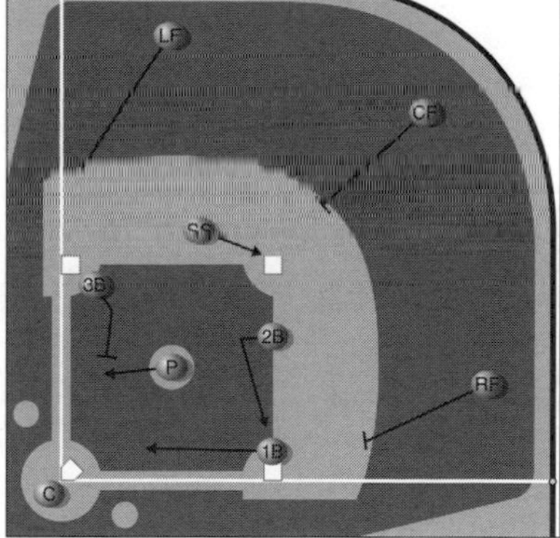

P Throws mid-low fastball for a strike when shortstop slaps glove and covers third-base side for bunt responsibility. If he can get the ball he calls "Mine, mine, mine," and fires to the third baseman. If he can't get the ball and the third baseman fields the ball, he goes in front of him and covers third base.

1B Starts 15 feet from first-base grass and charges hard when batter squares. Listens to catcher for the call.

2B Cheats toward first base from shallow second and covers first base from right-field side.

SS Holds runner close at second base. As pitcher comes to stretch he jabs hard with left foot toward second base and claps glove hard, indicating to the pitcher to pitch. If runner is too far off, opens glove and runs daylight pickoff.

3B Plays slightly in front of third base with view of runner, pitcher, and hitter. Takes a couple of steps in on pitch and reads bunted ball. If pitcher calls for ball, he covers third base. If he reads that pitcher can't get the ball, he calls for the ball and makes the play at first base.

C Covers in front of plate and calls where the ball should be thrown.

TABLE 14.13 Bunt Defense, Runners on First and Second, Second Baseman Charges

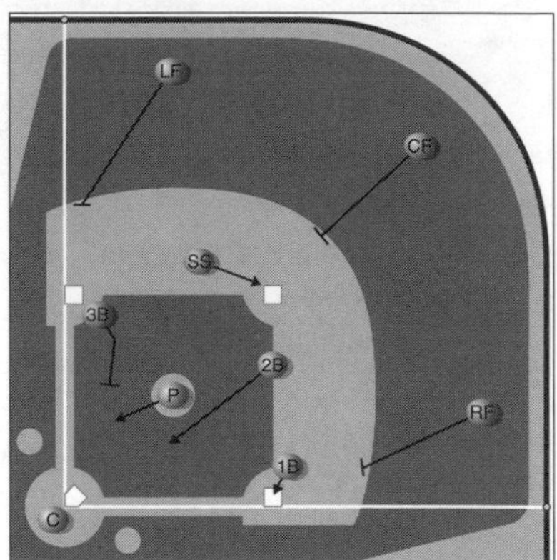

P Throws a mid-low strike when he sees second baseman out of corner of his eye. Covers third-base line and calls ball. If he can't field ball, covers third base.

1B Holds runner and stays on the bag.

2B When pitcher comes set, breaks hard to home plate.

SS Covers second base

3B Plays slightly in front of base and reads bunted ball. If pitcher calls for ball, he covers third base. If pitcher doesn't call for ball, he comes in, fields ball, and makes the play to first base.

C Calls play and has responsibility in front of plate.

TABLE 14.14 Runners on First and Second Base, Rotation Bunt Defense

P Throws a mid-low strike and delivers ball when shortstop reverses direction and has the base runner beat by at least four steps. He then charges ahead and has responsibility in front of the mound.

1B Charges toward home plate.

2B Jabs two steps hard to second base, then covers first base.

SS Starts in normal position. When pitcher gets down in stretch position, jabs two steps hard toward second base, slaps his glove in the same direction, and sprints to cover third base.

3B Plays slightly in front of third base with view of runner, pitcher, and hitter. Reads shortstop. If shortstop has runner beat, charges toward home plate. If the runner comes with the shortstop to third base, he retreats to third base and prepares for a throw from catcher. If hitter squares to bunt, he has left-side responsibility.

C Calls play and has short front responsibility.

You want to use this aggressive bunt defense when you are sure that the offense is bunting. The play is designed to get the out at third base.

Intentional Walks

An intentional walk is used as part of defensive strategy only when second base or second and third bases are occupied with less than two outs, and when the batter is not the potential tying or winning run.

In giving an intentional pass, the pitcher should not lob the ball to the plate but should instead throw medium-speed fast balls about three feet outside and shoulder high.

Because he cannot leave the catcher's area until the pitcher releases the ball, the catcher stands up and extends his arm (for a right-handed batter) or glove (for a left-handed batter) to the side, and then takes a lateral step to receive the ball.

The primary objective of the intentional pass is to pitch to a more logical opponent while setting up a force or double play. The intentional walk is used only with first base open.

Ways to Break the Opponent's Momentum

Through the course of a game, momentum, be it for your team or the opponent, can play a big role in the outcome of the day's event. You would like to think that how your opponent is playing that day will not affect the momentum of your team, but that is not always the case. Momentum is something that you want to keep on your side as much as possible; keep it in your dugout! Momentum can have a roller-coaster effect in which your team scores runs when emotions and intensity are high and gives up runs when intensity is low. This roller coaster can break a team down mentally and give them a feeling that they can't get over the hump. Keeping an even keel in your dugout is a sure way of getting the most out of your team that day. Breaking the opponent's momentum during the game can give them a topsy-turvy effect and give your team a win. Successful pitching and defense should set the tempo of the game.

Make Plays

Making plays on defense will keep your opponent from building momentum in a ballgame. Making a big play, such as a diving catch, a double play, or a strikeout to end an opponent's charge, can deflate the momentum of your opponent and give your team a big lift. Generally, you want a quick tempo when you are on defense.

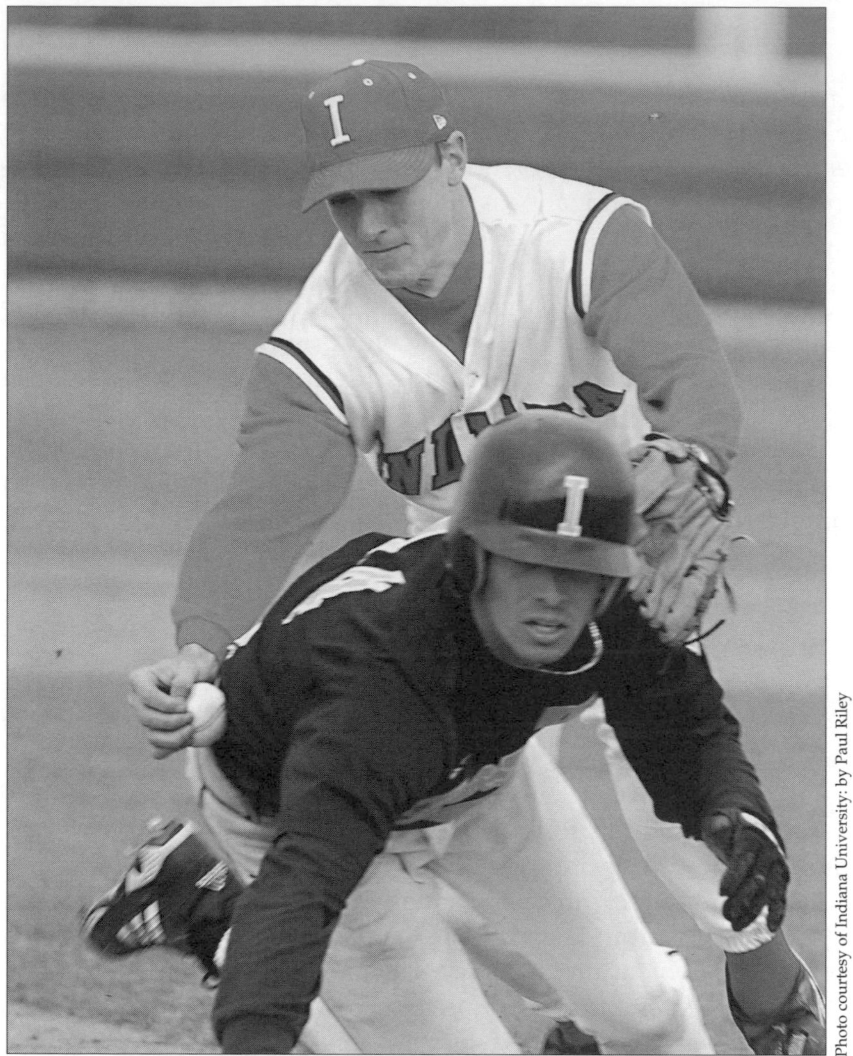

Photo courtesy of Indiana University: by Paul Riley

Making a big play on defense will help deflate your opponent's momentum.

Answer Back

Offensively, you can answer back to break your opponent's momentum. Suppose your opponent goes out and scores two runs in the top of the first inning. Answering with two or more runs in the bottom of that inning can cancel that charge. In the same situation, a pitcher can answer back in the top half of the second inning by shutting them down with no runs. Your team will then have an opportunity to build on the two runs they scored previously to answer back. Whether from an offensive standpoint or by pitching and defense, answering back is an effective way to break your opponent's momentum.

Minimize Runs Given Up

Minimizing the runs you allow in specific situations can stall or even stop your opponent's momentum. Pitching coaches always tell their pitchers to stay away from the big inning (giving up a lot of runs in one inning). If you check the box score, the big inning is usually what causes a loss. During a game you will have situations when the other team has the start of a big inning. Walks, errors, or hits may result in your opponent putting runners in scoring position. If you can minimize scoring by giving up just one run instead of two or three, you can slow the momentum and may even stop the opponent's charge.

Let the Starting Pitcher Set the Tempo

The starting pitcher for the next game can build momentum in baseball. Whether you are coming off a win or a loss, the starting pitcher can dictate the flow and pace of the game. Momentum from his standpoint is going out and establishing that he is going to throw strikes and get outs. If he can do this for a team coming off a win, momentum will stay on your side. If he can do this coming off a loss, he can break the momentum of the opponent.

Slow the Pace of the Game

The coach can use several methods to help break the momentum of an opponent. Let's say a team is building a big inning or is on the verge of scoring a bunch of runs. A coach can slow the pace of the game by having his catcher go out to talk to the pitcher and slow things down. When the catcher is done, the coach can call time-out and go talk to the pitcher. This all slows the pace of the game, lets the pitcher gather himself, and may slow the other team's momentum. A coach may also want to slow the pace when the opponent is making a late-inning charge to steal the lead. A coach can go out to talk to the pitcher, or he can make some substitutions in the middle of the inning that will take time and slow down the game. Another way to slow the other team's charge is for players to stall. A player can use the trick-knee gimmick and act as if he has an injury. Another ploy is to make an equipment adjustment, which will take time and slow the game down so that the team can regain its composure.

Getting the Lead Out Versus Taking the Sure Out

When talking about getting the lead out versus taking the sure out, you need to consider several factors:

- The defensive alignment
- The score
- The inning
- Whether you are the home or visiting team

With those in mind, you can start to break down what plays can be made from the infield or outfield, either getting the lead out or the sure out. Remember always that if you are trying to get the lead out and the play becomes impossible, you need to take the sure out. It is never a mistake to get an out, any out!

Defensive Alignment

Several factors influence defensive adjustments. As coaches we analyze several variables before making any defensive decision—pitcher's strengths, type of hitter, type of pitch, negative or positive count, number of outs, field conditions, inning, and whether the team is home or the visitor. When we move our players in or out of different positions, we consider these variables seriously.

Infield Depths

Coaches can use three different alignments for their infielders: back, in, and double-play depth.

- *Back*—When the infield is playing back, all four infielders are back to the cut of the grass and trying to keep the ball in the infield to make the sure out.
- *In*—If the infield is in, all four infielders are far enough in to make a throw to cut off the run at home and get the lead out. Attempting to get the lead out in this situation usually means your team is losing or you are in a close game and want to stop another run from scoring.
- *Double play*—If the infield is at double-play depth, they are positioned not at the back of the infield but cheating in a little so that they can cut down the distance that the ball will travel on the ground. This positioning will give the infielders more time to make the double play. In the double-play situation, you are trying to get the sure out at second base, which will also be the lead out if there is only a runner at first when the ball is hit. The sure out will not be the lead out if runners are at both first and second when the ball is hit. In this case you will almost always try to get the sure out at second and then have an opportunity to get the out at first by completing the double play. Taking the sure out at second in this situation can lead to getting two outs as opposed to just one if you choose to take the lead out

at third. In this situation the only time you will try to get the lead out at third is when there are already two outs or when the ball is hit in the hole between the third baseman and shortstop and the only play the shortstop can make is at third base.

Outfield Play

The outfield may play many different alignments during a game. They can play in, deep (so that nothing can get over their heads), shade to the right, or shade to the left. Outfielders are aligned depending on where the hitter may hit or the situation of the game. Regardless of the alignment, where the outfielder will throw depends on where the ball is hit and how far it is from the outfielder. When a hit ball takes the outfielder away from the lead runner, the throw should always go to second base to keep the sure out at first. If a hit ball takes the outfielder toward the lead runner or if he can make the play with a strong throw, he should throw to get the lead out.

Caught Ball in the Air When an outfielder can catch a fly ball by going toward the play, he should throw to try to get the lead out. When the out fielder catches a fly ball going away from the play on the lead runner, he should throw to second base (sure out) to keep the runner from advancing from first. The throw to second will keep the double play intact and keep the sure out at first if the next batter hits the ball on the ground. If the next batter hits the ball on the ground, you will have the opportunity to get a double play and stop the offensive charge.

Ball Hit on the Ground On ground balls hit directly at the outfielder or two or three steps to his right or left, he should throw to get the lead out because he can make a strong throw to the lead base. In the same situation with the ball on the ground and five or more steps to his right or left, the smart play would be to throw to second base (sure out). The throw will keep the batter from advancing to second and keep the double play intact. If the next batter hits the ball on the ground, there is a chance to turn a double play. In almost all situations the outfielder should try to keep the double play intact (take the sure out) and not let the runner advance. Always trying to throw out the lead runner is the biggest mistake an outfielder can make because doing so can extend the inning and lead to more runs for the opponent, rather than being able to break the back of an inning.

Winning or Losing, Early or Late in the Game

When your team is winning, the emphasis will be on getting sure outs. The winning team will take sure outs to minimize the number of offensive opportunities the opponent has to regain the lead. Whether early or late in the game the winning team should give a run to get as many sure outs as possible. Late in the game the winning team should trade runs for outs. Getting the lead out at second base in a double-play situation will be the best choice to get one or possibly two outs and stop the other team from advancing runners into scoring position. Getting the sure out at second in a double-play situation with the bases loaded or with runners at first and second may result in giving up a run, but it will draw the winning team closer to the 27 outs needed to end the game.

When your team is losing, the emphasis will be on stopping the opposing team from scoring any more runs. The team behind in the score will usually try to get the lead out if the runner is trying to score. A losing team will take the sure out early in a game if that out can be translated into a double play, even though a run may score. They will give up the run to get two outs, clear the bases, and stop any more runs from scoring that inning. Late in the game with a runner in scoring position, they will be trying to cut off the run by getting the lead out because they will not have many more opportunities to score runs. Cutting runs off late gives them a better chance to come back by scoring one or two runs.

Home or Visiting Team

The standard strategy in baseball is to play to win on the road and tie at home. If your team adheres to this strategy in the last inning of a game, you will need to make specific plays that translate into outs.

In this situation the home team will give up the tying run to get the sure out. They will concede the run because they know they have the bottom half of the inning to score a run and win a game. Getting the sure out, whether the front end of a double play or an out at first, will reduce the opponent's offensive opportunities to score the go-ahead run.

If you are the visitor in this situation, you must get lead outs or you will lose the game. Trying to turn a double play or taking an out at first without allowing the home team to score are the only two situations when the visiting team will take the sure out. Otherwise, the visitor will always try to cut off the winning run in the last inning of a game by getting the lead out.

Defending the Steal

A key to stopping the running game is to identify running situations and the players who can run. You should check the stat sheet for stolen bases and stolen bases attempted. In general, you can expect middle players or the one, two, and nine hitters in the lineup to be runners.

Good runners like to run early in the count, especially with two outs. Also, they often run with three balls on the hitter. They will run more in close games. Slower runners will try to run on breaking-ball counts and may try to delay steal, especially with a left-handed hitter at the plate.

Disrupting the base runner's timing. When a runner reaches base, the pitcher must upset his timing and rhythm. The simplest and most effective way to threaten a potential base stealer is to hold the ball and freeze the runner. The pitcher can disrupt the base runner's timing by varying the amount of the time he holds the ball on each pitch. On some pitches he can hold the ball longer, and on others he can go directly to the plate with only a slight pause. If the base runner is unsure when the pitcher will throw to the plate, he will become tense. His muscles will tighten up, and he is unlikely to get a good jump. Holding the ball until the base runner stops prevents the base runner from getting a walking lead. Additionally, the batter who is waiting will become anxious and begin to lose his concentration.

Statistics show that marginal base stealers have a significantly lower success rate when a pitcher throws to first at least once. A well-planned quick throw to first can be effective. Varying his moves is probably the best way for the pitcher to stop the running game. A quick step-off will chase the runner back to the bag and will often expose his intentions. When a runner slides headfirst back to first, it's a sign that he is going. A throw to first or a quick step-off will also cause the batter to tip his intentions.

Quickening the delivery to the plate. The pitcher can control the running game by speeding up his move to the plate and quickening his delivery to the plate. He should concentrate on minimizing arm and leg movement; the less wasted movement he has in his delivery, the easier it becomes to speed his release to the plate. He should think of his leg kick as a leg lift rather than vice versa. He should keep his arms close to his body and reduce the arc that his arm travels. He should get his arm up into a throwing position quickly. These techniques will speed up his delivery and improve his mechanics.

Slide step. The slide step is an effective way to slow down the running game. From the set position, the pitcher simply locks his hip and slides his lead leg close to the ground toward the plate. In essence, he is speeding up his time to home plate. If a normal leg lift is timed at 1.4 seconds, using the slide step would reduce the time to the plate to 1.2 seconds.

Pitchouts. Pitchouts are another way to slow down base runners. The purpose of the pitchout is to give the catcher an easy ball to handle so that he can get off a quick, accurate throw to second base. For a pitcher, the key on a pitchout is to stay compact, quicken the delivery, and throw a four-seam fastball high and away. He does not use a slide step when pitching out because the base runner will probably not go on the pitch. The pitcher can also use a modified pitchout, a pitchout thrown eye high just off the outside corner. A team that has the opponent's signals should use the modified pitchout because the opposition is less likely to suspect that their signs have been compromised. The modified pitchout is also used against teams who read pitchouts well.

Left-handers' advantages. Left-handers should have a good move to first base and be able to stop the running game better than right-handers can.

Photo courtesy of Indiana University: by Paul Riley

The pitcher can control the running game by quickening the delivery to the plate.

Many lefties have not developed a move to first base because most players do not run on lefties. The key is to keep all the actions of the pitch and pick the same so that the base runner has no key on an early read.

A left-handed pitcher can do a variety of things with his leg and arms. Left-handed pitchers must abide by two simple rules when picking to first base. The first rule concerns the leg lift. The stride leg must not cross the front plane of the rubber as it is being lifted. The second rule deals with the stride leg, which must land within a 45-degree angle from the center of the rubber.

Left-handed pitchers have the luxury of being able to freeze runners without throwing the ball to first base. One such move is called the shoulder turn. As the pitcher lifts his leg, he turns his right shoulder in toward the runner while keeping the left leg from crossing the plane of the rubber. He then delivers the pitch to the plate. This move will cause the runner to freeze or retreat to first base.

Read lift. The read lift is effective in slowing down the opponent's better base stealers. The read lift is a slow, deliberate lift of the leg without committing to either the base or the plate. The pitcher must read the runner and act accordingly. If the runner breaks toward second base, the pitcher steps down toward first and picks. If the runner freezes or retreats to first, the pitcher delivers the ball to the plate.

Step-back pitch. The step-back pick can be the quickest way for a left-hander to get the ball to the bag. The pitcher must step off the rubber with his left foot and throw the ball with a flicking action to the bag. A variation of this move would be not to throw the ball or to fake the throw. Because he has stepped off the rubber, a throw is not necessary.

Awareness of runners at second. When defending the steal, pitchers must be aware of runners occupying second base. Stealing third base can be much easier than stealing second for several reasons. Pitchers tend to have a slower count with a runner at second. Runners at second typically get bigger leads while taking walking leads. The runner will be in motion while taking his primary lead, which will increase his lead and make him quicker in getting a jump to run.

Inside move. The inside move is beneficial in deterring theft of third base. The pitcher executes the inside move by lifting the stride leg until it reaches its apex, turning the leg over and across the rubber, and stepping down to pick to second. This move can be effective only if the leg lift of the inside move resembles the leg lift of his normal delivery to plate. This particular move is great to use against aggressive runners, runners who put their heads down when they run, and in two-out, full-count situations when runners at first and second are running on movement.

Daylight, or open-glove, play. Other pickoffs to second or third are used with timing and communication within the team defense. One such strategy is the daylight, or open-glove, play at second. Either middle infielder will see daylight between the runner and bag. As the pitcher comes set, the shortstop will flash an open glove with his arm extended while he breaks to the bag. (The second baseman extends his right hand to execute the play.) The pitcher sees the open glove, immediately turns, and picks to the bag. This play takes timing, nonverbal communication, and the ability of the shortstop or second baseman to read daylight.

As we have seen in this section, defending the steal can involve a multitude of looks, counts, rhythm, and timing strategies. If a pitcher can learn to apply these techniques, he will surely be able to slow the running game of the opponent and control the game.

Buying Time for a Reliever

One of the most difficult situations for a coach during a game is changing pitchers. Many variables are involved in making this change, such as pitch count, struggling by the pitcher, and getting the relief pitcher warm. Sometimes a pitcher looks as if he is moving along well in a game, but in a matter of six or seven pitches, the opponent puts two or three runs on the scoreboard before the coach can get a reliever down to the bullpen. So how can we buy time for our relief staff to get ready?

When making a pitching change during a ballgame, the reliever usually comes into the game with runners on base in a tough situation. Therefore, the relief pitcher must be warm and ready to compete at his best. The best solution for giving your reliever time to prepare is to monitor your starting pitcher's pitch count. Once the starter has reached a certain number of pitches, you send the reliever to the bullpen to begin his warm-up. Although the starter may be pitching well, he is reaching a point of breaking down, and you are prepared when that begins to occur.

The most common strategy to buy extra time for your reliever is to stall. You and your players can use many stall tactics. The standard stall move is to send your catcher to talk to the struggling pitcher and follow that with a trip to the mound by a member of the coaching staff. The umpire usually will give the coach two to three minutes to confer with a pitcher before he walks out to break up the meeting. You have a choice of making the change or leaving the pitcher in the game. In this situation you have just enabled your relief pitcher to throw 15 to 20 more warm-up pitches.

In making a trip to the mound, the coach can either pull the starting pitcher or leave him in the game. If you leave the pitcher in the game, you cannot make another trip to the mound to make a change until the next batter comes to the plate. In essence, you have to roll the dice with that move. If you choose to leave the pitcher in the game and he makes it through that batter, you have given the reliever more time to warm up.

Players can talk to the pitcher to buy time for your reliever. An infielder can call time and confer with the pitcher. The catcher may then visit, followed by a coach, thus buying even more time.

Coaches can find themselves out of trips. In that case, using pitchouts and a series of pickoffs is a good tactic. Depending on the situation or where the base runner is positioned, pickoffs can give your relief pitcher time to get warm. Using inside moves to second base, pickoff throws to first base, or called picks with your infielders are good ways to gain extra warm-up time. Pitching around a hitter or calling pitchouts on consecutive pitches can lengthen time as well.

One of the most difficult ways to stall is slowing the starting pitcher's tempo. Tempo is how quickly the pitcher gets ready to throw the next pitch. We typically teach pitchers to have good, quick tempo. They get the ball, step on the rubber, and are ready to pitch. We have to teach our pitchers to change their tempo during the game.

When your starter begins to break down, he can take more time between pitches to gain time for the reliever. He can clean his spikes, walk around the mound, wipe the sweat off, tie his shoes, tuck his uniform in, use any way to buy time to give the relief pitcher more pitches.

In all our strategies for buying time for our relievers, we must remember the eight pitches he will receive when entering the game. The situations will dictate the moves you should consider making. You end up playing a game of cat and mouse to put your players in the best situation to be ready to perform. A relief pitcher should warm up in the stretch position and get two of his pitches game ready, or one if time is limited. Try to give your relievers a general idea of their roles and how you will use them during a ballgame.

Pickoff Plays

The primary objective of a pickoff is to keep base runners close to bases and make an aggressive team more tentative. Pickoffs are important in helping a team control the running game. Pickoffs can also be effective in uncovering a team's offense in a bunt situation.

We try to emphasize quick feet and a quick upper body, short arm action, and accurate location on all pickoffs. The target location is two feet over the inside corner of the bag.

At First Base

First base. The pitcher throws to the first baseman, who is playing behind the runner. The catcher puts the pickoff on and reads whether there is daylight between the runner and the first baseman breaking in behind the runner. If daylight appears, the catcher pops his mitt and the pitcher throws to first base. If the runner breaks back to first base with the first baseman, the catcher drops his mitt and the pitcher steps back. The pitcher reads the catcher. With a left-handed pitcher on the mound, the first baseman breaks when the pitcher picks up the nonpivot foot and throws automatically to first.

Go hard. The first baseman puts on this play by stepping in front of the runner. The pitcher comes set. If the runner leads off beyond the first baseman, the first baseman will break to the bag and the pitcher will throw over. If the runner stays even with the first baseman, the pitcher reads this and throws to the plate. With a left-handed pitcher on the mound, the throw to first base is automatic.

At Second Base

Daylight. No sign is needed for this play. When the pitcher comes set, the shortstop comes up behind the runner and bluffs him back to second base. If the runner doesn't step back toward second base, the shortstop opens his glove and breaks to second base. If the pitcher reads daylight between the shortstop and the runner at second base, he throws to the bag at second base. If the shortstop does get the runner to step back toward second base, he slaps his glove, which signals the pitcher to pitch, and the shortstop steps back to his normal position.

Count play. The pitcher gets the sign from second baseman or shortstop, depending on who is covering. This is a timing play based on the back of the pitcher's neck. When the pitcher starts his stretch, one of the infielders will bluff the runner back to second base (the one not covering the bag). As the pitcher comes to the set position, he looks home and counts one thousand one, one thousand two. He then turns and fires to the other infielder, who has broken to cover second base after counting one thousand one. Either the shortstop or the second baseman can put the play on and cover the bag.

Go hard. This play involves an inside reverse pivot from the pitcher, who throws to the shortstop covering second base. The shortstop puts the play on and breaks when the pitcher starts his leg lift. The pitcher should get to a balanced position before starting his inside pivot toward second base.

16. The catcher puts on this play. The pitcher is in a windup position and reads the catcher. If the catcher sees daylight between the shortstop and the runner, he pops his mitt and the pitcher throws to second. If the catcher drops his mitt, the pitcher steps back because they have no play. This pickoff is used with the bases loaded or runners at second and third. The pitcher must read the catcher.

14. The catcher puts on this play for a pickoff at second base. The second baseman reads the runner. When the runner takes his longest lead, the second baseman will break to the bag. The pitcher, in a stretch position and looking at home, must be ready to throw when the catcher lifts his glove.

At Third Base

Go hard. From the stretch position the right-handed pitcher steps at 45 degrees to third base and fires to the third baseman covering the bag. The infielder breaks when the pitcher lifts the nonpivot foot. The left-handed pitcher reads third base by looking over his left shoulder from the stretch position. When the infielder breaks, the pitcher fires to the third baseman covering the bag.

15. The catcher puts on this play. The pitcher in windup position throws to third base or steps back off the rubber, depending on the runner. If the infielder breaks to third base and the catcher sees daylight, the catcher pops his mitt and the pitcher jump turns and throws to third base. If the runner breaks back with infielder, the catcher drops his mitt and the pitcher steps back.

Other Pickoffs

31 and 32. We use another pickoff when runners are on second and third or first and third. We have our pitcher pitch from the stretch. He brings his leg up. As his leg comes down, his body should start moving toward third base. The pitcher fakes to third and throws to second or first, depending on where the runner is. With a runner at second base, the shortstop and second baseman should move a little farther from the bag to encourage the runner to take a maximum lead. The second baseman covers on this pickoff and breaks as the pitcher starts his kick. We have the ideal defense when the lead runner is sliding on the ground and we are making a play at second base. The pitcher must guard against moving his body to third base before his leg comes completely off the ground. The pitcher must make a good fake at third for two reasons. First, he must convince everyone he's going to third. Second, a good fake facilitates the pivot. During a first-and-third situation with two outs and a full count, this play is automatic. This pickoff with runners at first and third is very effective, especially with an aggressive base runner at first base.

Pickoff Plays off a Bunt Defense

When corners break early with a runner at first base and the bunt in order, we can have the second baseman circle into first base and cover first base, coming squared up to the pitcher for the pick.

The pitcher wants to make sure that he doesn't rush this so that the second baseman has time to get to first base. The pitcher will throw to first once he sees the first baseman pass by him out of the corner of his eye.

This same pickoff can be used at second base in a bunt situation. The corners will break early, and the shortstop will bluff and sprint for third base. If the runner goes with the shortstop, the pitcher will step back off the rubber. If the runner doesn't go with the shortstop, the pitcher will turn his head to home and count one thousand one, one thousand two. He then picks to the second baseman, who is covering second base. The second baseman will take two steps toward first and circle back to cover second base for the pickoff.

In the last pickoff off the bunt defense, the second baseman breaks early toward the hitter at home plate. After the second baseman passes the pitcher, the pitcher picks at first base to the first baseman, who is holding the runner on.

These pickoffs keep base runners from cheating on bunt coverages when the defense is breaking early. The idea is to make an aggressive base-running team more cautious.

Catchers can also put on pickoff plays to particular infielders. When the catcher puts on a pickoff to a particular infielder, he will be throwing to the base on the next swing and miss or bunt and miss. He will not throw unless he has received acknowledgment of the sign from the infielder. The best times to put on these plays are with a base runner who can run, in bunt situations, on 3-2 counts with less than two outs, or with a runner at third base and the infield playing in. You should never try a pickoff at a base with two outs and a weak hitter up behind in the count.

Offense can win you some games. Defense will win you more games. Defense and pitching will win you championships. An aggressive, communicating defense can control the flow of the game. As a coach you want to develop a team that plays consistent defense (making the routine play) and does not beat itself, meets every situation with poise, and is able to make a great play. Great defense can turn the momentum of a game and break the spirit of your opponent. Poor defense can dishearten a team, make it appear poorly coached, and prolong the game. In general, a defense breaks down when players try to do too much. Infielders go so fast that they are out of control, and outfielders try to make impossible throws. Teach players to be under control and make the average play. The defensive team that can make the routine play gives itself an excellent chance to win.

PART IV

Fine-Tuning Your Strategic Approach

15

Adjusting for Different Levels of Competition

John Herbold

1. Play catch.
2. Put the ball in play.
3. Throw strikes.
4. Have good team spirit.
5. Run the bases intelligently.
6. Know the rules.

These six axioms describe for players and coaches alike the secret to success at any level of baseball. Coach Wally Kincaid of Cerritos (California) Junior College originally outlined the first four. I added the last two later.

Coach Bill Powell of Long Beach Poly High then suggested a few more: "Try to score in the first inning because it's the most productive of all—and try to keep the other team from scoring in the first inning. And any time you score, it's important that you keep the opposition from scoring right after you do."

Coach Kincaid had some outstanding seasons, once going 39-1 and then 40-0! He did it by playing more games than anybody else and against the best opponents he could find, all the while stressing good fundamentals.

Of course, our next problem—after we know what to do—is deciding how to achieve it. No doubt, other chapters in the book will help you do this. Now let us ponder another statement with which at first reading many coaches, players, and fans may not agree: "Baseball at all levels is more similar than dissimilar!" A shocking and provoking thought, isn't it? But let's examine the issue. The history of baseball shows that it has been a consistent game. Three strikes and you're out, six outs per inning, no time limits, equal at-bats. Sure, the distances may vary: 40-foot bases or 75 or even 60. Seven innings or nine. Sometimes only five if the high school "mercy rule" creeps in. Certainly, at different levels the fences are not all the same distance. No doubt women's professional baseball failed because the women played in ballparks designed for males. Had the promoters brought in the fences, the game might have survived. Bats in the youth leagues are naturally smaller (and unfortunately usually metal), but players at all levels can surprise with demonstrations of power and arm strength. As Mr. Einstein once proved, it's all relative.

So now what of the game itself? It's not identical for all ages and sexes, but it's close. Players make errors of omission and commission at all levels. One team wins, one loses, and more often than not games are as much lost by the losing team as they are won by the victors.

Errors and umpires everywhere are all part of the winning and losing. As the great New York Giants manager John McGraw said long ago, "You take the errors and the umpires out of baseball, and the game would die in two weeks."

Players in high school often throw to the wrong base, but at a major-league game you may see the same mistake. While watching the St. Louis Cardinals play the Los Angeles Dodgers, I saw a lone Cardinals runner try to advance to third on a ground ball to short with one out! Easy out, dumb play. Later, with one out and Dodgers runners on first and third, the batter hit a fly ball to the Cardinals' center fielder, who then foolishly fired the ball home. Unfortunately, the throw not only cleared the head of the cutoff man but also flew over the catcher and even the pitcher backing him up! By the time the pitcher had retrieved the errant toss, the runner on first had gone all the way to third. A week later Cardinals manager Whitey Herzog resigned. I guess he'd seen enough.

So does strategy vary from level to level? Yes, of course, but not much. First, we need to realize that baseball is really a pyramid—of both success and failure! The bottom tiers of the pyramid are made up of the thousands of youngsters all over the world who begin playing the game at an early age. Johnny and Jenny at age six or seven come home and tell Mom and Pop they want to play T-ball down at the park because "all the kids are." Some of the youngsters then find that they like the game. Some love it, and some leave it.

Down through the ensuing years, our baseball pyramid becomes smaller as players strive to reach the top, our major leagues. We hope all will remember the game fondly through their experiences. As noted baseball expert Don Weiskopf wrote in his book *Baseball Play America,* "Often too much youth baseball is geared more to the adults than to the kids." He adds that in a rush to find national champions, for many players the summer season is all too abbreviated—finished by mid-July.

Often a good neighborhood playground can help in teaching the nuances of baseball, especially when the people in charge are baseball veterans with years of experience, putting fun into the word *fundamentals.*

Years ago, men such as Benny Lefebvre (Los Angeles Rancho Cienega Playground), Bill Duvernet (Los Angeles Manchester), and George Powles (Bushrod Park in Oakland) were key reasons behind the success of California high school powerhouses Dorsey, Washington, and Fremont in Los Angeles, and Oakland Tech and McClymonds in Oakland. Today Fremont High is tied with Long Beach Poly for producing the most major leaguers with 23 each, and Washington High once had six future AL or NL performers on one team! Powles for McClymonds in Oakland turned out such stars as Frank Robinson, Vada Pinson, basketball legend Bill Russell, and football whiz John Brodie.

As ex-major leaguer Chuck Stevens says of his youth, "On those Long Beach playgrounds, we learned to be 'playmakers,' of which there are very few today even in the big leagues."

I remember a Long Beach Poly High player of mine who, while receiving an intentional walk with the winning run on third, suddenly reached out and poked the third pitch into center field for the game clincher. Nobody *taught* him that! Certainly not I, who was as surprised as everyone else there. Kids learn such tricks at the park playing with and against each other, especially their elders.

Another time one of my players scooted home from third with a big run while the other team was making an appeal on him at second. Nobody taught him that either. But young players should be encouraged to try things on their own. Too much baseball today is robotic. Sadly, in high school ball now there are no more intentional walks and no appeal plays.

Ah, fundamentals. I remember Tommy Lasorda asking me after I had my head down after a losing effort in a close game, "John, did you lose the game because of a breakdown in fundamentals?" "No," I replied. "Then don't feel so bad," he said.

Certainly, the length of practice sessions will vary depending on your age group, but whatever the ages involved, practice should be carefully planned, executed by time blocks, and made competitive, realistic, and enjoyable. Make your practices like games, and then the games will be like practice.

Or, as the motorist asked the traffic cop, "How do I get to Carnegie Hall?" "Practice, practice, practice," was the reply.

By the time youngsters reach high school, the number remaining from those who started out in T-ball drops considerably. That number is cut in half when college rolls around, and it falls even more when the pro draft arrives. A fortunate few get a shot at the minor leagues. It is estimated that

7 percent of those drafted and signed will ever reach the majors, and of those who do, most will average about four years there. Still, hope springs eternal, and it should. Some are going to make it and become Yankees, A's, Astros, or whoever.

Ask, Listen, Observe

So, to help young people become more proficient in baseball or softball, coaches must do a lot of teaching and encouraging. As Ted Williams always said, "Hitting a baseball is the hardest thing to do in all sport."

Along this line, one of my ex-players, who went on to college and pro ball, once commented, "There are a lot more good *players* than there are good *coaches*!" Both should follow Yogi's advice, "You can observe a lot by watching," because baseball, more than any other sport, is a "monkey see, monkey do" game. Baseball is sort of an "individual team" game of chess played on grass and dirt.

For instance, as a beginning coach, I knew a lot about the art of catching because I had been a catcher, but I knew *nothing* about playing first base. So I studied first sackers and then asked questions about playing the bag from ex-major leaguers like Gordon Goldsberry, Chuck Stevens, and Jack Graham. Later, while discussing a flashy major-league first baseman with a pro shortstop, I told him how graceful I thought the first sacker was around the bag. To my dismay, the infielder blurted out, "We hate him! He never gives us a stationary target. He's just a 'hot dog' timing his arrival to catch the ball on the run to make himself look good." Hmmm. I learned something there—get to the bag quickly and stand *still*!

Mets scout Harry Minor once asked me, "When's the easiest time for a runner to get picked off base?" "Don't know. When?" "On a missed bunt," Harry answered.

Next question: "What should a base runner do if he gets picked off first base?" Same answer: "Don't know." "He does *not* try to get back to first or get in a rundown unless there's also a runner on third. Rather, he goes hard for second base and slides late, perhaps even head faking the receiving infielder." At Long Beach Poly High, we once beat a future major-league pitcher 1-0 on this technique, then went on to win the Southern California–CIF high school crown.

Minor's last question: "What does a runner on second do when there are two outs, two strikes on the batter, and the runner *sees* that the next pitch is going to be a strike?" For the third time I said, "Don't know." Minor answered, "He steals third!"

Makes sense doesn't it? Well, we once won our high school league championship on this play because I listened to Harry Minor, and my players listened to me.

On a very shallow pop fly that fell between the outgoing shortstop and the incoming left fielder, our runner barely scored the winning run because he was already racing to third on a pitch headed for the middle of the plate.

"What does the pitcher do on a pop fly between the first baseman and the catcher when both are going for the pop-up? The pitcher calls the name of one player, and then *tackles* the other so that they don't collide and perhaps drop the ball." Thank you, Scout Jackie Warner, many years ago. We've done it a few times.

"What does the second baseman do when he is prepared to cover first base on a sacrifice bunt?" What he does *not* do is sprint immediately in the direction of first base. Rather he cautiously moves straight forward so that he can move in either direction and not commit himself too early should the ball be hit behind him and go out into the outfield. Thank you, former Arizona State coach Bobby Winkles.

So ask, listen, observe. Yogi Berra had some pretty good messages for us, but I'm not so sure about his "When you get to the fork in the road, take it." When it comes to strategy, I don't think that one would be much help.

Six Steps to Success

And now, it's time for us to delve deeper into our half-dozen axioms: (1) play catch, (2) put the ball in play, (3) throw strikes, (4) have good team spirit, (5) run the bases intelligently, and (6) know the rules.

Play Catch

"Anybody can play catch!" you say. Whoa, not so! Branch Rickey once orated, "You don't *play* baseball, you *work* it." Brooks Robinson, the great Orioles third baseman, told Coach John Scolinos and me, "I often just bounce a baseball 50 times or more up against a cement wall and field the ricochets. Then I'll take 30 ground balls because fielders go into slumps just as hitters do."

All-star infielder Bobby Grich later added that Robinson showed him a good drill that Robinson's high school coach had once shown him. Two infielders stand facing each other, maybe four to five feet apart. One fielder would have his glove on while the tosser bounced difficult short hops to the fielder until he had made 25 in a row without a miscue. Then the pair would trade duties.

An old timer once told me, "Catch the ball as if you were catching a raw egg, and on ground balls think of your glove as a dustpan." Adds Coach Jerry Kindall, the former head man at the University of Arizona, "Fielders should field the *bottom* of a ground ball—glove beneath it."

So in practice we do fielding drills with dustpans as gloves, use square "baseballs" to detail the bottom part, and play catch with an egg, each player taking a step backward after each catch until something breaks. (Supposedly, the record throw and catch is over 300 feet—but not by us!)

One of the best catch-and-throw drills is the popular four-man relay-throwing contest in which the coach spreads out two or more squads of four players. The first man in line for each team has a ball, the coach yells, "Go!" and the race is on. The rules are that the ball must be caught on the fly by player number two, who like number three and number four, is spaced in a line a reasonable distance apart depending on the age level.

Number two then turns to his glove side and gives to number three, and then on to number four, who starts the ball going back in reverse with the ball returning to the first player, providing it hasn't been dropped or overthrown. If the ball ever hits the ground, that team loses right there, but the other squads must still complete their throws all in the air. To be victorious, the winning team must win by a two-game margin.

Put the Ball in Play

As the old saying goes, "Ya can't steal first base!" So there's not much strategy involved if the batter strikes out. And the worst strikeout is the called third strike. I've benched players who took a called third. You may be worried about teaching batters to swing at bad pitches, but I'm not. And I never criticize a player of mine for swinging at a ball over his head or in the dirt. I may not like it, but as a coach I can't have it both ways.

The Cuban players have a saying: "You can't walk off the island." (And don't let anybody tell you that "a walk is as good as a hit" either). Speaking of Cuban players, I once had a great talk with Tony Oliva, three-time AL batting champ and later the hitting coach for his Minnesota Twins. In that beautiful Cuban accent, he lectured, "You got to sweeng de bat. Don't be too peeky. You no know that de boll be outside a leetle beet. You can heet de peech ifn you sweeng at de boll."

In our Los Angeles State University dugout, we have several signs, one reading, "You can't hit the ball with the bat on your shoulder." Another says, "Close enough to call—close enough to hit."

Our players are also reminded that former player Doug Stodgel had but one strikeout in 229 times at bat one season (and that on a foul tip caught by the catcher on Doug's 123rd at-bat)!

Former La Verne University coach Ben Hines says, "Every pitch is a fastball strike until the batter finds out otherwise" (unless he had decided to look for a certain pitch from an off-speed pitcher with less than two strikes).

As the pitch comes toward the plate, the hitter must say to himself, 'Yes, yes, *yes*!' or 'Yes, yes, *no*!" (if he suddenly decides to lay off that pitch).

Photo courtesy of Cal State L.A. by Stan Carstensen

You can't hit the ball with the bat on your shoulder. To be successful, you must put the ball in play!

Coaches need to sell their players on the value of putting the ball in play. Maybe the following stats will help get the point across:

- Tony Gwynn, the great Padres hitter, swings and misses fewer than 10 times per every 100 swings, and that's against major-league pitching!
- Don Mueller of the New York Giants put the ball in play 93 times out of every 100 plate appearances, walking or striking out only 7 times per hundred.

- Reportedly, National Leaguer Manny Mota took only one called third strike in over 500 pinch-hitting trips while batting nearly .300 in so doing.
- Joe DiMaggio hit 11 home runs without an intervening strikeout, and he struck out only five times in his 56-game hitting streak.

Throw Strikes

"If pitching were easy, they wouldn't pay a man a million dollars a year to do it," once wrote the late Ron Squire, a great pitching guru some years back at Lynwood (California) High School. "And ya can't field a walk!" Jack Salveson, a former major leaguer out of Long Beach Poly High, once added, "Control is a state of mind." (Control is more mental than physical.)

I'm not sure about the secret of control. I once had at Lakewood High a pitcher named Mark Clabough who walked but two batters all season as a starter. In so doing, he threw a no-hitter against the Long Beach Poly High Gwynn brothers—Tony and Chris—using only 61 pitches, of which only 9 were balls!

That year we had three starters who gave up only 10 walks among them! We also had five hurlers who shared the 15 league wins, of which 10 were shutouts in which no walks were issued. (The team went undefeated in league.)

The so-called secret? Probably concentrating and focusing on the next pitch over and over. Or perhaps it was me constantly screaming "Throw strikes!"

If one wants a major-league record to shoot for, how about Red Barrett's 58-pitch, nine-inning shutout over Cincinnati in 1944? It can be done. Control *is* a state of mind, so work on it.

Sparky Anderson rates the 2-1 pitch the most important in baseball because the next pitch is going to be either 3-1 (bad) or 2-2 (good). Dean Stotts, the able pitching coach at Stanford University, advises, "A pitcher's objective is (a) to get at least one of his first two pitches over the plate for a strike, and (b) to get to a two-strike count on the hitter as soon as possible." Defensive strategy isn't a big concern when the other team doesn't have many runners on base. Only in T-Ball are walks not a big factor in the outcome of the game.

Yes, we do keep pitch counts with a clicker held by the pitching coach:

- 120 pitches maximum per week for high school, 80 to 85 per game.
- 135 to 145 per week for college, 90 to 105 per game.
- 70 pitches per game for ages 12 to 14 (don't count innings).
- 60 pitches per game for ages 9 to 11. An excessive number of pitches thrown in one bad inning is more damaging than an excessive number of pitches thrown in the entire game.

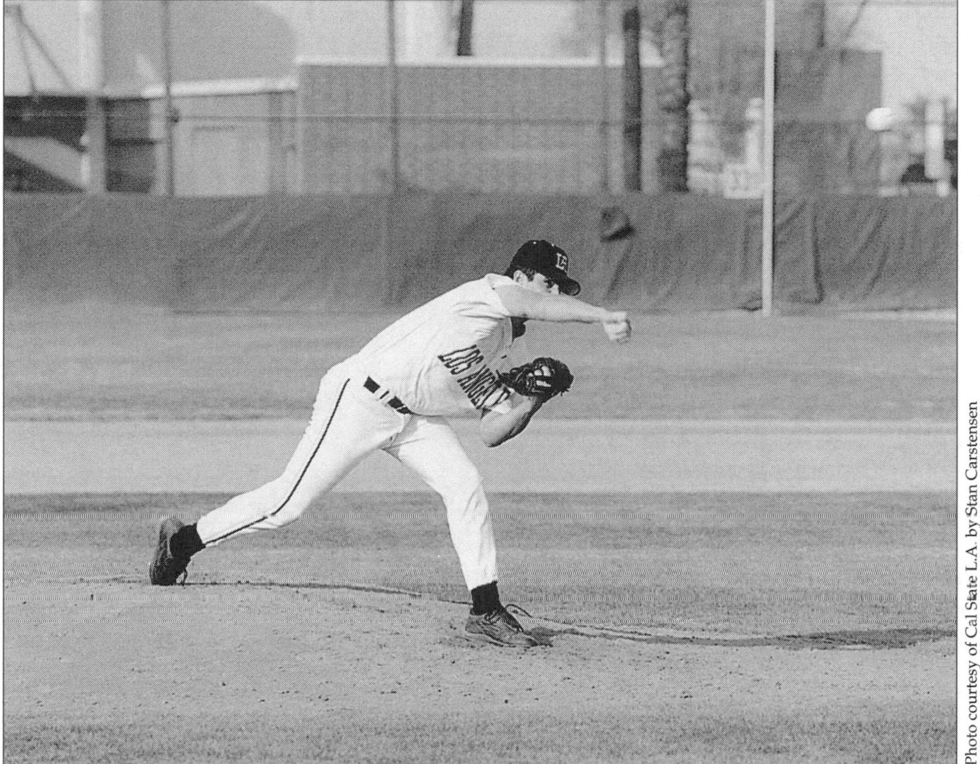

Photo courtesy of Cal State L.A. by Stan Carstensen

The key to a successful defense? Throw strikes!

Should the coaches call the pitches for the pitcher and catcher? For us? Not often—maybe 5 or 10 times a game when needed. Coach Gary Adams over at UCLA calls very few pitches, and some years he's had more players on major-league rosters than any other college coach. He lets his players *play* (and develop). He's not interested in playing master puppeteer. I wish my sons could have played for Gary Adams.

I'm not really in favor of young players ages 5 to 11 even facing other youth pitchers. I prefer to use tees for games or else have each coach "pitch" to his own players. More action, fewer walks, and fewer hit batters. Save the curveballs for high school. And nobody—especially players 6 to 12—enjoys getting hit by pitchers.

Have Good Team Spirit

Team spirit is a hard one to explain and equally hard to develop. Winning teams seem to have it, but which came first—the chicken or the egg?

Winning teams *expect* to win. Look at what Tommy Lasorda has accomplished with the Dodgers and the USA Olympians. Consider the Yankees under Joe Torre, USC under the legendary Rod Dedeaux, or LSU with Coach Skip Bertman.

I once saw a picture of Coach Ron Fraser's University of Miami team running across the outfield after practice, all holding hands together—bonding.

Another squad had its players fall one by one from a 10-foot platform into the arms of their teammates—trust.

Run the Bases Intelligently

Good base running can be taught by making home videos of the team and showing them on rainy days; these can be very instructional. Often, a picture is worth ten thousand words. Say it once, show it twice, and do it a thousand times!

For instance, we show our runners to run *through* the bag when running to first base, all the way to the outfield grass when legging out bunts and other balls hit in the infield. Track runners do not stop, turn off, slow down, or leap in the air when approaching the finish tape, and neither should ballplayers at the bag.

In publications like *Scholastic Coach* magazine and *Collegiate Baseball*, I have outlined our work on not foolishly running to third from second on ground balls to the shortstop when not forced, tagging up at third base properly to avoid being called out for leaving too early on fly balls, reading the ball off the bat and reacting correctly, and taking the proper position as a third-base coach with runners at third or second or both (down the line toward home so that the base runner can easily see him).

Any time we discuss base running, we must include the area of sliding, something we do extremely well at Los Angeles State because we practice and teach it more than most clubs do. We simply have the players take their shoes off, wet the grass, and then practice five to six different slides. We have two basic rules:

1. If in doubt, always slide.
2. He who changes his mind in the middle of a slide often trades a good leg for a broken one!

Know the Rules

It's never too early to learn the rules, but most players (and coaches and umpires) are pretty vague about them. Remember poor Fred Merkle of the New York Giants in 1908 who went down in baseball history (unjustly perhaps) for supposedly not touching second base on a force play and possibly costing his team the pennant? Only 20 years of age when he made his famous miscue, Merkle to his dying day was labeled a bonehead.

Let us just touch briefly on what all players and coaches should study:

- What is (and what is not) a legal catch? What about the force versus the double-off? Similar, yes. Identical, *no*!
- Why are there two lines three feet apart the last half of the way to first base?
- What's the difference between interference and obstruction?
- When does a catcher have to throw to first base or tag the batter on a missed third strike? When doesn't he?
- What exactly determines when the infield-fly rule is in effect? Where do the runners have to be? Can the ball be purposely dropped? No. Can the infielder allow the ball to hit the ground first and then make a play? Yes. Is a bunt an infield fly? No.
- What about thrown balls that hit an umpire? Batted balls?
- What happens when two players are on the same base at one time?
- What determines whether a batted ball is fair or foul?
- What are the special sliding rules and restrictions for your league?

General Strategy

In the ensuing section, I will be quoting Coach Al Weiner often because he has had 31 years of experience directing Pony and Colt League teams, has coached the Lakewood High (California) frosh-soph clubs for 15 years, and has directed AAU teams. Working out of Lakewood's Heartwell Park, Al has been a major factor in developing players for Lakewood High, which has had more players drafted by professional baseball than any other high school in the nation.

- At any level, I personally do not like to play my infield up, or in, unless it's the last inning of a tie game or unless we want to keep the opposition from tying it. In either case I don't like it, but we may be forced to do it. The drawback is that you make .500 hitters out of .250 hitters when you bring the infielders up.

  Assistant Coach Cliff Brown and I recently had an interesting talk on strategy with Hall-of-Fame manager Sparky Anderson, who said that when his teams were even or ahead in the game, he often would not play his infield at double-play depth. He would prefer to have them at normal position because as former Fresno State coach Bob Bennett notes, "What Anderson wanted were outs (even if only one) so as not to open up too many holes by playing close to the bag and thus getting even further behind in the score."

On the other side of the coin is former Los Angeles State assistant coach Jon Shuler, who just hated to have a single go between the middle infielders in a double-play situation. Thus we have some differences of opinion on strategy.

Speaking of the double play, Coach Bob Bennett relates that sometimes famed Fresno State coach Pete Beiden would play one infielder in and the other back depending on where he figured the batter would hit the ball. So he would play the shortstop back for a right-handed pull hitter but the second baseman in to cover the bag. Interesting.

- I use the intentional walk more than most high school or college coaches do. The free pass sets up more force plays, and it works more often than it fails.

- I like to hit-and-run with runners on first and third with none or one out. The hit-and-run keeps your team out of double plays and often guarantees a run if the batter gets the ball on the ground (or a double or triple play if he doesn't!)

  In defending the hit-and-run, many college-level teams will have the shortstop cover the bag if a right-handed batter is up because on a single through short, the runner from first probably will not advance to third, but on a single through second, he should.

- The four-man outfield works well against a powerful alley hitter in close games. We leave the third baseman in against bunt attempts but move the shortstop to the outfield, closing all the gaps (we hope). This maneuver, learned from a SABR (Society of American Baseball Research) study, also often upsets the hitter psychologically and may make him try to bunt or go the other way to overcome our defense, which can also work to our advantage. We'd rather have him bunt or single to the opposite field than hit for extra bases.

  A similar maneuver used when the game is really on the line is the five-man infield in which the coach brings in one of his outfielders and stations him either inside the second-base area to cut off a single up the middle or somewhere near the pitcher to cut off a possible squeeze bunt.

- Antisqueeze situation? Another technique to stop the squeeze is to have the catcher pitch out at least twice (or more if you dare) with an open base. Walking the runner won't hurt, and you may catch the runner coming home on a missed squeeze bunt.

  Offensively, I'm not much for ordering a squeeze bunt with the bases loaded at any amateur level—it's too easy to force the runner at home. Overall, I'm not much of a squeezer. As Earl Weaver once said, "If you play for one run, that's probably all you're going to get." (Well, maybe to *win* the game. Maybe.)

- On the double steal, catchers should be taught to throw to second base, not to third, because the trail runner has a momentary delay while he waits to see if the lead man is actually stealing. Thus the trailer is likely to lose a step or two and be thrown out. Often, too, he doesn't realize that the catcher is going after him rather than the lead runner.

  Coach Weiner points out, "Most of these plays are for high school varsity players on up as they are pretty advanced. The lower the age group, the more likely the players on defense will make throwing mistakes. Thus in Little League, a simple bunt anywhere in the infield is often mishandled."

- Both of us agree that being aggressive on the bases at any level is usually a positive factor in winning. For instance, with a runner on third and one out, at Los Angeles State we often send our runner home from third on a ground ball hit to third or first.

  With runners on second and third and none out, again we frequently send our third-base runner home on any ground ball, which he has learned to read as it comes downward off the bat. (But players must constantly practice this read.)

  You have runners at first and third, none or one out, and the batter hits a potential double-play ground ball to third. What should you do? Send the runner! He may be out at the plate, but that's better than a double play, especially if the runner stops near home plate and stays in a rundown if he sees that the catcher is going to tag him out. The other runners can then advance.

  Here Coach Weiner suggests that for players age 5 to 15, sending the runner home might not be a good play because the defense doesn't often shoot double plays. Sending those runners home from third on ground balls can get a coach a lot of criticism from the experts in the stands, but it will also bring in a lot of runs when, in his haste to make a play, the infielder kicks the ball for an error, lets it go by for a hit, makes a poor throw home, or hits the runner. In addition, the catcher may drop the ball, or the runner may just plain beat the play. But don't expect much praise when it works. Heck, often the infielder will be so surprised that the runner is going that the infielder will concede the run.

  Runners on second and first, none or one out, potential double-play ball hit? Many coaches will hold the runner coming from second. Me? I send him on home. Surprise!

- Here's a play that succeeds, especially for ages 12 on up. The opposing catcher has a good arm. One out, close game. You have a good runner at third and a leadfoot on first, who takes off on a "steal." The batter turns around as if to squeeze bunt while the third-base runner breaks hard just one or two steps toward home, yells, "Squeeze!" and then rapidly retreats to third. The catcher usually looks to third to stop the squeeze while the runner on first strolls untouched into second! Famed Coach John Scolinos of Cal Poly Pomona showed me this one.

Steals

Coach Weiner points out that it's difficult to rack up stolen bases at the Little League levels because base runners are not allowed to lead off. Just the opposite is true, however, at Pony League age because the bases are so close (80 feet apart), the pitchers are not too proficient at holding their runners, and young catchers are just learning how to throw well.

"In Pony, the key to winning is the stolen base and the squeeze," says Weiner, "because with the mound so close, the pitchers usually dominate. When the players get older, the distances from the mound to the plate and between the bases becomes greater."

"By the time the players reach Colt League age, they have learned to hit better because now they are a little stronger and have caught up with the pitching, and it's the same for the high school frosh-soph level. So here we bunt a little less and steal a little less, and besides, the catchers now throw better, plus the pitchers finally have learned how to hold their runners on base."

Speaking for high school and college squads, my teams have usually led the league in stolen bases (which doesn't mean we always lead the league in the standings!).

What's our steal sign? Usually we don't have any! It's "Go if you think you can make it, but you better make it!" (We do have a "don't go" sign).

Most coaches live in one of two camps: those who play for one run at a time with the small-ball philosophy and the Earl Weaver followers who subscribe to the three-run-homer creed. Me? I think you can often combine the two at all levels, leaning more one way or the other depending on your team composition, the score, and the park in which you are performing.

But #1, remember that if a player steals 40 bases but is picked off or thrown out 35 times, he's really only stolen 5 times!

Remember #2. When the rules permit players to lead off base, it is far better to be picked off first (and then go hard for second) than it is to be thrown out stealing! The catcher practices the throw to second more than the first sacker does.

And #3: a runner stealing third should be safe 19 times out of 20 tries. Being thrown out stealing third is a bad play. Oh, yes, I like to steal home too.

The Slash

The slash (also known as the fake-bunt-and-hit or the butcher boy) is a weapon I love at all levels of baseball. I've even seen pitchers like Orel Hershiser do it successfully in big-league ball.

The slash is a fun play, but few players know when and how to perform it because few coaches really know how to teach it. The maneuver takes place in a sacrifice-bunt situation, with a right-handed bunter (er . . . hitter) up against a pitcher with good control.

The slasher should usually take one strike because he may end up walking anyway. Many pitchers find it hard to pitch to a batter partially squared around as if to bunt.

We use the Branch Rickey bunt position. Rather than squaring around with both feet facing the pitcher, the bunter's feet remain in the hitting position, while only the upper body squares around. The slash batter goes into this position early. His not committing until the pitcher has thrown one strike plants a great deal of doubt in the minds of the defense about exactly what the offense is going to do next.

If the pitcher does get a pitch over, the bunter-slasher can choose to either bunt or slash the next strike.

The best time to bunt is with runners at first and second if the third baseman makes the mistake of backing up too soon to cover third on a force play. In that situation a well-placed bunt toward third will end up with everybody safe and the bases loaded!

But if the third-baseman charges, the batter should slash down on the ball, hoping to drive it by the oncoming third sacker. This is a good hit-and-run play too.

Even with two strikes, you may want to have the batter go ahead and bunt because of the surprise element. In this case the bunt doesn't have to be perfect—just so it's not foul for strike three.

The mistake made by most slashers is that they hold the bat down too close to the knob end and thus do not choke up enough to have good bat control. In addition, many wait too long to get the bat in proper position to slash. Just as the pitcher makes his very first move upward from the stretch, the slasher must cock his bat up to his ear, take a first step with his right foot toward the pitcher, and then take a step with his left foot—a sort of short, balanced one-two step forward. Then he swings downward, hits the top of the ball, and drives it hard at the feet of the oncoming infielder.

The best way to defend against the slash, by the way, is to move the right fielder in toward home about 30 feet because it's almost impossible for a slasher hitting right-handed to hit the ball over the right fielder's head. Further, the defense is already set up for a bunt, so have the pitcher throw a curveball, which is easier to bunt than to hit from the slash position.

Sacrifice Bunt

Some baseball people do not really like the sacrifice bunt, and I'm one of them, especially if we must use metal bats. The ball comes off metal too hard, and because the bat surface is also slippery, the bunter is more likely to pop up. Besides, using metal, game scores are usually so high that playing for one run can be a big mistake.

Some statisticians have even shown that a team is better off with a runner at first and none out than with a runner at second and one out. The same goes for a runner at second with none out as opposed to one at third with one down.

So 95 percent of the time in a sacrifice situation, we will either hit away, push bunt, slash bunt, slash hit-and-run, or just plain hit-and-run.

Hit-and-Run and Run-and-Hit

If I were coaching again in high school, I would do two things more often—base-hit bunt and hit-and-run (or better yet, run-and-hit).

We do it now a lot at Los Angeles State because the hit-and-run can

- help move a slow runner from first to third,
- move a faster runner perhaps from first all the way home (as in the winning play in the famed 1946 World Series), and
- keep the offensive team out of a double play.

Sometimes you may want to put the hit-and-run on for a timid hitter because it forces him to swing the bat—and it places the responsibility for failure on the coach!

If you played for Wally Kincaid and hit a ball out of the park for a home run when Wally had the hit-and-run on, you'd probably be benched because he demanded that the batter put the ball on the ground. But he had junior-college-age players and more hours of practice time than coaches at many other schools did.

In the hit-and-run situation the runners must never be picked off base. They should make sure that the pitch is actually on its way plateward. So the hit-and-run is not a steal situation, but one in which the runners have faith that the batter will hit the ball even if it's a pitchout (which is another situation which must be practiced).

Lately we have been leaning more to the run-and-hit, a play that does not force the batter to swing at the pitch. With power hitters at bat and fast runners on the bases, this is more of a steal situation in which the batter doesn't have to swing at the pitch and the runner must make second on his own if the batter decides not to offer at the pitch.

We agree with Coach Weiner that the slash, hit-and-run, or run-and-hit should be reserved only for high school varsity players on up.

We encourage our batters to swing at the 0-0 pitch because, contrary to the opinion of some, the stats at every level of baseball show that the 0-0 offering results in a batting average of over .300. And we often let hitters swing at the 3-0 pitch (here the stats are not so good), especially with runners on base and a batter up who has trouble hitting the curveball.

Well, so much for strategy at various age levels of baseball. If something works, the coach is a genius. If it doesn't, he's a goat. The same thing happens when the coach lets his cleanup hitter swing at the 3-0 pitch. Applause for the coach if the batter homers—boos if he pops out. Such is the nature of our national pastime.

Remember: "Every time you make three left turns, you go home!" And as that noted baseball sage Casey Stengel once quipped, "Ya touch that five-sided thing, and it adds up."

Good strategy and some luck will help you do just that. After all, it doesn't make any difference who wins as long as we do!

16

Adapting the Game Plan for Different Situations

Dick Birmingham

As coaches, we have all been in less-than ideal game situations. As the visiting ballclub, your team may have played on a surface that was less than adequate. Surely your team occasionally plays on a surface that they have never seen before. How do you and your players respond to inclement weather? Do your players complain about playing in the rain? What happens to your team, both physically and mentally, when you lose your star player for the season because of injury? Do your players, and you, make excuses for lack of success? How would your team react to playing in front of a capacity crowd for the first time? Would the cheers and jeers of the spectators distract them?

The previous examples are a few of the situations that players and coaches might have to respond to during a season. How does a coach help his team cope with these types of conditions and overcome them to be successful? The answer is simple. Successful coaches and teams have a strong yet adaptable game plan designed to conquer any obstacle they may encounter during the season. A solid game plan that is flexible will seldom land a coach or team in trouble when adversity strikes.

Developing a Successful Game Plan

A coach's overall game plan should be to have a well-disciplined and fundamentally sound ballclub. The goal is to have players so well trained that they meet any game situation or other circumstance that arises during the season with confidence and determination.

The key to having a successful game plan is to run highly structured practices that emphasize specifics and focus on player development. This approach will produce results. Just hitting groundballs doesn't deal with specifics.

No organization, whether it be in business, education, religion, or baseball, has any success without discipline. I do not mean military discipline, but subtle control through effective structure and organization. The entire operation, including all practices and drills, must form a structure based on team pride.

Team pride develops from what you are selling to your players—your program or your school. The players need to understand and buy into the idea that there is a wrong way to do things, a right way to do things, and *our* way to do things. Each individual team member harbors team pride in the form of individual discipline. He displays it in the way he carries himself, in his work habits, and in how he participates and executes in practice and games.

The structure of the game plan is founded in rigid practice organization. Two primary policies encompass all practice organization within the game plan:

1. *No-talk policy.* Idle chitchat should not occur during practice. This activity distracts players and gets them off task. If the talking is constructive and improvement related, then it is acceptable and tolerated. Otherwise, no talking is permitted. This approach allows players to concentrate on improvement, and it promotes intense and focused practices. Time is not wasted waiting for players to pay attention or answering questions that have already been answered. The no-talk policy focuses attention and effort.

2. *Sprint policy.* The sprint policy simply means that players run everywhere on the ballfield and to and from the dugout. The sprint policy set our program on a level above that of the opposition because nobody else ran as much as we did. Running kept us alert and involved in the game, and it was a great conditioner, especially for the outfielders.

Years ago, I saw a sign in an accounting office that said, "Good enough is never good enough." We all have a tendency to say, "That's good enough." You must train your players to avoid this attitude at all costs.

The game plan should center on hard work, discipline, and doing things correctly every time. If you do a drill several times poorly, you're better off not doing it at all. Every player must try to do drills better each time. Coaches and players must always remind themselves that they will play as they practice.

When the ball is hit, the only thing that players have to fall back on is their fundamentals. And the fundamentals may be good or bad.

When training the team, emphasize simple execution. Making the routine play should be valued and rewarded. Players should always be in the right position to make the play.

In developing the game plan, the coach must always keep in mind the four major skill areas in baseball:

1. running,
2. throwing,
3. fielding, and
4. hitting.

Every practice should center on these four major skill areas because most of the mistakes will come in these parts of the game. Players should strive relentlessly to improve daily in these areas. A day should not pass where they are not working on the four skill areas.

Focusing on Player Development

Building a successful program with a winning tradition begins with finding the right personnel for your team. The foundation of any team is pitching, both quality and quantity. A coach must try to develop at least two pitchers from every class. If he can do this, the team will always have eight pitchers, four of whom will be upperclassmen. In determining who the potential pitchers are, a coach should look for two things: general arm strength and the ability to throw in a pattern.

Although it helps, pitchers do not need to be the most physically gifted athletes on the team. But they do need to be able to develop a basic understanding of pitching mechanics and pitching strategy.

Every other year the coach should plan to develop a catcher, a middle infielder, and a center fielder. By doing that he will always have senior-sophomore or junior-freshman combinations at these positions. This plan does not always work, however, and a coach may need to be flexible in developing and assigning personnel. He may need to persuade some players to change positions for the good of the program. Most players will agree to a position change if it means more playing time.

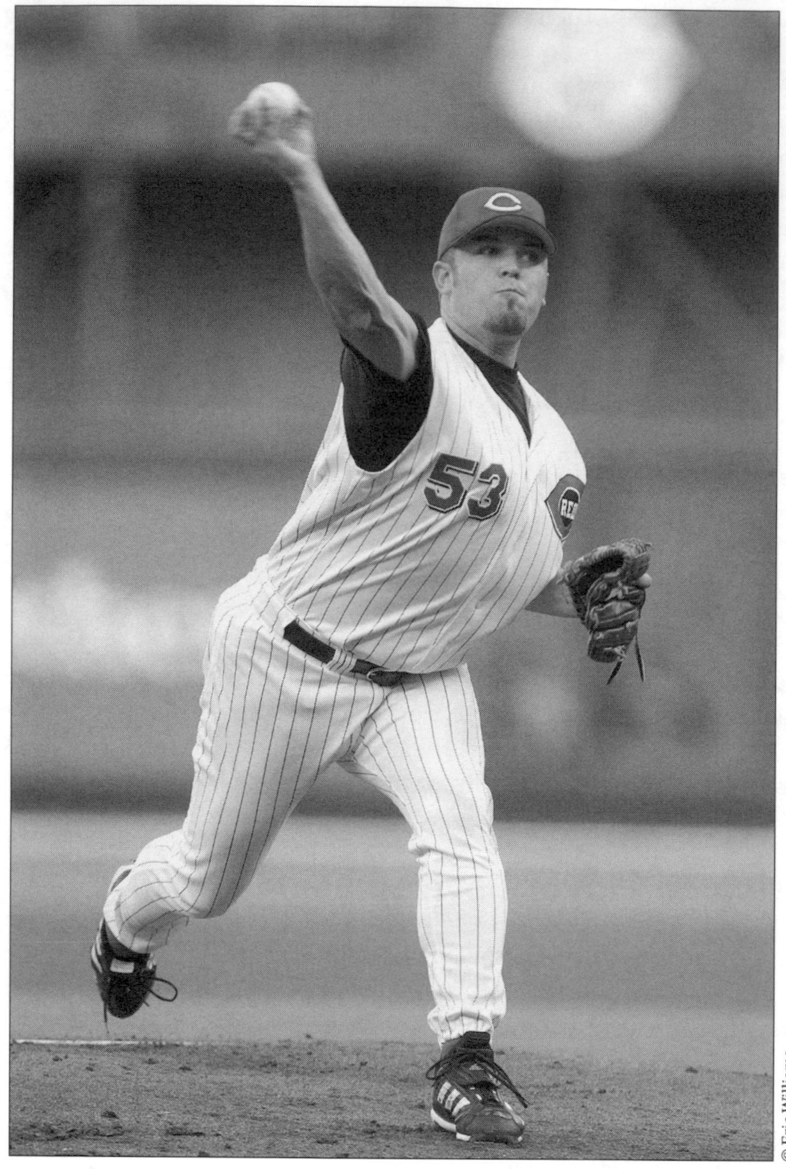

© Eric Williams

Pitching depth is essential for building and maintaining a successful program.

The corner-position players (first base and third base) need not be quite as skilled as the players at the middle-infield positions, but the coach should try to find a hard-nosed kid to fill each of these spots.

As mentioned previously, one of the keys to developing a successful game plan is to focus on player development. This is an everyday job for the coach of a successful program.

Getting to the Next Level

In helping his team and players reach the next level, a coach should understand how the following concepts interact with team and player development:

- *Talent.* Nobody moves to the next level without talent. Every coach is looking to add talented players to his squad.
- *Good fundamentals.* A fundamentally sound player is reliable and dependable on the field.
- *Strong work ethic.* Hustle can make up where talent is short. One of the roles of the coach in building the game plan for the ballclub is to inspire players to motivate themselves. We used three sayings, or slogans, in the game plan as part of our program:

    1. The five Ps was the first motto: Prior preparation prevents poor performance. We always tried to outwork our opponents. We focused on preparing for anything that might happen in a ballgame.
    2. The shortest route to success is *smart* hard work. We didn't just do drill after drill. Our game plan was to do the best and most effective drills until we mastered them.
    3. Success amounts to getting up one more time than you've been knocked down. No matter what the situation, teams must learn to overcome, and even thrive on, adversity if they are to be successful.

I have had former players write me letters years after having played in the program to say that these slogans were an integral part of their success in life, not just in baseball.

A coach usually has little say about what type of athlete shows up to tryouts or what type of talent is in the student body. In general, talent comes to a player through the genes he inherits from his parents.

But a coach can develop two other aspects—good fundamentals and a strong work ethic—so he must focus the majority of the game plan around them. Appropriate training can develop those attributes.

For example, most coaches spend most of their instructional time working with the most talented players on the team. These players are usually the easiest to work with because they are generally well skilled and can make the adjustments that the coach asks them to make. But to have a successful program, a coach must learn how to make his marginal players better. When the marginal players—the supporting cast—improve, the *team* improves. The best players will always perform at a high level because of their superior athletic talent. If a coach can get the marginal players to raise their level to average, the team stands a chance.

Educating Players by Position

A coach establishes a successful game plan through individual and team drills. Teams and players develop through drills. All drills should be a part of the game taken aside until players can perform it readily. The idea is to isolate parts of the game and teach players the correct reactions. You train them so their bodies are working for them, not against them. For example, you work on cutoffs and relays, slow rollers, double-play feeds and pivots, and so forth separately, away from game situations until players can demonstrate mastery. You can then incorporate the skills of the drill into more complex gamelike drills.

The next step in player development is making sure that players obtain and develop the particular skills and responsibilities that correspond with the position or positions they play. Players must understand the role and requirements for their positions and work on the requirements on a regular basis. The coach should emphasize the top three requirements of each position through drill work.

The coach must give daily attention to the three main areas of responsibility for each player according to the position requirements (table 16.1). Doing this will ensure that players can handle any situation they encounter during a game.

Developing the Defensive Side

We've all heard the cliche, "We beat ourselves." If this is true, then ballgames are lost, not won. A team must be able to stay in a game long enough to give the other team time to beat themselves. The great Bear Bryant said it best: "All championship teams begin on defense."

Players have to be trained to play good, basic defense. They must learn how to handle the ball and how to stay away from the big inning.

On defense, how does a team keep away from the big inning? Simple—they keep the double play in order. Every player has to be accountable for knowing his role in keeping the double play in order at all times.

For example, on a ground-ball single to the right side with less than two outs and a runner on first base, the right fielder must understand his role in keeping the double play in order. He must charge the ball hard and throw a strike to his cutoff man. If he does this, he prevents the runner at first base from going to third base. But more important, he keeps the batter-runner at first base and keeps the double play in order.

Two drills I have used with great success are the Starts Drill and the 21 Outs Drill. Both are essential to building a solid game plan as part of a successful program.

TABLE 16.1 Baseball Position Requirements

	PRIMARY RESPONSIBILITIES	SECONDARY RESPONSIBILITIES
Pitcher	1. Throw to spots (control) 2. Change speeds (change-up, breaking ball, fastball) 3. Get the ball to move (breaking ball, fastball, change-up)	1. Field position • Bunts (zones) • Pop-ups (zones) • Backup responsibilities 2. Hold runners close
Catcher	1. Handle the low ball and the pitch in the dirt (blocking) 2. Control runners (throwing) • Accuracy • Quickness • Strength 3. Handle pitchers • Soft hands • Framing • Psychological (control the pitchers, throw strikes, know pitching)	1. Bunts (zones) 2. Pop fouls (zones) 3. Run the club, be the field general
First base	1. Handle the slow roller 2. Guard the line 3. Move to the right	1. Bunts (zones) 2. Pop-ups • Communication with catcher • Sprint to barrier and work back 3. Cutoffs and relays 4. Hold and tag runners
Second base	1. Quick to the glove, side to the left 2. Make pivot on double play 3. Handle slow roller	1. Cover bag and tags 2. Cutoffs and relays 3. Pop-ups (zones)
Shortshop	1. Make play in the hole 2. Excellent in double-play situations (lead throw and pivot) 3. Handle slow roller	1. Cover bag and tags 2. Cutoffs and relays 3. Pop-ups (zones)
Third base	1. Handle slow roller 2. Range to the left 3. Guard the line	1. Bunts (zones) 2. Cutoffs and relays 3. Pop-ups (zones) • Communication with catcher • Sprint to barrier and work back

(continued)

TABLE 16.1 *(continued)*

	PRIMARY RESPONSIBILITIES	SECONDARY RESPONSIBILITIES
Left field	1. Go back on the ball 2. Quick to the line 3. Hit cutoff man	1. Execute deep angle into power alley 2. Backup responsibilities 3. Movement with the count and situation
Center field	1. Go back on the ball 2. Have excellent range to power alleys 3. Hit cutoff man	1. Backup responsibilities 2. Movement with the count and situation
Right field	1. Quick to the line 2. Hit cutoff man 3. Change the ball hard, under control, and make a quality throw to cutoff man to keep runner from going from first to third.	1. Backup responsibilities 2. Movement with the count and situation

Starts Drill

Tom Greenwade, the great New York Yankees scout who signed Mickey Mantle, said, "Offensively and defensively, the first two steps a player takes are the most important. And they must be explosive and correct." This was the basis for developing and using the Starts Drill. Defensively, baseball players must assume a good ready position and be prepared to go to left, right, forward, or backward. To do this effectively, players must execute the proper footwork and take the proper angle. A good start may make the difference in getting to the ball. This drill helps players establish angles that they will use in a game, and it trains them to do it explosively and correctly.

Here is how to set up the drill:

1. Put two players at each position. Catchers should be in full gear. Players will alternate.
2. The coach should kneel down on the grass behind the pitcher's mound, facing second base.
3. When the coach raises his arm, each player at each position assumes a ready position.

4. When the coach points to his right, the players break to their left and go hard for about seven yards; the catchers block to their right. When the coach points to his left, the players break to their right and the catchers block to their left. When the coach points to the fence, the players drop step, cross over, and sprint straight back about seven yards. The catchers break out in front of the plate to cover bunts. When the coach puts his hand on top of his hat, the players break in about seven yards. The catchers sprint to the backstop to cover a deep pop foul.

The coach should allow the first group of players to return to their backup positions from their start before he starts the second group.

The infielders and outfielders should work on different angles and techniques each turn.

21 Outs Drill

I developed this effective defensive drill in the 1960s. Players learn that they have to handle the ball to get outs.

Drill Rules

The drill does not include

bases on balls,
strikeouts,
curveballs (pitchers work on fastballs down the pipe),
bunting,
stealing (runners may advance on passed balls and wild pitches), or
sliding.

Purpose of the Drill

To make your defense handle the ball to get outs
To convince the pitching staff that a fastball thrown for a strike will be hit at someone most of the time

Advantage of the Drill

Gives the coach a drill for coaching team defense
Serves as batting practice for nonstarters
Conditions pitchers
Develops pride on defense

The coach and players must treat this drill with gamelike intensity.

A baseball coach's number-one job in relation to the defensive side of the game plan is to develop his pitchers. If he feels that he does not have the background in pitching to handle this responsibility, he must add a strong pitching coach to his coaching staff. This concept cannot be understated or ignored. If pitching is 70 to 90 percent of the game, as most experienced baseball people contend, then a coach must make sure that his pitchers are getting the attention and instruction they need.

The pitcher is the most important player on the field; he gets the win or the loss. The pitcher also must be the best-conditioned athlete on the team because he handles the ball on every play.

To be successful at any level of the game, a pitcher must be able to do the three primary responsibilities listed in the pitcher's position requirements. All activities set up to help develop the pitching staff should emphasize the following three things:

1. Control—Pitchers must learn to throw to spots with command and control. A well-located fastball is the best pitch in a pitcher's repertoire.
2. Movement for fastballs (particularly the two-seam fastball) and breaking balls—With the fastball, one inch of movement is worth three miles per hour. Develop spin drills for the breaking ball.
3. Change-up—If hitting is timing, then pitching is disrupting the hitter's timing. The change-up is the best pitch for destroying a hitter's timing and balance, especially when the pitcher can throw it in fastball counts.

Pitchers who can hold runners, know their backup responsibilities, cover unoccupied bases, and field their positions will win 25 percent more games than those who can't.

How do pitchers improve these skills? They do quality drill work—basic pitcher's fielding practice (PFP) drills—on a regular basis. The coach cannot train pitchers in these important parts of the game just during the preseason and expect them to be executing flawlessly in the last week of the season. Pitchers must practice and drill regularly to maintain their skills.

The coach must constantly build the mental attitude of the pitcher. He must foster confidence and competitive spirit in each pitcher. If the coach wants the pitching staff to have a bulldog mentality, then everything about practice and preparation should focus on developing this attitude.

The coach's role is to develop pitchers both physically and psychologically. He must remember to develop the whole pitcher, not just the guy who throws the ball.

Part of the development of the game-plan pitching philosophy should include the development of three-run pitchers, pitchers who give up no more than three runs in a ballgame. Pitchers should go into a game with the intention of throwing a shutout. If the opponent scores, however, not all is lost, and he tightens the reins a little. If a second run scores, the game is still in his control and he bears down. If a third run scores, the pitcher tells himself, "That's it, no more runs."

Pitchers must be able to read hitters and hitting flaws. A well-schooled or intuitive pitcher who can see hitters' weaknesses has the upper hand. A good coach teaches pitchers about hitting. Pitchers should remember that most amateur hitters hit off the last pitch they saw. This point emphasizes how important it is to throw set-up pitches and get ahead in the count.

Developing the Offensive Side

In developing the offensive side of the game plan, the coach must decide how to set the lineup. In general, a successful game plan includes the following ideas, although game situations or personnel issues may dictate deviations:

- *Leadoff hitter*—has a good eye, swings at few bad pitches, makes good contact, has good foot speed
- *Second hitter*—usually an excellent bunter, can put the ball in play, hits behind the runner, can run a little
- *Third hitter*—can put the ball in the air (even warning-track power) because runners will be in scoring position, generally the best hitter
- *Fourth and fifth hitters*—power guys, players with pop in their swings
- *Seven, eight, and nine*—the best of what's left, whatever you can get

The successful game plan requires that the entire lineup be trained to be good bunters. The coach never knows who will come up in a bunt situation with the game on the line; it may be the cleanup hitter.

Each player in the lineup must be able to move a man into better scoring position with a sacrifice bunt when the game is on the line. There are more ways to score from third than from second, and more ways to score from second than from first. Do not underestimate the importance of executing a sacrifice bunt.

Hitting

The hitting part of the offensive side of the game plan is divided into two halves, the physical and the mental.

Physical side (the mechanics of the swing). For the game plan to be successful in this area, the coach must emphasize, through practice and drill work, the following points of the swing.

- Setup, hitting position, stance. Call it what you will, each player must have a solid foundation to hit from. Everything starts from this position. Relaxation is the key.
- Stride. The stride has two purposes. First, it is a timing device that allows the hitter to recognize the pitch. Second, it puts the hitter in a position of attack. A good stride should take the hitter down, not forward, and it helps the hitter stay back. The hitter must remember that the swing is not part of the stride.
- Contact-point position. The hitter should be in a squared-up position with the belly button facing the pitcher. The front leg should be firm, and the back leg should look like the letter L with the toes pointed down. The top-hand palm should be facing up, and the bottom-hand should be knuckles down. The chin should be over the back shoulder, helping the hitter keep his eyes on the ball through contact.
- Extension and follow-through. The bat head should follow the ball as long as possible. Follow-through is the release to the front shoulder.

Mental side. The mental side of hitting includes two aspects—the intangibles and plate discipline.

- Intangibles. The intangibles include courage, concentration, confidence, and aggressiveness. A hitter who possesses all four will be a successful offensive player. The coach can have some say in the development of the intangibles. In the same way that the coach can develop the mental attitude of the pitching staff, he can develop the attitude of the hitters. The coach should always be trying to instill the four intangibles into hitters by putting them in practice situations where they can be successful.
- Plate discipline. Hitters must learn to distinguish between pitches they can drive and attack and pitches they must hold up on (balls in the dirt, high, or inside). Plate discipline is best developed in batting practice. The coach stands behind the batting-practice cage and gives the player reinforcement when he swings at a good pitch and corrective feedback when he chases a bad one.

The entire offensive side—the hitting program and drills—of the game plan should be built around developing the proper swing, instilling the intangibles, and acquiring plate discipline.

Different Game Situations

Keeping in mind that the goal throughout the season is to win ballgames, here are some points to consider when adapting your game plan to the situation.

Early, Mid-, and Late Season

Early in the year, practice work should focus on mastery of the fundamentals. Do not wear your pitchers down! Focus more on conditioning their arms, and ease them into their workloads. You should help protect pitchers' arms from injury by strictly monitoring throwing loads, including pitch counts, and emphasizing conditioning so that players will be strong for the late season and postseason.

Early in the season, the emphasis must be placed on setting both the defensive and offensive lineups. This is the time to establish who will be strongest where. Who are the leadoff guys, the power guys, etc.? The answers may not be immediately obvious; it takes time. You can start to answer these questions by playing a lot of games early in the season. Early season non-conference games give you the opportunity to experiment more with players to see if they can develop into being part of your overall scheme. This is especially true for the pitchers.

Like a scientist, you must do some experimenting to come up with the most productive lineup. This definitely requires playing different people in different places. Pay attention to the catching situation so you have at least two guys who will have some game experience. Later in the season it will be critical that you have two experienced catchers who can go out and perform at a high level.

Always remember, you should be trying to put the best team on the field, not just the best players. Every team is unique and will establish its own identity. Therefore, you must be concerned with figuring out how to utilize your personnel in the right way.

This being said, the key is to establish your pitching staff in the early part of the season. Figure out who the "stoppers" are, because they are the ones who will step up the last half of the season and carry the team into tournament time. You should know who the team's best two, three, or four starters are. You also need to know who you can count on to throw an inning or two and who will be the closer-type guy of the pitching staff.

On a daily and weekly basis during the midseason you can add increasingly more difficult or complex techniques and strategies to the offense and defense as part of the game plan. You should be refining and perfecting your bunt defense, cutoffs and relays, and defensive plays including first-and-third situations and pickoff plays.

During the mid- to second-half of the season and heading toward tournament play, you should be able to see a set lineup emerge and be able to fine-tune for particular needs (foot speed, offensive power, etc.) with substitutions when needed.

Rest is the most important factor during the latter part of the season. Workouts should taper down in terms of the physical demands required. Also, nutrition becomes a factor. Emphasize to your players the importance of watching what they eat and getting enough rest. The team is now in the "daily grind" part of the season, and every effort should be made to try and keep things fresh and exciting. You must keep the interest of the players. Daily quotes, stories, or words of inspiration either before or after practice can help keep players stimulated.

There is a lot to be said about having a team peak at the right time. This has to do with your coaching philosophy, how your practices are organized, how you approach games, and the discipline you have been establishing as you've gone along.

You're building toward what I call "team perfection." You are always trying to get your players to play better, whether it is early or late. They must keep improving each game as opposed to peaking too early and going downhill. The worst is to have a team that peaks too early. You have wasted all of your ammo before the real battle (postseason) begins.

In preparing for tournaments, you have to use all kinds of psychological weapons to motivate players. They must realize the importance of what they are doing and take pride in how they play individually as well as how they play as a team. There are many resources on the market today to help coaches motivate their players. The smart coach takes advantage of every opportunity to improve his team.

Keep driving home the importance of preparation. Stress how important tournament time is and what a great accomplishment it will be to advance deep into the postseason. Don't be afraid to use long-standing tradition to inspire your players to press on. Stressing the accomplishments of past teams can sometimes motivate players toward future achievements.

The mark of a good coach is one whose team improves every week. I've seen teams that played well early, but as the season rolled along they started to go backward. I've coached against some teams with serious "senioritis." Those teams were tough opponents in April, but as the middle of May rolled around, they got worse. The better the weather, the worse they played. They would just lose their focus. They were no longer thinking about baseball and about winning. They were thinking about the weather, girls, and summer vacation.

Getting ready for tournaments is actually a season-long event. It is not a situation where you say, "we've got a tournament next week and we're playing for the state championship so we better start getting ready." You build up to that point throughout the season. This is done by continuing to develop the pride, work ethic, team discipline, and all the other elements that go into pulling a team together. The goal is to play as a unit and have your players focused with the same goal in mind, while working toward that goal.

We all hope that our teams have performed well enough over the regular season to qualify for postseason or tournament play. During this time you must do your homework on your competition. You need to set your pitching according to the teams in the tournament. You should treat every game as if it is an elimination game and make a strong effort to stay in the winner's bracket, where the path to the championship requires fewer games.

Find out as much as you can about the opposing team's starting pitcher. If he is a low-run guy, you may have to change your game plan. You're going to have to try and throw a guy who is going to shut them down, because you are not going to get a lot of runs. Offensively, your kids can't be up there free-swinging. The team is going to have to be more patient at the plate. They may have to take a strike or two. In this situation, there is a need to simply put the ball in play. They're going to have to work to get one run.

Whatever you do, you've got to stay in the ball game. This may require putting the bunting game into effect, playing some "small ball," and just trying to get base runners. When the opposing pitcher is tough, do what you have to do to scratch a run across.The key is to always try to stay in the game. Stay close enough to give yourself a chance to win.

If you have no prior knowledge of the opponents your team will face, then apply the general philosophy to win the game you are in. You never know; it may rain for a week.

Home Versus Road Games

The home team should theoretically have an advantage, especially if the grounds or ballfield have irregular features that make them different from a typical baseball field. When on the road, take the players out early and let them roam the grounds.

There is definitely a mental factor involved when playing on the road. You are out of your element, and you are a guest at somebody else's place. To combat this, we played a lot of road games. We learned how to play on the road by developing the same mental toughness and discipline we have at home. That's about the only way you can really do it. You can't worry about the crowd, the umpires, etc. You've got to go out and play *your* game no matter where you are. You're always trying to beat the *game*. If you beat the game, you'll beat the opponent.

As mentioned earlier, there is a different mental state playing at home versus the road. Your players have to understand a lot of teams are tougher at home. They will play better, just as your team will, when they are more comfortable with the environment. So, when you go on the road and play one of those teams you have to take it up a notch. You have to play well. As the coach, you must establish that kind of mentality with your players about road games.

When we went on the road, my equipment manager carried a little plastic bucket with a mixture of dirt and clay. He also had a small scoop and a tamp. A lot of times, mounds are not well-groomed or maintained and there are large holes in front of the rubber or where the pitcher's striding foot lands.

© Mary Langenfeld Photo

The ability to cope with different game situations requires both excellent physical conditioning and mental toughness.

The pitcher will have a difficult time reaching a good balance or striding position because the footing is so uneven in front of the mound. So, our equipment manager would go out and repair the holes before the game began.

Ballpark Factors

The biggest thing you can do to combat ballpark factors is to go out early. Get to the field as early as possible so your players can walk around and size up the situation. The sooner they can see what they are up against, the sooner they can begin their physical and mental preparations. What type of ballpark is it? Is it a bandbox that requires the pitchers to adjust down in the strike zone with their pitches to keep routine fly balls from going out of the park? Is it a graveyard that may require the outfielders to play deeper than normal to minimize the chance for an extra-base hit? Determine what type of grass is on the field. Is it a slow track? What are the characteristics of the infield surface? Is there a warning track? How big is it? How much foul territory is there? What about the sun and the field layout? If it's a night game, where are the lights oriented?

If you have the luxury of having four or five outfielders and you're at a big park, you might have to sacrifice some offense by playing the three fastest outfielders on your roster. You might have an outfielder that hits a little better but doesn't have the foot speed of a backup outfielder. In a bigger park you're better with the three fastest outfielders in the lineup.

Years ago I coached a college all-star team that was a guest team at the Argentine National Championship. Our games were played in Buenos Aires in the largest stadium I've ever seen used for baseball. It was 425 feet down the lines! In talking with some of the Argentine federation officials, I learned that they had a hard time developing pitchers but they could develop outfielders who could really run and go get the ball. So, they built this ballpark extra large with the idea that no matter where their opponents hit the ball, the Argentine outfielders would be able to track it down. Good thinking.

However, this presented us with a challenge because it was hard to gauge where to play the outfielders. The park was so big we had to imagine the field was smaller and adjust our outfielders accordingly. It seemed our outfielders were playing in way too far, but in reality they weren't. It was just that the fence was so far behind them.

Conversely, in some ballparks routine fly balls are home runs. In these ballparks, it is a given that your pitchers have to keep the ball down in the strike zone. They must really work hard to keep the opponent from hitting the ball in the air. We played a best two-out-of-three series for the district title one year against a team whose home field resembled more of a phone booth than a baseball diamond. They beat us at our place in the first game of the series and we had to go to their place for the next two games. We proceeded to hit seven home runs in the doubleheader compared to their two—at *their* place. We came out victorious simply because our pitchers kept the ball down and their pitchers did not.

Odd-shaped contours and extraordinarily high fences can be a deciding factor during a ballgame. Again, the best weapon you have to combat these ballpark factors is to arrive early at the field and allow your players to practice going after balls in these areas. The more they can learn about the nuances of the ballpark, the better equipped they will be come game time.

Infield surface conditions can also be a factor during a game. Depending on whether the infield is fast or slow, you must prepare your players for that and adjust to it. If it is really slow, you are going to have to play up, closer to the hitter. Your players are going to have to concede a couple of steps, particularly the second baseman and shortstop.

If it is a slow track (high sand content), then you are not going to be able to utilize your running game quite as well. Your players will not be able to take the extra base or steal bases, and the bunting game will suffer somewhat. A fast track would be advantageous to your running game and your infielders would be able to play a little deeper than normal.

Sunfield and Twilight

Make sure *all* of your players understand that they need to be prepared with eye black and sunglasses. You never know who will be affected by the orientation of the sun at the field where you're playing.

Twilight time in some parks is a lot tougher than in others. This can be a real problem. Your pitchers must keep the ball down during twilight hours. They can't let the other team hit the ball up in the air because it is difficult to locate the ball against the twilight sky. A high sky (no clouds) is another time that requires pitchers to throw the ball down. Anything hit up will be more difficult to judge.

Practice with your players during these conditions to help them get better. Orient yourself so you are hitting fly balls or pop-ups to your fielders that are in the sun. Schedule a later practice every once in a while so your players can practice tracking the ball during twilight.

Weather Conditions

If it is raining or wet, the outfielders may need to be more secure in their throws and may want to use a three-finger grip on the ball. They won't get as much velocity on the throw, but with two fingers it is going to slip and slide more and players will make erratic throws from time to time. Also, the footing is going to be less sure so they may not be able to be as aggressive when charging ground balls.

Is it windy, requiring the infielders and outfielders to communicate more effectively on pop-ups and high fly balls? I've taken teams to play on the Caribbean Island of Aruba. The wind never stops blowing in Aruba. There is a constant breeze, day and night. Our players have always struggled even after they were warned about the wind.

Is it cold? Believe it or not, some people are allergic to cold. If you have players like this they will have a hard time functioning during games played in colder weather. Is it hot? During hot weather, players (especially pitchers) may want to bring an extra undershirt and towel to keep dry.

Injuries

The best way to adjust the game plan for injuries is to catch them early and get them treated. The two key defensive positions where injuries will be devastating to team success will be at center field and shortstop. What you have to do ahead of time is prepare another outfielder to play either center field or another outfield spot that would be vacated by a starting outfielder who takes the place of the injured center fielder. If the second best outfielder on your team is the left fielder and your center fielder runs into the wall, gets hurt, and has to be removed from the game, your left fielder has to move to center. You have to have someone come off the bench and do a great job in left field. You have to train them for this ahead of time. Prepare now for losing the key guy later.

The same thing is true at the shortstop position. If you never work anybody else at shortstop and your shortstop gets hurt before a game, you're in trouble. Once, during batting practice before a game, the infielders were taking fungos. Somehow the timing of the infield fungos and live-hit balls got messed up and when the shortstop came in to field a ground ball off the fungo, he was hit in the face by a live-hit ball. It broke his nose, and he obviously didn't play that night. A bad mistake and horrible accident. However, the third baseman was ready and took the shortstop's place.

In practice, and in some games, you need to move the second best infielder (usually the second baseman) to shortstop so he can play there and get comfortable at the position so if the unforeseeable happens, he can step in and contribute.

Even though my teams always had two catchers, I made the third baseman learn to catch. That way there was always a backup if both catchers went down.

A team must have pitching depth in order to protect the team against injuries to the pitching staff. The development of utility players is also a must for a successful game plan. Players who can play many positions are very valuable to a team.

The development of a successful game plan based on sound, fundamental philosophies grounded in team discipline and player development can help a team overcome any adversity or handle any situation it may encounter throughout the season. You will never be able to prepare for every possible setback you may encounter during a season. But what you can do is give your players the mental resolve to attack the problem with a positive attitude. If you have prepared them to adapt the game plan when the most common setbacks occur, they will have the skills to adjust when the unforeseen ones arise. It all begins with your preparations. You should always be stressing the five Ps: Prior preparation prevents poor performance. Prepare for the worst, just in case it happens. Doing so is time well spent and will pay off tenfold throughout the season.

17

Playing the Game the Right Way

Bobo Brayton

When you as a coach open the gates to your ballpark, you are assuming a great responsibility. We owe the game; it doesn't owe us. We owe the game identity; we owe the game integrity; we owe the game tradition; we owe the game perpetuity. We are committed to the game. To quote a 51-year-old player who plays baseball continuously on an amateur level, "The most important aspect in baseball is the love of the game. If you are playing for money or your ego, the game will eat you up."

Baseball is a great game, and how we approach the game is of utmost importance. The approach is so important that presentation becomes a big issue. It begins with how you treat the visiting coach and his team. Do you or your representative greet them at the motel or in the locker room or at the gate, whatever the case may be? Do you give them workout time on the field or nearby? Should there be some delay, such as inclement weather or a late bus, you should give up some of your field time to the visitor. Above all, don't hog the infield or hitting time; offer the visitor equal or more preparation time than you reserve for yourself.

Regardless of what happens, start your game on time. Fans and umpires will quickly come to know this about your program and will appreciate it. Make sure the visitors have training facilities and even a trainer. Make sure water and towels or whatever you think necessary is available in their dugout. If you are playing a double header, provide fruit, candy, or similar items between games as a courtesy. In other words, before the game even begins, show your class by being a good host. You have the responsibility of being Mr. Baseball in your area or at your school.

The park you play in, the field you play on, programs, lineup information, PA system, announcer, music, concessions, seating, the attitude of park personnel, groundskeepers, ball and bat shaggers, hostesses, umpires, scorers, and yes, your individual players, are all extensions of you and your program. As a coach you want the fans to enjoy your presentation. You want teams to look forward to competing in your park and against your team. You should strive to be the standard bearer of facilities in your area. Perhaps you cannot afford a new stadium or park, but your field can be well groomed and clean. Fans will want to come to your games because they know they will be comfortable and see a high level of competition. Coaches will want to play your team at your place because they know it will be a good game. They know the field itself will give them a chance to win. They know the officiating will be good. They know the bullpens, dugouts, and the field will all be first class. They know your attitude as a coach will be to play hard, play fair, and play to win. They know your players will emulate you and will play clean, doing and saying only positive things that make the game better.

An item that ranks near the top in your approach to the game is how your players look to others. Their personal appearance as reflected in jewelry, facial hair, and hairstyles is important. Their appearance in a baseball uniform is also important to fans, other teams, and other coaches. A great comment to hear about your team is that they always look and play the part, meaning that they look like traditional baseball players and play like traditional players. These issues may be controversial at times, but tradition always wins out.

The attitude of you and your players toward umpires is important to your total approach. Designate someone to meet the officials, direct them to their locker room, and issue them towels and baseballs. This is a good time to mention starting times, ground rules, and the ball resupply process. You can offer between-game or postgame snacks and attend to any other concerns. When addressing officials, use "Mr. Umpire" or "Sir." Those terms beat the heck out of "Blue" or "Hey, Ump." Umpires will appreciate that example of respect and work hard to keep the feeling going. A major-league coach recently mentioned that more players want to know the first name of the home-plate umpire. He thinks that players are attempting not only to know the umpire but also to improve working relations.

A cheerful or normal salutation between opponents is a good omen. When an opponent makes a great play or really scalds one, a positive comment cements good competition. A remark that I've remembered for almost 60 years occurred in a game I was playing as a 16-year-old kid against a high-quality team. The opposing first baseman was Art McLarney, a well-respected coach from the University of Washington. I ripped one back over the second baseman's head and as I rounded first base and came back to the bag, I said, "I thought he'd catch that one." Coach McLarney said, "Hey, kid, they don't catch those kind." Just a brief but correct comment brings

When it comes to appearance, attitude, and style of play, tradition always wins out.

out the respect the game deserves and, in this case, a lifetime memory. After all, that is what this game is all about—lifetime memories.

Hustle

A hustling approach is always a positive. Hustling is mental as well as physical. Being mentally alert whether you are on or off the field is important. As the coaches say, "Stay in the game, play nine!" Physically, hustling builds on your positive approach to the game, and everyone appreciates it. Some of the tried-and-true hustle plays are

- running out ground balls and fly balls;
- bouncing off and on the field between innings;
- returning to defensive position with a little pop after every play;
- backing up plays even when not directly responsible (a great example is the play by Yankees shortstop Derek Jeter in the 2001 World Series when he relayed a throw to the catcher from the right fielder from outside the first-base line and cut off an important run);
- throwing the ball around the infield from chest to chest with the accuracy required on a close play;
- accurate, forceful return throws from the outfield to the infield as opposed to some kind of flip throw that requires an infielder to retrieve the ball from someplace in the infield;
- accurate return throws from the catcher to the pitcher;
- bouncing out to the mound by the catcher for visits and brisk movement by the coaches to the coaching boxes; and
- giving maximum effort (the old college try) on every play.

Webster's definition of a hustler as one who gives energetic drive and effort at all times just about covers the preceding list. A team that hustles, both offensively and defensively, generates more problems for the opposition. An example of great hustle was displayed by a Lewiston (Idaho) High School player who ran to first base in four seconds flat—on a base on balls. When a player gets to first base that fast on a walk, what will he do when turned loose on the bases? That thought makes the pitcher hurry his pitch, the catcher becomes anxious about a potential steal attempt, the infielders all shorten up or move, and batted balls get through.

Two things that hurt the concept of hustle today are television and promotions between innings. In the College World Series and in professional baseball we are always waiting for the television advertising break. Thus the player doesn't have his glove ready at the right moment, the last-minute drink takes a little longer than anticipated, his appearance from the dugout is delayed, and the game is held up.

To encourage attendance in minor-league and college baseball, ballclubs run promotions between innings. When a player accustomed to hustling out on the field after the third out finds himself on the field all alone while two fake sumo wrestlers push each other around on the mound or some kids race a mascot somewhere, he can't help but be embarrassed. He is not likely to hustle out again.

Little Leaguers see this so they emulate the slowness of taking the field, and that action carries over to their play. Now this concept has moved into the parental ranks. Mom brings a sandwich or drink to her ballplayer just as the inning ends. Instead of hustling out, he eats the sandwich or takes a drink. Now he drags out onto the field. If the coach observes this lack of action, he may send a replacement out, which means that the mother is upset with the coach's insensitivity to his ballplayers' needs. This nonhustling concept seems to be creeping in throughout the sport.

Coaches must discourage the deterioration of the hustling attitude and image. The point here is that you are seldom right if you don't hustle and you are always right if you do. Fans, umpires, and other players appreciate a hustler. A major-league ballplayer who stands out in my mind as a real

Photo courtesy of Washington State University

A good player hustles on every play.

hustler was Mark Fydrich, pitcher for the Detroit Tigers. An injury early in his career was unfortunate because he might have changed baseball just by his hustle. Eddie Eraut, catcher for the Seattle Rainiers in the Pacific Coast League, and Pete Rose of the Cincinnati Reds, known as Charlie Hustle, were both famous for their hustle. Bobby Winkles, coach of Arizona State and manager of the Oakland Athletics, demanded hustle. Mark Marquess, an all-American player for Stanford and now coach at that university, is another great example of a hustler. The performance of David Eckstein and Darin Erstad in the 2002 World Series is an outstanding example of what hustle can do. Though these two players are not power hitters, their tremendous hustle set the tone for the Anaheim Angels team which resulted in the world championship. For those of us who love baseball hustle, these men are in a league of their own.

Practice Aggressive Base Running

Good base running is a powerful asset, and the defense must reckon with it. Base running is an area that coaches can teach, and because it is an integral tool of scoring, I feel they must teach it! First, you must determine the individual's attitude. Is he aggressive? Does he love to run? Does he love to slide? How badly does he want the next base? If these are all positive and he has reasonable speed and reaction time, he can be a good base runner. If he is very fast and has great reaction time, he can be a great base runner.

We start with the fundamentals of getting out of the batter's box and running through first base or rounding it. Next are the fundamental leads, the starts, and circling the bases. Reading the ball off the bat correctly, especially when the runner is on third base, is crucial.

The philosophy of where the runner should be at what time will reflect the attitude of the coach. To be a good base-running team, the players must practice all the fundamentals—both physical and mental. Coaches who take the time to concentrate on this phase of the game will find that it pays off big time. The Washington State Cougars had a prime example of a player being able to learn base running. A few years ago we had a big, overgrown catcher walk on to the program. His work ethic was so good that he soon became the number one catcher. His running speed was far below average, however, so every time he got on base in a situation when we needed a run, we sent in a pinch runner. As time went on, he became somewhat faster, and he learned to run bases exceptionally well. In his junior and senior years he did not need a pinch runner when he got on base. Everybody was comfortable with Hooper running instead of a faster pinch runner. The facts were that Hooper dedicated himself to base running just as he had with hitting and catching. He made up for a lack of speed by good fundamental base running.

A great example of aggressive base running occurred in a regional game we played against Stanford. John Olerud Sr., a catcher with medium running speed, was on first base when the batter hit a short grounder to center field. Ole challenged the outfielder's arm. With a great slide, he beat the throw to third base. As he got up and dusted himself off, he turned to me with a grin and said, "I burned 'em with my speed."

A third example occurred in an extra-inning playoff game with Oregon and a slow runner on third base. The Oregon infield was playing in when the hitter hammered a ground ball right to the first baseman, who juggled it just slightly and threw home. The base runner slid in safe at home to win the game. The opposing coach exclaimed, "He shouldn't even be trying to score in that situation." The point is that we had practiced the break from third base every day with every player, and it paid off.

Perfect the Fundamentals

New methods are sometimes frowned upon, but if they are sound and can be repeated to successful effect, the new techniques will eventually reach fundamental status. The evolution of equipment itself has led to many of these changes. One relatively new method that has been debated but has now almost gained fundamental status is the one-handed method of catching for catchers. This method—blended in with the old philosophy of keeping the ball in front, blocking pitches in the dirt, catching the ball in a near throwing position, and working the feet—has opened a whole new dimension to catching. With more pitchers developing the knuckleball, the knuckle curve, the split finger pitch, the turnover, and so on, the catcher must keep the ball in front of him. In the 2001 World Series, games were won or lost by catchers either blocking or not blocking the pitch. First-base play with one hand has extended the ability of the first baseman to make plays. I taught a present major-league Gold Glove first baseman to use one hand instead of two. The one-handed catch of fly balls, thrown balls, and grounders is now accepted and taught as an extension of basic two-hand play.

Coaches, scouts, and baseball people in general always appreciate good fundamental performance in catching, fielding, and throwing. Players can expertly exhibit these fundamentals in infield practice. Outfielders can work fly balls and ground balls in the proper way and finish with a low, strong overhand throw to the baseman or cutoff man. Infielders can work their feet, develop rhythm in their fielding, and make sound throws from chest to chest.

During an alumni game I was hitting infield to the alums. On the first ball I hit to the third baseman, the catcher, who had graduated 20 years earlier, played professionally for 9 years, and was presently a doctor in Seattle, yelled out, "Work your feet, work your feet, get on top of the throw."

That stuff must have been ingrained pretty deeply in those long-ago collegiate years. Catchers can also work their feet and get on top of their throws to the bases. A key to a sharp-looking infield is for the players to know where the ball is going before the fungo man ever hits it. They will get a good jump on the ball and maintain rhythm during the drills. A good fungo man is essential to good infield drills. Everything goes as planned—no bad hits, no surprises.

Develop Discipline

According to all the great teachers in the world of sport, such as Frank Leahy, Knute Rockne, John Wooden, and Frank Frisch, discipline is the difference between a gang and a team. On the field, discipline can be approached from the mental and physical aspects combined. Mentally, I tell myself that every ball is going to be hit to me, and I am going to get it. I must know that I need to be positioned correctly before the ball is pitched. I must approach the ball in the proper way to make the play. I must know what I can do with this ball. I must know what I need to do physically to field the ball and make an out.

There is a fine line between making a great play and trying to do something unachievable that will become a major mistake and in turn affect the outcome of the game. Players can locate this line only through experience and confidence developed by practice, practice, and more practice. We can avoid frustration by practicing good fundamentals and thereby gaining confidence to make the routine play all day, every day and to make the tough play whenever it is needed.

In the dugout and bullpen, the coach can keep discipline at a high level by keeping everyone involved in the game with tasks such as charting pitchers and hitters and timing base runners, pitchers' deliveries, double plays, and catchers' releases.

Know the Other Team

You've got to know who you are playing. Does the opposing team have an identity? Can they beat you with defense? Are they bulldogs who can beat you in the late innings? Can they beat you with the long ball or with base running? Do they sit back, play by the book, and count on superior talent to beat you, or are they aggressive and try to beat you with hustle and great execution? Will pressure affect them? Can you play better longer than they can?

Jim Wassem at Eastern Washington University was aggressive and coached with the phrase, "Don't let 'em throw a fastball by you." He won games with that philosophy, but we made a living using it against him. He also had some great running schemes that we had to shut down to beat him. We played a successful Big 12 team who wouldn't swing at a curveball unless they had two strikes on them. Our philosophy was to work at getting two curves over for strikes and then go from there. The tough part was getting that third strike past those hitters.

What can your opponent do against you defensively? How is each position manned? Are the players average, outstanding, or poor? Is there one player who you can beat by making him run, throw, or hit?

You must especially know the pitchers and catchers. Can they shut down your bats? Can they shut down your running game? You have to know what makes their pitcher tick. What is his personality? What is his game plan? What pitches does he throw and when? What is his out pitch? Where does he go when he is behind in the count or behind in the game? How does he field? How well does he hold runners on? What is his release time to the plate? Do we have to get to him early? Does he get better as the innings go by? Do we try to go deep into the count to get to him in the late innings? What is the release time for the catcher to first and second base?

Photo courtesy of Washington State University

The better you know your opponent, the easier it will be to shut down their strategy.

What is the opponent's offensive approach? When do they run? When do they hit-and-run? When do they steal? Do they squeeze? When? What other offensive maneuvers do they use as specialties—double steals, double squeezes, delayed steals, fake bunt and steal, fake bunt and hit, squeeze from second base, scoring from second on a ground ball? Do they have one or two guys who can beat you with their bats? If so, you must deal with them using a special philosophy. Do they have one or two guys who can hurt you with their speed? If so, you must keep them off base. What is their approach to the two-strike count? Do they swing for downtown, or are they contact hitters?

Be Ready to Play

To coach an intelligent game, you must have a sound approach and plan to deal with the opposing team. Have your team mentally and physically ready to play the game. Everyone should be on the same page, knowing your approach and how you plan to win the game. We know that if two baseball teams play each other enough times, each team will win some games. But you should not coach to "win some and lose some," but to win every game. Know what you must do defensively to shut down the other team. Know what you can do offensively against them. If you plan to use special maneuvers, practice them.

Your defense has a better chance of being consistent than your offense. If you can play defense, you can compete with anyone. Besides basic outfield and infield play, you must be able to execute a number of maneuvers, including

- bunt defense,
- double-steal defense,
- squeeze defense,
- cutoff and relay defense,
- double-play infield defense, and
- rundowns.

Your team will be judged by how well they execute these defenses.

One of my approaches to baseball has been that the game starts in the seventh inning. This thinking is similar to the philosophy of a famous basketball coach from Oregon State, Paul Valenti, who said at a regional basketball clinic, "In the last 30 seconds of a basketball game, get the ball in the hands of the basketball player." So in the seventh, eighth, or ninth inning we pinch run the best runner, pinch hit the better hitter, and make sure the strongest pitcher is on the mound. He may be the starter, or a right- or left-handed reliever, or a pitcher who is tough to bunt against, or a hard thrower who might get pop-ups or strikeouts, or any pitcher who may give the hitters a different look.

If it is a team unknown to us, we take the information that we have gathered during batting practice, infield, and the first six innings and apply it where we can. In the seventh inning we reexamine our approach. What has transpired for both teams and how? What is the score? We look for the defensive ability of the player that we can work against. If we are three or four runs ahead, we will probably continue an umbrella defense in which we cut off the four and six holes and the alleys. If the game is close, we may protect the lines with the infield to cut down the extra-base-hit area. If extra-base hits can really hurt us, we may play extra deep in the outfield. If the bases are loaded and a double play means more to us than one run, we will shorten up the infield and snuggle up a little closer to second base. If one run will win or tie or if we feel that we can't give away another run, we will bring the infield in. With runners on second and third we may bring our infield halfway in. This means the corners are up and the middle is back, which gives us a better chance at pop flies. With runners on second and third how we play will probably depend on what the runner on second means to us. We don't give them a bunch of runs; we want to stay close. Depending on the total situation, at any time we may show the infield in and then drop back on the pitch or vice versa. When the opponent has a runner on third with less than two outs and one run beats us, we bring the outfield in and adjust the infield to match up with the batter and the runner. We are always reluctant to bring the infield all the way in because of the broken-bat or pop-fly single.

Remember what happened in the 2001 World Series? The Yankees were forced to bring the infield in with the winning run on third. Gonzo Gonzales, a left-handed power hitter, hit a bloop pop fly into short left-center field. The ball fell in, and the Diamondbacks scored the winning run. Had the Yankees shortstop been in normal position for a left-handed power hitter, he may have made the catch, prolonging the game. This is baseball at its best. Even with the application of knowledge and extensive preparation, fate and luck have a place in this great game. John Zaephel, the great high school and American Legion coach from Yakima, Washington, once told me, "Bobo, sometimes before you even go out on the field, the big umpire in the sky has it all figured out who is going to win and how."

With runners on first and third we will defend the double steal in several ways. With the game-tying or game-winning run on third, our basic philosophy is to make them beat us with the bat. In other words, we won't throw a run in because that is what the opposition is counting on. They double steal because they don't have confidence in driving in the run.

Make Adjustments

Factors other than team personnel that may affect your approach are

- the park itself, small or large;
- contour of fences;
- warning track and distance from field to grandstand;
- park surface, whether dirt, grass, gravel, or artificial turf; if grass, note its condition—short or long, wet or dry; and
- weather—rain or wind and its effect on running and fielding conditions on the playing surface.

If these conditions change during the game, we must be ready to make adjustments. One example of an adjustment we made was in a game with the University of Idaho. In the 11th it had been raining for several innings, and the score was tied. Idaho had a catcher playing third base because of his strong bat. With a runner on third and slow-running Larry Schreck at bat with two strikes on him, I called for a bunt. Larry bunted the ball toward third, and it became a question of who would outslosh who. Larry won the contest, was safe at first, and we won the game.

Making adjustments can change the outcome of a game or even a season. Washington State University played an unusual Lewis & Clark team that booted a lot of ground balls. Coach Ed Cheff made an adjustment for the bad hands of his infielders, coaching them to be aggressive and charge the heck out of everything, picking up the grounders on the infield grass and throwing out the runners. Using this adjustment, they won the NAIA championship. We challenged them by having everyone run out ground balls as if they would be booted. The games we played against Lewis & Clark weren't pretty, but they were wars. The University of Oregon slapped the ball around, bunted, and ran. They were tough to beat. We adjusted by playing our infield in to about what coaches call halfway in. We began cutting down on four to six of these slap hits, drag bunts, and squeezes, resulting in our winning those games. The comments earlier had been, "How did they beat us when they never hit the ball out of the infield?" They beat us by being aggressive and scrappy.

In a series with Arizona State University, we were having trouble with left-hander Clay Westlake, a big, powerful hitter who had been killing everybody in left-center field. I placed my center fielder in left center and my right fielder in dead center. As predicted, Westlake hit a ball about 500 feet to straightaway center field. I had a man standing under it—my right fielder. Boy, what a great coaching adjustment—we had gotten Westlake out! Moments later everything fell apart when my man dropped the ball! Even when you make what you think is a great adjustment, the kids have to perform.

Rod Dedeaux, the great coach from the University of Southern California, won many games by adjusting his outfield play. In one College World Series game against Florida State, he jammed left-center field, took away about five doubles, and won the game. In a game against the Washington State University Cougars, Coach Dedeaux had every outfielder play toward left field in defense of Ron Cey. In a double header, Cey hit five doubles to right field. Dedeaux still wouldn't fault his strategy. He merely stated, "That Cey is the best unsigned hitter in America." Probably the greatest adjustment in modern baseball was made by the manager of the Anaheim Angels when he elected to walk Barry Bonds of the San Francisco Giants 14 times in crucial situations in the 2002 World Series and as a result won the series.

Do's and Don'ts

There are some real don'ts in the game that you see on occasion. As is usually the case, they are more easily copied than some of the do's are. Discourage an attitude of contempt toward your competition and encourage respect for their ability. Badgering the opposing team from the dugout is bad sportsmanship. Individual badgering on the field is an attitude thing. Threatening comments such as "We'll see how you can hit from your backside," or "You're going down next time up," or "You come hard into second again you had better be on the ground" are all better left unsaid. Some examples of physical actions you should discourage are

- spiking a first baseman,
- elbowing a baseman who happens to be near the bag,
- running over a pitcher covering the bag,
- sliding into the baseman with the spikes high,
- running over a baseman when there is no play and he may be looking elsewhere,
- interfering with the defense when running the bases,
- running over the catcher or baseman,
- swinging late to interfere with the catcher,
- intentionally getting hit by a pitch,
- throwing the bat, and
- throwing a helmet.

Other actions to discourage are mental strategies the offense might employ such as yelling "Look out" on a routine grounder or yelling "Cut it off" or "Let it go" when those plays would be the opposite what the defense should do. Discourage the defense from using a fake tag, telling the runner to slide when it is not necessary, standing in the base path to force a runner to take the longer route, and shielding the view of a base runner who is watching a fly ball on a tag-up play. Offensive players should assist defensive players who are attempting to make a play on or near the dugout, the bleachers, and the bullpens. The defense should signal or tell the runner to stand up if there is no play.

The home team is obliged to furnish a rosin bag and cleat cleaner for the pitcher. In case of rain, both teams should be prepared to help with the tarps and regroom the field so that play can resume.

To me, an important act concerns the exchange of the lineups. As a sign of respect, especially when the teams rarely play each other, the head coaches should do the exchange.

Important off-field etiquette includes arriving at and leaving the field fully dressed. A current movement in youth baseball has players wearing the least they can when they enter the field and stripping off the uniform as soon as the last out is made. A couple other poor behaviors are wearing spikes where it is prohibited and leaving the dugout or locker room in a disorderly condition. Coaches could also make an effort to clean up the language both on and off the field. A good example is a good teacher.

Improve the Game

As a personal challenge, you may want to take one or several elements of the game and make an effort to improve and encourage them or discourage and eliminate them from the game.

- Throwing and catching. What a challenge! This is the communication of baseball, and it must be improved.
- Double play. This is one of the most interesting elements of the defense. Keep it simple!
    1. Get there early.
    2. Make it simple.
    3. Get one out at a time.
- Pitchers. Keep them pitching. Eliminate the extracurricular activities on the mound.
- Catchers. Encourage pride in the position. You can win games with poor pitching, but you can't even play the game with poor catching.
- Infielders. Work for rhythm; it is almost extinct.
- Outfielders. A good outfielder must be able to hit, run, and throw, so he shouldn't jeopardize two-thirds of his game by not running and throwing properly. In the '40s and '50s, Al Lyons, the right fielder of

the Seattle Rainiers, took pride in making every throw split third base and home plate.

- Base running. Base runners should always be a threat to get to the next base. They should keep pressure on the defense.
- Between-inning delays. Do what you can to keep the game moving.
- Mound visits. Hustle.
- Poor PA system. Get a guy with a megaphone.
- Poor scoreboard. Improve on it.
- Poor music. Make it enjoyable to all involved.
- Ballpark. Make your park fan friendly.

A hustling team is a tough competitor and always has a chance to win. The statement, "They will hustle you right off the field," is a good thing to be said of your team.

- A courteous team, wearing uniforms properly, is acceptable on any field.
- A team strong on fundamentals will be a winner and appreciated by all who see them.
- A good base-running team can win.
- A sound batting philosophy will score runs.
- If you can play defense, you can compete with any team.

Two good cliches are particularly relevant here:

It isn't where we are; it is where we are going.

It isn't what we have; it is what we do with it.

Index

Note: The italicized *f* and *t* following page numbers refer to figures and tables.

A

Adams, Gary 287
adjustments, game 328–329
Anderson, Sparky 286
Argentine National Championship 313
arms, pitchers 179–181

B

backing up bases 151–154, 152*f*, 153*f*
balance-point drill 158–159
ball fake 247, 248*f*
ball four, base running and 65
ballpark factors 312–313
Barr pickoff play 126, 127*f*
base runners 115–138
  about 115–116
  aggressive 322–323
  bunt 135
  catchers 123
  catching and throwing skills 116–117
  coaches' tendencies 137–138
  delayed steal 134
  first-and-third situation 134–135
  glide step 125
  hit-and-run 135
  infielders 117–122
  looking at 125–126
  outfielders 122–123
  pickoff plays 127–132
  pitchers 123–124
  pitchout 126–127
  quickness to plate 124
  responsibilities 55
  run-and-hit 135
  running or walking leads 132–133
  stepping off rubber 126
  tendencies 136
  timing 125
base-running drill 6
base-running signals 25–30
base-running strategies 53–66, 78–88
  about 53
  ball four 65
  extended leads 65–66
  first base to third base 55–56
  foul fly balls 84, 85*f*
  hit-and-run play 66
  home to first base 53–55, 54*f*, 55*f*
  lead at second 60
  lead at third 60–61
  opposing coaches 88–89
  pitcher reading 61–62
  primary lead 56–57
  rundowns 65
  runner on first 79*f*, 79–80, 80*f*
  runner on second 80–82, 81*f*, 85, 86*f*
  runner on third 82, 83*f*, 85–86
  runners on first and third 83, 83*f*, 87*f*, 87–88, 88*f*
  runners on second and third 84, 84*f*
  secondary lead 57–60
  squeeze play 65
  steals 62–64
  tag-ups 64
bases, backing up 151–154, 152*f*, 153*f*
bases-loaded pickoff 131
bat-control drill 7
bat control of players, lineup 5
batting order position 77–78
behind the count, hitters 107–109
Bennett, Bob 290
Bertmand, Skip 160, 166, 174
book on opponents 169–170
bottom of lineup 11
breaking balls
  hitters 99–100
  out 105
bullpen use and pitchers 198–200
bunts
  base runners 135
  fielding 142–144
  hitting strategies 42–43
  pickoff plays 275–276
  tactics 259–262, 260*t*–262*t*

C

catchers
  base runners 123
  communication with catcher 173–176
  hitters and 111–112
  throwing ability 19
catching skills, base runners 116–117
chair drill 158
change-up, hitters 100
charting pitchers 194–195
Cheff, Ed 328
Clabough, Mark 286
Clemens, Roger 98
coaches' tendencies, base runners 137–138
commitment x

communication with catcher 173–176
competition levels 279–295
  about 279–281
  asking and observing 282–283
  ball in play 284–286
  hit-and-run 294–295
  play catch 283–284
  run-and-hit 294–295
  running bases 288–289
  sacrifice bunt 293–294
  slash 292–293
  steals 292
  team spirit 287–288
  throw strikes 286–287
composure, hitters 111
concentration x
count
  ahead in, hitters 106–107, 107*t*
  categories 41*t*
  hitting strategy 40–41
  pickoff plays 130
  pitchers and 195
  positioning outfielders 212
covering first, fielding 140–142, 141*f*
cutoff and relay system, defense 249–259, 251*t*–257*t*

D

D'Andrea, Mike 163, 165, 168
daylight method 130
daylight play 271
dead pull hitters 105
deception and hitters 96–97
Dedeaux, Rod 329
defensive positioning 219–241
  about 219–220
  consistency 221
  defensive alignment 266–267
  different signs and hitters 228–232, 230*f*, 231*f*
  double-play depth 233
  dugout communication system 238–241, 239*f*
  goals 225–226
  late adjustments 237–238
  positioning basics 227–234
  practice format 226–227
  priorities 232–234
  special coverage 234*f*, 234–237, 235*f*, 236*f*, 237*f*
  timing and signals 227
  zone defense 220–221
defensive tactics 243–276
  ball fake and throw to third 247, 248*f*
  breaking opponent's momentum 263–265
  bunt defense 259–262
  cutoff and relay system 249–259, 251*t*–257*t*
  defending steal 268–271
  defensive alignment 266–267
  first-and-third defense 243–249
  forced balk defense 248–249, 249*f*
  game plan 302–307, 303*t*–304*t*
  intentional walks 263
  pickoff plays 273–276
  relief pitchers 272–273
  second baseman as cutoff man 244, 244*f*
  straight to shortstop 245–246, 246*f*
  throw through to second base 245, 245*f*
  throw to pitcher 246–247, 247*f*
  winning or losing, early or late in game 267–268
delayed steals 63, 134
DiMaggio, Joe 286
discipline, game 324
Doubleday, Abner 219
double plays 144–148
  depth 233
drag bunt 42
dugout communication system 238–241, 239*f*

E

"eternal triangle" x*f*
ethics of game 317–319
extended leads, base running 65–66

F

fake-and-go method 130–131
fake bunting 42–43
fake bunt slash 42, 49
fake bunt slash hit-and-run 42, 49
fastball location, hitters 98–99
fielding bunts 142–144
fielding the position 139–154
  about 139–140
  backing up bases 151–154, 152*f*, 153*f*
  covering first 140–142, 141*f*
  double plays 144–148
  fielding bunts 142–144
  first-and-second bunt situation 148–151, 149*f*
fifth batter for lineup 10
first-and-second bunt situation, fielding 148–151, 149*f*
first-and-third situation
  base runners 134–135
  defense 243–249
  pickoff 132
first base
  pickoff plays 128–129, 273
  to third base, base-running strategies 55–56
first baseman 117–118, 118*f*, 119*f*
first-pitch strike 195–196
first strike, getting 163–165
fly balls
  base-running 58, 60
  lineup set 213–215, 215*f*
forced balk defense 248–249, 249*f*
foul fly balls 84, 85*f*
four-depth infield positioning 208–211, 209*f*
fourth batter for lineup 10

G

game pace, slowing 265
game plans 297–316
  about 297–299
  defensive side 302–307, 303*t*–304*t*
  offensive side 307–308
  21 outs drill 305–307
  player development 299–302
  starts drill 304–305
game situations 308–315
  adjustments 328–329
  administration 317–319
  aggressive base running 322–332
  ballpark factors 312–313
  discipline 324
  do's and don'ts 329–330
  early, mid, late season 309–311
  fundamentals 323–324
  home *versus* road games 311–314
  hustle 319–322
  improvement factors 330–331
  injuries 314–315
  lineup set 215–217
  opposing team knowledge 324–326
  play ready 326–327
  sunlight and twilight 314
  weather conditions 314
Gillespie, Gordie 73
Gillespie, Mike 174
Glavine, Tom 166
glide step 125
goals of defensive positioning 225–226
Greene, Charlie 163, 166
Greenwade, Tom 304
Grich, Bobby 283
groundballs 59
Gwynn, Tony 285

H

Herzog, Whitey 280
Hines, Ben 284
hip drill 158
hit-and-run plays
  base runners 135
  base-running strategies 66
  competition levels 294–295
  hitting strategies 46–47, 49–50
hitters 95–114
  adjustments, scouting 21–23
  ahead in count 106–107, 107*t*
  behind the count 107–109
  breaking ball 99–100
  calling pitches and pitch selection 112–114
  catcher and 111–112
  change-up 100
  classifying 104–106
  composure 111
  controlling tempo 109–110
  control of plate 40*f*
  deception and 96–97
  fastball location 98–99
  knowing pitchers 110
  mental toughness and 95–96
  pitching backward 109
  positioning outfielders 212
  practicing pitch location 100–101
  reading swings 101–106
  repeating pitches 109
  role in lineup 35–36
  strike zone and 96
  strike zones for right-handed hitters 102*f*–104*f*
  tendency chart 16*f*, 223*f*–224*f*
  zone 96
hitting signals 25–30
hitting strategies 31–51
  about 31–32
  bunting and fake bunting 42–43
  effective 32–34
  fake bunt slash 49
  fake bunt slash hit-and-run 49
  hit-and-run 46–47, 49–50
  hitters role in lineup 35–36
  man on second, no outs 44–45
  man on third, less than two outs 45–46
  overstrategizing 33
  patterns 34
  planning 36–40
  sacrifice bunt 47–48
  safety squeeze 50–51
  situational hitting 41–42
  suicide squeeze 51
  tempo 33
  work the count 40–41
home to first base, base running 53–55, 54*f*, 55*f*
home *versus* road games 311–314
hustle in games 319–322

I

improvement factors in games 330–331
infield depths 266–267
infielders 20
  base runners and 117–122
  positioning 204–205
injuries 314–315
innings, offensive decision-making 74–75
inside-out hitters 105
inside pitch 37*f*
intentional walks 263

J

jump turn 128

K

Kemble, Jay 160, 168
Kincaid, Wally 279, 294
Kindall, Jerry 283
Kotchman, Tom 89

L

Lasorda, Tommy 154, 281
lead at second, base-running 60
lead at third, base-running 60–61
leadoff base-running strategies 56–60, 59*f*
leadoff hitter for lineup 7–8
left-handed batters, pinch hitting 12
left-handed pitchers 146
Leyritz, Jim 113
line drives, base-running 58
lineups 3–13, 203–217
  about 3–4, 203–204
  bat control of players 5
  bottom of 11
  fifth batter 10
  fly ball system 213–215, 215*f*
  four-depth infield positioning 208–211, 209*f*
  fourth batter 10
  game-situation substitutions 215–217
  leadoff hitter 7–8
  offensive response of players 6
  one-depth infield positioning 205–206, 206*f*
  pitchers 184–186
  positioning infielders 204–205
  positioning outfielders 211–213, 213*f*
  power hitters 5
  second base coverage 211
  second batter 8
  sixth batter 10
  speed players 4–5
  third batter 8–10
  three-depth infield positioning 207, 208*f*
  two-depth infield positioning 206–207, 207*f*

M

Maddux, Greg 98, 113–114, 156
managers, pitchers and 199–200
man on second, no outs, hitting strategies 44–45
man on third, less than two outs, hitting strategies 45–46
Martinez, Pedro 156
matchups during games 89–91
Mauch, Gene 142, 146
McCovey, Willie 77
McGraw, John 280
mental attitude
  hitters 95–96
  pitchers 196
  relievers 176–177
  starters 167–168
Merkle, Fred 288
middle infielders 119–122, 120*f*–121*f*
  pickoff plays 129–132
middle of plate pitch 38*f*
mix hitter 105–106
Morris, Jim 174
Mota, Manny 286
Mueller, Don 285

O

offense 67–91
  about 67
  base-running strategies 78–88
  batting order position 77–78
  game plan 307–308
  hitting 307–308
  innings 74–75
  matchups during games 89–91
  other sports strategies 70–71
  outs number 75–77
  postgame wrap-up 91
  response of players for lineup 6–7
  score 71–74
  strategies ix
  their players' abilities 69–70
  your players' abilities 68–69
Olerud, John 323
Oliva, Tony 284
one, two, three drill 159
one-depth infield positioning 205–206, 206*f*
one-knee drill 157–158
open-glove play 271
opponents
  coaches 88–89
  momentum, breaking 263–265
  signals 27–30, 28*f*–29*f*
  team knowledge 324–326
outfielders 19
  base runners 122–123
  play 267
  positioning 211–213, 213*f*
out pitch 165–166
outs, number of 75–77
21 outs drill 305–307
outside pitch 37*f*
overstrategizing, hitting 33

P

patterns, hitting strategy 34
pickoff plays 127–132
  bases-loaded pickoff 131
  bunt defense 275–276
  count method 130
  daylight method 130
  fake-and-go method 130–131
  first-and-third 132
  first base 273
  pitchers and first basemen 128–129
  pitchers and middle infielders 129–132
  second base 274
  third base 274–275
  at third base 131
  Z-out method 131
pinch hitters 11–13, 216
  categories of 11–12
  right and left-handed batters 12
pitch count and number of pitches 170–171

pitch down the middle 37*f*
pitchers 161–166, 179–200
  about 179
  analyzing during game 171–173
  arms, monitoring 179–181
  base runners 123–124
  best pitch 165
  bullpen use and 198–200
  changing speeds 166
  charting 194–195
  control misses 192–193
  control of running game 19
  count and 195
  first-pitch strike 195–196
  getting first strike 163–165
  getting hitters out 193
  habits 18
  hitters knowledge of 110
  lineup 184–186
  managers and 199–200
  mastering pitch location 166
  mental focus 196
  mistakes 191
  monitoring pitchers' arms 179–181
  out pitch 165–166
  pickoff plays 128–129, 129–132
  reading 61–62
  rotation 181–184
  scouting opponents 186–190, 188*f*–189*f*
  starters 181–182
  from stretch 196–197
  tendencies and patterns 18–19
  tendency to use fastball 17*f*
  three-ball level 198
  tipping 191–192
  two-against-one mentality 194
  velocity complex 181
  zone 96
pitches
  backward 109
  calling 26–27, 112–114
  location, mastering 166
  location, practicing 100–101
pitchouts 126–127, 269
planning hitting strategy 36–40
plate, quickness to, base runners 124
play catch 283–284
players
  abilities 68–70
  being ready for games 326–327
  development 299–302
  strengths and weaknesses for lineup 4–7
positioning infielders, lineup 204–205
positioning outfielders, lineup 211–213, 213*f*
postgame wrap-up 91
Powell, Bill 279
power drill 6
power hitters 5
practice format, defense 226–227
practice sessions and strategy xi–xii
preparation methods, game 168–169
primary lead, base running 56–57

R

reading swings 101–106
relief pitchers 75
  defensive tactics 272–273
repeating pitches 109
rhythm, game 176
right-handed batters 12
  hitter zone 39*f*
Rigney, Bill 77–78
road games 311–314
rotation, pitchers 181–184
rulebook zone 96
run-and-hit
  base runners 135
  competition levels 294–295
rundowns, base running 65
runner on first, base running 79*f*, 79–80, 80*f*
runner on second, base running 80–82, 81*f*, 85, 86*f*
runner on third, base running 82, 83*f*, 85–86
runners on first and third, base running 83, 83*f*, 87*f*, 87–88, 88*f*
runners on second and third, base running 84, 84*f*
running bases, competition levels 288–289
running game, control 19
running or walking leads, base runners 132–133
runs, given up 265

S

sacrifice bunts 42
  competition levels 293–294
  hitting strategies 47–48
safety squeeze 42–43
  hitting strategies 50–51
Salveson, Jack 286
Scolinos, John 283
score, offensive decision-making 71–74
scoring percentages 78*t*
scouting opposition 15–23
  hitter's adjustments 21–23
  pitchers 186–190, 188*f*–189*f*
  umpires 20
secondary lead, base running 57–60, 59*f*
second base
  coverage lineup set 211
  pickoff plays 274
  tag-ups 64
second baseman as cutoff man 244, 244*f*
second batter for lineup 8
Sheehan, Chris 180
signals 25–30, 228–232, 230*f*, 231*f*
  indicators for 27
  opponents 27–30, 28*f*–29*f*
  system for 25–26
  who calls pitches 26–27

situational hitting 26, 41–42
sixth batter for lineup 10
slash 292–293
slide step 62, 269
slow bat 105
Soto, Mario 114
speed players lineup 4–5
speeds, changing, pitchers 166
squeeze play 65
starts drill 304–305
steals 62–64
  competition levels 292
  defending 268–271
  delayed steals 63
  home 63
  signals 28*f*–29*f*
  stealing home 63
  straight steals 62
  on your own strategy 62–63
Stengle, Casey 69
stepping off rubber, base runners 126
Stevens, Chuck 281
Stodgel, Doug 284
Stotts, Dean 286
straight steals 62
straight to shortstop, defensive tactics 245–246, 246*f*
strategies ix
  fine-tuning xi
  practice sessions and xi–xii
Strawberry, Darryl 114
stretch drill 160
strike zones
  hitters 96
  for right-handed hitters 102*f*–104*f*
success implementation x–xi
suicide squeeze 43, 51
sunlight and twilight game situations 314
Swift, Bill 164, 167, 169
swings, reading 101–106

T

tag-ups 64
talent x
team spirit 287–288
tempo, hitting strategy 33
tempo control, hitters 109–110
third basemen 19–20, 122
third base pickoff plays 274–275
third batter for lineup 8–10
three-ball level pitchers 198
three-depth infield positioning 207, 208*f*
throwing skills, base runners 116–117
throw strikes, competition levels 286–287
throw through to second base, defensive tactics 245, 245*f*
throw to pitcher, defensive tactics 246–247, 247*f*
throw to third, defensive tactics 247, 248*f*
tied score 73–74
timing
  base runners 125
  defensive positioning 227
two-depth infield positioning lineup set 206–207, 207*f*
two-knee drill 157

U

umpires
  scouting 20
  zone 96
uppercut swing with power 105

V

velocity complex, pitchers 181
vigilance 124

W

Wassem, Jim 324
weaknesses for lineup, players 4–7
weather conditions, games 314
Weaver, Earl 69
Weiner, Al 289, 291, 292
Weiskopf, Don 280
Westlake, Clay 328
wind, positioning outfielders and 213
Winkles, Bobby 283
Wohlers, Mark 113
Wolf, Randy 139
working a game 155–177
  about 155–156
  analyzing pitcher during game 171–173
  balance-point drill 158–159
  book on opponent 169–170
  chair drill 158
  communication with catcher 173–176
  hip drill 158
  mental attitude of relievers 176–177
  mental attitude of starters 167–168
  one, two, three drill 159
  one-knee drill 157–158
  pitch count and number of pitches 170–171
  pre-game experience 156–157
  preparation methods 168–169
  rhythm 176
  stretch drill 160
  two-knee drill 157

Z

Zaephel, John 327
zone defense 220–221
Z-out method 131

About the ABCA

The **American Baseball Coaches Association (ABCA)** is the largest baseball coaching organization in the world, including coaches from every state in the country and hundreds of international members. The association's mission is to improve the level of baseball coaching worldwide. The ABCA assists in the promotion of baseball and acts as a sounding board and advocate on issues concerning the game. In addition, the ABCA promotes camaraderie and communication among all baseball coaches from the amateur to professional levels. The ABCA also gives recognition to deserving players and coaches through several special sponsorship programs. It is an organization that has grown steadily in membership, prestige, and impact in recent years. The ABCA's headquarters is located in Mount Pleasant, Michigan.

About the Editors

Bob Bennett retired from coaching in 2002 with a career record of 1,302-759-4, ranking him seventh all-time on the Division I win list. In his 34 years as head coach at Fresno State University his teams had 32 winning seasons, won 17 conference championships, made 21 NCAA Regional Championship appearances, and played in two College World Series. Bennett was awarded 14 conference Coach of the Year Awards and an NCAA Coach of the Year Award in 1988. He coached 32 All-Americans, eight of whom were first-round draft picks. Bennett also served as head coach of the United States national team in 1983 and 1986. He lives in Fresno, California, with his wife, Jane. They have three children and eight grandchildren.

Jack Stallings finished his coaching career as the winningest active college coach with 1,258 victories. Stallings headed up baseball programs at Wake Forest University (1958-1968), Florida State University (1969-1975), and Georgia Southern University (1976-1999). He also coached the USA national baseball team in the 1979 Pan American Games, the 1970 and 1973 IBA World Tournament, the 1979 IBA International Cup, and the 1984 Olympic Games. Stallings is an associate professor in the department of health and kinesiology at Georgia Southern University. He and his wife, Norma, live near Statesboro, Georgia.

About the Contributors

Photo courtesy of University of Connecticut

Andy Baylock has coached the University of Connecticut Huskies for 39 consecutive years and has served as head coach for 23 years. With an overall record of 532-469-8, Baylock has led his teams to two Big East Conference Tournament Championships and three NCAA Regional appearances. He was named the New England Conference Division I Coach of the Year in 1990, the Big East Conference Coach of the Year in 1992, and the Northwest Region Coach of the Year in 1994. He has been inducted into five halls of fame, including the ABCA Hall of Fame.

Photo courtesy of Dick Birmingham

Dick Birmingham served as head coach at Hillcrest High School in Springfield, Missouri, Hillcrest American Legion Baseball, and the USA Junior Olympic team. Birmingham's teams have won more than 1,000 games, including a high school state championship, three legion state championships, and three medals—a gold and two silvers—at the Pan American Junior Baseball Championship. Birmingham is a member of several halls of fame, including the ABCA, the Missouri Baseball Coaches, the Iowa Baseball Coaches Hall of Fame, and the Missouri Sports Hall of Fame.

Photo courtesy of Washington State University

Bobo Brayton, a former All-American player and coach for Washington State University, compiled a record of 1162-523-8 and a .689 winning percentage before retiring in 1994 after serving as head coach for 33 years. He coached his team to 21 Pacific-10 Conference Championships and led them to the College World Series in 1965 and 1976. He is a member of several halls of fame, including the ABCA, Inland Empire, Washington State University, and Washington State Coaches Hall of Fame.

Photo courtesy of University of Southern California

Mike Gillespie has been at the University of Southern California for 17 years and has coached his teams to five Pacific-10 Southern Division Conference titles and the 1998 National Championship. He also coached the 2000 USA Baseball national team to a championship, posting a record of 27-3-1. Gillespie was named 1998 National Coach of the Year by both Collegiate Baseball and the ABCA.

Photo courtesy of Georgia Tech

Danny Hall, head coach at the Georgia Institute of Technology since 1994, has posted a record of 396-172. His teams captured two Atlantic Coast Conference Championships in 1997 and 2000 and appeared in the College World Series in 1994 and 2000. Hall was named ACC Coach of the Year in 1997 and 2000 and National Coach of the Year in 1997.

Photo courtesy of Virginia Tech

Chuck Hartman has coached baseball for 44 years and has spent 24 of those years at Virginia Tech. He ranks fourth in Division I baseball's top 20 winningest all-time coaches with 1,339 career wins. He posts an 856-481-7 record with the Hokies and has led his teams to three Atlantic-10 Tournament Championships. Hartman is also a member of the National Association of Intercollegiate Athletics Hall of Fame.

Photo courtesy of Cal State L.A. by Stan Carstensen

John Herbold, ABCA Hall-of-Fame member, began coaching at California State University at Los Angeles in 1984, after 28 years at Long Beach Poly and Lakewood high schools. Both schools ranked in the top four U.S. high schools for drafted players. Over 120 of his players have signed professional contracts. Herbold claimed two California Collegiate Athletic Association Conference Championships in 1997 and 1998 and earned a spot at the 1998 NCAA Division II Tournament.

Photo courtesy of Gonzaga University Baseball

Steve Hertz has served as head coach at Gonzaga University for 23 years after pitching for the Bulldogs for three years. He is the winningest coach in school history with more than 600 victories. Hertz has coached his teams to two NCAA Tournament appearances, and he has been named Conference Coach of the Year five times in four different conferences.

Photo courtesy of Cal-State Fullerton

George Horton has amassed a 259-116-1 record since taking over as head coach at California State University at Fullerton in the 1997 season. Horton's teams have won six Big West Conference titles by way of tournament or regular season play and have made two trips to the College World Series in 1999 and 2001. Horton has been honored as Big West Conference Coach of the Year twice, and National Junior College Coach of the Year three times.

Photo courtesy of Texas A&M Sports Information

Mark Johnson holds a 759-365-2 overall career record in his 17 years as head coach for Texas A&M and takes a place among Division I baseball's top 10 best winning percentage of active coaches. Johnson coached his teams to two Big 12 Conference Championships in 1998 and 1999; three Southwest Conference Championships in 1986, 1989, and 1993; and two trips to the College World Series in 1993 and 1999. Johnson was honored with Big 12 Conference Coach of the Year in 1998 and 1999. He served as ABCA president in 1994.

Photo courtesy of University of Illinois

Richard "Itch" Jones, one of Division I baseball's top 20 all-time winningest coaches and the 10th winningest active coach, boasts a 1,158-670-5 career record. Jones came to the University of Illinois from Southern Illinois University in 1991, where he made 10 NCAA Tournament appearances and three trips to the College World Series in 21 years. Jones' Illinois teams have captured a Big Ten Conference Championship and two NCAA Tournament bids.

Photo courtesy of University of Kentucky Baseball

Keith Madison began his head coaching career at the University of Kentucky, where he has coached for 24 years. He has compiled a record of 713-602-5 and has taken his teams to NCAA tournaments in 1988 and 1993. He is second in wins among active Southeastern Conference coaches. Madison has coached 10 All-Americans, and 83 of his players have been drafted or have signed professional baseball contracts. Madison served as president of the ABCA in 2000.

Photo courtesy of Indiana University

Bob Morgan, head coach at Indiana University, is ranked among Division I baseball's top 20 winningest active coaches and Division I baseball's top 20 best winning percentage of active coaches with a record of 990-504-6 in 27 years. As Indiana's all-time winningest coach, Morgan led his teams to the Big Ten Tournament championship and an appearance in the NCAA Tournament in 1996. In 1993, he was honored as Big Ten Coach of the Year.

Photo courtesy of University of Miami

Jim Morris, head coach at the University of Miami, posts a career record of 1,069-469-2 and claims the fifth spot in the Division I baseball's top 20 best winning percentage of active coaches. In his nine seasons with the Hurricanes, Morris led them to eight College World Series appearances including two National Championship titles in 1999 and 2001. In both 1999 and 2001, he was named Collegiate Baseball National Coach of the Year and the ABCA Coach of the Year.

John Winkin coached for 48 years in Maine, first at Colby College (1954-1974) and then at the University of Maine (1974-1996). Since 1996, he has been the pitching coach at Husson College. He amassed a 943-670 career record and appeared in 12 NCAA regional tournaments and 6 College World Series. Winkin received the College Division Coach of the Year award in 1965 and the prestigious Lefty Gomez award in 1986. He is a member of the ABCA Coaching Hall of Fame, Maine High School Baseball Coaches Hall of Fame, and the Maine Sports Hall of Fame.

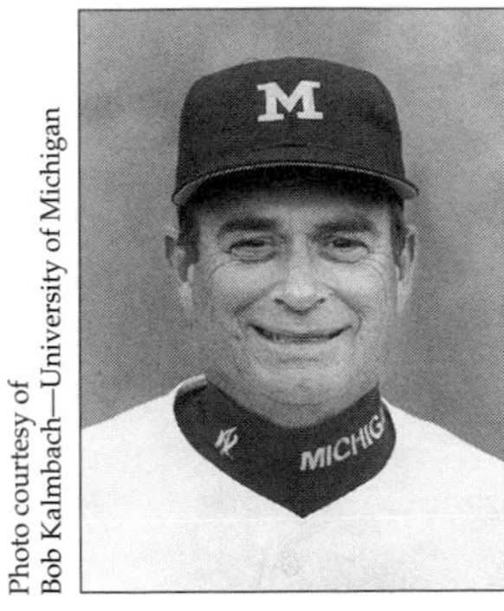

Photo courtesy of Bob Kalmbach—University of Michigan

Geoff Zahn served as head coach at the University of Michigan from 1995 until 2001 after earning his varsity letters there in 1966 and 1967. Zahn earned Big Ten Coach of the Year honors in 1997 after leading his team to a Big Ten title. The Wolverines also captured a Big Ten Conference Tournament Championship in 1999. Zahn spent 12 years pitching in the Major Leagues and was named Rookie of the Year for the Dodgers in 1974.